THE ARDEN SHAKESPEARE

GENERAL EDITORS:
RICHARD PROUDFOOT, ANN THOMPSON
and DAVID SCOTT KASTAN

MACBETH

THE ARDEN SHAKESPEARE

* Second series

THE ARDEN EDITION OF THE
WORKS OF WILLIAM SHAKESPEARE

MACBETH

Edited by
KENNETH MUIR

Arden Shakespeare

3 5 7 9 10 8 6 4 2

This edition of *Macbeth* by Kenneth Muir, first published
1951 by Methuen & Co. Ltd

Editorial matter copyright © 1962 and 1984 Methuen Drama

Arden Shakespeare is an imprint of Methuen Drama

Methuen Drama
A & C Black Publishers Ltd
36 Soho Square
London W1D 3QY
www.methuendrama.com
www.ardenshakespeare.com

A CIP catalogue record for this book is available from the British Library
ISBN: 978 1 9034 3648 6

The general editors of the Arden Shakespeare have been
W.J. Craig and R.H. Case (first series 1899-1944)
Una Ellis-Fermor, Harold F. Brooks, Harold Jenkins and
Brian Morris (second series 1946-82)

Present general editors (third series)
Richard Proudfoot, Ann Thompson, David Scott Kastan and H.R. Woudhuysen

Printed by C & C Offset, China

CONTENTS

GENERAL EDITOR'S PREFACE

When it was proposed, in 1946, to re-issue the Arden Shakespeare, little more was intended than a limited revision, bringing introductions and collations into line with the work of recent years and modifying appendices whenever additions were necessary or the material had been accepted into the common body of knowledge. In the main part of each volume the form of the original page was to be undisturbed, in order that the stereotype plates of those originals might still be used. This meant that practically no alterations could be made in the text, which was based on the Cambridge edition of 1863-6 (revised, 1891-3), and that any alterations in the commentary must be so arranged as to occupy the same space as the notes which they replaced.

It had been recognized from the first that in the case of a few plays it might be necessary to modify this restriction and it soon became clear that the first two volumes, *Macbeth* and *Love's Labour's Lost*, would prove more costly to produce if the stereotypes were retained than if they were abandoned. The two editors, therefore, who had gallantly endeavoured to preserve the original lay-out of the pages, found themselves freed from this necessity when their work was done or partly done, so that much of it had to be done again. As conditions became more stable, it became possible also to consider sparing their successors what they had experienced and at last to allow all editors to start afresh without tying them to the Cambridge text or to the lay-out of the original pages.

Thus a major change of policy came about by degrees, as the conditions of the years immediately after the war began to allow of it, and what had begun as a revision became a new edition.

This meant that publishers, editors, and general editor were faced with an entirely new responsibility: that of establishing the text of each play in place of a text which had hitherto been prescribed. Since we were unwilling to suspend activities until textual critics should be agreed that a text had been established as nearly authoritative for our day as that of the 1891-3 edition was held to be for its own, we decided to continue the work begun, in full awareness of the difficulties involved in publishing an edition such as this at a moment when there is not yet full agreement on a generally acceptable text. Each individual editor would thus be responsible for the text of his play, as well as for the introductions, collations, commentary, and appendices.

The policy of the original edition in respect of introductions, commentary, and appendices remains what it has always been; the lines laid down by those scholars who first designed its form have proved their worth throughout the past half-century. The introductions, though the emphasis must vary with the nature of the given play, include, together with the results of the editor's own thought and investigation, a survey of as many as possible of those studies which throw light upon the nature of the play or the problems surrounding it. The general commentary, which we have kept in its original position, at the foot of the page, provides such brief notes as may be required for the elucidation of specific passages or textual problems or for general comment and comparison; these often, therefore, serve to illustrate the general account given in the introduction.

The policy in respect of text is of necessity neither so simple nor so consistent as that of the editors of the original series, who were enjoined to use as their base the Cambridge text of 1891–3, and in most cases did so willingly, believing it to be as nearly authoritative as could be. Much has happened in the last fifty years, through the great extension of palæographical, bibliographical, and textual scholarship; and our better understanding of (among other things) the nature and relations of Folio and Quarto texts has led us not always into more certainty, but sometimes rather into wholesome and chastened uncertainty. Each editor's text must now be his individual concern, since each play presents its own group of problems. Some of us may prove to have solved these in a way which posterity will repudiate. But an attempt will be made in every case to present the evidence for the editor's decisions fairly and to give at the same time representation to solutions other than that editor's own.

UNA ELLIS-FERMOR

London, 1952

PREFACE

THE original Arden *Macbeth*, edited by Henry Cuningham, first appeared in 1912. The present edition owes much to its predecessor, many of the notes being used with little or no change; but there are substantial alterations. The introduction is new; the text (for which Mr Cuningham was not responsible) has been revised, and several hundred small alterations have been made in it—most of them consisting of a return to the First Folio; nearly all the notes contain alterations, and many are entirely new; and the appendices are new. There are, in fact, so many alterations that it was not possible to print from the old stereos.

Mr Cuningham disagreed with the General Editor of the series, and was not allowed to print his own text: he was thereby constrained to make a number of protests in the notes, which are happily now superfluous. Some of the differences between the present edition and Mr Cuningham's are caused by a change of attitude to the authenticity of the text. In 1912 it was still possible for Mr Cuningham to say:

> It is admitted by all competent scholars that the text of *Macbeth* has been more or less vitiated by the interpolation or additions of some dramatist other than Shakespeare.

But it is now generally agreed that such interpolations and additions are at least fewer than Mr Cuningham imagined.

It may be as well to mention one or two points about the present volume. First, the relevant parts of Holinshed's *Chronicle* are printed in the appendix, but, in order to save space, other parts have been curtailed. Secondly, the sections of the Introduction devoted to Date and Interpolations contain criticism necessary for the understanding of the final section, which is devoted to interpretation. Thirdly, though many of the annotations deal with questions of poetic imagery, I hope I have not lost sight of the fact that *Macbeth* is an acting play.

I am indebted to previous editors of the play, especially H. H. Furness, Jr (1903), Sir Herbert Grierson (1914), and Dr J. Dover Wilson (1947). I am grateful to many of my colleagues for assistance on different points, and particularly to Mr Harold Fisch who has checked the collations and criticized the introduction. Professor P. Alexander has generously given me advice on textual matters; Professor R. Peacock supplied me with useful information; Mr Roy Walker lent me the MS. of his valuable study, *The Time is Free*, and gave me permission to make use of it in my notes; Mr J. M. Nosworthy sent me some unpublished notes; and, above all, Professor U. Ellis-Fermor has been all that a General Editor should be. I should add that Cleanth Brooks's essay in *The Well Wrought Urn* arrived too late for me to use it, though we agree on a number of points.

KENNETH MUIR

University of Leeds
Christmas, 1950

NOTE TO TENTH EDITION

TWENTY years have elapsed since the publication of the Seventh Edition. I am greatly indebted to many colleagues, strangers, and friends for valuable suggestions, especially to the late John Dover Wilson. In the Ninth Edition passages from Buchanan and Leslie replaced those from Stewart. As the present edition has been reset, I have been able to introduce many changes. For the correction of many typographical anomalies, misprints, and minor errors my thanks are due to Miss Newland-Smith, the scholarly and indefatigable reader for the Broadwater Press.

K.M.

Liverpool 1971

NOTE TO 1984 REISSUE

THIS is the last revision for which I shall be responsible and I am glad of the opportunity of updating the work of my comparative youth. I have rewritten most of the introduction, altered many notes, and added others. I am grateful to the General Editor for his valuable suggestions and to many friends and colleagues.

K.M.

Liverpool 1984

ABBREVIATIONS

Barker   H. Granville-Barker, *Prefaces to Shakespeare*, 6 (1974).
Bradley   A. C. Bradley, *Shakespearean Tragedy* (1904).
Brown   *Focus on Macbeth*, ed. John Russell Brown (1982).
Bullough Geoffrey Bullough, *Narrative and Dramatic Sources of Shakespeare*, VII (1973).
Curry   J. C. Curry, *Shakespeare's Philosophical Patterns* (1937).
Greg   W. W. Greg, *The Shakespeare First Folio* (1955).
Kittredge G. L. Kittredge, '*Macbeth*', in *Sixteen Plays of Shakespeare* (1946).
Paul   H. N. Paul, *The Royal Play of 'Macbeth'* (1950).
Rogers   H. L. Rogers, '*Double Profit*' in Macbeth (1964).
Rosenberg Marvin Rosenberg, *The Masks of Macbeth* (1978).
Spurgeon Caroline Spurgeon, *Shakespeare's Imagery* (1955).
Walker   Roy Walker, *The Time is Free* (1949).
Wilson   *Macbeth*, ed. J. Dover Wilson (1947).

CHEL   *Cambridge History of English Literature.*
CSP   *Calendar of State Papers.*
EC   *Essays in Criticism.*
ELH   *English Literary History.*
ELN   *English Language Notes.*
ELR   *English Literary Renaissance.*
MLN   *Modern Language Notes.*
MLR   *Modern Language Review.*
NQ   *Notes and Queries.*
NV   New Variorum edition of *Macbeth*, ed. H. H. Furness (1963).
PMLA   *Publications of the Modern Language Association of America.*
RES   *Review of English Studies.*
SQ   *Shakespeare Quarterly.*
SS   *Shakespeare Survey.*
TLS   *The Times Literary Supplement.*

N   See additional note.

INTRODUCTION

I. TEXT

The Tragedie of Macbeth was first published in the First Folio of 1623, seven years after Shakespeare's death, and seventeen years after the play was first performed. The text follows *Julius Caesar* and precedes *Hamlet*. As it is mentioned in the *Stationers' Register* as one of those 'as are not formerly entred to other men',[1] it may be assumed that there was no quarto edition. Acts and scenes are indicated in Latin,[2] but there is no *dramatis personae*. It is by far the shortest of the tragedies, occupying only 21 Folio pages (compared with 30 for *Othello* and 31 for *Hamlet*). There is evidence, as we shall see, that there have been cuts in the text, as well as interpolations.[3]

The text was printed from the prompt-book, or more probably from a transcript of it prepared for the printers. It contains such indications of prompt-book origin as duplicated stage directions[4] and instructions for noises off (e.g. *Ring the Bell* and *Knock*)[5]; but there are also 'descriptive touches' in the stage directions 'to suggest the author'[6] and some vague touches characteristic of an author's manuscript which somehow got transferred to the prompt-book.

The textual problem is closely linked to the question of alterations made for different performances. The 1623 text contains passages which could not have belonged to the version performed in 1606; both differ from the version witnessed by Simon Forman in 1611; some critics believe[7] there was an earlier version dating from Elizabeth's reign; and almost all critics believe that one 1606 performance was at Court, and probably shortened for that reason.

1. S. Schoenbaum, *Records and Images* (1981), p. 221.

2. There are some inconsistencies, however. The first three scenes of Act II are virtually continuous, whereas the battle scenes of the last act are not divided.

3. See below, p. xxxii. 4. E.g. I. vi. S.D., I. vii. S.D.; v. viii. 34.

5. II. ii. 64; II. iii. 79. 6. Greg, p. 393. 7. See below, p. xvii.

It has been suggested that[1] the editors sent to the printers the version included in the First Folio because James I would have preferred it to the hypothetical longer version. But this was not the version performed at Court in 1606, and it seems more likely that when Hecate and the extra witches were introduced into the prompt-book, cut passages were discarded and were therefore not available in 1623.

The possibility that some whole scenes are missing from the extant text is discussed below.[2] Here it is necessary only to refer to the frequent mislineation, mainly in the second scene of the play, due possibly to the dislocation caused by cuts.[3]

It should be mentioned, however, that not everyone subscribes to these views on the text. Richard Flatter believed that the play showed no signs of editorial interference and that Shakespeare's Producing Hand may be discerned in it;[4] and D. A. Traversi warned us against the assumption that difficulties in the text can be explained by omissions:[5]

> The verse of *Macbeth* is often, at first reading, so abrupt and disjointed that some critics have felt themselves driven to look for gaps in the text. Yet the difficult passages do not look in the least like the result of omissions, but are rather necessary to the feeling of the play.

Here, surely, Professor Traversi was mistaken; but he wrote at a time when it was necessary to protest at the prevailing textual pessimism.

According to the standard work on the printing of the First Folio,[6] nine of the *Macbeth* pages were set by Compositor A, and twelve by Compositor B. A number of corrections were made in proof, but only two are of any consequence: *Roffe* was corrected to *Rosse* (IV. iii. 213) and 'on my with' to 'on with' (IV. iii. 154). As Hinman pointed out, the proof corrector did not usually refer to copy, his aim being merely to eliminate 'obvious typographical

---

1. Greg, p. 395.

2. See below, p. xxiv.

3. Not all the mislineation is the result of cuts. The last eleven lines of II. ii are printed as fifteen in the Folio. The stage directions necessitated the splitting of lines into two and this confused the compositor about lineation.

4. Richard Flatter, *Shakespeare's Producing Hand* (1948). His theories might have been more convincing if they had been applied to good quartos.

5. D. A. Traversi, *Approach to Shakespeare* (1938), p. 89.

6. Charton Hinman, *The Printing and Proof-reading of the First Folio* (1963). See I. 10–12 for an account of these two compositors and their characteristic habits. A was more accurate than B.

infelicities'.[1] In *Macbeth* he allowed twenty or more obvious errors to stand, and doubtless others which were not so obvious.

In most cases it is impossible to determine how these errors originated. Simple omissions, like that of 'break' (I. ii. 26), could be blamed on either the transcriber or the compositor. There are some misreadings, probably by the compositor (e.g. *Or* for *Are* (I. iv. 1), *sowre* for *sure* (II. ii. 56) and *Soris* for *Forres* (I. iii. 39), as well as a number of misunderstandings: e.g. *Heire* for *hair* (I. iii. 134). Dover Wilson thought[2] that 'Gallowgrosses' (I. ii. 13) could be explained as an actor's blunder strangely reproduced by the transcriber; and perhaps 'Barlet' (I. vi. 4) could be a blunder of the same kind. But it is impossible to suppose that an actor would say 'Can' for 'Came' (I. iii. 98).

2. DATE

In Simon Forman's manuscript[3] *The Bocke of Plaies and Notes therof per Formans for Common Pollicie* (i.e. affording useful lessons in the common affairs of life) there is a description of a performance at the Globe in the spring of 1611, as Forman states:

> In Mackbeth at the Glob, 16jo, the 20 of Aprill [Sat.], ther was to be obserued, firste, how Mackbeth and Bancko, 2 noble men of Scotland, Ridinge thorowe a wod, the[r] stode before them 3 women feiries or Nimphes, And saluted Mackbeth, sayinge 3 tyms vnto him, haille Mackbeth, king of Codon; for thou shalt be a kinge, but shall beget No kinges, &c. then said Bancko, what all to mackbeth And nothing to me. Yes, said the nimphes, haille to thee Bancko, thou shalt beget kings, yet be no kinge. And so they departed & cam to the Courte of Scotland to Dunkin king of Scots, and yt was in the dais of Edward the Confessor. And Dunkin bad them both kindly wellcome. And made Mackbeth forth with Prince of Northumberland, and sent him hom to his own castell, and appointed mackbeth to prouid for him, for he wold Sup with him the next dai at night, & did soe. And mackbeth Contrived to kill Dunkin, & thorowe the persuasion of his wife did that night Murder the kinge in his own Castell, beinge

1. Hinman, *ibid.*, p. 227. Owing to the normal method of type-setting, a compositor could be ignorant of the context and so fall into error: e.g. 'Lady Lenox' in II. i. 10 S.D., instead of 'Lady Macbeth as Queen, Lenox'.

2. Wilson. p. 89. I do not agree with him that *stuffed* (v. iii. 44) and *rooky* (III. ii. 51) should be blamed on Burbage's faulty memory. See notes to these lines.

3. Ashmolean MS. 208. Facsimile in S. Schoenbaum's *Records and Images* 1981).

his gueste. And ther were many prodigies seen that night
& the dai before. And when Mackbeth had murdred the
kinge, the blod on his hands could not be washed of by Any
means, nor from his wiues handes, which handled the bloddi
daggers in hiding them, By which means they became moch
amazed and Affronted. the murder being knowen, Dunkins 2
sonns fled, the on to England, the other to Walles, to saue
themselues. They being fled, they were supposed guilty of the
murder of their father, which was nothinge so. Then was
Mackbeth crowned kinge, and then he for feare of Banko, his
old companion, that he should beget kings but be no kinge him
selfe, he contriued the death of Banko, and caused him to be
Murdred on the way as he Rode. The next night, being at
supper with his noble men whom he had bid to a feaste to
the whiche also Banco should haue com, he began to speake of
Noble Banco, and to wish that he wer there. And as he thus
did, standing vp to drincke a Carouse to him, the ghoste of Banco
came and sate down in his cheier behind him. And he turninge
About to sit down Again sawe the goste of banco, which
fronted him so, that he fell into a great passion of fear and
fury, vtterynge many wordes about his murder, by which,
when they hard that Banco was Murdred they Suspected
Mackbet.

Then Mack dove fled to England to the kings sonn, And soe
they Raised an Army, And cam into scotland, and at dunston
Anyse ouerthru Mackbet. In the mean tyme whille macdouee
was in England, Mackbet slewe Mackdoues wife & children,
and after in the battelle mackdoue slewe mackbet.

Obserue Also howe mackbets quen did Rise in the night in
her slepe, & walke and talked and confessed all, & the doctor
noted her wordes.

Forman gives an impossible date since 20 April did not fall on
a Saturday in 1610; his account of the play was apparently mixed
with memories of Holinshed;[1] the indelible stains of blood were
presumably suggested by Macbeth's speeches after the murder
and Lady Macbeth's in the sleep-walking scene; he makes a bad
mistake in supposing that Macbeth was created Prince of Northumberland (or Cumberland);[2] he makes no mention of the
cauldron scene although, as an astrologer, he should have been
interested in the prophecies in this scene. Nevertheless there is no

---

1. E.g. '3 women feiries or Nimphes'. See J. M. Nosworthy, 'Macbeth at
the Globe', *The Library*, II (1947–8), 108–18; Leah Scragg, 'Macbeth on
Horseback', *SS 26* (1973), pp. 81–8; Peter Thomson, *Shakespeare's Theatre*
(1983), pp. 137–9.
2. Northumberland is mentioned in III. vi.

reason to believe that the play witnessed by Forman was substantially different from that performed before the King five years previously. Forman was inaccurate in his account of other plays and he may have recorded his impressions after a lapse of days or weeks.[1]

Although this performance, in 1611, is the first of which we have a definite record, we can be fairly certain that the play was in existence four years before, because of echoes of it in contemporary plays. In *Lingua* (1607), there are possible echoes of II. i, and what seems to be a parody of the sleep-walking scene. There are references to Banquo's ghost in *The Puritaine* (IV. iii. 89):[2]

> and in stead of a Iester, weele ha the ghost ith white sheete sit at vpper end a'th'Table . . .

and in Beaumont and Fletcher's *The Knight of the Burning Pestle* (v. i. 22–8),[3]

> When thou art at thy Table with thy friends
> Merry in heart, and fild with swelling wine,
> Il'e come in midst of all thy pride and mirth,
> Invisible to all men but thy selfe,
> And whisper such a sad tale in thine eare,
> Shall make thee let the Cuppe fall from thy hand,
> And stand as mute and pale as Death it selfe.

The Puritaine was published, and *The Knight of the Burning Pestle* probably acted, in 1607. Allowing for the necessary interval for the writing, performing, and publishing of the former play, it is fairly certain that *Macbeth* was being performed in 1606. It is also certain that the reference to the King's Evil (IV. iii) and to the two-fold balls and sceptres of Banquo's descendants (IV. i) must have been written after the accession of James I in 1603.

If these passages were interpolations, the play as a whole might have been written earlier. It has, indeed, been argued by several critics that the play was originally written in the reign of Elizabeth I and revised in 1606. J. Dover Wilson believed[4] that Shakespeare visited Scotland and there perused William Stewart's *The Buik of the Croniclis of Scotland*, though he later retracted his

---

1. Forman does not mention Hermione's survival, nor the Queen in *Cymbeline*. Although some scholars suspected that the Forman MS. was a Collier forgery, its authenticity was established by Dover Wilson and R. W. Hunt, *RES* (1947), 193 ff.
2. Halliwell (*NV*).   3. Clarendon (*NV*).
4. Wilson, p. xli.

view, propounded originally by Mrs C. C. Stopes,[1] that this was a source of the play. Apart from that, he argued that numerous obscurities in the Folio text were caused by cuts in the original play, and that George Saintsbury was right to maintain that portions of the play and in particular 'the second scene are in verse and phrase whole stages older than the bulk of the play'.[2] Wilson believed that the second scene of the play must have been written soon after the Hecuba speeches in *Hamlet*;[3] but the resemblance can better be explained as a deliberate attempt on Shakespeare's part to adopt a style suitable for 'epic' narrative on the model of Marlowe's account of the fall of Troy in *Dido, Queen of Carthage* and Kyd's account of the battle in *The Spanish Tragedy*.[4] Nothing can be deduced about the date when the *Macbeth* scene was written.

Arthur Melville Clark agreed[5] with Dover Wilson that the play was written in 1601, his main reason being that the play contained allusions to the Gowrie conspiracy of the previous year. None of these allusions is convincing and, even if they were, they could have been derived from the anonymous play, *Gowrie*, performed by Shakespeare's company in 1604.[6] If Clark had read H. N. Paul's *The Royal Play of 'Macbeth'*[7] he could hardly have thought that the Gunpowder Plot was less relevant to the play than the Gowrie conspiracy.[8]

A third critic, Daniel Amneus, has argued[9] for an even earlier date, 1599, for the composition of the play, partly because Shakespeare would not have dared to write a play which gave approval to a rebellion against a reigning monarch after he had

1. C. C. Stopes, *Shakespeare's Industry* (1916), pp. 93, 102–3. The relevant Stewart passages were reluctantly included in my original edition of *Macbeth*, and afterwards withdrawn.

2. George Saintsbury, *CHEL*, v. 203.

3. Wilson, p. xl.

4. J. M. Nosworthy, *RES* (1946), 126–30.

5. A. M. Clark, *Murder under Trust* (1982), pp. 109–13, 120–4. It should be mentioned that through age and infirmity Clark was unable to see his book through the press. Presumably for the same reason he seems to have consulted no book or edition of the play published during the last thirty years.

6. Performed December 1604. As there were official objections to it, Shakespeare would not have been encouraged to associate his play with the Gowrie conspiracy.

7. But Michael Hawkins, 'History, politics and *Macbeth*', in *Focus on Macbeth*, ed. John Russell Brown (1982), pp. 185–8, argues that there is ambiguity in the political 'lessons' in *Macbeth* and that Paul is wrong to assert that it was written by royal command.

8. Paul, pp. 226–47.

9. Daniel Amneus, *The Mystery of Macbeth* (1983).

learned of James's strong views on the matter. Against this it may
be urged that Macbeth was a usurper and that Malcolm, having
been made Prince of Cumberland, could be regarded as Duncan's rightful successor. Amneus is on stronger ground when he
lists nineteen unsolved problems connected with the play,[1] which,
he thinks, are due to the cuts and alterations made in 1606.
Some of these problems may rather be due to carelessness on
Shakespeare's part—there are similar discrepancies in many of
his plays. The report by Forman may be influenced by memories
of Holinshed;[2] and it is surely improbable that in the performance he witnessed Shakespeare's fellows used the 1599, not the
1606, version of the play, the earlier version being nevertheless
unavailable to the Folio editors.

More significant are the apparent changes with regard to the
murder of Duncan. Lady Macbeth first decides to incite her
husband to commit the deed; then she decides to use her keen
knife herself; then she apparently proposes a joint murder, and
finally Macbeth does the deed on his own. When Marvin
Rosenberg carried out an experiment[3] on people who were
ignorant of the play, they assumed at the end of the fifth scene
that Lady Macbeth would herself carry out the murder.

Amneus argues ingeniously that in the original play Macbeth,
not Malcolm, was made Prince of Cumberland—Forman's
'Northumberland' is a slip—and as this meant that he would
succeed Duncan in due course, he decided not to murder him.
He is later persuaded to murder Duncan in collaboration with
his wife, and this murder took place on stage at 2 a.m. (cf.
v. i. 33) not, as in the present text, soon after midnight. Amneus's
theory is well-argued and the clues are marshalled with great
skill; but from the nature of things it comes short of proof. It may
be doubted whether Shakespeare could ever have intended
Lady Macbeth to do the deed, whatever *her* intentions: it would
have gone against the sources and against the poet's conception
of the tragic hero. We may doubt, too, whether the murder ever
took place on stage, or that this was altered to avoid giving
offence to the King. The discrepancy between the times given
for the murder would not be noticed by the audience. Shakespeare could not allow Lady Macbeth in the sleep-walking scene
to count *twelve* strokes. In any case the murder is a joint operation
since Lady Macbeth drugs the possets of the grooms. Above all, I

1. Amneus, pp. 2–4.
2. Nosworthy. See p. xvi, n. 1.
3. Rosenberg. p. 242.

cannot believe that Shakespeare could have written the verse of
Macbeth before that of *Hamlet* and *Othello*.[1]

There were cuts and topical additions in the version of the play
performed in the summer of 1606; and, as we shall see, between
1606 and 1623 there were other changes, but for these Shakespeare was probably not responsible.

The play was therefore written, we may assume, between 1603
and 1606. The allusions to equivocation (II. iii. 9 ff.) and to the
hanging of traitors (IV. ii. 46 ff.) were presumably written after
the trial of Father Garnet (28 March 1606) for complicity in the
Gunpowder Plot. The words 'yet could not equivocate to heaven'
imply that the speech was written after 3 May, when Garnet was
hanged. Equivocation had been mentioned in *Hamlet* (v. i), but in
the spring and summer of 1606 it had become a burning topic.
John Chamberlaine wrote to Winwood on 5 April:[2]

> So that by the Cunning of his Keeper, *Garnet* being brought
> into a *Fool's Paradise*, had diverse Conferences with *Hall, his
> fellow Priest in the Tower*, which were overheard by *Spialls* set on
> purpose. With which being charged he stifly denied it; but
> being still urged, and some Light given him that they had
> notice of it, he *persisted still, with Protestation upon his Soul and
> Salvation, that there had passed no such Interlocution: till at last being
> confronted* with *Hall*, he was driven to *confess*; And being now
> asked in this Audience how he could salve this *lewd Perjury*, he
> answered, *that so long as he thought they had no Proof he was not
> bound to accuse himself: but when he saw they had Proof, he stood not
> long in it*. And then fell into a large Discourse of defending
> *Equivocations*, with many weak and frivolous Distinctions.

Garnet admitted that equivocation was justifiable only when used
for a good object;[3] but he argued that if the law be unjust, then
there is no treason.[4] He prayed 'for the good Success of the great
Action, concerning the Catholick Cause in the beginning of the
Parliament' and then denied that this referred to the Gunpowder
Plot.[5] He claimed that he could not reveal the plot because he
was told of it in confession, though, as James I pointed out:[6]

---

1. Not so much because of the metrical tests worked out in the nineteenth
century and tabulated by E. K. Chambers, but because of the impression of
most critics of Shakespeare's stylistic development. See *Shakespeare's Styles*, ed.
P. Edwards, I.-S. Ewbank and G. K. Hunter (1980).

2. Winwood, *Memorials*, II. 205–6.

3. *CSP (Domestic)* (1603–10), p. 306.

4. *Ibid.*, p. 308.   5. *State Trials*, I. 254.

6. *Political Works*, ed. McIlwain (1918), pp. 156–7.

For first, it can neuer be accounted a thing vnder Confession, which he that reueals it doth not discouer with a remorse, accounting it a sinne whereof hee repenteth him; but by the contrary, discouers it as a good motion, and is therein not dissuaded by his Confessor, nor any penance enjoyned him for the same . . . at the last hee did freely confesse, that the party reuealed it vnto him, as they were walking and not in the time of Confession . . . he confessed, that two diuers persons conferred with him anent this Treason; and that when the one of them which was *Catesby*, conferred with him thereupon, it was in the other parties presence and hearing; and what a Confession can this be in the hearing of a third person?

When Garnet was asked if it were well to deny on his priesthood that he had written to Greenwell, or had conference with Hall, knowing his denial to be false, he replied that in his opinion, and that of all the schoolmen, equivocation may be confirmed by oath or sacrament, without perjury, 'if just necessity so require'.[1] At his trial Garnet excused a man who had perjured himself on his death-bed with the words: 'It may be, my Lord, he meant to equivocate'.[2] Finally, I may quote Dudley Carleton, who in a letter to John Chamberlaine on 2 May mentions the postponement of Garnet's execution and his surprise when told he was to die. Carleton tells his correspondent that the Jesuit shifts, falters, and equivocates, but 'will be hanged without equivocation'.[3] This grim jest, worthy of the Porter, is quoted by A. N. Stunz in his article on the date of *Macbeth*.[4] He goes on to argue that the Porter's references to drunkenness and lechery are also aimed at Garnet, who comforted himself with sack to drown sorrow, and was falsely accused of fornication with Mrs Vaux, a slander he repudiated in a speech he made on the scaffold. We may doubt, however, that there was any such implication in the passages about drink and lechery. Some critics have pretended that Shakespeare inserted allusions to equivocation to please the taste of James I or of the public; but there is every reason to believe that Shakespeare, even if he had secret sympathies with the old religion, would have been horrified at the 'dire combustion' of the Gunpowder Plot and would have agreed with his royal master on the subject:[5]

And so the earth as it were opened, should haue sent foorth of the bottome of the *Stygian* lake such sulphured smoke,

1. *CSP*, p. 313.
2. A. N. Stunz, *ELH*, ix (1942), pp. 95–105.
3. *State Trials*, i. 266.   4. *CSP*, p. 315.
5. James I, *Workes* (1616), p. 224.

furious flames, and fearefull thunder, as should haue by their
diabolicall *Domesday* destroyed and defaced, in the twinkling of
an eye, not onely our present liuing Princes and people, but
euen our insensible Monuments . . .

It has been pointed out[1] that many of the conspirators came
from the neighbourhood of Stratford-upon-Avon, including
Catesby; that they trained at Clopton Hall; that some of them
frequented the Mermaid Tavern in London; and that therefore
the plot must have come as a shock to Shakespeare. Nor is there
reason to doubt that Shakespeare agreed with the King and most
of his subjects on the damnableness of equivocation. Devout
Catholics like Anne Vaux were equally scandalized by Garnet's
conduct: she remarked that she was sorry to hear that he was
privy to the plot, as he had made many protestations to the
contrary. At about the time *Macbeth* was first performed, the
King, saved from death by what he regarded as a miracle,
praised the wisdom of the Venetian Republic for the measures
she had taken against the Jesuits:[2]

> 'O blessed and wise Republic . . . how well she knows the
> way to preserve her liberty; for the Jesuits are the worst and
> most seditious fellows in the world. They are slaves and
> spies, as you know.' He then embarked on a discourse about
> the Society. By an able induction from all the kingdoms and
> provinces of the world he demonstrated that they have always
> been the authors and instruments of all the great disturbances
> which have taken place.

These quotations will give some idea of the climate of opinion in
which *Macbeth* was written. Lord Salisbury's *Answer to Certain
Scandalous Papers*, attacking equivocation, was being 'greedily
read' as early as 5 February 1606;[3] and equivocation became a
still more burning topic at the time of Garnet's trial and execution.

There are other scraps of evidence about the date. The price of
wheat was low in 1605–7; but as the farmer who hanged himself
was an old joke,[4] we cannot assume that the Porter's allusion
refers to any particular year. The reference to French hose (II.
iii. 14) seems to imply that it was close-fitting, but the joke was an

1. J. L. Hotson, *I, William Shakespeare* (1937), pp. 197–8.
2. *CSP (Venetian)* x. p. 361.
3. *CSP (Domestic)*, p. 286. Cited by E. K. Chambers.
4. Sordido in Jonson's *Every Man Out of His Humour* (1605) hangs himself
on the expectation of plenty. See also Beatrice D. Brown, 'Exemplary Materials
underlying *Macbeth*', *PMLA*, L (1935), 712.

old one, and too much reliance cannot be placed on it.[1] Shake-speare was probably in Oxford in the summer of 1605[2] and he would then have heard that James I, on the occasion of his visit in August, approved of Matthew Gwinn's Latin entertainment, *Tres Sibyllae*, with its prophecies to Macbeth and Banquo and its allusions to James's supposed ancestry. Shakespeare may also have heard that James disliked long plays. One such play, Samuel Daniel's *Arcadia Reformed*—later entitled *The Queenes Arcadia*—was witnessed by the Queen, but not by the King, on 30 August. As there seem to be two echoes of the play in *Macbeth* (see notes on III. ii. 49–50 and v. iii. 39–45), Shakespeare may have been in the audience. He may also have heard that two of the subjects proposed for debate before the King were 'whether the imagination can produce real effects' and whether the morals of nurses are imbibed by babes with their milk.[3]

We may suppose that the poet began his play on his return to London in the autumn of 1605. The discovery of the Gunpowder Plot of 5 November and the subsequent trials inevitably left their mark on some scenes. Although the influence of the Profanity Statute of 27 May has been discerned in the last two acts, the purging is likely to have taken place at a later date. The play was probably performed at Hampton Court on 7 August 1606 before King Christian of Denmark and James I. This was either the first performance or, most likely, as J. G. McManaway argued,[4] 'the first performance of Shakespeare's abbreviated version'.

There are, however, two difficulties about this dating. As Bradley pointed out,[5] there are a number of parallels between *Macbeth* and Marston's *Sophonisba* and these persuaded Sir Edmund Chambers to put Shakespeare's play early in 1606 and to support Dover Wilson's argument that the references to Garnet were added for the Court performance. As *Sophonisba* was entered in the *Stationers' Register* on 17 March, it may be doubted whether Marston could have got his play written and performed in the few weeks which were supposed to have elapsed between the first performance of *Macbeth* earlier in the year and the entry of *Sophonisba*. The relevant passages in Marston's play are all an integral part of the text, and most of them are in

1. See II. iii. 14 n.
2. Paul, pp. 15–24.
3. *Ibid.*, pp. 18 ff.
4. *SS 2* (1949), p. 149. But there is no proof that *Macbeth* was the play performed at Hampton Court.
5. Bradley, p. 471.

Act I. But need we assume that Marston was the debtor? By far
the most striking parallel is the following:

>   three hundred saile
> Upon whose tops the *Roman* eagles streachd
> Their large spread winges, which fan'd the evening ayre
> To us cold breath, for well we might discerne
> *Rome* swam to *Carthage*   (I. ii)
>   From Fife, great King,
> Where the Norweyan banners flout the sky,
> And fan our people cold.   (I. ii. 49–51)

The Marston passage is more straightforward than Shakespeare's;
for whereas eagles, quibbling on the bird, can readily be imagined
as fanning cold air to the enemy, it is more difficult to see the
aptness of the lines in which the inanimate banners actively fan
the Scottish army. It is more likely that Shakespeare picked up
one of Marston's best images than that Marston imitated several
passages from one of the weakest scenes in *Macbeth* while he remembered nothing from later and greater scenes.

One other parallel remains to be mentioned.[1] In the anonymous play, *Caesar's Revenge*, there are lines which resemble the
last lines of Macbeth's soliloquy in I. vii:

> Why thinke you Lords that its ambitions spur
> That pricketh *Caesar* to these high attempts.   (1468–9)

This play was entered in the *Stationers' Register* in June 1606; but
it is old-fashioned in style and may have been written in the previous reign. Shakespeare, if anyone, was probably the borrower;
but the association of *spur*, *prick*, and *ambition* is a natural one.

From these probable or possible echoes it is reasonable to
assume that *Macbeth*, at least in the form we have it, dates from
1606; but some passages, as Dover Wilson and others have
noted,[2] appear to be interpolations—the passage about the
hanging of traitors (IV. ii. 44–63), the 'milk of concord' passage
(IV. iii. 99–100), and possibly the King's Evil episode (IV. iii.
140–59).[3] But there need not have been any great lapse of time
between the writing of the original scenes and these interpolations.

Dover Wilson argued[4] that a number of scenes must have
been cut: a scene between Macbeth and his wife between I. iii
and I. iv; a scene in Act II in which Lady Macbeth went knife in

---

1. Malone (*NV*).   2. Wilson, pp. xxxi ff.
3. See above, p. xvii.   4. Wilson, pp. xxxiv ff.

hand to murder Duncan, and another dialogue between her and her husband; a speech in which Banquo, after Macbeth's accession, made it clear that he was not acquiescing in the murder because of the promise that he would beget kings; a scene to explain the presence of the Third Murderer; a scene in which Macduff explained why he had left his wife unprotected. Apart from the fact that there is no positive evidence for any of these cuts, the play would greatly suffer from any one of these speculative additions. More dialogues between Macbeth and his wife before the murder of Duncan would be dramatically disastrous; Banquo's conduct requires no explanation beyond what we are given; and any explanation of Macduff's 'desertion' would detract from the atmosphere of suspicion so necessary in this part of the play.

In all Shakespeare's plays there are loose ends, references to scenes which were deliberately left unwritten, and conflicting impressions of motives and characters. Nor are these dramatic weaknesses, but rather devices to create the illusion of life. Attempts to improve on Shakespeare by turning him into a naturalistic dramatist should be resisted.

3. THE PORTER SCENE

Although Pope and Coleridge agreed[1] that the Porter scene was interpolated by the players, enough has been said to indicate its topical significance; and although its topicality is not a proof that Shakespeare wrote it, a further consideration of the scene may establish his authorship, as well as having wider implications about the interpretation of the play.

The scene is theatrically necessary, if only because the actor who plays Macbeth has to wash his hands and change his clothes, and, as Capell suggested, it was necessary 'to give a rational space for the discharge of these actions'. Shakespeare was fully conversant with theatrical necessities and he always bowed to them; but if these were the sole reason for the scene's existence, it might have been added by another hand. Some scene, then, there had to be between the exit of Macbeth and the entrance of Macduff; but this does not explain why Shakespeare should introduce a drunken porter, or one suffering from a hangover, when a sober porter, singing an aubade, as in one of the German versions,[2]

---

1. Pope's edition of Shakespeare; *Coleridge on Shakespeare*, ed. T. Hawkes (1969), p. 215.
2. Schiller's.

might seem to serve as well. 'Comic relief' is a convenient, but question-begging term; for Shakespeare, we might suppose, could have used lyrical relief, if relief were needed. As Coleridge pointed out, Shakespeare never introduced the comic except when it may react on the tragedy by harmonious contrast. A good dramatist does not laboriously create feelings of tension and intensity only to dissipate them in laughter. Sometimes he may use the comic as a laughter-conductor, so as to prevent the audience from laughing at the wrong place and at the wrong things. Lear's sublimity is preserved for us by the Fool. In the present case it is impossible to agree with those critics who suppose that the function of the Porter is to take the present horror from the scene. On the contrary, the effect of the Porter scene is almost the exact opposite: it is there to increase our feelings of horror. We are never allowed to forget throughout the scene that a murder has been committed, and that it is about to be discovered. If we laugh, we never forget.

In his opening words the Porter identifies himself with the Porter of hell-gate,[1] who was expected to make jests, but who was something more than a jester. The plays in which he appears are on the theme of the harrowing of hell in the York, Chester, and Townley cycles, and it has been suggested by two recent critics[2] that the knocking on the gate and the entrance of Macduff recall the entrance of Christ into hell. The Townley porter, named Ribald, when he answers Christ's knocking, calls to Belzebub, as Macbeth's porter asks 'Who's there i'th' name of Belzebub?'

The purpose of recalling this traditional character was complex. First, it transports us from Inverness to the gate of hell, without violating the unity of place: Shakespeare has only to tell us the name of the place we were in before. It is hell because Lady Macbeth has invoked the murdering ministers, because Macbeth has called on the stars to hide their fires, and because hell is a state, not a place, and the murderers might say with Faustus's tempter,

> where we are is hell,
> And where hell is, there must we ever be.

1. W. E. Hales, *Notes and Essays on Shakespeare* (1884), pp. 273–90.

2. John B. Harcourt, 'I pray you remember the Porter', *SQ*, xii (1961), 393 ff.; Glynne Wickham, 'Hell Castle and its Door-Keeper', *SS 19* (1966), pp. 68–74 (reprinted in *Aspects of Macbeth*); W. A. Armstrong, *Shakespeare's Typology: Miracle and Morality Motifs in 'Macbeth'* (1970); Michael J. B. Allen, 'Macbeth's Genial Porter', *ELR*, iv (1974), 326–36, which, drawing on the classical links between porters and genii, suggests that the Porter symbolizes Macbeth's evil genius.

Shakespeare's second reason for recalling the miracle plays was that it enabled him to cut the cable that moored his tragedy to a particular spot in space and time, so that on the one hand it could become universalized, or on the other become contemporary. Macbeth's tragedy might therefore appear as a second Fall, with Lady Macbeth as a second Eve; or it could appear as terrifyingly topical. As S. L. Bethell put it,[1]

> the historical element distances and objectifies what is contemporary, and the contemporary element gives current significance to an historical situation . . . The whole atmosphere of treason and distrust which informs *Macbeth* found a parallel in the England of the Gunpowder Plot, so that a passing reference serves to define an attitude both to the Macbeth regime and to contemporary affairs.

The reference to treason in the Porter's speech looks back to the executed Thane of Cawdor, the gentleman on whom Duncan had built an absolute trust; and it looks forward to the dialogue between Lady Macduff and her son, and to the long testing of Macduff by Malcolm, which shows the distrust and suspicion which grow from equivocation. Later in the play, Macbeth complains of

> th'equivocation of the fiend
> That lies like truth:

and of those juggling fiends

> That palter with us in a double sense;
> That keep the word of promise to our ear,
> And break it to our hope.

Indeed, as Dowden pointed out,[2] Macbeth, on his first appearance after the discovery of the murder, is compelled to equivocate; and later in the same scene there is an even more striking equivocation:

> Had I but died an hour before this chance,
> I had liv'd a blessed time; for, from this instant,
> There's nothing serious in mortality;
> All is but toys: renown, and grace, is dead;
> The wine of life is drawn, and the mere lees
> Is left this vault to brag of.

---

1. S. L. Bethell, *Shakespeare and the Popular Dramatic Tradition* (1944), p. 46. Peter Ure pointed out (*NQ*, 28 May 1949) that the section added by Warner to *Albion's England* in 1606 on the Macbeth story was immediately followed by one on the Gunpowder Plot.

2. E. Dowden, *New Sh. Soc. Trans.* (1874).

The audience knows, as Macbeth himself was to know (though he here intended to deceive) that the words are a precise description of the truth about himself. Macbeth's own equivocation, by an ironical twist, becomes merely an aspect of truth. It is a brilliant counterpart to the equivocation of the fiend that lies like truth: it is the equivocation of the murderer who utters truth like lies. Equivocation therefore links up with one of the main themes of the play, and the equivocator would have earned his place in the Porter scene if Father Garnet had never lived or become involved in the Gunpowder Plot.

Similarly, the unnaturalness of the avaricious farmer is contrasted with the images of natural growth and harvest which are scattered through the play; and he is connected with the equivocator because Garnet went under the alias of Farmer. Even the tailor has his place in the scheme of the play, because of the clothing imagery which is so abundant in it.[1]

Nor is the style of the scene un-Shakespearian. Bradley pointed out[2] resemblances between Pompey's soliloquy on the inhabitants of the prison in *Measure for Measure* (IV. iii. 1–18) and the Porter's soliloquy, and between the dialogue of Pompey with Abhorson (IV. ii. 22 ff.) and the dialogue that follows the Porter's soliloquy. We may go further and suggest that one of the Porter's speeches, often bowdlerized out of existence, provides a valuable clue to one theme of the play. He is speaking of the effects of liquor, in answer to Macduff's question: 'What three things does drink especially provoke?'

> Marry, Sir, nose-painting, sleep, and urine. Lechery, Sir, it provokes and unprovokes: it provokes the desire, but it takes away the performance. Therefore, much drink may be said to be an equivocator with lechery: it makes him, and it mars him; it sets him on, and it takes him off; it persuades him, and disheartens him; makes him stand to, and not stand to: in conclusion, equivocates him in a sleep, and giving him the lie, leaves him.

Drink 'provokes the desire, but it takes away the performance'; and this contrast between *desire* and *act* is repeated several times in the course of the play. Lady Macbeth, in invoking the evil spirits, begs them not to allow compunctious visitings of nature to shake her fell purpose,

---

1. Spurgeon, *Shakespeare's Imagery* (1935), p. 324. H. L. Rogers has pointed out, *RES* (1965), 44, that the tailor may refer to a man associated in the public mind with the Garnet trial.
2. Bradley, p. 397.

> nor keep peace between
> Th'effect and it!

(i.e. intervene between her purpose and its fulfilment). Two
scenes later she asks her husband:

> Art thou afeard
> To be the same in thine own act and valour,
> As thou art in desire?

In IV. i. Macbeth gives some variations on the same theme:

> The flighty purpose never is o'ertook
> Unless the deed go with it. From this moment,
> The very firstlings of my heart shall be
> The firstlings of my hand. And even now,
> To crown my thoughts with acts, be it thought and done . . .
> This deed I'll do, before this purpose cool.

The passage is linked with one at the end of the banquet scene,
where Macbeth tells his wife:

> Strange things I have in head, that will to hand,
> Which must be acted, ere they may be scann'd.

The opposition between the hand and the other organs and senses
recurs again and again. Macbeth observes the functioning of his
own organs with a strange objectivity: in particular, he speaks of
his hand almost as though it had an independent existence of its
own. He exhorts his eye to wink at the hand; when he sees the
imaginary dagger he decides that his eyes have been made the
fools of the other senses, or else worth all the rest; later in the
same speech his very footsteps seem, as it were, to be divorced
from himself:

> Hear not my steps, which way they walk, for fear
> The very stones prate of my where-about;

and, after the murder of Duncan, both criminals are obsessed by
the thought of their bloody hands, as Forman noticed. Macbeth
speaks of them as 'a sorry sight' and as 'hangman's hands'—the
hangman had to draw and quarter his victim; Lady Macbeth
urges him to wash the 'filthy witness' from his hand; and in the
great speech that follows her exit, Macbeth asks:

> What hands are here? Ha! they pluck out mine eyes.
> Will all great Neptune's ocean wash this blood
> Clean from my hand? No, this my hand will rather
> The multitudinous seas incarnadine,
> Making the green one red.

In the first line of this quotation the hand–eye opposition appears in its most striking, most hallucinated form. Lady Macbeth persists in her illusion that a little water clears them of the deed— an illusion she has to expiate in the sleep-walking scene. Just before the murder of Banquo, Macbeth invokes Night:

> Scarf up the tender eye of pitiful Day,
> And, with thy bloody and invisible hand,
> Cancel, and tear to pieces, that great bond
> Which keeps me pale!

The bloody hand has now become completely detached from Macbeth and become a part of Night. Later in the play we are reminded of the same series of images when Angus declares that Macbeth feels

> His secret murders sticking on his hands.

The hand–eye opposition may have been suggested by the biblical injunctions to pluck out the eye that offends, and to cut off the offending hand;[1] for these occur in chapters which are echoed elsewhere in the play.

The Porter's words on lechery have yet another significance. They consist of a series of antitheses: *provokes—unprovokes; provokes—takes away; desire—performance; makes—mars; sets on— takes off; persuades—disheartens; stand to—not stand to*. Here concentrated in half a dozen lines we find one of the predominant characteristics of the general style of the play, multitudinous antitheses. The reader has only to glance at any scene of the play. We may link this trick of style with the 'wrestling of destruction with creation' which Wilson Knight has found[2] in the play, and with the opposition he has pointed out between night and day, life and death, grace and evil. Kolbe likewise spoke[3] of the play as a 'picture of a special battle in a universal war' (i.e. the war between sin and grace) and he declared that

> this idea is portrayed and emphasized in words and phrases more than 400 times . . . Not a single scene in the play is without the colour. And the whole effect is enhanced by the two-fold contrast we have already observed,—Darkness and Light, as a parable, Discord and Concord as a result.

1. I.e. Matt. v, vi, xviii, Mark ix, Luke xi. See II. ii. 58 n.; also Roy Walker pp. 71–2, and Rogers, p. 41.
2. *The Imperial Theme*, p. 153. See also G. I. Duthie, 'Antithesis in *Macbeth*', *SS 19* (1966), pp. 25 ff.
3. F. C. Kolbe, *Shakespeare's Way* (1930), pp. 21–2.

But the play contains many antitheses which are not to be found under such headings as Angel and Devil, good and evil. It may even be suggested that the iterative image of ill-fitting garments is a kind of pictorial antithesis, a contrast between the man and his clothes, as in the lines—

> Now does he feel his title
> Hang loose about him, like a giant's robe
> Upon a dwarfish thief.

Another recurrent image may be regarded as a contrast between the picture and the thing depicted:

> The sleeping, and the dead,
> Are but as pictures; 'tis the eye of childhood
> That fears a painted devil.

> This is the very painting of your fear.

> Shake off this downy sleep, death's counterfeit,
> And look on death itself!—up, up, and see
> The great doom's image!

These images are linked with the equivocation, deceit, and treachery which have been noted by more than one critic as constituting one of the main themes of the play.[1] These too are a contrast between appearance and reality, the favourite resource of many interpreters of Shakespeare.

The style of the Porter's speech is therefore not alien to that of the remainder of the play. It possesses the antithetical characteristics of the verse, suitably transprosed for semi-comic purposes. The whole scene is linked so closely with the rest of the play, in content as well as in style, that it is clearly impossible to regard it as a barbarous interpolation by the actors. The antithetical style is a powerful means of suggesting the paradox and enigma of the nature of man,

> The glory, jest, and riddle of the world,

the conflict within him between sin and grace, between reason and emotion, and the shadow which falls

> Between the potency
> And the existence
> Between the essence
> And the descent.

---

1. Cf. G. Wilson Knight, *The Wheel of Fire* (1949), pp. 140–59; L. C. Knights, *Explorations* (1946), pp. 18 ff.; Theodore Spencer, *Shakespeare and the Nature of Man* (1943), pp. 153–62.

This discussion of the authenticity of the scene has led us imperceptibly into a consideration of the play as a whole; and this in itself may serve to show that the Porter is an integral part of the play.

4. INTERPOLATIONS

The Porter scene is not the only part of the play which has been regarded with suspicion. There are at least nine other passages or scenes which earlier editors have branded as spurious on insufficient grounds.

(1) I. i.	Written by Middleton (Cunningham)
(2) I. ii.	Written by Middleton (Clarendon; Cunningham)
(3) I. iii. 1–37.	Written by Middleton (Clarendon; Cunningham)
(4) III. v.	Spurious, probably Middleton (many critics)
(5) IV. i. 39–43, 125–32.	Spurious, probably Middleton (many critics)
(6) IV. ii. 30–63.	Interpolation (Cunningham)
(7) IV. iii. 140–6.	Interpolation (Clarendon)
(8) V. ii.	Dubious (Clarendon)
(9) V. ix.	'evident traces of another hand' (Clarendon)

There is now no need to authenticate 1, 2, 3 and 9, since they are universally accepted as Shakespeare's, with the exception of Granville-Barker who thought that Shakespeare's genuine work began with the entrance of Macbeth.[1] No. 8 contains examples of Shakespeare's characteristic imagery and is certainly his. Nos 6 and 7 (on the hanging of traitors and on the King's Evil) are probably interpolations, but by Shakespeare himself.

There remain to be considered Nos 4 and 5, and here there is good reason to suppose that Shakespeare was not responsible. Middleton has often been regarded as the author of these interpolations since two songs from his play *The Witch* were sung at III. v. 32 and IV. i. 43. This play was not printed until 1778, but it has come down to us in a transcript made by Ralph Crane, one of the scriveners of the King's Men. He states that the play was 'long since acted by His Majesty's servants at the Blackfriars'; and, as the company did not act there before the autumn of 1609, the play was presumably written after that date. The tran-

1. Barker, p. 61.

script has been roughly dated 1620–7, so that 'long since' is likely to have been before 1620, and perhaps before 1615.[1]

W. J. Lawrence argued that *The Witch* was written soon after Johnson's *Masque of Queenes* which was performed on 1 February 1609, and that the professional performers (as opposed to the aristocratic amateurs), the same dances, and the same costumes were used in Middleton's play. This seems a plausible hypothesis, but we cannot tell how long the costumes would be available, if indeed they were available at all. Perhaps the King's Men acquired them. Dover Wilson regarded 1609–10 as a 'highly probable date' for *The Witch*; but if Middleton began writing for the King's Men only in 1614, the play must have been later,[2] but it is now thought that his association with the company began as early as 1606.

Nor is it possible to determine when the two songs were added to *Macbeth*. Forman does not refer to the cauldron scene, so his account does not enable us to tell whether the interpolations were in the 1611 performance. Presumably not. One would like to think that Shakespeare was dead and buried, or at least living in retirement, before his play was spoiled. It is reasonable to suppose that Shakespeare, if he had been available, would have been asked to carry out the revisions.

The Hecate passages were clearly invented to introduce the songs and Middleton is usually blamed for these insertions. But, as J. M. Nosworthy pointed out,[3]

> The Hecate of Middleton's *The Witch* is a very different creature from the *prima donna* and *prima ballerina* of Macbeth. She is coarse, brusque and colloquial, speaking mainly in blank verse . . . and never in octosyllabic couplets . . . There is no reason why the Hecate so rudely thrust into *Macbeth* should not have had all the properties of her namesake in *The Witch*. Close comparison of the two plays has convinced me that, of all contemporary claims to the Hecate scenes, Middleton's is, in fact, the weakest.

I concur with this verdict and believe that the Hecate passages were written by a writer, not without poetic talent, in order to

1. W. W. Greg, *Elizabethan Dramatic Documents*, pp. 358–9; Greg and F. P. Wilson, eds, *The Witch* (1950); F. P. Wilson, *The Library*, VII, 194–215; E. K. Chambers, *Elizabethan Stage*, II. 510; J. Dover Wilson, pp. xxvii ff.

2. R. C. Bald, *MLR*, XXXII (1937), 43; W. J. Lawrence, *Shakespeare's Workshop* (1928), pp. 28–33. R. V. Holdsworth (in a forthcoming book) is said to argue that Middleton was responsible for parts of *Macbeth* and *Timon of Athens*.

3. J. M. Nosworthy, 'The Hecate Scenes', *RES*, XXIV (1948), 138–9, and Rogers, p. 29, believe that the scenes may be Shakespeare's.

explain and introduce the two songs and the dance. It was then
found necessary to make certain other alterations. This would
account for the cuts in Act I and the possible rearrangement of
some scenes later in the play.

It was pointed out long ago[1] that III. vi should chronologically
follow IV. i, and that it was probably shifted to its present position,
when the Hecate scene was interpolated, to prevent the juxtaposition of two witch scenes. Lenox and the anonymous Lord
converse on matters which have not yet occurred and of which
Macbeth was ignorant till the end of IV. i. At the end of the
banquet scene Macbeth had decided to go early the next morning
to consult the Weird Sisters; IV. i. presumably takes place only a
few hours after this decision. Macbeth also declares that he will
send to Macduff; yet in III. vi we hear that his messenger has
already been repulsed by Macduff and that the latter has fled to
England. Lenox appears in III. vi as a savage critic of Macbeth
and in IV. i as an apparently loyal follower. Possibly his lines in
IV. i were originally spoken by another character, or his feigned
loyalty could exemplify the fact that Macbeth can trust no one.
If III. vi followed IV. i it would be an effective means of expanding
the brief announcement that Macduff had fled, without spoiling
Lady Macduff's feelings of bewilderment in IV. ii. There is one
slight difficulty. The banquet scene and the cauldron scene would
thereby be juxtaposed, and the furniture of the former would have
to be replaced by the cauldron. This operation could be effected
either by an interval at the end of the act or by a lost intervening
scene.[2]

Charles Lamb, in a famous paragraph, described the differences
between Middleton's witches and Shakespeare's Weird Sisters:[3]

> His witches are distinguished from the witches of Middleton
> by essential differences. These are creatures to whom man or
> woman plotting some dire mischief might resort for occasional
> consultation. Those originate deeds of blood, and begin bad

---

1. G. Crosse, *NQ*, 22 October 1898.
2. Cf. III. iv. 131–2 n. and Wheelock *MLN*, xv, 81. Rogers, p. 28, ingeniously
suggests that lines in III. vi have been transposed, and that they should be
printed in the following order: 37 '. . . pine for now.', 39 'Sent he to Macduff?',
40–3 'He . . . answer.', 37–9 'And this . . . war.', 43 'And that well might'. It
should be mentioned that knowledge of Macduff's flight enables the audience to
react to the irony of the words of the first apparition. Emrys Jones, *Scenic Form in
Shakespeare* (1971), p. 196, shows that if III. v is omitted, the Weird Sisters open
both the main parts of the play, 'and if an interval were to follow the third act,
the essential structural arrangement could be made clear to the audience'.
3. Charles Lamb, *Works*, ed. E. V. Lucas, *Miscellaneous Prose*, p. 55.

impulses to men. From the moment that their eyes first met Macbeth he is spellbound. That meeting sways his destiny. He can never break the fascination. These witches can hurt the body; those have power over the soul. Hecate, in Middleton, has a son, a low buffoon: the hags of Shakespeare have neither child of their own, nor seem descended from any parent. They are foul Anomalies, of whom we know not whence they are sprung nor whether they have beginning or ending. As they are without human passions, so they seem to be without human relations. They come with thunder and lightning, and vanish to airy music. This is all we know of them. Except Hecate, they have no names; which heightens their mysteriousness. Their names, and some of the properties, which Middleton has given to his hags, excite smiles. The Weird Sisters are serious things. Their presence cannot co-exist with mirth. But in a lesser degree, the Witches of Middleton are fine creations. Their power, too, is, in some measure, over the mind. They raise jars, jealousies, strifes, *like a thick scurf o'er life.*

It may be observed, however, that the Weird Sisters do not plant the seeds of evil in Macbeth; that they have no power over the innocent; that they are not without human passions; and that Lamb had no reason to suppose that the Hecate scenes were spurious—as they doubtless are.

Farnham showed that both *hag* and *witch* could mean a demon, as well as a human being who had made a compact with the devil; and that in the three spurious passages Shakespeare's superhuman witches are changed into human ones. 'They are compared to fairies when they cease to be fairies'.[1]

Another point was made by D. L. Chambers.[2] The genuine speeches of the Weird Sisters 'are prevailingly tetrameter with a trochaic cadence'. The spurious passages, on the other hand, are in iambic measures, 'dull, mechanical, regular', in striking contrast with 'the grotesqueness, the freedom, the bold roughness of the colloquies and incantations of the weird sisters'.

It may be added that Middleton was influenced by *Macbeth* when he wrote *The Witch*;[3] and that there are also a number of parallels between the witch scenes of the two dramatists, doubtless because they drew on the same sources for their information.

1. W. Farnham, *Shakespeare's Tragic Frontier* (1950), pp. 74 ff.

2. D. L. Chambers, *The Metre of 'Macbeth'* (1903), p. 18. Cited W. J. Lawrence.

3. Several parallels between *Macbeth* and *The Witch* were pointed out by Steevens (*NV*): 'I spic'd them lately with a drowsy posset' (cf. II. ii. 6); 'There's no such thing' (cf. II. i. 47). Two others were pointed out in Clarendon ed.: 'The innocence of sleep' (cf. II. ii. 35); 'I'll rip thee down from neck to navel' (cf. I. ii. 22).

5. SOURCES

Since 1951, when the New Arden *Macbeth* was first published, there have been several discussions of the sources of the play, including my own (1957, 1977), and Geoffrey Bullough's (1973).[1]

William Kemp in *Kemps Nine Daies Wonder* (1600) refers to what was apparently a ballad on the subject of *Macbeth*, when he speaks of 'a penny Poet whose first making was the miserable stolne story of Macdeol, or Macdobeth, or Mac-somewhat, for I am sure a Mac it was, though I neuer had the maw to see it'.[2] On the following page he proceeds to advise its author to 'leaue writing these beastly ballets, make not good wenches Prophetesses, for litle or no profit'. As ballads were frequently based on plays and as the remark about prophetesses could refer to the Weird Sisters, there may have been a Macbeth play before 1600; and if there was one, Shakespeare may have known it. But, even so, Holinshed provided Shakespeare with his main source. As Grierson suggested,[3] he derived from the *Chronicles*

> the tone and atmosphere of the Celtic and primitive legends of violent deeds and haunting remorse . . . Story after story told him of men driven by an irresistible impulse into deeds of treachery and bloodshed but haunted when the deed was done by the spectres of conscience and superstition.

Shakespeare combined the story of Macbeth with the earlier account of the murder of King Duff by Donwald and his wife, thus replacing an open conspiracy, in which Banquo was an accomplice, with a secret murder of a royal guest. It would have been impossible to have depicted James I's reputed ancestor in such a role; but the dramatic advantages of the change were equally obvious. The fusion of the two stories was made easier by the fact that both men were driven to commit murder by their ambitious wives.

Shakespeare may have taken some hints from Holinshed's story of the noblemen who conspired with witches against King Duff,[4] and he took a number of details from the account of the murder by Donwald and his wife—the incitement by the wife, the fact that the King was a guest of the murderer and had just given him presents, the murder of the chamberlains whom Donwald and his wife had sent to bed drunk. But in Holinshed's

1. *The Sources of Shakespeare's Plays; Narrative and Dramatic Sources of Shakespeare.*
2. Ed. G. B. Harrison (1923), pp. 30–1.
3. *Macbeth*, ed. Grierson and Smith (1914), pp. xviii-xix.
4. See p. 164 below.

account the murder is carried out by Donwald's servants who remove the body from the castle. Holinshed's marginalia read almost like a running commentary on the play, and they may have suggested the dramatic treatment of the subject:

> A guiltie conscience accuseth a man . . . Donwald's wife counselled him to murther the king . . . The womans euill counsell is followed . . . Donwald a verie dissembler . . . Prophecies mooue men to vnlawfull attempts . . . women desirous of high estate . . . Mackbeth's guiltie conscience . . . Macbeth's dread . . . His crueltie caused through feare . . . Macbeths confidence in wizzards . . . Mackbeth recoileth [cf. v. ii. 23] . . . Mackbeths trust in prophecies.

The voice that cried 'Sleep no more' was probably suggested by the voice heard by King Kenneth after he had murdered his nephew[1]—as described by Holinshed (or Buchanan). One or two details were derived from the account of Edward the Confessor's reign, and by a lucky chance touching for the King's Evil was topical as well as historically accurate. But the main plot was taken from Holinshed's account of Macbeth, though with many alterations, made for dramatic reasons.[2] Shakespeare keeps close to the chronicler in his account of Macbeth's meeting with the Weird Sisters (except for their physical appearance) and in the scene between Macduff and Malcolm in England, partly because in both places Holinshed uses direct speech. Elsewhere Shakespeare occasionally uses single words which may have been suggested by the *Chronicles*, but not many.

The following are the most striking alterations: (i) Duncan, as depicted by Holinshed, is younger than in the play, and he is depicted as a feeble ruler. By making the victim old and holy, and by passing over his weaknesses as a ruler, Shakespeare deliberately blackened the guilt of Macbeth. (ii) There are three campaigns described in Holinshed which are condensed into one in the play: the defeat of Macdonwald's rebellion, the defeat of Sweno, and the defeat of Canute, who came with a new fleet to avenge his brother Sweno's overthrow. (The telescoping may be due partly to cuts.) (iii) Macbeth, according to Holinshed's account, has a genuine grievance against Duncan who, by proclaiming his son Prince of Cumberland, went against the laws of succession, and took away from Macbeth the prospect of the throne; which he had every reason to hope for, since he could

1. See p. 166 below.

2. R. A. Law, *University of Texas Studies in English* (1952), has a useful list of 35 incidents in the play which are not in Holinshed.

claim it on behalf of his wife and her son by her first husband. Shakespeare suppresses these facts, because he wished for dramatic reasons to accentuate Macbeth's guilt and to minimize any excuses he might have had. We hear nothing of a previous marriage of Lady Macbeth, though she states that she has given suck. It has been suggested, too, that because of 'the triumph of primogeniture during the twelfth and thirteenth centuries'[1] the method of succession which existed in Macbeth's day was not understood in Shakespeare's, even by Holinshed. (iv) Banquo and others were accomplices in the murder of Duncan. It was much more dramatic to have Macbeth and his wife solely responsible, and this safeguarded the reputation of James's ancestor. The King had a particular dislike of political assassination, even of manifest tyrants, such as Nebuchadnezzar and Nero. 'The wickednesse therefore of the King can neuer make them that are ordained to be iudged by him, to become his Iudges.'[2] Shakespeare therefore took the details of the murder from the Donwald story. (v) Shakespeare omits the ten years' good rule by Macbeth between the murder of Duncan and the murder of Banquo. The omission was dramatically necessary. (vi) Shakespeare apparently invented the banquet scene and the appearance of Banquo's ghost. (vii) He omits the story of Macduff's refusal to assist in the building of Dunsinane Castle. (viii) Although the cauldron scene is based on the three prophecies mentioned by Holinshed, Shakespeare for reasons of dramatic economy substitutes the Weird Sisters for 'a certeine witch, whom hee had in great trust'. (ix) In the *Chronicles*, Macbeth surrounded Macduff's castle with a great power. It was more economical to use murderers. (x) The testing of Macduff by Malcolm is given in full by Holinshed (and it is also in Boece, Bellenden, and Stewart); but Shakespeare omits the fable of the Fox and the Flies, omits Malcolm's self-accusation of dissimulation, and adds other vices to those mentioned by Holinshed. In the *Chronicles* the testing of Macduff occurs after he has heard of his wife's death. Shakespeare's alteration made Malcolm's suspicions more understandable. (vi) Macbeth flees from Dunsinane Castle and is pursued by Macduff to Lunfannaine. This would have been dramatically irrelevant. (xii) Shakespeare invents the sleep-walking scene and the presumed suicide of Lady Macbeth. Holinshed says nothing about the fate of Macbeth's wife. or of Donwald's.

1. Wilson, p. ix.
2. James I, *The Trew Law of Free Monarchies*, in *Political Works*, ed. McIlwain (1918), pp. 60-1, 66.

Other sources have been suggested for the plot of *Macbeth*. Mrs C. C. Stopes argued[1] that Shakespeare was acquainted with William Stewart's *Buik of the Croniclis of Scotland*, an enormous poem of over 42,000 lines which remained in manuscript until 1858. It was written 1531–5 by order of Queen Margaret, for the use of her son, James V. Mrs Stopes's theory was propounded in 1897,[2] accepted temporarily by Dover Wilson,[3] who later expressed doubts, and accepted more recently by Arthur Melville Clark.[4] The case seems to me to be very weak. Mrs Stopes fails to provide a single convincing verbal parallel between Stewart and Shakespeare. Although 'till the warldis end' resembles 'the crack of doom' (iv. i. 117) it was a common idea in the early years of James I's reign. Lancelot Andrewes, in his sermon on the coronation, spoke of the King's descendants, 'who shall (wee trust, and pray they may) stretch their line to the world's end'.

It seems to me that the resemblances between Stewart and Shakespeare are accidental, and that any poet expanding the bare facts of the story would tend to develop Lady Macbeth's character in the same way. From Holinshed Shakespeare would learn that Donwald committed the murder of Duff *through setting on of his wife*, who *bare no lesse malice in hir heart towards the king* and showed Donwald *the meanes wherby he might soonest accomplish it*. Although Donwald *abhorred the act greatlie in heart, yet through instigation of his wife* he bribed the servants to do the deed. In the section of the *Chronicles* relating to Macbeth himself Shakespeare would have read that *his wife lay sore upon him to attempt the thing, as she was verie ambitious, burning in unquenchable desire to beare the name of a queene*. From these hints of the ambition and determination of the wife and the moral scruples of the murderer, it would not be difficult for any competent dramatist to depict a Lady Macbeth who called her husband a coward, bade him play the hypocrite, and who herself pretended great indignation after the murder to cover up their guilt. Even the swoon of Lady Macbeth, whether real or feigned, does not need to have a source. Nor would it be difficult for two poets independently to have arrived at the idea of Banquo's descendants reigning till the end of the world. Holinshed's 'long order of continuall descent' and Matthew Gwinn's prophecy to Banquo's descendants of *imperium sine fine* express the same idea. No one, moreover, has provided any

---

1. *Shakespeare's Industry* (1916), pp. 102–3.
2. When her theory appeared in a periodical.
3. Wilson, pp. xviii ff.   4. *Murder Under Trust* (1981).

plausible explanation of how Shakespeare obtained access to the manuscript of Stewart's poem.

It is much more likely, as M. H. Liddell[1] and H. N. Paul have argued, that Shakespeare had read Buchanan's *History of Scotland* in its original Latin. His hero is, perhaps, closer to Buchanan's portrait of Macbeth than to Holinshed's. According to Buchanan,

> he was a man of penetrating genius, a high spirit, unbounded ambition, and, if he had possessed moderation, was worthy of any command however great; but in punishing crimes he exercised a severity, which, exceeding the bounds of the laws, appeared oft to degenerate into cruelty.

Holinshed speaks of him merely as a 'valiant gentleman'. The account given by Buchanan of King Kenneth's remorse is likewise closer than Holinshed's to Macbeth's:

> His soul disturbed by a consciousness of his crime, permitted him to enjoy no solid or sincere pleasure; in retirement the thoughts of his unholy deed tormented him; and, in sleep, visions full of horror drove repose from his pillow. At last, whether in truth an audible voice from heaven addressed him, as is reported, or whether it were the suggestion of his guilty mind, as often happens with the wicked, in the silent watches of the night, he seemed thus to be admonished.

Buchanan's statement that 'the command of Cumberland was always considered the next step to the crown' is nearer to Macbeth's lines (I. iv. 48–50) than the corresponding passage in Holinshed.

Paul has also argued[2] that Shakespeare knew Leslie's *De Origine, Moribus et Rebus Gestis Scotorum* (1578), in which the Weird Sisters are devils disguised as women, as they may be in Shakespeare's play, and in which there is a genealogical tree of Banquo's descendants with roots, leaves, and fruit. This may well have caught Shakespeare's eye and left its mark on the imagery of Act III.[3] Leslie, moreover, makes no mention of Macbeth's accomplices, he stresses the way in which Lady Macbeth persuaded her husband by showing him how the deed could be successfully accomplished—as Donwald's wife does in Holin-

---

1. Ed. *Macbeth* (1903). Rogers, pp. 6–7, doubts whether Shakespeare read Buchanan or Leslie.

2. Paul, pp. 171 ff.

3. Cf. 'root' (III. i. 5); 'Stick deep' (III. i. 49); 'seed' (III. i. 69); 'snake', 'serpent' (III. ii. 13, III. iv. 28), the last three being suggested by the fruit and the serpentine trunk of the genealogical tree.

shed—he speaks of 'the most holy king Duncan', and he gives a more vivid account than Holinshed of Macbeth's reign of terror. Paul also thought[1] that Shakespeare consulted Skene's *Scots Acts* (1597); but he did not need to read this book in order to depict Duncan as 'a good and modest prince' and Macbeth as 'a cruel tyrant'.

Sir James Fergusson of Kilkerran pointed out[2] that the Table of all the Kings of Scotland in *Scots Acts* was reprinted in London in *Certeine Matters concerning the Realme of Scotland* (1603), where it was more accessible to Shakespeare. He also suggested that *Macbeth* may have been influenced by some details in the career of James Stewart of Bothwellmuir, who fell from power in 1585 and met his death in 1595. He became Earl of Arran and was spurred on by the ambition of a wicked wife. The 'highland oracles' had shown her that Gowrie should be ruined, but she 'helped the prophecy forward as well as she could'. Stewart was slain after he had tried to avoid the circumstances 'which it had been prophesied would attend his death', and his head was cut off and set on a pole. Stewart's wife was suspected of trafficking with witches and she was described as 'a meete matche for such a spouse, depending upon the response of witches, and enemie of all human societie'.[3] Shakespeare was probably ignorant of these matters, but they provide further evidence that the atmosphere of the play was not alien to Shakespeare's contemporaries.

B. J. Burden has pointed out to me (privately) a number of resemblances between *Macbeth* and *Arden of Feversham*. The conscience-stricken soliloquies of Michael before Arden's murder (II. ii, III. i), Mosbie's soliloquy after the murder (III. v), and the knocking at the door (v. i) may be compared with Macbeth's speeches before and after the murder of Duncan. But knocking on the door occurs after the murder of Desdemona.

It is more certain that three of Shakespeare's early works had some influence on *Macbeth*. The theme of witchcraft in *2 Henry VI* and the equivocating prophecy in the first act of that play seem to have called up a number of associations in Shakespeare's mind.[4] More significant are the echoes in *Lucrece*, such as the stage imagery pointed out by Walter Whiter,[5] the setting of Duncan's murder resembling that of Lucrece's rape, as Macbeth

---

1. Paul, pp. 220 ff.
2. *Shakespeare's Scotland* (1957), p. 6.
3. Wardlaw MS. 182.
4. See G. Wilson Knight, *The New Adelphi* (1927).
5. *A Speciment of a Commentary*, ed. A. Over and M. Bell (1967), p. 136.

himself recognizes (II. i. 55), and as Warburton pointed out, and the realization by both Macbeth and Tarquin that their crimes will make them lose the blessings which should accompany old age (v. iii. 24–5; *Lucr.*, 141–7). Shakespeare uses some of the same imagery in both works, and in both he shows the conflict between temptation and conscience.[1]

There are many echoes of *Richard III*.[2] In both plays the hero wades through slaughter to a throne; both are tyrants, usurpers, and murderers; both courageous, cruel, and treacherous. But Richard chooses evil without reluctance, Macbeth only after an agonizing conflict, his conscience operating before, during, and after his crimes. We hear of Richard's timorous dreams, as we know of Macbeth's insomnia; but it is not until the eve of the battle of Bosworth that we see Richard display any consciousness of his guilt. (See below, p. lii.)

Richard III and *Macbeth* have been regarded as the most Senecan of Shakespeare's plays, in which he made use of the *Tenne Tragedies* translated by Heywood, Studley, and others, but also, at times, referring to the originals.[3] There seem to be echoes of five of Seneca's plays, scattered through nearly all Shakespeare's scenes.[4] These include versions of popular quotations,[5] but others coloured his treatment of scenes and characters. Lady Macbeth is modelled partly on Clytemnestra,[6] but her invocation of evil spirits, her wish to be unsexed, and her pretended willingness to dash out the brains of her infant are clearly influenced by Seneca's portrait of Medea.[7] Cassandra's foreseeing of the murder of Agamemnon has affinities with two famous speeches of Macbeth.[8] She declares that

> No vision fond fantasticall my senses doth beguile;

and Macbeth, overwhelmed by temptation in the third scene of the play, speaks of his 'thought, whose murder yet is but fantastical', and just before the murder, when he sees the imaginary dagger, asks

---

1. See M. C. Bradbrook, *SS 4* (1951); reprinted in *Aspects of Macbeth*.
2. F. M. Smith, *PMLA* (1948), pp. 1003 ff., compares the two plays and discusses a number of parallel passages.
3. Wilson, p. xliii.
4. *Hercules Furens, Hercules Oetaeus, Agamemnon, Medea*, and possibly *Phaedra*. For *Hercules Oetaeus* see E. B. Lyle in *English Studies*, LIII (1972), 109–12.
5. See G. K. Hunter, *Dramatic Identities and Cultural Tradition* (1978), pp. 159 ff., for a critical account of the Senecan influence.
6. Muir, *The Sources of Shakespeare's Plays*, and Bullough.
7. I.-S. Ewbank, 'The Fiend-like Queen', *SS* 19 (1966), pp. 82 ff.
8. Muir, *op. cit.*, p. 214.

> Art thou not, fatal vision, sensible
> To feeling as to sight?

Finally, it should be mentioned that Shakespeare took the trouble to read more than one of James I's works. There are several echoes of *Daemonologie*[1] and one from his *Counterblast to Tobacco*.[2] It is possible that Shakespeare also perused *The True Law of Free Monarchies, Basilikon Doron*, and *A Fruitfull Meditation*,[3] but the parallels with these are more dubious.

6. THE PLAY

> 'This dead butcher and his fiend-like queen.'

Malcolm's epitaph on the murderers of his father is understandably harsh. Whereas Hamlet has flights of angels to sing him to his rest, Antony and Cleopatra are eulogized by their chief enemy, Coriolanus is praised by his assassin, and even the wife-murderer Othello is complimented after his suicide on his greatness of heart, the hell-hound Macbeth has no one to speak for him; and when Samuel Johnson commented on the play in his edition (1765), he expressed the general view that 'The passions are directed to their true end. Lady Macbeth is merely detested; and though the courage of Macbeth preserves some esteem, yet every reader rejoices at his fall.'[4]

Although the play has been described as Shakespeare's 'most profound and mature vision of evil',[5] 'a statement of evil',[6] and 'a play about damnation', it is plain that in order to show how the hero comes to be damned, Shakespeare had to describe and create the good which Macbeth had sacrificed. Few modern critics share Johnson's attitude to the protagonists.

In some ways, as we have seen, Macbeth resembles the murderer and usurper, Richard III;[7] and like Claudius, he is led

---

1. Muir, *op. cit.*, p. 217.   2. Muir, *Shakespeare's Sources* (1957), p. 177.
3. Jane H. Jack, *ELH* (1955), pp. 173 ff. Ann Pasternak Slater, *EC*, XXVIII (1978), 112–28, points out a number of parallels with Thomas Nashe's *The Terrors of the Night*, of ideas more than of words. J. J. Tobin, *The Aligarh Journal of English Studies*, VII (1982), 72–8, argues that there are parallels with Nashe's *Christ's Tears over Jerusalem*. They include the following: base, pluckt, bone, gums (ed. Mckerrow, pp. 70–1; cf. I. vii. 54–7); bankes, shole, come (p. 68; cf. I. vii. 6–7); birdes doe, the Pyt-fal, the nette, the Ginne (p. 169, cf. IV. iii. 32–5).
4. *Dr Johnson on Shakespeare*, ed. W. K. Wimsatt (1969), p. 133.
5. G. Wilson Knight, *The Wheel of Fire* (ed. 1949), p. 140.
6. L. C. Knights in 'How Many Children Had Lady Macbeth?'; reprinted in *Explorations* (1946), p. 18.
7. See above, p. xlii.

from crime to crime in the attempt to achieve security. Macbeth is a humanized version of the previous villains. Shakespeare wished to get under the skin of a murderer, and to show that the Poet for the Defence, though extenuating nothing, can make us feel our kinship with his client, can make us recognize that if we had been so tempted, we too might have fallen. In Donne's words, applied by Peter Alexander,[1]

> Thou knowest this man's fall, but thou knowest not his wrast-ling; which perchance was such that almost his very fall is justified and accepted of God.

So, although Macbeth is 'a miserable, and a banished, and a damned creature', yet he is God's 'creature still and contributes something to his glory even in his damnation'.[2] Macbeth is a noble and gifted man who chooses treachery and crime, not believing he has any justification for his deeds, but knowing them precisely for what they are. In altering his sources in this respect, Shakespeare deprived his hero of mitigations and excuses. In the tragedy immediately preceding *Macbeth*, evil is concentrated in the savage quartet of Goneril, Regan, Cornwall, and Edmund, who are able to bring about the ruin of their moral superiors by making use of their weaknesses in the shape of lust, credulity and pride. In *Macbeth*, the evil is transferred from the villains to the hero and heroine, influenced, if not dominated, by the evil embodied in the Weird Sisters.

Yet there is no play which puts so persuasively the contrasting good. Shakespeare makes Duncan venerable and saintly, Malcolm an image of perfection, Macduff a righteous avenger. The long scene in England contrasts the portrait of a good king (as Malcolm will be) with that of the tyrant he pretends to be, and the account of Edward the Confessor's powers presents a good supernatural to counterbalance the evil of the Weird Sisters.[3] Apart from these things, it is by the imagery and symbolism that the good is presented.[4] The contrast between light and darkness symbolizes a general contrast between good and evil, devils and angels, hell and heaven. The disease images clearly reflect both the sin which is a disease and Macbeth himself who *is* the disease,

1. *Shakespeare's Life and Art* (1939), p. 173.
2. *Donne Poetry and Prose*, ed. J. Hayward, p. 663.
3. L. C. Knights, *Explorations*, p. 32.
4. See Kenneth Muir, 'Image and Symbol in *Macbeth*', *SS 19* (1966) (reprinted in *Aspects of Macbeth* [1977]) and the longer essay in *Shakespeare the Professional* (1973), pp. 128–57.

from which Scotland suffers. Wilson Knight has an effective chapter[1] on the 'life-themes' of the play, in which he makes the point that Lady Macbeth 'wins largely by appealing to Macbeth's valour'; and Cleanth Brooks in a well-known essay[2] writes on her appeal to his manliness. All through the play Shakespeare continually juggles with the different meanings of 'honour'— military honour, honour bestowed by a king, free honours, mouth-honour. The ambiguity in the word is brought out in the exchange between Macbeth and Banquo just before the murder of Duncan:

> If you shall cleave to my consent, when 'tis,
> It shall make honour for you.
> So I lose none
> In seeking to augment it, but still keep
> My bosom franchis'd, and allegiance clear,
> I shall be counsell'd.

Closely connected with 'honour' are the feudal ideas of 'duties' and 'service', the repetition of which helps to create a picture of an orderly and closely knit society, in contrast to the disorder consequent upon Macbeth's initial crime. The naturalness of that order, and the unnaturalness of its violation by Macbeth, are emphasized by the images of planting and sowing;[3] and the images of sleep and milk contrast with the images of unnatural disorder and the reiteration of fear and blood. The contrast is most apparent in the lines which express so violently Lady Macbeth's violation of her sex:[4]

> I have given suck, and know
> How tender 'tis to love the babe that milks me:
> I would, while it was smiling in my face,
> Have pluck'd my nipple from his boneless gums,
> And dash'd the brains out, had I so sworn . . .

By such means Shakespeare builds up the order of Nature and examines the nature of Order; so that the violation of order in the state by the murder of Duncan is seen to be an unnatural horror, a deed too terrible to behold,[5] inevitably attended by

1. *The Imperial Theme* (ed. 1951), p. 125.
2. *The Well Wrought Urn* (1947), pp. 22–49. See also Helen Gardner, *The Business of Criticism* (1957), pp. 61 ff.
3. Andor Gomme has suggested (privately) that the idea of planting was derived from its biblical use in e.g. Jer. xii. 2, xxiv. 6, and 2 Sam. vii. 10.
4. See n. 2 above.
5. See II. ii. 53; II. iii. 71; III. iv. 60; IV. i. 113.

portents.[1] Caroline Spurgeon recorded[2] four reverberation images which, she argued, suggest the 'overwhelming and unending nature of the consequences or reverberations of the evil deed'.[3]

Nevertheless the presentation of the good which counterbalances the evil is done most effectively through Macbeth and his wife, who are unwilling witnesses to the good they renounce. Macbeth is aware from the very beginning that the deed he contemplates is evil. He admits that its 'horrid image' makes his hair stand on end, and his heart knock against his ribs. Although he never discusses with his wife the morality of the murder, which she always mentions euphemistically,[4] and although he hardly faces it himself, every word he speaks shows that he is struck to the soul with a realization of the horror of the deed. The half-demented language he uses immediately after the murder expresses fear, but not of detection; and although he fears Banquo partly for prudential reasons, he fears him also because of his own sense of guilt. Macbeth is never in doubt of the difference between good and evil; nor is Lady Macbeth, not even in the speech in which she deliberately chooses evil as a means of achieving the 'good' of the crown; nor, indeed, is the audience. Inexorably the action rams home the moral that all the perfumes of Arabia will not sweeten the little hand of the murderess, and that, to those who destroy life, life itself becomes merely 'a tale told by an idiot'.

To some critics, however, the play has seemed to be lacking in inevitability and coherence. Robert Bridges complained[5] that the Macbeth we have cause to admire could never have committed the murder of Duncan, and that Shakespeare deliberately throws dust in the eyes of the audience, not clearly telling them whether Macbeth decided to murder Duncan before the beginning of the play, or whether the idea was imposed upon him by the witches, or whether he was urged to it by his wife:

We may combine the two latter motives, and see hell and home

1. John Masefield, 'Shakespeare and Spiritual Life', reprinted in *Recent Prose* (1932), pp. 270 ff., discusses the significance of the portents.

2. *Shakespeare's Imagery* (1935), p. 329.

3. Erasmus in the colloquy Shakespeare echoed in III. i has the following passage on the reverberation of good deeds: 'I would desire to have a certain honourable renown of my name, which may Echo again throughout the whole world, and which may become more famous with my age, and at last may grow more renowned after my death' (trans. H. M., 1671, p. 478).

4. See I. v. 66–8, I. vii. 48, 73.

5. *The Influence of the Audience on Shakespeare's Dramas* (ed. 1927), p. 14.

leagued against him: the difficulty lies in the unknown quantity of the first motive, his predisposition; which, if it be allowed to be only in the exact balance required for these two agencies to carry it, is still contradictory to the picture of nobility impressed upon us by Shakespeare.

A Macbeth who feels the horror of the deed as Shakespeare's hero would not, Bridges thought, be able to commit it. The argument is that Shakespeare sacrificed psychological consistency to theatrical effect. Edgar Elmer Stoll made[1] a similar point, though without regarding this characteristic of the play as a fault. He pointed out that if Macbeth had had a better title to the throne than Malcolm, or if Duncan had been depicted as a feeble rather than as a holy king, 'Macbeth's conduct in killing him would have been more reasonable and more psychologically in keeping, to be sure, but less terrible, less truly tragic'. Shakespeare was not so much concerned with the creation of real human beings, but with theatrical or *poetical* effect. He was fascinated by the very difficulty of making the psychologically improbable, by sheer virtuosity, appear possible. As Schücking said,[2] Shakespeare made 'the bold experiment of a character with a strongly marked mixture of qualities of which the one seems almost to preclude the other'—a brave warrior who is a moral coward, a brutal murderer who is racked by feelings of guilt, and so on. Maurice Morgann made the same point[3] when he wrote of the conflicting impressions of a character deliberately set in motion by the dramatist.[4]

It is only fair to Shakespeare to add, and Stoll did not always make full allowance for this, that ideas about what is psychologically possible change from age to age, and that what Bridges thought impossible seemed perfectly possible to the readers of Timothy Bright and even, to judge from criticism of the play, right down to the end of the nineteenth century. Eighty years after Bridges' complaint, it is his conception of psychology which seems simplistic.[5] For he underestimates the potentialities for

1. E. E. Stoll, 'Source and Motive in *Macbeth* and *Othello*', *RES*, xix (1943), 27.

2. L. L. Schücking, *The Baroque Character of the Elizabethan Tragic Hero* (1938), pp. 21–2.

3. Maurice Morgann, *Shakespearian Criticism*, ed. Daniel A. Fineman (1972), *passim*.

4. Kenneth Muir, *The Singularity of Shakespeare* (1977), pp. 1–19, and 'Shakespeare's Open Sceret', *SS* 34 (1981), pp. 1–9.

5. There is a good reply to Bridges in J. I. M. Stewart's *Character and Motive in Shakespeare* (1949), Chapter V.

evil in the virtuous, and for virtue in the wicked. The sheep and
goats of our 'judgement here' are not necessarily the divisions
of the life to come. 'Our life', remarked a wise character in *All's
Well that Ends Well*, 'is of a mingled yarn, good and ill together'.
Besides all this, there is something artificial in Bridges' assumption
that if Macbeth has enough predisposition to be driven to murder
by wife and witches combined, he is too ignoble to be the tragic
hero envisaged by the dramatist. For it is never possible to determine the exact share of blame to be allotted after a crime in the
real world to the three factors, heredity, environment, and personal weakness; and, in a play, between three comparable factors,
fate, external evil, and the character of the hero. We cannot
divide the world into potential murderers and those who are not.
It consists of imperfect human beings, more or less ignorant of
their own selves, and not knowing (though they have been told
often enough) the way to be happy. If they commit evil it is
because they hope thereby to avoid another evil, which seems to
them for the moment to be worse, or obtain another good, which
seems attractive only because it is not in their possession. The
direct cause of sin, Thomas Aquinas thought,[1] is the

> *adherence to a mutable good*, and every sinful act proceeds from an
> inordinate desire for some temporal good; and that one desires
> a temporal good inordinately is due to the fact that *he loves
> himself inordinately*.

Macbeth has not a predisposition to murder; he has merely an
inordinate ambition that makes murder itself seem to be a lesser
evil than failure to achieve the crown and so satisfy his wife. They
both misjudge, destroying themselves for the sake of the other.

Lady Macbeth, however, accuses her husband of having proposed the murder before Duncan announced his intention of
being their guest, before time and place cohered. This made
Coleridge argue[2] that the murder had been discussed before the
opening of the play, and led Bradley to suggest[3] ingeniously that

> If they had had ambitious conversations, in which each felt
> that some half-formed guilty idea was floating in the mind of
> the other, she might naturally take the words of the letter, as
> indicating much more than they said.

---

1. Curry, pp. 111–12. The italicized words are quoted from Thomas
Aquinas.
2. *Coleridge on Shakespeare*, ed. T. Hawkes (1969), p. 209.
3. Bradley, pp. 480–4.

Dover Wilson used[1] this passage (1. vii. 47–52) to support his theory that in the original play there was another scene between Macbeth and his wife, after the meeting with the Weird Sisters, and before he knew that Duncan was coming to Inverness. He rejected Coleridge's view of a prior discussion because he felt that Macbeth's aside (1. iii. 130 ff.) 'depicts the terror of Macbeth's soul when the idea of murder *first* comes to him'; and that Lady Macbeth's soliloquy at the beginning of 1. v proves that 'so far he has refused to entertain any but honourable thoughts'. But Macbeth's aside, by a common Shakespearian convention, does not so much express the birth of murderous thoughts (though it still may do that) as refer back to the guilty start to which Banquo calls attention earlier in the scene (I. iii. 51), a start which could not be explained earlier without holding up the action.[2] It could either represent the birth of guilt, or else show that Macbeth's mind has been 'rendered temptable by a previous dalliance of fancy with ambitious thoughts'. Lady Macbeth's soliloquy does not prove that her husband did not have those thoughts, or what Bradley called 'some vaguer dishonourable dream': they prove only that she believed, and rightly it appears, that Macbeth's conscience or conventionality was liable to prevent him from achieving the crown by foul means, even though he may have proposed the murder when the question was merely theoretical. I do not find, therefore, the inconsistency of which Bridges spoke; nor do I think there is sufficient evidence to support Dover Wilson's theory of an earlier version of the play, in which all was clear. Even if Lady Macbeth refers to a time between 1. iii and 1. iv Shakespeare might (and, in my opinion, would) have left the scene unwritten.[3]

In the same essay Bridges speaks of Macbeth's poetic imagination.[4] In this opinion he was following Bradley, who had argued[5] that

---

1. Wilson, p. xxxvi.

2. Cf. the soliloquy at the end of Act II of *Hamlet*, which tells us what had been passing through the hero's mind during the recitation of the Hecuba speeches.

3. See above, p. xxv.

4. *Op. cit.* p. 13.

5. Bradley, p. 352. Is this wholly true? For Macbeth's imagination also feeds his ambition. G. Bullough, *Narrative and Dramatic Sources of Shakespeare*, VII (1973), 458, quotes from Burton's *Anatomy of Melancholy* on the force of imagination: 'Some ascribe all vices to a false and corrupt imagination, anger, revenge, lust, ambition, covetousness, which prefer falsehood before that which is right and good, deluding the soul with false shows and suppositions'.

Macbeth's better nature—to put the matter for clearness'
sake too broadly—instead of speaking to him in the overt
language of moral ideas, commands and prohibitions, incor-
porates itself in images which alarm and horrify. His imagination is thus the best of him, something usually deeper and
higher than his conscious thoughts; and if he had obeyed it he
would have been safe.

Sir Herbert Grierson went even further,[1] paradoxically comparing Macbeth to Bunyan, in that

his own deepest thoughts and feelings come to him as objective
experiences, as visions of the bodily eye, as voices that ring in
the ear. . . The obscure processes of his own soul translate
themselves into the voices and visions, and their significance is
a better clue to the working of his moral being than are his
articulate statements. He may profess contempt of moral
scruples and supernatural inhibitions, and declare that if he
were safe in this world he would 'jump the life to come'. The
voices that he hears and the visions that he sees give him the
lie.

Now it was perfectly legitimate to disagree with Moulton who,
by ignoring the poetry, had argued that Macbeth's soliloquy in
I. vii shows that he was deterred only by fear of the consequences;[2] for the imagery of the speech shows that Macbeth is
haunted by the horror of the deed, that he impresses that horror
on the audience, and that he resolves not to go ahead with the
murder. But such an argument has to be used with great caution.
If we go further and pretend that this poetic imagery is a proof
that Macbeth had a powerful imagination, that he was in fact a
poet, we are in danger of confusing real life and drama. Every
character in a poetic play may speak in verse, may speak poetry:
but this poetry does not necessarily reflect their poetic disposi-
tions—it is merely a medium. The bloody Sergeant utters bombastic language, not because he is himself bombastic, but because
such language was considered appropriate to epic narration. The
First Murderer (to give an extreme example) echoes Samuel
Daniel and gives us a lovely vignette of twilight,[3] not because he
was of a literary turn of mind, but because his creator was a poet,
and in the second passage required some verbal scene-painting
on the bare Jacobean stage. So, too, with Macbeth, we may say
that his imagery expresses his unconscious mind (that poetry can

1. *Ed. cit.*, pp. xxv ff.
2. R. G. Moulton, *Shakespeare as a Dramatic Artist* (ed. 1892), pp. 151–3.
3. III. i. 11, III. iii. 4 and nn.

do this is one of the greatest advantages it has over naturalistic drama) but we must not say that he is therefore a poet. Hamlet, despite the sublime poetry of his soliloquies, and despite his reputation for his pen as well as his sword, tells Ophelia that he is a bad poet: 'I am ill at these numbers.'[1]

Maeterlinck, in words echoed by Granville-Barker, spoke[2] of the way in which the 'essence of the dramatic poet's art consists in speaking through the mouth of his characters without appearing to do so'; and he declared that the mode of life in which the protagonists of *Macbeth*

> are steeped penetrates and pervades their voices so clearly, animates and saturates their words to such a degree that we see it much better, more intimately and more immediately than if they took the trouble to describe it to us. We, like themselves, living there with them, see from within the houses and the scenery in which they live; and we do not need to have those surroundings shown to us from without any more than they do. It is the countless presence, the uninterrupted swarm of all those images that form the profound life, the secret and almost unlimited first existence of the work. Upon its surface floats the dialogue necessary to the action. It seems to be the only one that our ears seize; but, in reality, it is to the other language that our instinct listens, our unconscious sensibility, our soul, if you like; and, if the spoken words touch us more deeply than those of any other poet, it is because they are supported by a great host of hidden powers.

The characters are thus subordinated to the poetry, rather than (as in much earlier criticism) the poetry to the characters. But the danger which has been mentioned above remains. Lascelles Abercrombie in his *Idea of Great Poetry* has a brilliant discussion[3] of why we enjoy tragedy which seems a version of 'the mere evil of life'. In answering this question he gives a generally convincing analysis of *Macbeth*. In the last act of the play, the hero's world 'turns into a blank of imbecile futility'; yet he

> seizes on the appalling moment and masters even this: he masters it by knowing it absolutely and completely, and by forcing even this quintessence of all possible evil to live before him with the zest and terrible splendour of his own unquenchable mind.

After quoting Macbeth's speech when he hears of his wife's death, Abercrombie comments:

1. *Hamlet*, II. ii. 119.
2. *Fortnightly Review*, April 1910, pp. 696–9.
3. *The Idea of Great Poetry* (1925), pp. 176–7.

Tragedy can lay hold of no evil worse than the conviction that life is an affair of absolute inconsequence. . . And precisely by laying hold of this and relishing its fearfulness to the utmost, Macbeth's personality towers into its loftiest grandeur. . . We see not only what he feels, but the personality that feels it; and in the very act of proclaiming that life is a tale told by an idiot signifying nothing personal life announces its virtue, and superbly signifies itself.

Abercrombie seems here to be confusing the powers of expression supposed to be possessed by Macbeth with the poetic powers of his creator. Once again it must be emphasized that because Shakespeare makes Macbeth talk as only a great poet could write, we are not to deduce that Macbeth is a great poet: he is merely part of a great poem. His consummate expression of the meaninglessness of life signifies only that life is meaningless to him: it cannot be taken to signify that he has overcome that meaninglessness by the very act of expressing it. Nor, of course, does it mean, as Bernard Shaw and others have surmised,[1] that Shakespeare was expressing his own pessimistic ideas about the universe. What gives satisfaction to the spectator or reader is not the comprehension of experience by Macbeth, but that the poet is revealing experience through the mouth of his hero. Macbeth, by his own actions, has robbed life of meaning: Shakespeare restores meaning to life by showing that Macbeth's nihilism results from his crimes.

Not, of course, that he is merely a callous criminal. As James pointed out,[2] tragic heroes must be 'finely aware' and this '*makes* absolutely the intensity of their adventures, gives the maximum of sense to what befalls them'. Macbeth arouses our sympathies more than Richard III does precisely for this reason. The difference between the two characters is partly the result of Shakespeare's increased understanding of human nature. All his mature tragedies may be regarded as 'melodrama humanized'. Richard is a conscious villain and admired only for his commitment to evil. Macbeth embarks on his career of crime with anguish and reluctance, 'as if it were an appalling duty'.[3] He is humanized by his fears,[4] which prove him to be a man, and not the monster his oppressed subjects believe him to be. 'Those are my best dayes,' he might have said, 'when I shake with fear'.[5]

1. *Shaw on Shakespeare*, ed. Edwin Wilson (1969), p. 27.
2. Henry James, *The Princess Casamassima*, Preface.   3. Bradley, p. 358.
4. Hardin Craig, *The Enchanted Glass* (1936), p. 232.
5. John Donne, Holy Sonnets, xix.

Richard, though he suffers from the same terrible dreams, is depicted from the outside, and not without appreciation of his sardonic humour;[1] but as Macbeth goes the primrose way to the everlasting bonfire, we see with his eyes. Richard is the villain as hero; Macbeth is a hero who becomes a villain.

It should be remembered that the Elizabethans, bred on Seneca, did not adhere to Aristotle's view that the overthrow of a bad man is not a tragedy at all. They were content with Sidney's statement, with Seneca in mind, that 'high and excellent Tragedie . . . maketh Kings feare to be tyrants'.[2] This does not mean that Shakespeare's imagination was cabined, cribbed, and confined by this conception, any more than he was bound within the Senecan form and structure. His imaginative perception of the human heart made it necessary for him to investigate the steps by which a noble and valiant man is brought to his damnation, and to present the process in such a way as to arouse our pity and terror.[3] For although, in the last resort, Macbeth is responsible for his damnation, he is sorely tempted. 'The power of divels', wrote George Giffard in 1603,[4]

> is in the hearts of men, as to harden the heart, to blind the eyes of the mind, and from the lustes and concupiscences which are in them, to inflame them vnto wrath, malice, enuie, and cruell murthers: . . . And about these things they work continually, and with such efficacy, that without the power of the glorious passion and resurrection of our Lord Jesus Christ, which we haue by faith, they cannot be withstood.

So James I himself declared[5] that the devil allures persons,

> euen by these three passions that are within our selues: Curiositie . . . thirst of reuenge, for some tortes deeply apprehended: or greedy appetite of geare.

Shakespeare concentrated on the third passion; but he could not represent devils in a tragedy because they had acquired comic associations. Witches served his turn. They were tragic creatures who, 'for the sake of certain abnormal powers, had sold themselves to the devil'.[6]

We do not know Shakespeare's private opinion of witchcraft— whether he accepted the tenets of James's *Daemonologie*, or whether

1. H. B. Charlton, *Shakespearean Tragedy* (1948), pp. 24 ff.
2. Sir Philip Sidney, *The Defence of Poesie*, E4ᵛ. Cited Dover Wilson.
3. Charlton, *op. cit.*, p. 182.
4. *A Dialogue Concerning Witches* (ed. 1843), pp. 22–3.
5. James I, *Workes* (1616), p. 98.   6. Curry, p. 61.

he adhered to the sceptical position of Reginald Scot, which seems to us to be so much more sane. But, whatever his views, the belief in witchcraft could be used by him for dramatic purposes at a time when most people supposed that witches were 'channels through which the malignity of evil spirits might be visited upon human beings'. W. C. Curry argued[1] that the Weird Sisters are not witches, but demons or devils in their form. Nevertheless,

> whether one considers them as human witches in league with the powers of darkness, or as actual demons in the form of witches, or as merely inanimate symbols, the power which they wield or represent or symbolize is ultimately demonic.

Kittredge, however, believed[2] that the Weird sisters were Norns, 'great powers of destiny, great ministers of fate. They had determined the past; they governed the present; they not only foresaw the future, but decreed it'. 'Weird Sisters' was Gavin Douglas's translation of *parcae*.[3] Witches, devils, fates—the conflicting interpretations reflect the elusive ambiguity of Shakespeare's creations. It should be noted, however, that the Weird Sisters tempt Macbeth only because they know his ambitious dreams—and 'in dreams begins responsibility'[4]—and that even so their prophecy of the crown does not dictate evil means of achieving it—it is morally neutral. 'Chance may crown me / Without my stir', Macbeth admits, and he never thinks of blaming the Weird Sisters for tempting him to the murder of Duncan, though he later blames the 'juggling fiends' who have lulled him into a false sense of security. As the author of III. v says:

> And you all know, security
> Is mortals' chiefest enemy.

He knows that the first step along the primrose path was taken on his own responsibility.

Macbeth's first crime is inspired by ambition and carried through by his wife's determination; the remainder, from the murder of the grooms to the slaughter of Macduff's family and the reign of terror of which this is an example, are inspired by fear, fear born of guilt. Timothy Bright, writing of neurotic fears,[5] distinguished them from those caused by the pangs of conscience:

1. *Ibid.*, pp. 59, 61.   2. *Complete Works of Shakespeare*, p. 1114.
3. *Aeneid*, tr. Gavin Douglas, III. vi. 24. Cf. Surrey's translation of Book IV. 581.
4. W. B. Yeats, Epigraph to *Responsibilities*.
5. Timothy Bright, *A Treatise of Melancholy* (1586), p. 193.

Whatsoeuer molestation riseth directly as a proper object of the mind, that in that respect is not melancholicke, but hath a farther ground then fancie, and riseth from conscience, condemning the guiltie soule of those ingrauen lawes of nature, which no man is voide of, be he neuer so barbarous. This is it, that hath caused the prophane poets to haue fained Hecates Eumenides, and the infernall furies; which although they be but fained persons, yet the matter which is shewed vnder their maske, is serious, true, and of wofull experience.

These are the terrible dreams that nightly shake Macbeth and his wife; and the apocalyptic imagery that precedes and follows the murder of Duncan may be ascribed to the same cause, rather than to Macbeth's poetic temperament. Plutarch, in his *Morals*, declared[1] that

wickednesse ingendering within it selfe . . . displeasure and punishment, not after a sinfull act is committed, but euen at the very instant of committing, it beginneth to suffer the pain due to the offence . . . whereas mischievous wickednesse frameth of her selfe, the engines of her owne torment . . . many terrible frights, fearfull perturbations and passions of the spirit, remorse of conscience, desperate repentance, and continuall troubles and vnquietnesse.

Before the end of the play Macbeth, having 'supped full with horrors', is no longer tortured by such 'fearfull perturbations': this is the measure of his damnation. As Curry says,[2] 'in proportion as the good in him diminishes, his liberty of free choice is determined more and more by evil inclination and . . . he cannot choose the better course.'

Although, as we have seen, the murders after the first are all motivated by a frantic desire for security, there are differences between them. The murder of Banquo is not merely due to his knowledge of the Weird Sisters' prophecy, which makes him a menace to Macbeth; nor is it due merely to the promise that Banquo's descendants would inherit the throne, powerful though both motives be. Macbeth fears Banquo's 'royalty of nature', the 'dauntless temper of his mind', and his wisdom. He fears them because they are a standing reproach to his own character, now stained with crime—'under him / My Genius is rebuk'd'. He hopes that by murdering Bánquo he will rid himself of this reproach; yet the act merely ensures that the reproach will be

1. *Morals*, tr. P. Holland (1601), pp. 545–6; cited Lily B. Campbell, *Shakespeare's Tragic Heroes* (1930).
2. Curry, p. 105.

eternal. We may, perhaps, apply what J. P. Sartre says of murder to the killing of Banquo. He argues[1] that the murderer per-petuates the intolerable situation for which he did the deed by the act itself; for he kills his victim because he hates being the other's *object*, and by the murder this relationship is rendered irremediable. The victim has taken the key of this alienation into the tomb with him. 'So hatred is transformed into frustration even in its triumph.'

Some think that Banquo scarcely deserves the compliment of admiring hatred, in that he seems to have come to terms with evil. Before the murder, he is determined to lose no honour in seeking to augment it; and after the murder, with suspicion of Macbeth in his mind, he declares:

> In the great hand of God I stand; and thence
> Against the undivulg'd pretence I fight
> Of treasonous malice.

Yet at the beginning of the third act we find that he has done nothing to implement his vow; and Bradley argued[2] that

> He alone of the lords knew of the prophecies, but he has said nothing of them. He has acquiesced in Macbeth's accession, and in the official theory that Duncan's sons had suborned the chamberlains to murder him.

Although Dover Wilson was right to protest that we should not treat a playwright as though he were a historian, although this interpretation of Banquo's character that 'he has yielded to evil' seems to be contradicted by Macbeth's tribute later in the scene, unless irony is intended, and although James I would not have approved of an unflattering portrait of his reputed ancestor, yet there is no need to suppose that an uncut version of the play (in which, for example, Banquo was in secret communication with Malcolm) would have made all plain.[3]

What ought Banquo to have done? It could be argued that he ought to have behaved loyally to Macbeth until Malcolm had set foot on Scottish soil. James condemned rebellion even against manifest tyrants. As he says in *The Trew Law of Free Monarchies*,[4]

> The wickednesse therefore of the King can neuer make them that are ordained to be iudged by him, to become his Iudges. . .
> Next, in place of relieuing the commonwealth out of distresse

---

1. *L'Etre et le Néant* (1943), p. 483.
2. Bradley, pp. 384-5.   3. Wilson, p. xvi.
4. *Political Works*, ed. McIlwain (1918), p. 66.

(which is their onely excuse and colour) they shall heape double distresse and desolation vpon it; and so their rebellion shall procure the contrary effects that they pretend it for.

Even a bad king maintains order in the commonwealth, and except where his lusts or passions are involved, he will generally favour justice. If there is no king, James argued, there is a breakdown of morality: 'nothing is vnlawfull to none'.

On the other hand James was careful to point out that[1]

the duty and alleageance, which the people sweareth to their prince, is not only bound to themselues, but likewise to their lawfull heires and posterity . . . it is alike vnlawfull (the crowne euer standing full) to displace him that succeedeth thereto, as to eiect the former: For at the very moment of the expiring of the king reigning, the nearest and lawful heire entreth in his place: And so to refuse him, or intrude another, is not to holde out vncomming in, but to expell and put out their righteous King.

The situation was different in the Scotland of Duncan's time. Malcolm had been made Prince of Cumberland, but Macbeth had been elected by the thanes. Banquo had strong suspicions about the murder of Duncan; he feared that Macbeth had played most foully for the throne; but his duty was not by any means certain.

The long dialogue between Macbeth and the murderers of Banquo recalls John's temptation of Hubert and Claudius's temptation of Laertes. It shows us a Macbeth we had only glimpsed before and could not have foreseen before his first murder. He is revealed as a smooth-tongued 'politician', well able to 'beguile the time'. If it be said that the two murderers would have been content to do the deed without all this persuasion—that they only wanted the cash—it may be answered that Macbeth[2]

wanted to subdue their wills. One sees him pacing the floor and weaving words like spells round the two wretches, stopping every now and then to eye them hard and close.

He wants them to do the deed out of hatred of Banquo, and not out of the need of money, so that he himself shall be relieved of some part of the guilt—so that he can cry, 'Thou canst not say I did it.' His speech about dogs, regarded by some as the least necessary speech in the play, serves to present one aspect of the order which he himself is destroying. There is a further signifi-

1. *Political Works*, ed. McIlwain (1918), p. 69.   2. Barker, p. 75.

cance of the scene: the cluster of echoes from the Sermon on the Mount make Macbeth bear witness, apparently unconsciously, to the ethic he is violating.

The later massacre of Macduff's family is not calculated to achieve a particular end. Destruction, though originating in fear, has come to be an end in itself. It has the effect of turning the man Macbeth fears into a determined avenger.

We must turn now to consider the other protagonist, the accomplice as well as the temptress of Macbeth. According to Coleridge,[1] she is not the monster, the fiend-like queen, that most eighteenth-century critics assumed her to be. On the contrary

> her constant effort throughout the play was to *bully* conscience. She was a woman of a visionary and day-dreaming turn of mind; her eye fixed on the shadows of her solitary ambition; and her feelings abstracted, through the deep musings of her absorbing passion, from the common-life sympathies of flesh and blood. But her conscience, so far from being seared, was continually smarting within her; and she endeavours to stifle its voice, and keep down its struggles, by inflated and soaring fancies, and appeals to spiritual agency.

Coleridge is reading back into the early scenes of the play the evidence provided by the sleep-walking scene. But although it is true that Lady Macbeth is not naturally depraved or conscienceless (any more than Satan was) she deliberately chooses evil, her choice being more deliberate than her husband's. Macbeth speaks of his ambition being his only spur; but he would never have overcome his reluctance to commit regicide without the chastisement of his wife's tongue, and she persuades him only after she has invoked the powers of darkness to take possession of her. The invocation is not metaphorical or symbolical, but in deadly earnest, and with belief in its efficacy. Curry argued:[2]

> Her prayer is apparently answered; with the coming of night her castle is . . . shrouded in just such a blackness as she desires. She knows also that these spiritual substances study eagerly the effects of mental activities upon the human body, waiting patiently for evidences of evil thought which will permit them entrance past the barriers of the human will into the body to possess it. They tend on mortal thoughts. For, says Cassian: 'It is clear that unclean spirits cannot make their way into those bodies they are going to seize upon, in any other way than by first taking possession of their minds and thoughts.'

1. *Coleridge on Shakespeare*, ed. T. Hawkes (1969), p. 218.
2. Curry, pp. 86–7.

Thus, instead of guarding the workings of her mind against the assaults of wicked angels, Lady Macbeth deliberately wills that they subtly invade her body and so control it that the natural inclinations of the spirit toward goodness and compassion may be completely extirpated... And without doubt these ministers of evil do actually take possession of her body even in accordance with her desire.

W. Moelwyn Merchant more recently has argued[1] that Lady Macbeth's 'willed submission to demonic powers, her unequivocal resolve to lay her being open to the invasion of witchcraft, is held in dramatic contrast to the painful, casuistic deliberations of Macbeth'.

Mrs Siddons likewise declared[2] that Lady Macbeth, 'having impiously delivered herself up to the excitements of hell . . . is abandoned to the guidance of the demons she has invoked'. The great actress's belief is one of the reasons why her performance of the part has probably never been surpassed. In our own day Judi Dench's triumph in the part depended largely on the sense she gave of horrified belief in the spirits that tend on mortal thoughts. We need not assume that Shakespeare himself believed in demoniacal possession, any more than we need decide whether he followed Reginald Scot in his views of witchcraft,[3] or King James in his views on Divine Right. But in writing *King Lear* he had depicted Poor Tom as a feigned demoniac and he drew on Harsnett's *Declaration of Egregious Popishe Impostures*[4] for details of the portrait, and this book would have made most readers sceptical. Yet there can be little doubt that he intended Lady Macbeth to believe herself to be possessed. In addition we can suppose that diabolical possession explains the unnatural portents on the night of the murder and what Curry calls[5] the 'demoniacal somnambulism' of the sleep-walking scene.

Some critics have sentimentalized the character of Lady Macbeth. She has been depicted as the loving wife with an affectionate and gentle disposition, a maternal figure, a sensual woman, and a neurotic.[6] Some have argued that her cry 'The

---

1. *SS* 19; reprinted in *Aspects of Macbeth*, ed. K. Muir and P. Edwards (1977).

2. Thomas Campbell, *Life of Mrs Siddons* (1834), II. 10 ff. For Judi Dench's performance (1977), see G. Lloyd Evans in Brown, p. 108.

3. Reginald Scott, *The Discoverie of Witchcraft* (1584).

4. *King Lear*, ed. Kenneth Muir (1952), Appendix.   5. Curry, p. 90.

6. Rosenberg, pp. 158 ff. For stage history of the play see also Dennis Bartholomeusz's *Macbeth and the Players* (1969) and G. Lloyd Evans's chapter in Brown.

Thane of Fife had a wife' shows that 'as a woman she can still feel for a murdered woman'. On the other hand, Bradley agreed[1] with Campbell when he insisted that 'in Lady Macbeth's misery there is no trace of contrition'. But this, surely, is to take the sleep-walking scene too literally. Although Lady Macbeth's obsession with the blood stains on her hand, and particularly with the *smell* of the blood, might be interpreted as a mere fear of detection, it also symbolizes, as Forman noticed,[2] her consciousness of guilt and the outrage she had committed on her own soul. It must be admitted, however, that a second personality which speaks through the patient's mouth, confessing sins and sometimes relating memories, was thought to be a characteristic of demoniacal somnambulism.[3] It may be retorted that the starless night, the prodigies accompanying the murder, the voice that cried 'Sleep no more' and the sleep-walking can all be explained without bringing in the supernatural at all. This may reflect an ambiguity in Shakespeare's mind, which he cultivated for dramatic reasons. The audience could take it either way, though the supernatural was to most of Shakespeare's original audience the more natural.

On the other hand it must be admitted that the wonderful scene in the third act where we see that the crime has not brought the criminals closer together, but has set an impassable barrier between them—this picture 'of the haunted desert of their souls'[4] which reveals that Lady Macbeth now realizes (what her husband knew at the time of the murder) what it is they have done—does not require, and may even be thought to exclude, that she should still be actively possessed; and the banquet scene, in which she recovers for a while and for the last time some semblance of her indomitable will, is not easy to reconcile with the demoniac theory; for in that case Satan would seem to be divided against himself, on the one hand driving Macbeth to exhibit his guilt, and on the other enabling Lady Macbeth to shield him. So in the sleep-walking scene, whether her involuntary confessions are the outpourings of her repressed conscience, or the treacherous words of the demon within her, we need not deny her (what Shakespeare must have given her) pity, as well as the terror she has never failed to arouse. The scene is so poignant that, as Bradley remarked,[5] for the moment 'all the language of

1. Bradley, p. 378.
2. See above, p. xvi. It recalls Pilate's symbolic washing of his hands.
3. Curry, p. 90.   4. Barker's phrase, but untraced.
5. Bradley, p. 400.

poetry . . . seems to be touched with unreality, and these brief toneless sentences seem the only voice of truth'. The language is almost that of the nursery:[1]

> One; two: why, then 'tis time to do't. . . . Yet who would have thought the old man to have had so much blood in him?. . . The Thane of Fife had a wife: where is she now?. . . What, will these hands ne'er be clean?—No more o'that, my Lord, no more o' that. . . Here's the smell of the blood still.

The fact that we no longer believe in demons , and that Shakespeare's audience mostly did, does not diminish the dramatic effect for us; for with the fading of belief in the objective existence of devils, they and their operations can still symbolize the workings of evil in the hearts of men. It is not only the superstitious, but the guilty, to whom sleep is 'a verie hell and a place of damned persons', for it presents unto them[2]

> Terrible visions and monstrous fancies; it raiseth diuels, fiends and furies, which torment the poore and miserable soule; it driueth her out of her quiet repose by her owne fearfull dreames, wherewith she whippeth, scourgeth and punisheth herselfe (as it were) by some other, whose cruell and vnseasonable commandements she doth obey.

The changes in custom and belief do not seriously detract from the universality of the tragedy. A. A. Smirnov, for example, had no difficulty in interpreting the play so as to make it conform to modern ideas of the supernatural:[3]

> The conversations of Macbeth with the witches and phantoms, like the famous dialogue of Ivan Karamazov with the devil, are but the inner dialectical struggle of Macbeth with himself. The struggle is projected on the supernatural plane, just as the socio-historical events arising from Macbeth's concrete actions are projected on the spiritual plane.

The trouble with such an interpretation is that the Weird Sisters on their first appearance were seen and addressed by Banquo; and although the ghost of Banquo has been regarded as a mere hallucination, like the air-drawn dagger, it was clearly more than a projection of guilt. Shakespeare is again ambiguous. The appearance to Macbeth alone would have seemed the same whether the ghost was indeed Banquo's, or imaginary, or (as Curry

1. Kenneth Muir, *Shakespeare's Tragic Sequence* (1972), p. 153.
2. Plutarch, *Morals*, tr. P. Holland (1601), p. 260.
3. A. A. Smirnov, *Shakespeare* (1937), p. 72.

argues[1]) an infernal illusion created by devils to bring about
Macbeth's ruin. Devils 'are able to assume bodies of air, condensing it by virtue of their angelic natures insofar as is necessary
for the forming of assumed bodies. . . Demons are enabled to
induce in the imaginations of men, either waking or asleep,
whatever visions and hallucinations they please.'

It is sometimes stated that, apart from the Macbeths, Banquo,
and Macduff, the characters are 'flat' and lacking in individu-
ality, and that some scenes are undramatic and (compared with
the scenes in which Macbeth appears) rather dull. The flattening
of the minor characters, however, is a legitimate dramatic device,
used consistently by Shakespeare in order to focus attention on
the protagonists.[2] Rosse, Angus, the Old Man, Lenox, Another
Lord, the two Doctors, and the Waiting Gentlewoman, although
depicted with few individualizing touches, together act as a kind
of chorus. The words and actions of Rosse and Lenox are confusing, if not confused. Possibly some points have been obscured
by cuts;[3] but any audience would obtain a general impression,
which is all that is needed, of the gradual desertion of the thanes
to Malcolm, so that at the end Macbeth is virtually alone. Two
scenes which are most obviously choric (ii. iv, iii. vi) are by no
means dull. The second of them, indeed, begins with a masterly
exercise in irony.

It is not altogether accidental that some of the scenes which
earlier critics regarded as of doubtful authenticity, or as irrelevant
compliments to a king they dislike, or as concessions to the taste
of the groundlings, or even as pieces of relaxed writing, have now
come to be regarded as essential to the understanding of the play.
The Porter scene, the passage about dogs, the speech on the King's
Evil, and the first two scenes of the play have been discussed
elsewhere.[4] But something may be added about the scene in
England, particularly the self-accusation of Malcolm, which
has been condemned as long-drawn-out and absurd. Harley
Granville-Barker, while admitting what he regarded as lack of
spontaneity in the writing, pointed out[5] the importance of the
scene in the scheme of the play. It is the starting-point of the
play's counter-action, the audience needs a breathing-space, and

> That Malcolm might be what his self-accusation would make
> him, that Macduff might be Macbeth's spy, that each then

1. Curry, pp. 73, 75.
2. U. Ellis-Fermor, *Shakespeare the Dramatist* (1961), p. 85.
3. See above, p. xxv.   4. See above, pp. xxv ff.
5. H. Granville-Barker, *Prefaces 6* (1974), p. 81.

should turn from the other in loathing, and that Macduff should not be too easily convinced of the truth—all this is necessary as a solid foundation for the moral dominance of the rest of the play by these two. And the whole matter must be given space and weight to the measure of its importance.

The scene can also be defended as a 'mirror for magistrates', a discussion on the contrast between true royalty and tyranny that is very germane to the matter, and which readers of Holinshed would expect to be dramatized.[1] It would have pleased James I, who wrote on that subject in *Basikilon Doron*:[2]

> For a good King (after a happie and famous reigne) dieth in peace, lamented by his subjects, and admired by his neighbours; and leauing a reuerent renowne behinde him in earth, obtaineth the Crowne of eternall felicitie in heauen. And although some of them (which falleth out very rarelie) may be cut off by the treason of some vnnaturall subiects, yet liueth their fame after them, and some notable plague faileth neuer to ouertake the committers in this life, besides their infamie to all posterities hereafter: Where by the contrarie, a Tyrannes miserable and infamous life, armeth in end his owne Subiects to become his burreaux: and although that rebellion be euer vnlawfull on their part, yet is the world so wearied of him, that his fall is little meaned by the rest of his Subiects, and but smiled at by his neighbours. And besides the infamous memorie he leaueth behind him here, and the endlesse paine hee sustaineth hereafter, it oft falleth out, that the commiters not onely escape vnpunished, but further, the fact will remaine as allowed by the Law in diuers aages thereafter.

Perhaps, too, as L. C. Knights suggested,[3] the scene acts as a choric commentary:

> We see the relevance of Malcolm's self-accusation. He has ceased to be a person. His lines repeat and magnify the evils that have already been attributed to Macbeth, acting as a mirror wherein the ills of Scotland are reflected. And the statement of evil is strengthened by contrast with the opposite virtues.

Above all, the scene demonstrates effectively how Macbeth's misrule has made even the good suspect each other of treachery. It is worth remembering that the scene came over with painful vividness in the years immediately preceding World War II, at a

1. See IV. iii. Headnote.
2. James I, *Political Works* (1918), p. 19.
3. L. C. Knights, *Explorations* (1946), p. 28.

time when refugees were arriving in Britain with poignant tales of the effect of totalitarianism, with its terror, treachery, and suspicion, on family loyalty and the trustfulness of friends. Lastly, it should be stressed that the scene needs no apology in the theatre. The idea that the scene provides choric commentary rather than dramatized action is based, as Marvin Rosenberg points out,[1] on hindsight:

> If we know the outcome, we may be tempted to agree that Malcolm's antics with Macduff are 'tedious', a 'dull . . . perfunctory paraphrase from Holinshed'; a conventional exercise in deception leading without suspense to a foregone conclusion. To the *naive* spectator, however, the first half of the scene points dangerously to possible disaster, and the later part is charged with emotion.

The audience knows, as Malcolm and Macduff do not, that news is about to arrive of the extermination of the latter's family. Even with knowledgeable spectators, the scene is always successful, and it is greeted with prolonged applause. For the first time their moral sentiments and their aesthetic responses are able to coincide.

When the seventh edition was published in 1951, I was unduly anxious to defend imagistic criticism from attacks by admirers of Bradley, who complained that by concentrating on themes and images the new critics were leading readers away from action and character. Although Leavis and Knights campaigned against what they regarded as Bradley's weaknesses, Wilson Knight regarded himself as a follower. Of course the poetic dramas of Shakespeare are plays to be performed, not poems to be read— nearer to Ibsen's *Rosmersholm* than to *The Waste Land*.[2] Wilson Knight, who had played Shakespeare's major roles and had written on Shakespeare production, was never in danger of forgetting this.[3] Shakespeare wrote plays which are great poetry, as well as poetry which is embodied in great drama—and it is not always easy to preserve a nice balance between the two halves of this statement. Then, again, in the process of analysing one of the tragedies, and separating their themes, we are apt to fossilize the living substance, and to impose a modern, psychological, or an Elizabethan, meaning on its stranger and less formulable

---

1. Rosenberg, p. 543.

2. Knights, *op. cit.*, p. 18. '*Macbeth* has greater affinity with *The Waste Land* than with *The Doll's House*.'

3. Nor was I: in three different productions I have played three different parts.

significance. For what the groundlings and even the 'judicious' thought in Shakespeare's day may fall—did fall—as far short of a comprehensive and Shakespearian understanding of *Macbeth* as the speculations of Andrew Bradley or Wilson Knight.

The plays are so vast and so complex that we can make statements about them which seem contradictory, while both express some aspect of truth. We may, indeed, call *Macbeth* the greatest of morality plays, at the same time as we are aware that Shakespeare transcends the sublime story of a human soul on the way to damnation and that he shows us also indomitable energy, cherubim *horsed upon the sightless couriers of the air, Pity, like a naked new-born babe, striding the blast,* the very *frame of things disjoint,* and human life, a brief candle quenched in the dust of death, in all its splendours and miseries, and even in its crimes, not

>   a tale
> Told by an idiot, full of sound and fury,
> Signifying nothing.

We may not agree with Campbell when he spoke of *Macbeth* 'as the greatest treasure of our dramatic literature'[1] or with Masefield who called it 'the most glorious'[2] of Shakespeare's plays; but, despite its weaknesses (for which Shakespeare was probably not responsible), glory it certainly has, of a peculiar richness and intensity, which the poet seldom equalled and 'the achieve of, the mastery of the thing' which he surpassed, perhaps, only in *King Lear*.[3]

1. Thomas Campbell, *Life of Mrs Siddons* (1834), II. 6.
2. John Masefield, *Poetry* (1931), p. 13.
3. One is tempted to add, 'before the cuts made in the First Folio'.

MACBETH

DRAMATIS PERSONÆ

DUNCAN, *King of Scotland.*

DONALBAIN, } *His Sons.*
MALCOLM,

MACBETH, } *Generals of the King's Army.*
BANQUO,

MACDUFF,
LENOX,
ROSSE, } *Noblemen of Scotland.*
MENTETH,
ANGUS,
CATHNESS,

FLEANCE, *Son to Banquo.*
SIWARD, *Earl of Northumberland, General of the English Forces.*
YOUNG SIWARD, *his Son.*
SEYTON, *an Officer attending on Macbeth.*
BOY, *Son to Macduff.*
AN ENGLISH DOCTOR.
A SCOTTISH DOCTOR.
A SOLDIER.
A PORTER.
AN OLD MAN.
LADY MACBETH.
LADY MACDUFF.
GENTLEWOMAN *attending on Lady Macbeth.*
[HECATE].
THREE WITCHES.

Lords, Gentlemen, Officers, Soldiers, Murderers, Attendants, and Messengers.

The Ghost of Banquo, and other Apparitions.

SCENE: *In the end of the Fourth Act, in England; through the rest of the play, in Scotland.*

THE TRAGEDY OF MACBETH

ACT I

SCENE I.—[*An open place.*]

Thunder and lightning. Enter three WITCHES.

1 *Witch.* When shall we three meet again?
  In thunder, lightning, or in rain?
2 *Witch.* When the hurlyburly's done,
  When the battle's lost and won.

ACT I
Scene 1

1. again?] again *Hanmer.*   2. or] and *Hanmer, Capell.*

Scene 1] Cuningham thought that this scene was spurious, because no dramatic object was gained by its introduction. Granville-Barker (*Preface,* xxvi) concurred: 'Apart from such an opening being un-Shakespearean, the lines themselves are as little like Shakespeare as Hecate is, and have indeed all the tang of the Hecate lines... The scene ... is a poor scene and a pointless scene.' But, as Coleridge remarked (*Shakespearean Criticism,* ed. Raysor, I. 68), 'the true reason for the first appearance of the Weird Sisters, [is to strike] the keynote . . . of the whole play. . .' Coleridge likewise suggests that the opening of the play should be contrasted with that of *Hamlet*: 'In the latter the gradual ascent from the simplest forms of conversation to the language of impassioned intellect, yet still the intellect remaining the *seat* of passion; in the *Macbeth* the invocation is made at once to the imagination, and the emotions connected therewith' (*op.*

cit., I. 67). So Knights, *Explorations,* p. 18, declares that each theme of the play 'is stated in the first act. The first scene, every word of which will bear the closest scrutiny, strikes one dominant chord.'

1.] Hanmer's emendation, though generally accepted, is superfluous.

3. *hurlyburly*] uproar, tumult, confusion, esp. the tumult of sedition or insurrection. See Halle, *Chronicle* (1548), *Hen. VIII,* 231 *a*: 'In this tyme of insurrection, and in the rage of horley borley'. The word occurs in Golding's *Ovid,* ix. 510, and in Marlowe, *Dido,* IV. I. 10, and there is a close parallel in Seneca, *Agam.* (tr. Studley), 1, Chor., 'One hurly burly done'. Cf. note v. iii. 45 *post.* Knights (*op. cit.,* p. 18) suggests that the word 'implies more than the tumult of insurrection. Both it and "When the Battaile's lost, and wonne" suggest the kind of metaphysical pitch-and-toss which is about to be played with good and evil.'

3

3 *Witch.* That will be ere the set of sun.   5
1 *Witch.* Where the place?
2 *Witch.*   Upon the heath.
3 *Witch.* There to meet with Macbeth.
1 *Witch.* I come, Graymalkin!
2 *Witch.* Paddock calls.
3 *Witch.* Anon!   10
All. Fair is foul, and foul is fair:
        Hover through the fog and filthy air.   [*Exeunt.*

9–11. Paddock . . . fair] *so Singer (1856), Hunter, Globe, Kittredge, Wilson; one line spoken by All* Padock calls anon: faire is foule, and foule is faire *F; two lines, the first ending* anon! *Pope;* Paddock calls.—Anon! *Rowe and Capell, subst.*

8. *Graymalkin*] or Grimalkin, a grey cat; with the toad, a common witches' familiar. Cf. 'brinded cat' (IV. i. 1 *post*). 'Malkin' is a diminutive of Mary. Upton observes that 'to understand this passage we should suppose one familiar calling with the voice of a cat, and another with the croaking of a toad.' Cf. James I, *Dæmonologie (Workes,* 1616), p. 103: 'either in likenes of a Dog, a Cat, an Ape, or such-like other beast; or else to answere by a voice onely'. Cf. Scot, *Discouerie of Witchcraft*, ed. 1930, p. 6: 'Some say they can keepe divels and spirits in the likenesse of todes and cats.'

9–11. *Paddock . . . fair*] printed as one line in the Folios. Most editors retain the speech-prefix, *All,* and divide into two lines. Hunter's re-arrangement, which I have adopted, allows the witches to speak in turn. It is obviously improbable that Shakespeare intended all the witches to address the paddock, the familiar of one.

9. *Paddock*] a toad. The word is still found in provincial English. But Cot-

grave seems to regard the word as equivalent to *grenouille*, a frog, and not to *crapaud*, a toad. Topsell, *History of Serpents*, 1608, p. 187, refers to the 'Padock or crooked back Frog'—'It is not altogether mute, for in time of perrill . . . they have a crying voyce, which I have often times prooved by experience' (quoted by Furness, Jr.).

11. *Fair . . . fair*] Farmer pointed out the proverbial character of this phrase, and quoted Spenser's *Faerie Queene*, IV. viii. 32: 'Then faire grew foule, and foule grew faire in sight.' R. Walker, *The Time is Free*, p. 9, points out that the picture of Sclaunder in stanza 26 may have contributed to Shakespeare's picture of the witches. Furness, Jr., quotes Nashe, *Terrors of the Night* (1594, ed. McKerrow, I, p. 361): 'euery thing must bee interpreted backward as Witches say their Pater-noster, good being the character of bad, and bad of good.' The line is the first statement of one of the main themes of the play, of 'the reversal of values' (Knights).

SCENE II.—[*A camp.*]

Alarum within.　*Enter* KING DUNCAN, MALCOLM, DONAL-
BAIN, LENOX, *with Attendants, meeting a bleeding Captain.*

Dun.　What bloody man is that? He can report,
　As seemeth by his plight, of the revolt
　The newest state.
Mal.　　　　　　This is the Sergeant,
　Who, like a good and hardy soldier, fought
　'Gainst my captivity.—Hail, brave friend!　　　　5

Scene II
S.D. *Duncan*] *Capell;* King *F1.*　*Captain*] *F;* Sergeant *Old Camb.*　5. Hail,
brave friend] Haile: haile brave friend *F2–4.*

The authenticity of this scene has been questioned by Cuningham, following Clark and Wright; but it has been successfully defended by modern critics, inc. Knights, Nosworthy, *R.E.S.*, April 1946, and Flatter, *Shakespeare's Producing Hand* (1948). It may, however, have been badly cut. See Introduction, p. xx.

Theobald and Capell, followed by most modern editors, deduced from I. iii. 39 and from Holinshed that Sc. ii was laid at Forres. But Macbeth—assuming he is Bellona's bridegroom—was fighting in Fife (l. 49) which, as Wilson points out, is 100 miles from Forres, and could not be in two places at once. The two battles have been run together in place as well as in time. Cf. note on I. iii. 91. The Captain begins to tell the story of the second phase of the battle (ll. 29–43), i.e. with the Norweyan lord; and Rosse completes the tale (ll. 51–9). But not even an audience of Scotsmen would notice the geographical difficulties.

R. Walker, *op. cit.*, pp. 19–30, argues for the authenticity of this scene by showing that in Sc. iii 'Shakespeare means us to give most of our attention to Macbeth's reception of the news,

not to the news and its bearers. He achieves this by a measure of repetition.'

1. *bloody*] Kolbe points out, *Shakespeare's Way*, p. 3, that 'blood' is mentioned over 100 times in the course of the play. Dowden makes a similar observation.

3. *Sergeant*] Steevens suggests that Shakespeare borrowed the term from Holinshed, who mentions that Duncan sent a Sergeant at Arms to bring up the chief rebels to answer the charges preferred against them, but they slew him. Cf. Appendix, p. 168.

3, 5, 7.] The various attempts which have been made to regularize the metre are superfluous. The gap in 5 may indicate a pause for a gesture, and there might be a pause in 7 while the wounded captain collects himself to speak. Flatter (*op. cit.*) defends many of the irregularities in the metre in a similar way.

5. *my captivity*] This may have been suggested by Holinshed's mention of a Captain Malcolme, who was beheaded by Makdowald in an earlier phase of the revolt. But Case thinks that Malcolm merely means that the Captain had resisted an attempt to take him prisoner.

Say to the King the knowledge of the broil,
As thou didst leave it.

Cap.   Doubtful it stood;
As two spent swimmers, that do cling together
And choke their art. The merciless Macdonwald
(Worthy to be a rebel, for to that   10
The multiplying villainies of nature
Do swarm upon him) from the western isles
Of Kernes and Gallowglasses is supplied;
And Fortune, on his damned quarrel smiling,
Show'd like a rebel's whore: but all's too weak;   15

---

6. the knowledge] thy knowledge *Walker.*
F2–4.   10. for to that] for, to that, *Capell.*
13. Gallowglasses] *F2;* Gallowgrosses *F1.*
F.

9. Macdonwald] Macdonnell
11. villainies] villaines *F2–3.*
14. quarrel] *Hanmer;* quarry

---

6. *broil*] Cf. *1H4*, i. i. 3, and *Oth.*, i. iii. 87.

7–23.] According to Cuningham this is 'a corrupt piece of bombast'. It may be corrupt; but, as Nosworthy has argued (*op. cit.*), its style may be compared with the 'epic' style of the Pyrrhus speeches in *Hamlet* and the corresponding passage in Marlowe's *Dido.* Coleridge, *Shakespearean Criticism* (p. 67), makes the same comparison: 'the epic is substituted for the tragic, in order to make the latter be felt as the *real-life* diction.' Cf. Bradley, *Shakespearean Tragedy*, pp. 389–90.

9. *Macdonwald*] Holinshed's form is Makdowald. Knights, *Explorations*, p. 20, suggests that Shakespeare 'consciously provided a parallel with the Macbeth of the later acts'.

10. *to that*] i.e. to that end.

11–12. *The . . . him*] i.e. like lice.

13. *Kernes and Gallowglasses*] See Holinshed, Appendix, p. 168. The 'kern' was a light-armed foot-soldier; one of the poorer class among the 'wild Irish', from whom such soldiers were drawn. Stanihurst in his Introduction to Holinshed's *Irish Historie* (p. 45*a*) says that 'Kerne signifieth ... a shower of hell, because they are taken for no

better than for rakehels, or the diuels black gard, by reason of the stinking sturre they keepe, wheresoeuer they be.' The 'gallowglass' was a horseman armed with a sharp axe, defined by *O.E.D.* as 'one of a particular class of soldiers or retainers formerly retained by Irish chiefs'. According to Stanihurst (*op. cit.*) the gallowglass uses 'a kind of pollax for his weapon. These men are commonlie weieward rather by profession than by nature, firm of countenance, tall of stature, big of lim, burlie of body, well and stronglie timbered, cheeflie feeding on beefe, porke and butter.' Both words occur in *2H6*, IV. ix. 26–7: 'A puissant and a mighty power of gallowglasses and stout kerns'. N.

14. *quarrel*] This, the emendation of Hanmer, inasmuch as it occurs in the corresponding passage in Holinshed, may be regarded as certain. The Clar. Edd. point out that Fairfax in *Godfrey of Bulloigne* uses 'quarry' (xi. 28) as well as 'quarrel' (vii. 103) for the square-headed bolt of a cross-bow. The Folio printers, therefore, may readily have printed *quarrel* as *quarry*.

15. *rebel's whore*] Nosworthy compares *Ham.*, II. ii. 515: 'strumpet, fortune'.

For brave Macbeth (well he deserves that name),
Disdaining Fortune, with his brandish'd steel,
Which smok'd with bloody execution,
Like Valour's minion, carv'd out his passage,
Till he fac'd the slave;   20
Which ne'er shook hands, nor bade farewell to him,
Till he unseam'd him from the nave to th'chops,
And fix'd his head upon our battlements.
Dun. O valiant cousin! worthy gentleman!
Cap. As whence the sun 'gins his reflection,   25
Shipwracking storms and direful thunders break,
So from that spring, whence comfort seem'd to come,
Discomfort swells. Mark, King of Scotland, mark:
No sooner justice had, with valour arm'd,
Compell'd these skipping Kernes to trust their heels,   30

19. carv'd] *F;* carved *Rowe.*   21. Which] *F;* Who *Pope;* And *Capell.*   ne'er]
never *F4.*   bade] bid *F4.*   22. nave] nape *Hanmer, Warburton.*   th'chops]
F; the chaps *Reed (1803).*   26. thunders break] *Pope;* Thunders: *F;* thunders
breaking *F2–4.*   28. Discomfort swells] Discomforts well'd *Johnson (conj.*
Thirlby); Discomfort wells *Capell.*   29. had,] *F1–3;* had *F4, Globe.*

17–20. *Disdaining . . . slave*] Paul
suggests that 'Like Valour's minion'
should be substituted for 'Disdaining
Fortune'.

20.] Half a line, and probably more,
seems to be missing here, perhaps
deliberately cut. The *Which* of the following line may refer either to Macbeth, or to Macdonwald, or to
Fortune (whose slave he is). If it refers
to Macbeth, the polite expression contrasts with the impolite action.

21. *shook hands*] i.e. bade farewell.
Cf. Lyly, *Euphues* (ed. Arber, p. 75):
'you would inueigle me to shake hands
with chastitie.'

22. *unseam'd*] Note the tailoring
metaphor, of which there are many in
the course of the play.

nave] i.e. navel, but not so used elsewhere. The words were perhaps confused in Elizabethan English. Cf.
Massinger, *Parliament of Love,* II. iii:
'His body be the navel to the wheel'.
Steevens quoted Marlowe, *Dido,* II. i.
256: 'Then from the navell to the

throat at once / He ript old *Priam.*'
chops] i.e. jaws.

24. *cousin*] Macbeth and Duncan
were both grandsons of King Malcolm.

25–8. *As . . . swells*] Nosworthy compares *Ham.,* II. ii. 506–11. R. Walker,
op. cit., p. 31, suggests that 'the storms
and thunders at once recall the
witches, and inform us from what
source the danger threatens; and we
remember that the Witches go to meet
Macbeth. "Shipwracking" storms is
the very subject of the Witches' next
consultation. Macbeth is the source
whence comfort seemed to come.
From just that quarter danger
threatens. . . Let the King of Scotland
mark the omen! . . The Sergeant . . . is
of course unconscious of the undertone
of meaning.'

25. *reflection*] turning back at the
vernal equinox (Paul).

27. *spring*] i.e. source, but possibly
suggested by day-spring with its com-
forting associations.

But the Norweyan Lord, surveying vantage,
With furbish'd arms, and new supplies of men,
Began a fresh assault.

Dun.   Dismay'd not this
Our captains, Macbeth and Banquo?

Cap.   Yes;
As sparrows eagles, or the hare the lion.   35
If I say sooth, I must report they were
As cannons overcharg'd with double cracks;
So they
Doubly redoubled strokes upon the foe:
Except they meant to bathe in reeking wounds,   40
Or memorize another Golgotha,
I cannot tell—
But I am faint, my gashes cry for help.

Dun. So well thy words become thee, as thy wounds:
They smack of honour both.—Go, get him surgeons.   45
                       [*Exit Captain, attended.*

---

32. furbish'd] (furbisht) *Rowe;* furbusht *F.*   33–4. Dismay'd . . . Banquo?]
verse Pope; prose F.   34–5. Yes; . . . lion] *so Pope; lines end* Eagles; / Lyon: *F.*
37. overcharg'd with] overcharg'd; with *Theobald.*   38. So they] *Steevens;*
begins 39 F; ends 37 Globe (1878), Kittredge; They so *conj. Keightley.*   39. upon]
on *F2–4.*   40. reeking] recking *F2–3.*   42–3. I cannot . . . help] *Rowe;*
lines end faint, / help *F.*

31. *Norweyan*] Shakespeare, in de-
ference to King Christian, omits
mention of the Danes (Paul).

surveying vantage] i.e. seeing his
opportunity (Wilson). Cf. *R3*, v. iii.
15: 'Let us survey the vantage of the
ground.'

33–4.] Duncan's speech is printed as
prose in the Folio, and though the
Clar. Edd., following Douce, assumed
that 'captains' should be pronounced
'capitains' to make the line regular (cf.
3H6, iv. vii. 30: 'A wise stout captain,
and soon persuaded'), the word is
nearly always dissyllabic in Shakespeare, and it might be better to print
the speech as prose. In which case the
Captain's 'Yes' would be printed with
35.

38. *So they*] Abbott suggests that this
short line should be detached from the
beginning of 39 (as it is in the Folio)
and added to 37—reading *o'ercharg'd*
for the sake of the scansion. But I suspect that a line or more is missing
between 36 and 37, 37 beginning a
new sentence.

39. *Doubly redoubled*] Cf. *R2*, I. iii.
80.

42–3. *I . . . help.*] Flatter, *op. cit.*,
p. 101, defends the F arrangement of
these lines on the grounds that the
broken line ('I . . . faint') allows the
captain to exhibit faintness, and that
the short line at the end marks the
place where attendants go to his assistance. Wilson thinks the whole speech
is the ruin of a longer one. Perhaps a
wounded soldier may be forgiven
some slight incoherence.

Enter ROSSE *and* ANGUS.

Who comes here?
Mal.   The worthy Thane of Rosse.
Len. What a haste looks through his eyes! So should he look
    That seems to speak things strange.
Rosse.   God save the King!
Dun. Whence cam'st thou, worthy Thane?
Rosse.   From Fife, great King,
    Where the Norweyan banners flout the sky,   50
    And fan our people cold. Norway himself,
    With terrible numbers,
    Assisted by that most disloyal traitor,
    The Thane of Cawdor, began a dismal conflict;
    Till that Bellona's bridegroom, lapp'd in proof,   55

---

45. *Enter Rosse and Angus*] F; *Enter Ross, Steevens; Enter Ross and Angus, after*
strange (48) Dyce; after here? (*46*) *Old Camb., Wilson.*   47–8. What . . . King!]
so Hanmer; lines end eyes? | *strange.* | King. F.   47. a haste] hast *F2–4.*
48. seems] teems *conj. Johnson;* comes *Collier (ed. 2).*   51–2. And . . . numbers,]
so Singer, Globe, Chambers, Grierson, Kittredge, etc.; lines end cold. | numbers, F,
Arden (ed. 1), Wilson, etc.   54. began] 'gan *Pope.*

---

45. Enter . . . Angus] Steevens says
that 'as Ross alone is addressed, or
is mentioned in this scene, and as
Duncan expresses himself in the singular number as in line 49, Angus may be
considered a superfluous character.
Had his present appearance been
designed, the King would naturally
have taken some notice of him.' But
cf. I. iii. 100 which makes it certain that
his presence in this scene was intended.

47–9. *What . . . King*] Hanmer's arrangement of these lines is probably
correct.

47. *a haste*] The line would be better
without the article.

look] perhaps copied in error from
'looks', which in F is in the previous
line. Cf. *Ant.*, v. i. 50: 'The business of
this man looks out of him.'

48. *seems*] i.e. 'whose appearance
corresponds with the strangeness of his
message'. Cf. I. v. 29 *post*, and *1H4*,
III. ii. 162: 'thy looks are full of speed.'

50. *flout*] Elwin, quoted in the New

Variorum, suggests that Rosse 'describes the previous advantages of the
rebels in the present tense, in order to
set the royal victory in the strongest
light of achievement'. Keightley re-
arranges the lines and inserts 'did'
before 'flout'. The meaning must be
that the Norweyan banners made the
Scots cold with fear, and not, as
Malone supposed, that the captured
banners serve to cool the conquerors.
Cf. Marston, *Sophonisba*, i. ii: 'Upon
whose tops the *Roman* eagles stretch'd /
Their large spread winges, which
fanned the evening ayre / To us cold
breath'. See Introduction, p. xxiv. Cf.
also *John*, v. i. 72.

53. *traitor*] Holinshed says the Thane
of Cawdor was condemned at Forres
for treason; but makes no mention of
his having assisted the invaders.

55. *Bellona's bridegroom*] i.e. Macbeth. Chapman, *Iliad*, v. 590, cited by
Wilson (from P. Simpson), speaks of
'great Mars himselfe, matcht with his

Confronted him with self-comparisons,
Point against point, rebellious arm 'gainst arm,
Curbing his lavish spirit: and, to conclude,
The victory fell on us;—

Dun.   Great happiness!

Rosse. That now   60
Sweno, the Norways' King, craves composition;
Nor would we deign him burial of his men
Till he disbursed at Saint Colme's Inch
Ten thousand dollars to our general use.

Dun. No more that Thane of Cawdor shall deceive   65

---

57. point, rebellious arm] *F;* point rebellious, arm *Theobald, Globe, Chambers.*
60–1.] *so Johnson, Steevens (1778); lines end* King, / *composition:* F; *one line*
(*omitting* That) *Pope.*   63. Inch] ynch, *F1;* hill *F2–4.*

---

femall mate, / The drad Bellona'.
Douce remarks that 'Shakespeare has
not called Macbeth . . . the *God of War*,
and there seems to be no great impro-
priety in *poetically* supposing that a
warlike hero might be *newly married* to
the Goddess of War'. Shakespeare
knew that 'the fire-eyed *maid* of smoky
war' (*1H4,* IV. i. 114) was not a bride.
Granville-Barker suggests that Bellona's bridegroom may not be Macbeth. But though Shakespeare was
condensing three campaigns into one,
there would have been no point in
making some other general responsible for the victory over Sweno, in
defiance of his source. Nosworthy compares *Ham.,* II. ii. 512.

lapp'd in proof] i.e. clad in armour of
proof—approved or tested. Cf. *R3,*
II. i. 115.

56. *Confronted . . . self-comparisons*] i.e.
faced him with equal courage and
skill; 'gave him a Roland for his
Oliver', as Craig says. But R. Walker,
op. cit., chap. 2, points out that Macbeth is to match the Thane of Cawdor
in treachery as well as in valour.

57.] Theobald's punctuation, wisely
rejected by Cuningham, the New Clar.
Edd., Kittredge, and Wilson, 'obli-
terated a characteristic feature of
Shakespeare's style' (Simpson, quoted

Wilson). Nosworthy compares *Ham.,*
II. ii. 492.

58. *lavish*] i.e. insolent. Cf. *2H4,*
IV. iv. 63: 'When rage and hot blood
are his counsellors, / When means and
lavish manners meet together'.

to conclude] To Wilson 'this sudden
conclusion suggests abridgement'; but
if one were not looking for evidence of
abridgement, one would not suspect it
here.

60. *That now*] For the construction
cf. II. ii. 7, 23, *post.*

61. *Sweno*] Steevens thought, from
the irregularity of the metre, that
Sweno was only a marginal reference,
thrust into the text, and that the line
originally read 'That now the Norways' king craves composition'.

63. *Saint Colme's Inch*] Steevens says
that 'Colmes' is here a dissyllable.
Colmes'-ynch, now called Inchcomb, is
a small island lying in the 'Frith of
Edinburgh' (i.e. the Firth of Forth).
Saint Colmes'-kill Isle (Pope's emendation) is Iona, in the Hebrides, a
totally different place. Cf. Appendix,
p. 171.

64. *dollars*] first coined *c.* 1518, some
five hundred years later.

King Christian gave 10,000 dollars
to 'the officers above the stairs', of
whom Shakespeare was one (Paul).

Our bosom interest.—Go pronounce his present death,
And with his former title greet Macbeth.
Rosse. I'll see it done.
Dun. What he hath lost, noble Macbeth hath won.   [*Exeunt.*

SCENE III.—[*A heath.*]

Thunder.   Enter the three Witches.

1 *Witch.* Where hast thou been, Sister?
2 *Witch.* Killing swine.
3 *Witch.* Sister, where thou?
1 *Witch.* A sailor's wife had chestnuts in her lap,
    And mounch'd, and mounch'd, and mounch'd: 'Give
      me,' quoth I:—   5
    'Aroynt thee, witch!' the rump-fed ronyon cries.

66. interest.—Go] trust. *conj. Capell.*   67. greet] great *F2–4.*

Scene iii
5. And ... I] *so Pope; two lines, the first ending* mouncht *F.*   6. Aroynt] Anoynt *F3.*

67. *former title*] R. Walker, *op. cit.*, p. 35, points out that the last title applied to the Thane of Cawdor was 'that most disloyal traitor'.

Scene iii
2. *Killing swine*] Steevens quotes from *A Detection of Damnable Driftes*, etc., 1579: 'She came on a tyme to the house of one Robert Lathburie . . . who, dislyking her dealying sent her home emptie; but presently after her departure, his hogges fell sicke and died, to the number of twentie.'
6. *Aroynt thee*] Cf. *Lr.*, iii. iv. 129: 'And aroint thee, witch, aroint thee'; the only other passage where the word seems to occur. The origin of the word is unknown, though it has been the subject of numerous conjectures. Ray, in his *North Country Words*, 1691, thus explains: 'Ryntye, by your leave, stand handsomly'; as ' "Rynt you, witch," quoth Bessie Locket to her mother; Proverb: Cheshire.' Halli-

well, *Dict. of Archaic and Provincial Words*, says that, according to Wilbraham, 'rynt thee' is an expression used by milkmaids to a cow when she has been milked, to bid her get out of the way. Hilda M. Hume, 'Shakespeare's Language' in *Shakespeare's World*, ed. J. Sutherland and J. Hurstfield (1964), p. 148, quotes the phrase 'arent the wich' from a Stratford-upon-Avon record and suggests a connection with Anglo-French *aloyner*, 'go far away'.
rump-fed] This is variously explained. (i) 'fed on offals' (Steevens). Cf. Jonson, *Staple of News*, ii. iii. 78: 'And then remember, meat for my two dogs; / Fat flaps of mutton, kidneyes, rumps of veale, / Good plentious scraps.' (ii) 'fat-bottomed; fed or fattened in the rump' (Nares). (iii) 'Nut-fed' (Dyce. Cf. Killan's Dictionary: '*Rompe*. Nux myristica vilior, cassa, inanis.' The sailor's wife was eating chestnuts. (iv) 'fed on the best joints, pampered' (Clarendon). Though

Her husband's to Aleppo gone, master o'th' *Tiger:*
But in a sieve I'll thither sail,
And like a rat without a tail;
I'll do, I'll do, and I'll do.   10
2 *Witch.* I'll give thee a wind.

Cuningham points out that this explanation does not go well with
'ronyon', the first does not suggest the
wife of a master of the *Tiger*. I incline
to (iv).

ronyon] a mangy, scabby creature,
and hence a term of abuse. Cf. *Wiv.*,
IV. ii. 195: 'You witch, you hag, you
baggage, you polecat, you ronyon!'

7. *th'Tiger*] a favourite name for
ships in Shakespeare's day. Cf. *Tw.N.*,
v. i. 65.

8.] Several quotations are given by
Steevens in the 1821 Variorum as to
the powers of witches in this respect.
The New Variorum quotes from
Pitcairn, *Criminal Trials*, I. ii. 217,
about Agnis Tompson (Sampson),
who confessed that, accompanied by
200 other witches, 'all they together
went to Sea, each one in a riddle or
cive, and went into the same very
substantially, with flaggons of wine,
making merry and drinking by the
way in the same riddles or cives, to the
Kirke of North Barrick in Lowthian.'
Cf. *Newes from Scotland*, 1924, p. 13.

9. *tail*] Steevens mentions it as a
belief of the times, that though a
witch could assume the form of any
animal she pleased, the tail would still
be wanting, and that the reason given
by some old writers for such a defi-
ciency was, that though the hands and
feet by an easy change might be converted into the four paws of a beast,
there was still no part about a woman
which corresponded with the length
of tail common to almost all our four-
footed creatures.

10. *I'll do*] Kittredge, *Witchcraft in
Old and New England*, p. 13, explains:
'she will take the shape of a rat in order
to slip on board the *Tiger* unnoticed.
This, and not to use her teeth, is the

object of the transformation. Then she
will bewitch the craft and lay a spell
upon the captain. There is no question
of scuttling the ship.' This is doubtless
correct, though some editors have
supposed that the witch in the shape
of a rat would gnaw through the hull
and make the ship spring a leak
(Clarendon) or through the rudder
and make the ship drift helplessly
(Grierson, prob. from Paton, *Few
Notes on Macbeth*).

11. *a wind*] Witches were supposed
to sell winds. See Nashe, *Terrors of the
Night*, 1594 (ed. McKerrow, I. 359):
'Farre cheaper maye you buy a winde
amongst them than you can buy wind
or faire words in the Court. Three
knots in a thred, or an odde (? olde)
grandams blessing in the corner of a
napkin, will carrie you all the world
ouer.' Also his *Will Summers Last Will
and Testament*, 1600 (ed. McKerrow,
III, ll. 1219–22): 'For, as in *Ireland* and
in *Denmarke* both / Witches for gold
will sell a man a winde, / Which, in the
corner of a napkin wrapt, / Shall blow
him safe unto what coast he will'.
Hunter quotes G. Fletcher, *The Russe
Commonwealth*, 1591 (inc. in Hakluyt's
Voyages, Everyman ed., II. 326–7) on
the Laplanders: 'Though for enchant-
ing of ships that saile along their
coast . . . and their giving of winds
good to their friends, and contrary to
other, whom they meane to hurt by
tying of certaine knots upon a rope
(somewhat like to the tale of Æolus his
windbag) is a very fable, devised (as
may seeme) by themselves, to terrifie
sailers for comming neere their coast.'
See also Drayton, *The Moon Calfe*, 865
ff. (ed. Hebel, III. 188): 'She could sell
windes to any one that would, / Buy
them for money, forcing them to hold /

1 *Witch.* Th'art kind.

3 *Witch.* And I another.

1 *Witch.* I myself have all the other;
　　　And the very ports they blow,　　　　　　　　　15
　　　All the quarters that they know
　　　I'th'shipman's card.
　　　I'll drain him dry as hay:
　　　Sleep shall neither night nor day
　　　Hang upon his penthouse lid;　　　　　　　　　20
　　　He shall live a man forbid.
　　　Weary sev'n-nights nine times nine,
　　　Shall he dwindle, peak, and pine:
　　　Though his bark cannot be lost,

---

15. very] various *conj. Johnson.*　　　ports] points *Pope.*　　　18. I'll] (Ile) *F;* I will *Pope, etc.*　　　22. sev'n-nights] *Theobald;* Seu'nights *F;* se'nnights *Globe, etc.*

What time she listed, tye them in a thrid, / Which ever as the Sea-farer undid / They rose or scantled, as his Sayles would drive, / To the same Port whereas he would arive.'

14. *other*] i.e. others. Cf. Philip., ii. 3.

15. *very . . . blow*] 'the exact ports the winds blow upon' (Cuningham); but the meaning is rather that contrary winds keep the ship out of every port, and we must assume either that 'from' is understood (Abbott), or else that 'ports' is the subject (Wilson).

17. *shipman's card*] The circular piece of stiff paper on which the 32 points of the compass are marked, and hence the compass itself. But as Hunter (*New Illustrations of Shakespeare*, II. 167) points out, the word also meant *chart*; and Dyce likewise quotes Sylvester, *Du Bartas, The Triumph of Faith*, 1641, where 'my Card and Compasse' translates 'Mon Quadrant et ma Carte marine'. Cf. *Ham.*, v. i. 149: 'we must speak by the card.'

18. *I'll*] Most editors unnecessarily accept Pope's sophistication.

19–20. *Sleep . . . lid*] Cf. Macbeth's later insomnia.

20. *penthouse lid*] The eyelid slopes like the roof of a penthouse. Malone

quotes Dekker, *Gul's Horne Booke* (ed. McKerrow, p. 33): 'The two eyes are the glasse windowes at which light disperses itselfe into every roome, having goodly penthouses of haire to overshadow them'; and Drayton, *David and Goliath*, 373: 'His brows like two steep penthouses hung down / Over his eyelids.'

21. *forbid*] 'as under a curse, an interdiction' (Theobald).

23. *dwindle*] The passage may have been suggested by the account in Holinshed of the bewitchment of King Duff (Appendix, p. 164). Scot, *Discouerie of Witchcraft*, XII. 16, has '*A charme teaching how to hurt whom you list with images of wax, etc.*' Waxen figures were stuck with needles or melted before a slow fire; and as the figure wasted, so wasted the person intended to be harmed. Cf. Webster, *Duchess of Malfi*, IV. i. 73: 'It wastes me more, / Than were't my picture, fashion'd out of wax, / Stucke with a magical needle, and then buried', etc.

peak] i.e. become emaciated. Cf. *Ham.*, II. ii. 594.

24–5.] Knight, *The Wheel of Fire* (1949), p. 157, applies this couplet to Macbeth; but surely *his* bark is lost.

Yet it shall be tempest-tost.   25
Look what I have.

2 *Witch.* Show me, show me.

1 *Witch.* Here I have a pilot's thumb,
Wrack'd, as homeward he did come.   [*Drum within.*

3 *Witch.* A drum! a drum!   30
Macbeth doth come.

All. The Weïrd Sisters, hand in hand,
Posters of the sea and land,
Thus do go about, about:
Thrice to thine, and thrice to mine,   35
And thrice again, to make up nine
Peace!—the charm's wound up.

Enter MACBETH *and* BANQUO.

Macb. So foul and fair a day I have not seen.

29. Wrack'd] (wrackt) *F;* wreckt *Theobald (ed. 2), Globe, Chambers.*   32.
Weïrd] *Theobald, Wilson;* weyward *F;* weyard *Keightley;* weird *modern Edd.*
generally.

30. *drum*] It is curious that though
Banquo and Macbeth are alone, their
arrival is announced by a drum.

32. *Weïrd*] I have adopted Theobald's spelling. Compositor A's spelling, *wayward,* is repeated at I. v. 8 and
II. i. 20. It is also to be found in
Heywood and Brome's *The Late
Witches of Lancashire* (1634), 'one of
the Scottish wayward sisters' (ed.
Shepherd, IV. 184). Compositor B's
spelling *weyard,* probably indicates
how the word was pronounced. The
word comes from O.E. *wyrd,* M.E.
werd (i.e. fate). Cf. Holinshed, Appendix, p. 171, 'the weird sisters,
that is (as ye would say) the goddesses of destinie'.

33. *Posters*] i.e. persons who travel
post, swiftly.

35–6. *Thrice . . . nine*] Odd numbers,
and especially multiples of three and
nine, were affected by witches. Cf.
IV. i. 2 *post.* The Clar. Edd. cite Ovid,
Metam., xiv. 58 and vii. 189–91.
Golding translates the latter: 'The
starres alonly faire and bright did in

the welken shine. / To which she lifting
up her handes did thrise hir selfe en-
cline: / And thrise with water of the
brooke hir haire besprincled shee: /
And gasping thrise she opte her
mouth.'

37. *wound up*] i.e. 'set in readiness
for action' (*O.E.D.*).

38. *So . . . seen*] Cf. I. i. 11. Dowden
(p. 249) comments on this parallel that
Shakespeare intimated by it 'that,
although Macbeth has not yet set eyes
upon these hags, the connection is
already established between his soul
and them. Their spells have already
wrought upon his blood.' Elwin,
Shakespeare Restored, 1853, thinks it
means '*Foul* with regard to the *weather,*
and *fair* with reference to his *victory*'.
But Wilson quotes James I, *Dæmonologie,* 1924, p. 39, to the effect that the
Devil can 'thicken and obscure so the
aire, that is next about them [witches]
by contracting it strait together, that
the beames of any other mans eyes
cannot pearce thorow the same, to see
them' [*Workes,* 1616, p. 114].

Ban. How far is't call'd to Forres?—What are these,
     So wither'd and so wild in their attire,   40
     That look not like th'inhabitants o'th'earth,
     And yet are on't? Live you? or are you aught
     That man may question? You seem to understand me,
     By each at once her choppy finger laying
     Upon her skinny lips: you should be women,   45
     And yet your beards forbid me to interpret
     That you are so.
Macb.   Speak, if you can:—what are you?
1 *Witch.* All hail, Macbeth! hail to thee, Thane of Glamis!
2 *Witch.* All hail, Macbeth! hail to thee, Thane of Cawdor!
3 *Witch.* All hail, Macbeth! that shalt be King hereafter.   50
Ban. Good Sir, why do you start, and seem to fear
     Things that do sound so fair?—I'th'name of truth,
     Are ye fantastical, or that indeed
     Which outwardly ye show? My noble partner
     You greet with present grace, and great prediction   55
     Of noble having, and of royal hope,

---

39. Forres] (Foris) *Pope;* Soris *F.*   44. Choppy] (choppie) *F;* chappy *Collier.*

39. *How . . . call'd*] Stopes, *Shake-speare's Industry,* p. 98, says this is a 'peculiarly Scottish idiom'. Mr David D. Murison, however, editor of *The Scottish National Dictionary,* informs me privately that though 'an old speaker in N.E. Scotland might use those very words' it might also have been used in England. Brougham, quoted in Webster's *New International Dictionary* for a similar use of the word 'call', '*might* have picked it up in Edinburgh'. Murison concludes that it is 'most highly improbable that Shakespeare meant it for a Scotticism'.

43. *question?*] 'Are ye any beings with which man is permitted to hold converse, or of whom it is lawful to ask questions?' Wilson refers to *Ham.,* I. i. 45 and I. iv. 43, and points out that 'Spirits might not speak unless first addressed.'

44. *choppy*] i.e. chapped. Cotgrave, *Dictionary,* 1611, has 'Fendu: *gaping, chappie.*' Wilson, following Bradley,

suggests that the gesture means that the witches refuse to speak to Banquo; they reply directly to Macbeth.

46. *beards*] Cf. *Wiv.,* IV. ii. 202: 'By yea and no, I think the 'oman is a witch indeed. I like not when a 'oman has a great peard.'

48. *Glamis*] To Shakespeare the word was dissyllabic. Cf. I. v. 15, 54; II. ii. 41, etc.

51. *start*] a sign of guilty thoughts (Coleridge). N.

53. *fantastical*] imaginary. The word is used by Holinshed in the context ('some vaine fantasticall illusion') and Craig quotes Scot, *Discouerie of Witchcraft,* 'these prestigious things which are wrought by witches are fantasticall.'

55–6. *present . . . hope*] 'There is here a skilful reference to the thrice repeated "Hail" of the witches' (Hunter).

56. *having*] estate, possession, fortune. Cf. *Tw.N.,* III. iv. 379.

That he seems rapt withal: to me you speak not.
If you can look into the seeds of time,
And say which grain will grow, and which will not,
Speak then to me, who neither beg, nor fear,   60
Your favours nor your hate.

1 *Witch.* Hail!
2 *Witch.* Hail!
3 *Witch.* Hail!
1 *Witch.* Lesser than Macbeth, and greater.   65
2 *Witch.* Not so happy, yet much happier.
3 *Witch.* Thou shalt get kings, though thou be none:
So all hail, Macbeth and Banquo!
1 *Witch.* Banquo and Macbeth, all hail!
Macb. Stay, you imperfect speakers, tell me more.   70
By Sinel's death I know I am Thane of Glamis;
But how of Cawdor? the Thane of Cawdor lives,
A prosperous gentleman; and to be King
Stands not within the prospect of belief,
No more than to be Cawdor. Say from whence   75
You owe this strange intelligence? or why

---

57. rapt] *Pope;* wrapt *F.*   59. not] rot *conj. Porson MS.*   68–9.] *given to all three witches, Lettsom apud Dyce ed. 1866, Hudson, and conj. Cuningham.*

57. *rapt*] i.e. *extra se raptus* (Steevens). Cf. 143 *post.* The Folio was inconsistent in the spelling of this word (Clarendon).

58. *seeds of time*] 'Demons', says Curry, *Shakespeare's Philosophical Patterns,* p. 48, 'know the future development of events conjecturally though not absolutely... If time is the measure of movement of corporeal things and if corporeal things move and develop according to the impulses latent in that treasury of forces called *rationes seminales,* then these seeds of matter may literally be called the seeds of time and demons have the power of predicting which grain will grow and which will not.'

68, 69.] I am inclined to agree with Cuningham that both these lines should be assigned to *all* the weird sisters.

71. *Sinel's*] Shakespeare got the name from Holinshed (cf. Appendix, p. 171). The word 'Finele' was mistranscribed 'Synele' by Boece, and so the name reached Holinshed (Wilson).

73. *prosperous*] Cawdor's aid to the invader was secret and not discovered until after Macbeth had left the battlefield. This would seem to be the only way of explaining this epithet and Macbeth's surprise. But the point is not made clear, and there may have been a bad cut. An audience would not notice that anything was wrong.

74. *prospect*] range of vision. Cf. *Tw.N.,* III. iv. 90: 'the full prospect of my hopes'.

75–6. *whence . . . intelligence*] rhyme, presumably accidental. Cf. II. iii. 128–9 *post.*

76. *owe*] own.

Upon this blasted heath you stop our way
With such prophetic greeting?—Speak, I charge you.

[*Witches vanish.*

Ban. The earth hath bubbles, as the water has,
  And these are of them.—Whither are they vanish'd?   80
Macb. Into the air; and what seem'd corporal,
  Melted as breath into the wind. Would they had stay'd!
Ban. Were such things here, as we do speak about,
  Or have we eaten on the insane root,
  That takes the reason prisoner?   85
Macb. Your children shall be kings.
Ban.   You shall be King.
Macb. And Thane of Cawdor too; went it not so?
Ban. To th'selfsame tune, and words. Who's here?

78. With . . . you] *so Pope; two lines, the first ending* greeting? *F.*   81–2. Into . . . stay'd!] *three lines, ending* corporall, / Winde. / stay'd *F; two lines, ending* melted / stay'd; *Capell and most modern Edd.*   84. on] *of F4.*

78.] The Folio line-division leaves room for a necessary pause after 'greeting!'

79. *bubbles*] Wilson interprets this to mean 'illusions' and refers to *O.E.D.*, which, however, quotes this line as an illustration of the ordinary meaning of the word. Banquo simply means that the witches have vanished like a bubble.

81–2. *Into . . . stay'd*] The lines are easier to speak if 'melted' is placed at the beginning of the line as in F. The second of these lines is printed as two by F to indicate the significant pause after *wind*.

81. *corporal*] i.e. corporeal, a form which Shakespeare never uses. Cf. *Ham.*, III. iv. 118: 'incorporal air'.

82. *as . . . wind*] Coleridge, *Shake-spearean Criticism*, I. 69, notes the appropriateness of the simile to a cold climate; and Wilson adds that it is also apt to a Scotch mist.

84. *on*] For this common usage, cf. v. i. 60 *post* and *MND.*, II. i. 266.

the *insane root*] i.e. which produces insanity. This may be hemlock, henbane, or deadly nightshade. Steevens quotes Greene, *Never Too Late* (ed.

Grosart, p. 195): 'you haue eaten of the rootes of Hemlock, that makes men's eyes conceipt vnseene obiects.' Cf. IV. i. 25 *post.* Malone quotes Plutarch, *Life of Antonius* (Temple ed., p. 63). The Roman soldiers in the Parthian War were driven by hunger 'to tast of rootes that were never eaten before; among the which there was one that killed them, and made them out of thir wits. For he that had once eaten of it, his memorye went from him, and he knew no manner of thing.' Douce quotes Batman, *Uppon Bartholome de propriet. rerum*, XVIII. 87: 'Henbane . . . is called *Insana*, mad, for the use thereof is perillous, for if it be eate or dronke, it breedeth madness . . . is called commonly *Mirilidium*, for it taketh away wit and reason.' The Clar. Edd. suggest that Shakespeare was thinking of the Mekilwort berries, mentioned by Holinshed (Appendix, p. 170). Boece speaks of them as deadly nightshade, which 'troubleth the minde, bringeth madnes if a fewe of the berries be inwardly taken' (Gerard, *Herball*).

88. *To . . . words*] Banquo quibbles on 'went' (Wilson). J. M. Nosworthy

Enter ROSSE *and* ANGUS.

Rosse. The King hath happily receiv'd, Macbeth,
    The news of thy success; and when he reads   90
    Thy personal venture in the rebels' fight,
    His wonders and his praises do contend,
    Which should be thine, or his: silenc'd with that,
    In viewing o'er the rest o'th'selfsame day,
    He finds thee in the stout Norweyan ranks,   95
    Nothing afeard of what thyself didst make,
    Strange images of death. As thick as hail,
    Came post with post; and every one did bear
    Thy praises in his kingdom's great defence,
    And pour'd them down before him.

Ang.   We are sent,   100
    To give thee from our royal master thanks;
    Only to herald thee into his sight,
    Not pay thee.

Rosse.   And, for an earnest of a greater honour,
    He bade me, from him, call thee Thane of Cawdor: 105

---

91. rebels'] *Theobald;* Rebels *F;* rebel's *Johnson.*   96. afeard] afraid *F4.*
97–8. hail, Came] *Rowe;* tale Can *F;* tale, Came *Malone (conj. Johnson).*
102–3. Only . . . pay thee] *one line, Singer.*

points out that in all accounts of the
episode Macbeth and Banquo joked
about the 'prophesies'.

  91, 95.] referring to the two phases
of the fight, against Macdonwald, and
against Norway.

  92–3. *His wonders . . . his*] There
is a conflict in Duncan's mind between his astonishment at the achievement and his admiration for Macbeth.

  93. *Which . . . his*] R. Walker, p. 14.
comments that 'in Macbeth's rebel
heart that is the very question.'

  that] 'the mental conflict just described' (Clarendon).

  97. *images of death*] Cf. Virgil, *Aen.*,
II. 369: 'plurima mortis imago'
(Sprague). See Empson, *Seven Types of
Ambiguity*, 1930, pp. 58–9.

  thick as hail] Rowe's emendation is

generally accepted. Though Johnson
retained the Folio reading, and explained, 'posts arrived as fast as they
could be counted', Dyce showed that
whereas 'thick as tale' is unknown,
'thick as hail' is common. It is twice
used by Holinshed, not far from
Macbeth sources. H. M. Hume, *op.
cit.*, p. 155, defends 'tale'.

  100. *pour'd*] continues image of
'hail' (Wilson).

  104. *for . . . honour*] R. Walker, p. 15,
suggests that as Rosse has been given
no message from Duncan which would
justify this phrase, he 'has become an
oracle, repeating the greatest promise
of the Witches'. At least Macbeth may
take it as such.

  earnest] 'mony giuen for the conclusion, or striking vp, of a bargaine'
(Cotgrave).

In which addition, hail, most worthy Thane,
For it is thine.

Ban.　　　　　　What! can the Devil speak true?

Macb. The Thane of Cawdor lives: why do you dress me
In borrow'd robes?

Ang.　　　　　　Who was the Thane, lives yet;
But under heavy judgment bears that life　　　　　110
Which he deserves to lose. Whether he was combin'd
With those of Norway, or did line the rebel
With hidden help and vantage, or that with both
He labour'd in his country's wrack, I know not;
But treasons capital, confess'd and prov'd,　　　　115
Have overthrown him.

Macb. [*Aside.*]　　　　Glamis, and Thane of Cawdor:
The greatest is behind. [*To Rosse and Angus*] Thanks
for your pains.—
[*To Banquo*] Do you not hope your children shall be
kings,
When those that gave the Thane of Cawdor to me
Promis'd no less to them?

108–9. The Thane ... yet;] *so Capell; three lines, ending* liues: / Robes? / yet. *F.*
109. borrow'd] his borrowed *F2–4.*　　111–14. Which ... know not;] *so
Malone; five lines, ending* loose, / Norway, / helpe, / labour'd / not: *F; four lines,
ending* was / Rebell / both / not; *Pope.*　　112. did] else did *F2–4.*　　114.
wrack] wreck *Theobald.*　　116. S.D.] *Rowe.*　　117. S.D.] *White.*

106. *addition*] 'a Title given to a Man over and above his Christian and Sirname, shewing his Estate, Degree, Mystery, Trade, Place of dwelling, etc.' (Blount, Law Dict. (1670)).

108–9. *dress ... robes*] This image recurs throughout the play. Cf. Spurgeon, *Shakespeare's Imagery*, pp. 325–7.

111–14.] Wilson remarks that the mislineation in the Folio suggests adaptation. But there is a good deal of mislineation in F where adaptation is not suspected. Granville-Barker (*Preface*, p. xxvii) remarks that it is strange that Angus should say these words of Cawdor. 'Shakespeare was not apt to leave things in such a muddle at the beginning of a play.' But perhaps the muddle helps to create the atmosphere

of 'deceitful appearance, and consequent doubt, uncertainty, and confusion' (Knights, *op. cit.*, p. 18).

R. Walker, *op. cit.*, p. 23, explains: 'The poet is shifting the emphasis from the former thane of Cawdor's particular faults which are past to a statement in general terms which ostensibly describes those faults but actually foreshadows also the faults, the "treasons capital" that will "overthrow" the new thane of Cawdor. He achieves his purpose by casting this slight haze of doubt over the particular faults and speaking in the most positive and arresting terms of the general sins that are common to both cases.'

112. *line*] strengthen, reinforce. Cf. *H5*, II. iv. 7: 'To line and new repair our towns of war'.

Ban.   That, trusted home,   120
   Might yet enkindle you unto the crown,
   Besides the Thane of Cawdor. But 'tis strange:
   And oftentimes, to win us to our harm,
   The instruments of Darkness tell us truths;
   Win us with honest trifles, to betray's   125
   In deepest consequence.—
   Cousins, a word, I pray you.
Macb.   [*Aside.*] Two truths are told,
   As happy prologues to the swelling act
   Of the imperial theme.—I thank you, gentlemen.—
   [*Aside.*] This supernatural soliciting   130
   Cannot be ill; cannot be good:—
   If ill, why hath it given me earnest of success,
   Commencing in a truth? I am Thane of Cawdor:
   If good, why do I yield to that suggestion
   Whose horrid image doth unfix my hair,   135
   And make my seated heart knock at my ribs,
   Against the use of nature? Present fears
   Are less than horrible imaginings.
   My thought, whose murther yet is but fantastical,

120. trusted] thrusted *conj. Malone.*   125. betray's] betray us *Rowe.*   126–7.
In . . . you] *one line, Capell.*   127. S.D.] *Rowe.*   131–2. good . . . success,]
so F; lines end ill, / success, *Rowe, etc.*   135. hair] *Rowe;* Heire *F.*   139.
murther] murder *Steevens (1778).*

120. *home*] thoroughly, fully, largely
(Cotgrave). Cf. *Cym.*, III. v. 92.
   121. *enkindle you*] 'excites you to hope
for' (Bradley). Banquo does not think
of foul play.
   122–6. *But . . . consequence*] The ap-
plication to Macbeth is obvious.
   123. *to win . . . harm*] Cf. James I,
Dæmonologie, in *Workes,* 1616, p. 98:
'for that old and craftie serpent being a
Spirit, he easily spies our affections,
and so conformes himself thereto to
deceiue vs to our wracke'.
   128. *the swelling act*] Cf. *H5,* Prol.,
3–4: 'A kingdom for a stage, princes to
act, / And monarchs to behold the
swelling scene'.
   130–1.] The 'sickening sea-saw
rhythm completes the impression of
"a phantasma, or a hideous dream" '

(Knights, *op. cit.,* p. 20). Flatter also
supports the F lineation. Knight, *The
Wheel of Fire,* 1949, p. 153, comments:
'This is the moment of the birth of evil
in Macbeth—he may indeed have had
ambitious thoughts before, may even
have intended the murder, but now
for the first time he feels its oncoming
reality.'
   135. *horrid image*] i.e. of himself
murdering Duncan.
   137. *Against . . . nature*] contrary to
my natural habit (Kittredge).
   fears] objects of fear. Cf. *MND.,*
v. i. 21: 'Or in the night, imagining
some fear'.
   139–41. *My . . . surmise*] Kenneth
Muir, *N.Q.,* June 1956, suggested that
these lines and II. i. 36–47 were both
influenced by Cassandra's prophecy

Shakes so my single state of man,   140
That function is smother'd in surmise,
And nothing is, but what is not.

Ban. Look, how our partner's rapt.

Macb. [*Aside.*] If Chance will have me King, why, Chance
    may crown me,
Without my stir.

Ban.   New honours come upon him,   145
Like our strange garments, cleave not to their mould,
But with the aid of use.

Macb.   [*Aside.*] Come what come may,
Time and the hour runs through the roughest day.

140–3. Shakes . . . rapt.] *so F; lines end* function / is / rapt. *Pope and most modern*
Edd.   144. If . . . crown me,] *so Rowe; two lines, the first ending* King F.

---

in Studley's translation of Seneca's
Agamemnon, Act v.

139. *fantastical*] imaginary. Cf. I. iii.
53 *ante.*

140–2.] I have restored the F arrangement of these lines, as nearly
every actor speaks them thus and, I
think, correctly.

140. *single . . . man*] Steevens observes that '*double* and *single* anciently
signified *strong* and *weak*'. Cf. *Oth.,*
I. ii. 14: 'As double as the Duke's', and
2H4, I. ii. 207: 'Is not . . . your wit
single?' and cf. I. vi. 16 *post.* But
Grierson—I think rightly—says that
single here means 'indivisible' and the
phrase as a whole 'my composite
nature—body, spirits, etc., made one
by the soul'. Though Wilson regards a
reference to the microcosm pointless in
this context, I believe that such a
reference is made. Cf. *Caes.,* II. i. 63–9,
where the same phrase, 'state of man'
occurs, and where the reference to the
microcosm is explicit.

141. *function*] The intellectual activity which is revealed in outward
conduct: but the word is applied to
action in general, whether physical or
mental. 'All powers of action are oppressed and crushed by one overwhelming image in the mind, and
nothing is present to me but that which

is really future. Of things now about
me I have no perception, being intent
wholly on that which has no existence'
(Johnson).

142. *nothing . . . not*] Knight, *The*
Wheel of Fire, 1949, p. 153, says this is
'the text of the play. Reality and unreality change places.' Coleridge, *op.*
cit., I. 69–70, says: 'So truly is the guilt
in its germ anterior to the supposed
cause and immediate temptation . . . a
confirmation of the remark on the
early birth-date of guilt'.

143. *rapt*] Cf. line 57 *ante.* According
to Flatter's rules, Banquo should not
be made to complete Macbeth's line;
but it is difficult to regard Banquo's
speeches as linked together metrically.

145. *come*] probably the participle,
not the finite verb.

146. *Like . . . mould*] another image
taken from clothes.

148. *Time . . . hour*] Grant White,
Words and their Uses, 1871, p. 237, says:
'Time and the hour in this passage is
merely an equivalent of time and tide
—the time and tide that wait for no
man.' Shakespeare may use 'runs' in-
transitively; but Cuningham thinks it
is used transitively, meaning, 'runs the
roughest day through'. Dyce, *Few*
Notes, etc., 1853, p. 119, remarks that
'this expression is not infrequent in

Ban. Worthy Macbeth, we stay upon your leisure.

Macb. Give me your favour: my dull brain was wrought   150
  With things forgotten. Kind gentlemen, your pains
  Are register'd where every day I turn
  The leaf to read them.—Let us toward the King.—
  [*To Banquo*] Think upon what hath chanc'd; and
    at more time,
  The Interim having weigh'd it, let us speak   155
  Our free hearts each to other.

Ban.   Very gladly.

Macb. Till then, enough.—Come, friends.   [*Exeunt.*

SCENE IV.—[*Forres. A room in the palace.*]

Flourish. Enter DUNCAN, MALCOLM, DONALBAIN, LENOX,
and Attendants.

Dun. Is execution done on Cawdor? Or not
  Those in commission yet return'd?

150–4. Give . . . time,] *so Pope; seven lines, ending* fauour / forgotten / registred, / leafe, / them / vpon / time, *F; six lines, ending* favour: / forgotten. / register'd / them / King / time *Knight.*   154. S.D.] *Rowe.*   155. The] I' th' *conj. Steevens;* In the *Keightley.*   157. Till . . . friends] *so Pope; two lines, the first ending* enough.— *F.*

Scene IV

S.D. *Forres . . . palace.*] *Capell; not in F.*   1–2. Is . . . return'd?] *so Capell; two lines, the first ending* Cawdor? *F.*   1. Or] *F1;* Are *F2–4.*

Italian'—e.g. '*il tempo e così l'ora*' (Pulci).

150. *favour*] pardon.
  wrought] agitated. Cf. *Oth.*, v. ii. 345.
  151. *things forgotten*] i.e. which he is trying to recall. He is lying.
  152–3. *register'd . . . them*] i.e. in his brain.
  155. *The Interim*] Steevens says, 'Thus the intervening portion of time is personified; it is represented as a cool impartial judge; as the *pauser Reason*.' Malone, however, believes it is used adverbially. The word is here printed in the Folio with a capital letter and in italics, as in *Caes.*, II. i. 64, but not elsewhere in the Folio.

Scene IV

This scene, says Knights, *Explorations*, p. 21, 'suggests the natural order which is shortly to be violated. It stresses natural relationships . . . honourable bonds and the political order . . . and the human "love" is linked to the more purely natural by images of husbandry.' Cf. Knight, *The Imperial Theme*, p. 126, and Traversi, *Approach to Shakespeare*, 1938, p. 88.

  1. *Or*] Cuningham suggests that the reading of the First Folio may be correct, the verb being understood.
  2. *in commission*] charged with the duty.

Mal.   My Liege,
     They are not yet come back; but I have spoke
     With one that saw him die: who did report,
     That very frankly he confess'd his treasons,   5
     Implor'd your Highness' pardon, and set forth
     A deep repentance. Nothing in his life
     Became him like the leaving it: he died
     As one that had been studied in his death,
     To throw away the dearest thing he ow'd,   10
     As 'twere a careless trifle.
Dun.   There's no art
     To find the mind's construction in the face:
     He was a gentleman on whom I built
     An absolute trust—

          Enter MACBETH, BANQUO, ROSSE, *and* ANGUS.

                                                O worthiest cousin!
     The sin of my ingratitude even now   15
     Was heavy on me. Thou art so far before,
     That swiftest wing of recompense is slow
     To overtake thee: would thou hadst less deserv'd,
     That the proportion both of thanks and payment
     Might have been mine! only I have left to say,   20
     More is thy due than more than all can pay.
Macb. The service and the loyalty I owe,

2–8. My . . . died] *so Pope; seven lines, ending* back. / die: / hee / Pardon, /
Repentance: / him, / dy'de, *F.*   9–10. studied . . . To] studied, . . . death, To
Keightley; studied . . . death To *Dyce (ed. 2).*   17. That] The *Jennens.*   wing]
F1; wine *F2–4;* wind *Rowe.*

9. *studied*] a theatrical term, meaning 'learnt by heart'.
   10–11. *To . . . trifle*] R. Walker compares III. i. 67–8 *post.*
   11–12. *There's . . . face*] 'We cannot
construe or discover the disposition of
the mind by the lineaments of the face'
(Johnson). Baldwin compares Juve-
nal, *Satires,* ii. 8 ff., '*Frontis nulla fides*'.
The irony of the speech is pointed by
the immediate entrance of Macbeth,
as critics have observed.
   19–20. *That . . . mine*] i.e. that I

might have been able to give you
thanks and reward in proportion to
your merits. *O.E.D.* quotes this passage and defines 'proportion' as 'the
action of making proportionate'.
   22–7.] Coleridge, *Shakespearean Criticism,* I. 70, declares that 'Macbeth
has nothing but the commonplaces of
loyalty, in which he hides himself. . .
Reasoning instead of joy . . . the same
language of *effort* . . . at the moment
that a new difficulty suggests a new
crime.'

In doing it, pays itself. Your Highness' part
Is to receive our duties: and our duties
Are to your throne and state, children and servants;   25
Which do but what they should, by doing everything
Safe toward your love and honour.

Dun.   Welcome hither:
I have begun to plant thee, and will labour
To make thee full of growing.—Noble Banquo,
That hast no less deserv'd, nor must be known   30
No less to have done so, let me infold thee,
And hold thee to my heart.

Ban.   There if I grow,
The harvest is your own.

Dun.   My plenteous joys,
Wanton in fulness, seek to hide themselves
In drops of sorrow.—Sons, kinsmen, Thanes,   35
And you whose places are the nearest, know,
We will establish our estate upon

23–7. In . . . honour] *so Pope; six lines, ending* selfe. / Duties: / State, / should, /
Loue / Honor. *F.*   27. Safe] Shap'd *Hanmer;* Fief'd *Warburton;* Fiefs *conj.
idem;* Serves *conj.* Heath; saf'd *conj.* Malone; Slaves *conj. Kinnear;* Sole *conj. Orson.*
your] you *conj. Blackstone.*   love] Life *Warburton.*   30. That] Thou *Pope.*
nor] and *Rowe.*   35. Sons] Sons and *conj. Cuningham.*

27. *Safe . . . honour]* 'with a sure
regard to your love and honour'
(Clarendon) or 'to confer security on
you whom we love and honour'.

28. *plant]* Cf. *All's W.,* II. iii. 163: 'It
is in us to plant thine honour where we
please to have it grow.'

33–5. *My . . . sorrow]* Cf. *Rom.,* III. ii.
102–14; *Ado,* I. i. 26–9; and *Wint.,*
v. ii. 49–50. Malone quotes Lucan,
Phars. ix. 1038: '—lacrymas non
sponte cadentes / Effudit, gemitusque
expressit pectore laeto / Non aliter
manifesta potens abscondere mentis /
Gaudia, quam lacrymis.'

34. *Wanton]* unrestrained, perverse.

35. *Sons, kinsmen]* Cuningham
wanted to mend the metre by inserting
'and' between these two words. But
there must be a pause while Duncan
masters his emotion. Adams thinks
that two scenes have been run together

or at least that portions of the text are
lost because (i) we lose a day while
Macbeth makes enquiries about the
weird sisters; (ii) the weak Duncan
suddenly exhibits strength by ar-
ranging for his son to succeed him; and
(iii) announces in an unexpected and
brief clause—almost unintelligible—
that he proposes to visit Macbeth at
Inverness. Bradley and Wilson also
suspect a cut. But see Thaler, *Shakespeare and Democracy,* pp. 88–105, for a
refutation of Adams. (i) Shakespeare
was not realistic in his treatment of
time; (ii) Duncan was not weak, and
even if he were, a sudden announcement is not incompatible with weakness; (iii) the clause is intelligible
enough—though I too suspect there
may have been a cut here.

37. *establish our estate]* settle the
succession.

Our eldest, Malcolm; whom we name hereafter
The Prince of Cumberland: which honour must
Not unaccompanied invest him only,   40
But signs of nobleness, like stars, shall shine
On all deservers.—From hence to Inverness,
And bind us further to you.
Macb. The rest is labour, which is not us'd for you:
I'll be myself the harbinger, and make joyful   45
The hearing of my wife with your approach;
So, humbly take my leave.
Dun.   My worthy Cawdor!
Macb. [*Aside.*] The Prince of Cumberland!—That is a step
On which I must fall down, or else o'erleap,
For in my way it lies. Stars, hide your fires!   50
Let not light see my black and deep desires;
The eye wink at the hand; yet let that be,
Which the eye fears, when it is done, to see.   [*Exit.*
Dun. True, worthy Banquo: he is full so valiant,
And in his commendations I am fed;   55
It is a banquet to me. Let's after him,

---

48. S.D.] *Rowe.*   51. not] *F;* no *Hanmer.*   light] Night *Warburton.*   56.
Let's] *F;* Let us *Pope, etc.*

---

39. *The . . . Cumberland*] 'The crown
of Scotland was originally not heredi-
tary. When a successor was declared in
the life-time of a king, as was often the
case, the title of *Prince of Cumberland* was
immediately bestowed on him as the
mark of his designation. Cumberland
was at that time held by Scotland of the
crown of England as a fief' (Steevens).

45. *harbinger*] an officer of the household whose duty it was to provide
lodgings for the king, hence 'fore-
runner'.

48–53.] Granville-Barker, *Preface,*
p. xxvii, remarks that 'the disclosure
of Macbeth's mind, not in a soliloquy,
but in two rather ineptly contrived
asides, is surely, in such a play and with
such a character, un-Shakespearean.'
Fleay suspected this passage was
written by Middleton. But the imagery
is Shakespearian. Compare 49 with
I. vii. 27; 50 with I. v. 50 and II. i. 5;

and 52 with several passages in which
eye and hand are opposed. See Introduction, p. xxvii, and cf. Spurgeon,
Shakespeare's Imagery, pp. 329.

50. *Stars*] 'Macbeth apparently appeals to the stars because he is con-
templating night as the time for the
perpetration of the deed. There is
nothing to indicate that this scene took
place at night' (Clarendon). Cf. Lady
Macbeth's speech I. v. 50–4. R. Walker
p. 40, compares 41 *ante* and comments: 'it is the signs of nobleness in
his own nature that he would obscure.'

52. *wink at*] seem not to see, connive.
Cf. Introduction, p. xxix.

be] i.e. be done.

56. *banquet*] Cuningham suggests
that this is what we now call dessert—
a slight refection, consisting of cakes,
sweetmeats, and fruit, and generally
served in a room to which the guests
removed after dinner; but as the

Whose care is gone before to bid us welcome:
It is a peerless kinsman.   [*Flourish. Exeunt.*

SCENE V.—[*Inverness. A room in* MACBETH'S *castle.*]

Enter LADY MACBETH, *reading a letter.*

Lady M. 'They met me in the day of success; and I have
learn'd by the perfect'st report, they have more in
them than mortal knowledge. When I burn'd in
desire to question them further, they made themselves air, into which they vanish'd. Whiles I stood   5
rapt in the wonder of it, came missives from the
King, who all-hail'd me, "Thane of Cawdor"; by
which title, before, these Weïrd Sisters saluted me,
and referr'd me to the coming on of time, with "Hail,
King that shalt be!" This have I thought good to   10
deliver thee (my dearest partner of greatness) that
thou might'st not lose the dues of rejoicing, by being
ignorant of what greatness is promis'd thee. Lay it
to thy heart, and farewell.'

Scene v

S.D. *Inverness . . . castle.*] *Capell.*   8. Weïrd] *Cf. 1. iii. 32.*   10. be!] be
hereafter *conj. Upton.*   12. the] thy *conj. Capell.*

ordinary sense of the word is common
in Shakespeare and as several critics
have stressed the importance of
banquets in the play, as a visible sign
of the concord violated by Macbeth's
crimes—see, e.g., Knight, *The Imperial
Theme*—it is unlikely that Shakespeare
here intended the restricted sense of the
word.

58. *kinsman*] Macbeth was Duncan's
first-cousin.

Scene v

1. *success*] Although the common
sense of this word in Shakespeare's day
was 'issue', 'sequel', or 'consequence'
of a thing, it is used here and at 1. iii. 90
ante in the modern sense. Cf. note to
1. vii. 4 *post.*

2. *the perfect'st report*] 'the best intelligence' (Johnson); 'my own experience' (Clarendon); Rosse's report
of the King's intention to invest Macbeth with the thaneship of Cawdor
(Leighton). Johnson's explanation,
implying that Macbeth had made enquiries about the weird sisters, is
clearly right.

6. *missives*] messengers. Cf. *Ant.*,
II. ii. 74: 'Did gibe my missive out of
audience'.

7. *all-hail'd*] Florio, *Worlde of Wordes*,
1598, gives as meanings of *salutare*, 'to
greet, to salute, to recommend, to
all-haile'.

14. *farewell*] R. Walker, *op. cit.*, p. 43,
comments that Macbeth does not
mention Banquo. 'He has suppressed

Glamis thou art, and Cawdor; and shalt be   15
What thou art promis'd.—Yet do I fear thy nature:
It is too full o'th'milk of human kindness,
To catch the nearest way. Thou wouldst be great;
Art not without ambition, but without
The illness should attend it: what thou wouldst highly,

15. be] be— *Kittredge.*   17. human] *Rowe;* humane *F.*   human kindness]
humankindness *conj. Moulton.*

the one piece of news that would show the flaw in the plot against Duncan, and deliberately made his wife believe that the prophecy . . . is a secret of which he was the sole possessor.' But we only hear the second half of the letter.

15–30. *Glamis . . . withal*] Stewart, *M.L.R.*, 1945, p. 173, points out that 'the speech will be satisfactory if we only admit that the portrayal of Lady Macbeth, and of her relations with her husband, are factors in it; and that a certain distortion of Macbeth's character is entailed in this. On Macbeth himself the speech does indeed throw new and useful light, such as is desirable in an exposition, for we chiefly gather from it that he is not likely to be immediately wholehearted in villainy and that some spiritual struggle is to be expected of him. But the speech is also charged with certain feelings of Lady Macbeth's which lead her to exaggerate what she pervertedly regards as her husband's insufficiencies, and this renders more striking and terrible our first impression of her.' Lady Macbeth suddenly realizes 'forces in his nature that may militate against her designs. These she does not review "objectively" but magnifies in passion and scorn. And this should be clear to us. For we already know that Macbeth has murder in his thoughts.'

15. *shalt be*] Lady Macbeth, in repeating the words of the Third Sister, instinctively checks herself at the word *King*, and substitutes a reticent phrase (Kittredge).

17. *th'milk . . . kindness*] Cuningham points out that it is essential to remember the radical signification of the words *kind, kindness,* as meaning *natural* and *nature.* Moulton, *Shakespeare as a Dramatic Artist*, p. 149, therefore suggests that we should read *humankind* as meaning *human nature*; 'and that the sense of the whole passage would be more obvious if the whole phrase were printed as one word, not "human kindness" but "humankind-ness" '— that shrinking from the unnatural which is a marked feature of the practical man. 'The other part of the clause, *milk* of humankindness, no doubt suggests absence of hardness: but it equally connotes natural inherited traditional feelings imbibed at the mother's breast.' But cf. *Lr.*, i. iv. 364: 'This milky gentleness and course of yours', and line 48 *post* ('take my milk for gall') which certainly suggest that *milk* implies an absence of hardness; and *humane* was the only spelling down to the end of the eighteenth century, when *human* was substituted in certain senses, leaving *humane* as a distinct word, with distinctive meanings. There is therefore no reason for altering the text. Lady Macbeth implies that her husband is squeamish and sentimental. She may also imply that he is bound by traditional feelings. See headnote to Sc. iv *ante* and the reference to 'the milk of concord' (IV. iii. 98). Cf. Appendix A, p. 181.

One of the subjects debated at Oxford in August 1605 was the nurse's influence on a baby's character (Paul).

20. *illness*] evilness, wickedness. The word was not used for 'sickness' in Shakespeare's day.

That wouldst thou holily; wouldst not play false,   21
And yet wouldst wrongly win; thou'dst have, great
    Glamis,
That which cries, 'Thus thou must do,' if thou have it;
And that which rather thou dost fear to do,
Than wishest should be undone. Hie thee hither,   25
That I may pour my spirits in thine ear,
And chastise with the valour of my tongue
All that impedes thee from the golden round,
Which fate and metaphysical aid doth seem
To have thee crown'd withal.

Enter a Messenger.

                            What is your tidings?   30
Mess. The King comes here to-night.
Lady M.   Thou'rt mad to say it.
Is not thy master with him? who, were't so,

22-3. And . . . it;] *so Pope; three lines, ending* winne. / cryes, / it; *F.*   23. 'Thus
. . . do'] *so Hunter; final inverted comma placed after* undone, *Pope; placed after* have
it; *Hanmer, Capell.*   25. Hie] *F4;* High *F1-3.*   28. impedes thee] thee
hinders *F2-3.*

22-5. *thou'dst . . . undone*] The chief
difficulty here is the extent of the
quotation. Pope put the whole passage
in inverted commas, and he has been
followed by most editors (i.e. 'Thus
. . . undone'). Hanmer, Capell, Verity,
Wilson, and others end the quotation
at the end of line 23. Hunter (*Illustrations*, II. 172) only marks 'Thus thou
must do' as such. I think he is right,
because that which cries is the crown,
and if 'it' were part of the quotation,
one would expect 'me' instead. As
Verity explains, 'thou'ldst have' has
two objects, the crown (23) and the
murder by which the crown may be
obtained (24-5). Cuningham wished
to follow Keightley and emend the
second 'thou' in 23 to 'thou'ldst'. But
Shakespeare wisely avoided the more
logical form because he already had a
plethora of *wouldsts* and there could be
no doubt of the meaning.
   27. *chastise*] The accent is on the

first syllable. Cf. *R2*, II. iii. 104.
   28. *golden round*] Cf. IV. i. 88.
   29. *metaphysical*] supernatural.
   seem] Cf. I. ii. 48 *ante.*
   30. *tidings*] singular or plural, like
'news'. Cf. *AYL.*, v. iv. 159: 'these
tidings'; *Ant.*, IV. xiv. 112: 'this
tidings'. Flatter suggests that Lady
Macbeth's question should form a line
with the messenger's speech which
follows, so as to allow for a dramatic
pause after *say it.*
   31. *The King . . . to-night*] R. Walker,
op. cit., p. 46, makes the ingenious suggestion that as Lady Macbeth has been
thinking of her husband as King, she
thinks for a moment that the messenger refers to him and not to Duncan.
   31-3. *Thou'rt . . . preparation*] Lady
Macbeth, in replying to the messenger,
discloses what has been passing in her
own mind, and then, observing the
man's surprise, she adds a not very
convincing explanation.

Would have inform'd for preparation.
Mess. So please you, it is true: our Thane is coming;
    One of my fellows had the speed of him,   35
    Who, almost dead for breath, had scarcely more
    Than would make up his message.
Lady M.   Give him tending:
    He brings great news. [*Exit Messenger.*] The raven
        himself is hoarse,
    That croaks the fatal entrance of Duncan
    Under my battlements. Come, you Spirits   40

38. He . . . hoarse] *so Rowe; two lines, the first ending* news. *F.*

33. *inform'd*] absolute or intransitive.

35. *had the speed of*] Cf. *Ado.*, I. i. 142: 'I would my horse had the speed of your tongue.' But the phrase in *Macbeth* means 'out-distanced', in *Ado*, 'went as fast as'.

37. *tending*] Shakespeare does not elsewhere use this word as a substantive.

38–9. *The raven . . . croaks*] Some think that the reference is to the breathless messenger, but lack of breath does not cause hoarseness. As Hunter says, the phrase means 'even the raven . . . has more than its usual harshness'; or perhaps, as Manly suggests, the implication is that 'the approach of an ordinary guest might be announced by a magpie, but for such a visit as Duncan's the hoarse croaking of a raven would alone be appropriate.' Cf. Hamlet's words 'The croaking raven doth bellow for revenge' (III. ii. 248), parodying *The True Tragedy of Richard III* (1891–2), 'The screeking Rauen sits croking for reuenge. / Whole heads of beasts comes bellowing for reuenge.' Cf. also *Oth.*, IV. i. 21: 'As doth the raven o'er the infected house, / Boding to all'; and Nashe, *Terrors of the Night* (ed. McKerrow, I. 346) on the raven also: 'A continuall messenger hee is of dole and misfortune.'

39. *entrance*] This word is a trisyllable. The retention of *e* is frequently required *metri gratia*, when a

mute is followed by a liquid. Cf. III. vi. 8 and *Tw.N.*, I. i. 32, 'remembrance'.

40–54. *Come . . . hold!*] Inga-Stina Ewbank has suggested (*S.S.*, XIX. 82 ff.) that Shakespeare in these lines, and also in I. vii. 54–8, was influenced by Studley's translation of Seneca's *Medea*.

40. *Come, you Spirits*] Wilson comments: 'All critics have noticed the effect of the metrical pause before "Come" and the tremendous lines that follow.' But to judge from the fact that editors have followed Davenant in reading 'Come, all you spirits,' the statement is an exaggeration. Darmesteter supports this emendation by comparing Hughes, *Misfortunes of Arthur*, I. ii (an echo of the opening lines of Seneca's *Medea*): 'Come, spiteful fiends, come heaps of furies fell, / Not one by one, but all at once!' Steevens suggested a repetition of 'Come'; and Cuningham argued for 'Come, you ill spirits.' Nevertheless these emendations spoil the effectiveness of the passage and deprive the actress of the chance of taking the long breath she obviously needs. Malone quotes Nashe, *Pierce Penilesse*, ed. McKerrow, I. 230, where he thinks 'Shakespeare might have found a particular description of these spirits and of their office': 'The Second kind of Diuels, which he most imployeth, are those Northerne *Marcij*, called the spirits of reuenge, & the authors of

That tend on mortal thoughts, unsex me here,
And fill me, from the crown to the toe, top-full
Of direst cruelty! make thick my blood,
Stop up th'access and passage to remorse;
That no compunctious visitings of Nature   45
Shake my fell purpose, nor keep peace between
Th'effect and it! Come to my woman's breasts,
And take my milk for gall, you murth'ring ministers,
Wherever in your sightless substances
You wait on Nature's mischief! Come, thick Night,   50

46. peace] pace *Travers (conj. Johnson);* space *conj. Bailey.*   47. it] *F3–4;* hit *F1–2.*

massacres, & seedesmen of mischiefe; for they haue commission to incense men to rapines, sacriledge, theft, murther, wrath, furie, and all manner of cruelties, & they commaund certaine of the Southern spirits (as slaues) to wayt vpon them, as also *Arioch,* that is tearmed the spirite of reuenge.'

Burton, *Anatomy of Melancholy,* I. ii. 1, 2 mentions nine kinds of bad spirits. See Introduction, p. lviii, for a comment on this invocation.

41. *mortal thoughts*] 'murderous, deadly, or destructive designs' (Johnson). Cf. III. iv. 80 and IV. iii. 3.

42. *crown . . . toe*] Baret's *Alvearie* has: 'From the top to the toe, *a capite ad calcem usque*'.

top-full] Cf. *John,* III. iv. 180.

43. *make . . . blood*] Wilson compares *Wint.,* I. ii. 171, and *John,* III. iii. 42–7. She means 'so that pity cannot flow along her veins' and reach her heart (Bradley).

44. *remorse*] compassion, tenderness. Cf. *Mer.V.,* IV. i. 20. 'Used anciently to signify repentance not only for a deed done but for a thought conceived' (Clarendon).

45. *compunctious*] not used elsewhere by Shakespeare.

46–7. *nor . . . it*] 'use the restraining power of a peacemaker . . . between my purpose and the achievement of it' (New Clarendon). Steevens quotes Brooke, *Romeus and Juliet* (1562),

1781 ff.: 'the lady no way could / Kepe trewse betweene her greefes and her.'

48. *take . . . gall*] 'Take away my milk, and put gall into the place' (Johnson); 'Nourish yourselves with my milk which . . . has turned to gall' (Delius); take = infect (Keightley). The last explanation is the best. Cuningham compares *1H6,* v. iv. 27: 'I would the milk / Thy mother gave thee when thou suck'dst her breast, / Had been a little ratsbane for thy sake!'

ministers] attendant spirits (Wilson).

49. *sightless*] invisible. Cf. I. vii. 23.

50. *Nature's mischief*] According to Johnson this means 'mischief done to nature, violation of nature's order committed by wickedness'; Elwin thinks it means 'both injury engendered in human nature and done to it'; and Cuningham thinks it may mean 'mischief wrought by any natural phenomenon, such as storm, tempest, earthquake, etc.' Curry's explanation of the whole clause, *Shakespeare's Philosophical Patterns,* p. 86, is 'objective, substantial forms, invisible bad angels, to whose activities may be attributed all the unnatural occurrences of nature'.

50–4. *Come . . . hold*] Cf. Munday, *The Downfall of Robert, Earl of Huntington,* 1601: 'Muffle the eye of day, / Ye gloomie clouds (the darker than my

And pall thee in the dunnest smoke of Hell,
That my keen knife see not the wound it makes,
Nor Heaven peep through the blanket of the dark,
To cry, 'Hold, hold!'

Enter MACBETH.

Great Glamis! worthy Cawdor!
Greater than both, by the all-hail hereafter!   55
Thy letters have transported me beyond
This ignorant present, and I feel now
The future in the instant.

53. blanket] blank height *conj. Coleridge.*

deedes, / That darker be than pitchie sable night) / Muster together on these high topt trees, / That not a sparke of light thorough their sprayes / May hinder what I meane to exccute.' See *M.L.N.*, 1931, and cf. III. ii. 46–7 *post*.

51. *dunnest*] an epithet criticized by Johnson (*Rambler*, no. 168) as 'mean'; but the criticism was apparently recanted in his *Dictionary*.

52. *my*] Wilson and Adams assume that Lady Macbeth originally intended to do the deed herself. Cf. 68, 73 *post* and note on II. ii. 12–13. See Introduction, p. xix.

53. *blanket*] Johnson also objected to the meanness of this word, and so did Coleridge (*Shakes. Crit.*, I. 73); but many parallels have been quoted including: 'The sullen night in mistie rugge is wrapp'd' (Drayton, *Mortimeriados*, l. 694, ed. Hebel, I. 329); 'Spread thy close curtain, love-performing night', *Rom.*, III. ii. 5); *1H6*, II. ii. 2; and *Lucr.*, 788. Whiter, in his *Specimen of a Commentary*, 1794, pp. 153–84, quotes so many passages which link *pall*, *hell*, *knife*, and *dark* with the stage that it is impossible not to believe that they were associated in Shakespeare's mind. 'The peculiar and appropriate dress of *Tragedy* is a *pall* and a *knife*. When Tragedies were represented, the stage was hung with black . . . on the same occasions, the

Heavens, or the Roof of the Stage, underwent likewise some gloomy transformation.' But although the passage as a whole was suggested by the stage, the metaphor of the blanket is quite simple, and can only refer to the blanket spread by the dark over the earth. It implies a 'sleeping world' (Clarendon).

55. *all-hail hereafter*] Lady Macbeth 'speaks as if she had heard the words as spoken by the witch, and not merely read them as reported in her husband's letter' (Clarendon). Yet the audience would not notice the discrepancy, and it may be noted that the letter does use the phrase 'all-hail'd' (7) and that Lady Macbeth reads only the second half of the letter. Wilson interprets 'hereafter' to mean 'that followed': and the New Clar. Edd. assume that 'All-hail' is an adjective. But surely hereafter = in the future. Mrs Siddons accepted this reading; so, I imagine, do most actresses.

57. *This . . . present*] i.e. this present which is ignorant of the future (ignorant = unknowing). Cf. *Wint.*, I. ii. 397.

57–8. *I . . . instant*] 'I feel by anticipation those future honours, of which, according to the process of nature, the *present time* would be *ignorant*' (Johnson). Several critics have supposed that a word is missing between 'feel' and

Macb.   My dearest love,
    Duncan comes here to-night.
Lady M.   And when goes hence?
Macb. To-morrow, as he purposes.
Lady M.   O! never   60
    Shall sun that morrow see!
    Your face, my Thane, is as a book, where men
    May read strange matters. To beguile the time,
    Look like the time; bear welcome in your eye,
    Your hand, your tongue: look like th'innocent flower,
    But be the serpent under't. He that's coming   66
    Must be provided for; and you shall put
    This night's great business into my dispatch;
    Which shall to all our nights and days to come
    Give solely sovereign sway and masterdom.   70

---

62. a] *not in F2.*   63. matters. To . . . time,] *Theobald;* matters, to . . . time. *F1–2;*
matters to . . . time. *F3–4.*

'now'. Cuningham suggested 'even' and quoted v. ii. 10 *post.* This is possible, but not necessary; and it would slow up the line, where impetuosity is required.

62. *face*] Mrs Siddons here looked at Macbeth's face for the first time in this scene.

63. *strange*] Cf. I. ii. 48 *ante.*

beguile the time] i.e. deceive the world, delude all observers. 'The time' often means 'the present age, i.e. men and things generally'. Cf. I. vii. 82 *post.* Steevens cites Daniel, *Civil Wars,* VIII. 709: 'He drawes a trauerse 'twixt his greeuances: / Lookes like the time: his eye made not report / Of what he felt within.' In *Tw.N.,* III. iii. 41, Shakespeare uses the phrase to mean 'while away the time'.

65–6. *look . . . under't*] Cf. Chaucer, *Squire's Tale,* 512; *2H6,* III. i. 228; *Rom.,* III. ii. 73, and *R2,* III. ii. 19. The idea is ultimately derived from Virgil, *Ecl.,* iii. 93: 'latet anguis in herba.' This quotation appears in Whitney, *Choice of Emblemes,* 1586, p. 24, with a picture of a serpent and a strawberry

plant and the following explanation: 'Of flattringe speeche, with sugred wordes beware, / Suspect the harte, whose face doth fawn and smile, / With trusting theise, the worlde is clog'de with care, / And fewe there bee can scape these vipers vile: / With pleasinge speche they promise, and protest, / When hatefull heartes lie hidd within their brest.' Wilson thinks the image shows that Lady Macbeth intended her husband to play a passive role (p. l). But the serpent does more than hide behind the flower—he also stings. The medal commemorating the discovery of the Gunpowder Plot depicts a serpent lurking amid flowers (Paul).

67. *provided for*] Cf. *1H6,* v. ii. 15.

68. *my dispatch*] This does not necessarily mean that Lady Macbeth intended to do the actual deed, but merely that she intends to manage the whole affair. Cf. Introduction, p. xix. Wilson points out that there is a pun on the word 'dispatch'.

70. *solely*] 'for us alone' (New Clarendon); 'absolutely' (Wilson).

Macb. We will speak further.
Lady M.   Only look up clear;
    To alter favour ever is to fear.
    Leave all the rest to me.   [*Exeunt.*

SCENE VI.—[*The same. Before the castle.*]

Hautboys and torches. Enter DUNCAN, MALCOLM, DONALBAIN,
BANQUO, LENOX, MACDUFF, ROSSE, ANGUS, *and Attendants.*

Dun. This castle hath a pleasant seat; the air
    Nimbly and sweetly recommends itself
    Unto our gentle senses.
Ban.   This guest of summer,

---

72. to fear] and fear *Theobald (ed. 2).*

Scene VI
S.D. *The . . . castle.*] *Theobald, subst.*   1–2. the air . . . itself] *so Rowe; lines end*
seat, / itself *F.*   3. senses] sense *Capell (conj. Johnson).*

71. *speak further*] The old formula for
refusing the royal assent to a bill in
Parliament was 'le roi s'avisera'
(Clarendon).

72. *To alter . . . fear*] 'When a person
shows a disturbed countenance, it is
always inferred he has something on
his mind—and that may rouse suspicion' (Kittredge).

favour] countenance. 'Lady Macbeth detects more than irresolution in
her husband's last speech' (Clarendon).

73. *Leave . . . me*] Cf. notes to 65–6,
68 *ante.*

Scene VI
    Knights, *op. cit.*, p. 22, remarks that
'the key words of the scene are . . . all
images of love and procreation,
supernaturally sanctioned, for the
associations of "temple-haunting"
colour the whole of the speeches of
Banquo and Duncan.' Cf. Knight, *The
Imperial Theme*, p. 142, and Leavis,
Education and the University, appendix.

S.D. Hautboys and torches] used
for the *player* of the instrument and the
bearer of the torch, as well as for the instrument and the torch. Cf. II. i. *init.*
Wilson omits the torches, on the
ground that they are inappropriate to
one of the few sunlit scenes in the play.
But at sundown, torches would be
needed inside the castle, even though
it was still light outside.

1. *seat*] Reid compares Bacon, *Essays*,
Of Building: 'Hee that builds a faire
House, upon an *ill Seat*, Committeth
himself to Prison. Neither doe I reckon
it an *ill Seat* only where the Aire is un-
wholesome, but likewise where the
Aire is unequal; as you shall see many
fine Seats set upon a Knap of Ground
environed with higher Hills round
about it.'

3. *gentle senses*] probably a proleptic
construction, in which the epithet of
the object is the result of the previous
action (cf. III. iv. 75 *post*); but Duncan
may mean that his senses have become
gentle through age.

The temple-haunting martlet, does approve,
By his loved mansionry, that the heaven's breath   5
Smells wooingly here: no jutty, frieze,
Buttress, nor coign of vantage, but this bird
Hath made his pendent bed, and procreant cradle:
Where they most breed and haunt, I have observ'd
The air is delicate.

Enter LADY MACBETH.

4. martlet] *Rowe;* Barlet *F;* Marlet *Collier* (*MS.*).   5. mansionry] *Theobald;*
Mansonry *F;* masonry *Pope.*   6–10. Smells . . . delicate] *five lines, ending*
buttress, / made / they / air / delicate. *Steevens* (*1793*).   6. wooingly here: no]
wooingly: here is no *Travers* (*conj. Johnson*); wooingly: there is no *conj.*
Cuningham.   jutty, frieze] *Steevens* (*1793*); Iutty frieze *F;* jutting frieze *Pope.*
8. his] this *F4.*   8–9. cradle: . . . haunt,] *Rowe;* Cradle, . . . haunt: *F.*
9. most] *Rowe;* must *F;* much *Collier* (*ed. 2*).

4. *martlet*] This is now the swift, but seems to have been the house-martin in Shakespeare's day. According to *O.E.D.* the bird was 'formerly often confused with the swallow and the house-martin'; but even Gilbert White thought that the martlet was another name for house-martin, though he would not confuse the swift with the martin. B. K. Harris points out (*T.L.S.*, 16/3/51) that there were martlets on Edward the Confessor's shield. Braithwaite, *Survey of History* (1638), says that 'the martin will not build but in fair houses.' Cf. 'temple-haunting'. Spurgeon, *Shakespeare's Imagery*, pp. 187–90, compares *Mer.V.*, II. ix. 28: 'like the martlet / Builds in the weather on the outward wall'. She points out that in both contexts a guest arrives who is to be fooled or deceived, the hidden connection in Shakespeare's mind being that 'martin' was a slang term for 'dupe', the word being so used by Greene and Fletcher. This supports the view that martlet = martin.

approve] prove. Cf. *Mer.V.*, III. ii. 80: 'Will bless it and approve it with a text'.

5. *By . . . mansionry*] 'by making it his favourite abode' (New Clarendon).

Staunton's conj. 'love-mansionry' was supported by Cuningham and is not unattractive.

6. *Smells . . . frieze*] Some think that one or two words have dropped out of this line; but there are five stresses as it stands.

jutty] 'iuttie, or part of a building that iuttieth beyond, or leaneth ouer, the rest' (Cotgrave, *Dict.*, 1611); 'An outnooke or corner standing out of a house; a iettie' (Florio, *Worlde of Wordes*, 1598); '*Sporto*, a porch, a portall, a baie window, or outbutting, or iettie of a house that ietties out further than anie other part of the house, a iettie or butte. Also the eaues or penteis of a house' (*ibid.*). Cf. *H5*, III. i. 13: 'jutty'.

7. *coign of vantage*] 'a position (properly a projecting corner) affording facility for observation or action' (*O.E.D.*). Old French *coing* or *coin* is the corner-stone at the exterior angle of a building; and perhaps, as Johnson explained, the phrase means merely 'convenient corner'. Hunter mentions that in *Porta Linguarum Trilinguis* an advantage is described as 'a something added to a building, as a jutting'.

10. *delicate*] soft. Cf. *Wint.*, III. i. 1.

Dun.   See, see! our honour'd hostess.— 10
The love that follows us sometime is our trouble,
Which still we thank as love. Herein I teach you,
How you shall bid God 'ild us for your pains,
And thank us for your trouble.
Lady M.   All our service,
In every point twice done, and then done double,   15
Were poor and single business, to contend
Against those honours deep and broad, wherewith
Your Majesty loads our house: for those of old,
And the late dignities heap'd up to them,
We rest your hermits.
Dun.   Where's the Thane of Cawdor? 20
We cours'd him at the heels, and had a purpose
To be his purveyor: but he rides well;
And his great love, sharp as his spur, hath holp him
To his home before us. Fair and noble hostess,
We are your guest to-night.
Lady M.   Your servants ever   25
Have theirs, themselves, and what is theirs, in compt,
To make their audit at your Highness' pleasure,
Still to return your own.
Dun.   Give me your hand;

---

10. See, see!] See! *Hanmer.*   11. sometime] sometimes *Theobald.*   13. God
'ild] *Globe;* God yield *Steevens;* God ild *Dyce;* God-ild *Capell;* God-eyld *F;*
Godild *Hanmer;* God-yield *Johnson;* God shield conj. *Johnson.*   17–20. Against
. . . hermits] so *Pope;* lines end broad, / House: / Dignities, / Ermites. *F.*   23. as]
at *F2.*   26. theirs, in compt,] *Hanmer;* theirs in compt, *F;* theirs, in compt: *Capell.*

11–14. *The love . . . trouble*] a difficult
speech, but not corrupt. It means:
'Love sometimes occasions me trouble,
but I thank it as love notwithstanding;
this should teach you to pray God to
reward me for the trouble you yourself are taking.'

13. *God 'ild us*] i.e. God reward us.
Hunter refers to a passage in Palsgrave's *Lesclarcissement*, 1530, p. 441*b*:
'We use "God yelde you" by manner
of thanking a person.' Cf. *AYL.*, v. iv.
56, and *Ant.*, IV. ii. 33.

16. *single*] simple, weak. Cf. I. iii. 140.

20. *We . . . hermits*] 'We as *hermits* or
beadsmen shall always pray for you'
(Steevens). Cf. *Tit.*, III. ii. 41, and
Gent., I. i. 17.

22. *purveyor*] provider (Cotgrave).
His office was to travel before the King
in his progresses to different parts of
the realm, and to see that everything
was duly provided, and generally, to
make provision for the royal household. The office was restrained by 12
Chas. II, c. 24.

26. *in compt*] subject to account
(Steevens).

Conduct me to mine host: we love him highly,
And shall continue our graces towards him.   30
By your leave, hostess.   [*Exeunt.*

SCENE VII.—[*The same. A room in the castle.*]

*Hautboys and torches. Enter, and pass over the stage, a Sewer, and
divers Servants with dishes and service. Then enter* MACBETH.

Macb. If it were done, when 'tis done, then 'twere well
It were done quickly: if th'assassination
Could trammel up the consequence, and catch

29. host:] Host *F1–2.*   30. continue] continue, *F;* continue in *conj. Cuningham.*

Scene VII

1–2. well It . . . quickly: if] well, It . . . quickly: If *F;* well. It . . . quickly, if
Travers.

30.] This line scans awkwardly and
it is probable, as Cuningham urges,
that it should read 'continue in'. Cf.
Tp., ii. i. 184; *Meas.,* ii. i. 276, 196; and
v. i. 28 *post.*

31. *By your leave*] 'As the custom was,
he kisses Lady Macbeth's cheek. What
better climax and ending could the
scene have?' (Granville-Barker).

Scene VII

S.D. Enter . . . a Sewer] from the
French *essayeur,* and meant originally
one who tasted of each dish to prove
that there was no poison in it. Afterwards it was applied to the chief servant, who directed the placing of the
dishes on the table.

1–28.] Macbeth's soliloquy has been
taken as the supreme expression of his
'visual imagination' (Wilson) and as
a proof that he was worried only by
practical considerations (Moulton).
See Introduction, p. l, and Empson,
Seven Types of Ambiguity, 1930, pp.
64–5.

1–2. *If it . . . if*] The notion of placing
a full stop at the end of the first line and
taking 'It were done quickly' as part

of the next sentence is ingenuity mis-
placed, though Kemble, Macready,
and Irving adopted it.

1–7. *If it . . . come*] This passage must
be considered as a unit. 'If the assassination were ended once for all as
soon as accomplished, then it were
well to do it quickly: if it could prevent
any consequences and obtain success
by his death, in such a way that this
blow might kill Duncan and not lead
to any reprisals, here, only here, in this
world, we would risk what might
happen in the next world.' Or, as
Bethell puts it more briefly: 'If there
were no ill-consequences in this life I
should be quite satisfied, for I should
ignore the question of a future state.'

2. *It . . . quickly*] R. Walker compares
John, xiii. 27: 'And after the soppe,
Satan entered into him. Then said
Iesus vnto him, That thou doest, doe
quickly.' Both Duncan and Jesus have
'almost supped', when the betrayer
leaves the chamber. The allusion to
the Last Supper may have suggested
to Shakespeare the chalice, 11 *post.*

3. *trammel up*] i.e. entangle as in a net.
A trammell (Fr. *tramail*) was a net for

With his surcease success; that but this blow
Might be the be-all and the end-all—here,   5
But here, upon this bank and shoal of time,

4. surcease success] success, surcease *conj. Johnson.*   5. end-all—here,] end all.
Heere, *F;* end-all here, *Hanmer;* end all—Here, *Rowe (ed. 1);* end-all—Here.
Warburton; end-all . . . here, *Wilson.*   6. shoal] *Theobald;* Schoole *F1-2.*

partridges (Cotgrave) or for catching
fish. But *trammel* also meant to fasten
the legs of horses together, so that they
could not stray, or to teach them to
amble; and Cuningham thought that
Shakespeare may have been thinking
of an iron device for suspending pots
over a fire, the meaning being 'hang
up' the consequences.

catch] metaphor suggested by 'trammel'.

4. *his surcease*] Cuningham, following Clarendon, thought that 'his'
must refer to consequence rather
than to 'Duncan'. *Surcease* (O.Fr.
sursis, from *surseoir*), a legal term,
meaning the stop or stay of proceed-
ings, is not elsewhere in Shakespeare
used as a substantive. But in *Lucr.,*
l. 1766 ('If they surcease to be that
should survive') it is used in a phrase
meaning 'die', and I believe the word
here is a euphemism for death—one
of several in the play—and that 'his'
refers to Duncan.

success] Cuningham suggests that the
word is not used here in the more modern sense of 'prosperous issue', but rather meaning simply the issue, sequel,
or consequence of an action, whether
good or bad. This would make 'trammel up the consequence' and 'catch . . .
success' almost identical in meaning,
as indeed Staunton takes them to be.
It seems to me better to take *success* in
its usual modern sense. Cuningham
further suggests that the word may
have the sense of 'succession' as in
Wint., I. ii. 394: 'Our parents' noble
names, / In whose success we are
gentle'. Perhaps, like *surcease,* an
Empsonian ambiguity.

5. *end-all—here*] Rowe's punctuation. The Folio full-stop after 'end-all'

cannot be retained in a modern text;
but most editors have debased Shakespeare's intentions. As Simpson points
out, *Shakespeare's Punctuation,* pp. 82–3,
'The meaning as well as the movement
of the verse suggest the close connection of the words "Heere, But heere."
The pause is the most powerful of
which blank verse is capable. At that
final monosyllable the rhythm gathers
like a wave, plunges over to the line
beyond, and falls in all its weight and
force on the repeated word. The check
given to the line fits in admirably with
the brooding, hesitating mood of the
speaker.'

6. *bank and shoal*] Theobald's brilliant emendation for 'Schoole' is now
generally accepted, especially as
'schoole' is a possible seventeenth
century spelling of 'shoal'. Theobald
explained, 'This *Shallow,* this *narrow
Ford,* of humane Life, opposed to the
great Abyss of Eternity'. Heath, however, *Revisal of Shakespeare's Text* (1765)
argued for bank (= bench) and
school. So also did Elwin, *Shakespeare
Restored* (1853): 'If here only, upon
this bench of instruction, in this school
of eternity, I could do this without
bringing these, my pupil days, under
suffering, I would hazard its effect on
the endless life to come.' Bethell, *The
Winter's Tale* (1947), pp. 126–7, is one
of the few modern critics to defend
'school'. He adopts the suggestion of
the Rev. G. Shaw that 'bank' is the
judicial bench, probably from O.F.
banc. The word was certainly current
in this sense in Shakespeare's time.
Bethell says: 'Time is thus seen as the
period of judgement, testing, or
"crisis", and as a school; corresponding to these meanings we have later in

We'd jump the life to come.—But in these cases,
We still have judgment here; that we but teach
Bloody instructions, which, being taught, return
To plague th'inventor: this even-handed Justice   10
Commends th'ingredience of our poison'd chalice
To our own lips. He's here in double trust:

10–11. th'inventor . . . Commends] *not in F2–4, Rowe.*   10. this] thus *conj.*
Mason.   11. ingredience] *F, Kittredge, Wilson;* ingredients *Pope.*

the speech, "judgment here" and "teach Bloody instructions"'.' If we reject this interpretation, it should not be because it is less *poetic* in the stock sense—cf. Keats's parable of the world as a school (*Letters*, 1935, p. 336) —but because Shakespeare often couples words together like 'bank and shoal' (though Bethell denies this) and the preposition 'upon' fits 'bank' but not 'school'. It seems to me probable that Shakespeare intended 'shoal'; but that, by an unconscious pun, 'bank' suggested 'judgment' and 'schoole' suggested 'teach . . . instructions . . . taught' a few lines below.

7. *jump*] i.e. risk. Cf. *Cym.*, v. iv. 188: 'Jump the after-enquiry at your own peril'. But it might perhaps mean 'skip over' or 'evade' (the thought of the life to come).

life to come] i.e. the future life, though Keightley thought it meant the remaining years of Macbeth's own life on earth and compared *Troil.*, III. ii. 180: 'True swains in love shall in the world to come / Approve their truths by Troilus.' But this means the world generations hence, not during the lifetime of Troilus. Some think that in *Wint.*, IV. iii. 31 ('For the life to come I sleep out the thought of it'), Autolycus was speaking of his future life on earth. But surely Shakespeare was echoing the prayer-book phrase ('the life of the world to come') both here and in *Macbeth*.

8. *have judgment*] i.e. receive sentence. See Hall, *Chronicles*, 244: 'He confessed

the inditement and had judgment to be hanged.'

here] referring back to 'here' (5, 6).

that] i.e. 'so that', or 'in that'.

10. *plague th'inventor*] Wilson compares Seneca, *Hercules Furens*, 735–6: 'Quod quisque fecit, patitur: auctorem scelus / Repetit suoque premitur exemplo nocens.' Heywood translates: 'What eche man once hath done, he feeles: and guilt to th'author theare / Returnes, and th'hurtfull with their owne example punisht bee.'

Grierson suggests that the adjacent description of the good king (739–41) may have been echoed in Macbeth's description of Duncan (16 ff.). Heywood translates: 'what man of might with fauour leades his lande, / And of his own lyfe lorde reserues his hurtlesse handes to good, / And gently doth his empyre guide without the thyrst of blood, / And spares his soule . . .'

Malone quotes (from a different text), Bellenden's translation of Boece (1941, II, p. 154): 'traisting all pepill to doo siclike cruelties to him as he did afoir to vtheris'. This passage introduces the murder of Banquo.

even-handed] impartial.

11. *Commends*] offers.

ingredience] For the spelling cf. IV. i. 34. Originally a misspelling of the plural, it was subsequently confused with the singular, *ingredient*.

poison'd chalice] Cf. Holinshed, Appendix, p. 173, 'least he should be serued of the same cup'.

12. *double trust*] N.

First, as I am his kinsman and his subject,
Strong both against the deed; then, as his host,
Who should against his murtherer shut the door,   15
Not bear the knife myself. Besides, this Duncan
Hath borne his faculties so meek, hath been
So clear in his great office, that his virtues
Will plead like angels, trumpet-tongu'd, against
The deep damnation of his taking-off;   20
And Pity, like a naked new-born babe,
Striding the blast, or heaven's Cherubins, hors'd
Upon the sightless couriers of the air,
Shall blow the horrid deed in every eye,

16. bear] bare *conj. Daniel.*   17. his] this *F2–3.*   faculties] Faculty *F3.*
22. Cherubins] Cherubin *F, Grierson, Kittredge;* cherubim *D'Avenant.*   23.
couriers] *Pope* (Curriors *F*)*;* coursers *Theobald (Warburton).*

17. *faculties*] powers, prerogatives of
the crown. Still used in this sense in
ecclesiastical law.
18. *clear*] free from guilt or stain.
19. *Will ... trumpet-tongu'd*] 'suggests
the Last Judgment' (Wilson). Garrick
used to make a long pause after
'Angels' to indicate that the epithet
agreed with 'virtues'. But this is unlikely; 'trumpet-tongu'd' means either
'using their trumpets for speech' or,
more likely, 'with voices as clear,
penetrating, and musical, as trumpets'.
20. *taking-off*] Cf. III. i. 104 *post*, and
Lr., v. i. 65.
21. *Pity*] R. Walker, *op. cit.*, p. 55,
notes that 'the babe whose brains the
she-devil would dash out is pity,
striding the blast of the storm of evil.'
22. *Striding*] i.e. bestriding.
blast] Wilson comments: 'i.e. (*a*) of
the trumpet, (*b*) the tempest of horror
and indignation aroused by the deed'.
But I do not understand how Pity—
and still less how a naked new-born
babe—can stride the blast, i.e. the
sound, of a trumpet. But 'blast', by a
hidden pun, was doubtless suggested
by '*trumpet*-tongu'd'—and perhaps
Wilson meant this.
Cherubins] Cf. 'He rode vpon the
Cherubyns and did flye; he came
flyenge with the winges of the wynde'

(Ps. xviii. 10—Coverdale). The Psalter
of Shakespeare's day had 'Cherubims
... flying vpon the winges'; the Metrical
Psalter read 'On Cherubes and on
Cherubins'; but Shakespeare always
uses the form *cherubins*. Cf. Spenser,
Hymne on Heavenly Beautie, 92–4.
Although 'from the beginning of the
seventeenth century *cherubim* began to
be preferred by scholars to *cherubims*'
(*O.E.D.*), Shakespeare is unlikely to
have known that *cherubim* was a plural;
and a knowledge of Hebrew could not
have been called into being by a desire
to avoid an excess of sibilants. *Cherubins*
involves less change in the text than
cherubims, besides being Shakespeare's
invariable form of the plural. But see
N.Q. (25/12/1886) where it is pointed
out that Batman in 1582 speaks of the
'order of Cherubin' and says that
'Cherubin are the highest companies
of Angelles.'
23. *sightless couriers*] invisible run-
ners, i.e. the winds. Cf. I. v. 49 *ante*.
Steevens cites Warner, *Albion's England,* 1602, II. xi: 'The scouring winds
that sightless in the sounding air do
fly'. Elwin interprets 'blind and invisible'; and the horses in Blake's
painting 'Pity' are blind.
24–5. *blow ... wind*] 'Alluding to the
remission of the wind in a shower'

That tears shall drown the wind.—I have no spur   25
To prick the sides of my intent, but only
Vaulting ambition, which o'erleaps itself
And falls on th'other—

Enter LADY MACBETH.

                                        How now! what news?
Lady M.   He has almost supp'd. Why have you left the
        chamber?
Macb.   Hath he ask'd for me?
Lady M.   Know you not, he has?   30
Macb.   We will proceed no further in this business:
        He hath honour'd me of late; and I have bought
        Golden opinions from all sorts of people,
        Which would be worn now in their newest gloss,
        Not cast aside so soon.
Lady M.   Was the hope drunk,   35
        Wherein you dress'd yourself? Hath it slept since?

27. itself] its sell *conj. Landor.*   28. th'other—] *Rowe;* th' other. *F;* th' other
side *Hanmer, Kittredge (subst.) ;* the other. *Globe.*   30. not, he has?] not? He has.
conj. Capell.   33. sorts] sort *Theobald.*

(Johnson) and 'also to an object
blown into the eye, causing it to fill
with tears' (Elwin). Cf. *Lucr.,* 1788-90;
Troil., IV. iv. 55.
    25-8. *I have ... other*—] 'I have no
spur to stimulate my guilty intention
except ambition—ambition which is
like a too eager rider, who in vaulting
into the saddle o'erleaps himself and
falls on the other side of the horse.'
Hunter explains: 'lights on the opposite side of what was intended; that is,
dishonour and wretchedness, instead
of glory and felicity'. Wilson mentions
that vaulting into one's saddle was a
much-admired feat. But Grierson,
following Steevens, suggests that
'Shakespeare may be thinking of a too
furious rider who, leaping too high at
an obstacle, clears it indeed but falls
on the other side.' Cf. I. iv. 48-50 *ante.*
Cuningham wanted to insert 'side'
after 'other' to regularize the metre;
but the entrance of Lady Macbeth

interrupts the soliloquy and fills in the
gap. I cannot agree with Wilson that
'Macb. is exhausted by his passion' and
that *therefore* Shakespeare 'makes him
end with an unfinished sentence; a
weary gesture supplying the gap'. The
images from horsemanship, *spur* and
vaulting, were suggested by *hors'd* and
couriers above. N.
    34. *would*] i.e. should. Cf. IV. iii. 23
post.
    worn] another clothing image. Cf.
dress'd (36).
    35-6. *Was ... since*] Cf. *John,* IV. ii.
116-17: 'O where hath our intelligence been drunk? / Where hath it
slept?'
    36. *dress'd*] another clothing image
which has been altered by some editors
to '*dressed* (= addressed) and *bless'd,* so
as to avoid a mixed metaphor. But
dress'd is clearly suggested by *worn* and
may be intended by Lady Macbeth as
a sarcastic reference to it (Abbott).

And wakes it now, to look so green and pale
At what it did so freely? From this time
Such I account thy love. Art thou afeard
To be the same in thine own act and valour,   40
As thou art in desire? Would'st thou have that
Which thou esteem'st the ornament of life,
And live a coward in thine own esteem,
Letting 'I dare not' wait upon 'I would,'
Like the poor cat i'th'adage?
Macb.   Pr'ythee, peace.   45
I dare do all that may become a man;
Who dares do more, is none.
Lady M.   What beast was't then,
That made you break this enterprise to me?
When you durst do it, then you were a man;
And, to be more than what you were, you would   50
Be so much more the man. Nor time, nor place,

---

39. afeard] afraid *F4*.   41, 43. have . . . And] leave . . . And *or* have . . . Or
conj. Johnson.   45. adage?] *Capell;* Addage. *F*.   47. do] *Rowe;* no *F*,
Hunter, who gives the whole of 47 to Lady M.   51. the] than *Hanmer*.

---

37. *green and pale*] i.e. with a hang-over.

38. *did*] Bulloch's conj. 'dared' is attractive at first sight; but 'did' refers to the orgy of which Hope repents.

39. *afeard*] Cf. I. iii. 96 *ante*.

40–1. *act . . . desire*] Cf. II. iii. 29–35 and Introduction, p. xxviii.

42. *ornament of life*] i.e. the crown.

45. *cat i'th'adage*] Heywood, *Three Hundred Epigrammes* (Spenser Society, p. 28) 'The cate would eate fyshe, and would not wet her feete.' Cf. 'Le chat aime le poisson, mais il n'aime pas à mouiller la patte.'

47. *do more*] Rowe's emendation is supported by *Meas.*, II. iv. 134: 'Be that you are, / That is, a woman; if you be more, you're none.'

none] i.e. 'superhuman or devilish' (Wilson) or 'subhuman'.

beast] The whole force of the passage lies in the direct dramatic contrast to *man* in the previous line. Cf. *Rom.*,

III. iii. 109–13: 'Art thou a man? . . . fury of a beast'.

48. *That . . . me?*] Chambers and others use this to show that the murder was discussed before the action of the play or in a lost scene (Koester, Wilson). Thaler, *Shakespeare and Democracy*, pp. 88–105, remarks: 'Macbeth's *letter*, written when neither place not time yet "adhered", is sufficient to explain Lady Macbeth's nervous and not necessarily accurate allusion to earlier passages between them on this subject. . . If a scene must be sought in which Macbeth definitely yielded to his wife's urgings, this scene—*unwritten*, i.e. compressed to a mere suggestion, for reasons of artistic economy in an opening action consciously keyed to a swiftly tense crescendo —would logically come *between scenes*, after I. v. which closes with Macbeth's promise, "We will speak further."' Cf. Bradley, *Shakespearean Tragedy*, pp. 480–4, and Introduction, p. xlviii.

Did then adhere, and yet you would make both:
They have made themselves, and that their fitness now
Does unmake you. I have given suck, and know
How tender 'tis to love the babe that milks me: 55
I would, while it was smiling in my face,
Have pluck'd my nipple from his boneless gums,
And dash'd the brains out, had I so sworn
As you have done to this.

Macb.   If we should fail?

Lady M. We fail?   60
But screw your courage to the sticking-place,

55. me:] *Capell;* me— *Rowe;* me, *F.*   58-9. And . . . this] *F; lines end* you /
this, *Steevens (1793).*   59. fail?] *F;* fail,— *Theobald (ed. 2);* fail! *Singer (ed. 2).*
60. We fail?] *most editors give these words as part of line 59;* We fail! *Rowe, Delius,
Craig, Arden (ed. 1);* We fail. *Capell.*

52. *adhere*] i.e. 'not the *coherence* of
time with *place,* but the *adherence* of these
two with the murder' (Capell).

54. *I . . . suck*] Cf. IV. iii. 216. This
raises the unprofitable question of how
many children had Lady Macbeth?
Wilson wisely quotes Eckermann,
Conversations, 18 April 1827: 'Whether
this be true or not does not appear; but
the lady says it, and she must say it, in
order to give emphasis to her speech.'
There is no reason to think that Shakespeare was referring to Lady Macbeth's child by her first husband, who
is not mentioned by Holinshed. Cf.
I. v. 48 *ante.*

57. *pluck'd . . . gums*] Coleridge says
that this passage 'though usually
thought to prove a merciless and un-
womanly nature, proves the direct
opposite: she brings it as the most
solemn enforcement to Macbeth of the
solemnity of his promise to undertake
the plot against Duncan. Had *she* so
sworn, she would have done that
which was most horrible to her feelings,
rather than break the oath; and as the
most horrible act which it was possible
for imagination to conceive, as that
which was most revolting to her own
feelings, she alludes to the destruction
of her infant, while in the act of sucking

at her breast. Had she regarded this
with savage indifference, there would
have been no force in the appeal; but
her very allusion to it, and her purpose
in this allusion, shows that she considered no tie so tender as that which
connected her with her babe' (*op. cit.,*
II. 271).

58. *the brains*] 'The' frequently takes
the place of the possessive pronoun
'his'.

58-9. *sworn . . . this*] Flatter, *op. cit.,*
p. 127, pleads for a restoration of the
Folio lineation. This makes a less
awkward enjambement, allows for a
greater emphasis on the words *dash'd,*
brains out, and *sworn,* and leaves room
for a pause after Lady Macbeth's
scornful question in the following line.

60. *We fail?*] Mrs Siddons tried 'We
fail?', then '*We* fail!' and finally 'We
fail.' Critics have argued in favour of
all three. I have kept the Folio punctuation, though 'the note of interroga-
tion in the Folio is frequently equivalent to the note of exclamation'
(Cuningham).

61. *But . . . sticking-place*] But = only.
Murry, *Shakespeare,* pp. 328-9, describes the significance of this image,
derived perhaps from the screwing up
of the strings on a viol. Cf. *Tw.N.,*

And we'll not fail. When Duncan is asleep
(Whereto the rather shall his day's hard journey
Soundly invite him), his two chamberlains
Will I with wine and wassail so convince,   65
That memory, the warder of the brain,
Shall be a fume, and the receipt of reason
A limbeck only: when in swinish sleep
Their drenched natures lie, as in a death,
What cannot you and I perform upon   70
Th'unguarded Duncan? what not put upon
His spongy officers, who shall bear the guilt
Of our great quell?

69. lie] *F2;* lyes *F1.*   72-3. officers, . . . quell?] Officers? . . . quell. *F.*

v. i. 125. But Paton and Liddell think the metaphor was suggested by a soldier screwing up the cord of his cross-bow to the 'sticking-place'. Cf. l. 80 below.

64. *chamberlains*] gentlemen-of-the bedchamber.

65. *convince*] overpower, *convincere.* Cf. IV. iii. 142.

66-8. *memory . . . only*] The old anatomists divided the brain into three ventricles, in the hindmost of which, viz. the cerebellum, they placed the memory. Cf. *LLL.,* IV. ii. 70. Memory, the warder of the cerebellum, warns the reason against attack; and where converted by intoxication into a fume of smoke, it fills the brain, the receptacle of reason, which thus becomes like an 'alembic' or cap of a still. Cf. *Tp.,* v. i. 67: 'the ignorant fumes that mantle / Their clearer reason'.

E. Schanzer, *M.L.R.,* 1957, p. 223, argues that as warder was not used in the sense of jailor in Shakespeare's day, we should emend to 'warden'. He then gives an interpretation based on Davenport's: 'The full meaning of the alchemic methaphor that follows seems never to have been brought out by commentators. "Receipt" appears to comprise both the meaning of "container", suggested by the theory that reason occupies a separate ventricle of the brain, and that of the

receiver at the bottom of the still in which the end-product is gathered and condensed. "Limbeck" here clearly refers not to the head or cap of the still, the alembic proper, as it is often explained, but to the retort or cucurbit, the vessel in which the liquids to be distilled are heated. This seems to have been the more common use of "limbeck" or "alembic" in Shakespeare's day. The full meaning of the image is therefore that the receptacle which should collect only the pure drops of reason, the final distillate of the thought-process, will be turned into the retort in which the crude undistilled liquids bubble and fume.'

68. *limbeck*] the corrupt form of 'alembic', a word adopted into most European languages from the Arabic of the Moorish alchemists of Spain. Cf. previous note.

69. *drenched*] drowned. Wilson suggests a pun on 'drench' = a dose of medicine administered to an animal. Cf. 'swinish' (68).

72. *spongy*] drunken. Cf. *Mer.V.,* I. ii. 108.

73. *quell*] i.e. murder. Used as a substantive only in this passage by Shakespeare. It is from the same root as 'kill', i.e. O.E. *cwellan.* Florio, *Worlde of Wordes,* 1598, has 'Mazzare: to kill, to slay, to quell.' Cf. *2H4,* II. i. 58: 'a man-queller'.

Macb.   Bring forth men-children only!
For thy undaunted mettle should compose
Nothing but males. Will it not be receiv'd,   75
When we have mark'd with blood those sleepy two
Of his own chamber, and us'd their very daggers,
That they have done't?
Lady M.   Who dares receive it other,
As we shall make our griefs and clamour roar
Upon his death?
Macb.   I am settled, and bend up   80
Each corporal agent to this terrible feat.
Away, and mock the time with fairest show:
False face must hide what the false heart doth know.
                                              [*Exeunt.*

77. and] *not in, conj. Capell.*

74. *mettle*] i.e. material, spirit. The same word as 'metal' from which it had not been distinguished.

75-8. *Will . . . done't*] As Curry has pointed out, *Shakespeare's Philosophical Patterns*, p. 119, Macbeth becomes entirely converted to the murder as soon as his wife puts forward a practical scheme. It is irrelevant, as Wilson says, p. lix, that the plan is absurd. It satisfies him, which is all that matters to her. *receiv'd* = accepted as true. Cf. *Meas.*, I. iii. 15-16: 'For so I've strew'd it in the common ear, / And so it is receiv'd.'

78. *other*] otherwise. Cf. *Oth.*, IV. ii. 13.

79. *As*] inasmuch as. Wilson com-

pares this scheme with Lady Macbeth's fainting after the murder.

80. *bend up*] Kittredge suggests that the metaphor from a crossbow is linked with line 61 *ante.*

81. *Each . . . agent*] Cf. I. iii. 81 and *H5*, III. i. 16: 'Hold hard the breath and bend up every spirit / To his full height!'

82-3. *Away . . . know*] echoing her advice of I. v. 64-5. Hunter absurdly suggested that the final couplet should be spoken by Lady Macbeth. She would not speak in this regretful tone at this point.

82. *mock the time*] i.e. delude all observers.

ACT II

SCENE I.—[*The same. Court within the castle.*]

Enter BANQUO, *and* FLEANCE, *with a torch before him.*

Ban. How goes the night, boy?
Fle. The moon is down; I have not heard the clock.
Ban. And she goes down at twelve.
Fle.   I take't, 'tis later, Sir.
Ban. Hold, take my sword.—There's husbandry in heaven;
Their candles are all out.—Take thee that too.   5
A heavy summons lies like lead upon me,
And yet I would not sleep: merciful Powers!
Restrain in me the cursed thoughts that nature
Gives way to in repose!—Give me my sword.

Enter MACBETH, *and a servant with a torch.*

Who's there?   10

ACT II

Scene 1

S.D. *Court within the castle. Capell.*   4. Hold . . . heaven;] *so Rowe; two lines, the
first ending* sword: *F.*   7–9. And . . . repose!] *so Rowe; lines end* sleepe: /
thoughts / repose. *F.*

S.D. a torch] Dyce remarks that 'in
the stage-direction of old plays, "a
Torch" sometimes means a *torch-
bearer*.' Cf. I. vi. *init*. But here Fleance
probably acts as torch-bearer.

4. *husbandry*] thrift, economy. Florio,
Worlde of Wordes, 1598, has 'Parsi-
monia, *parcimonie, sparing, husband-
rie*.'

5. *Their*] referring presumably to
the inhabitants of heaven.

candles . . . out] Cf. *Rom.*, III. v. 9:
'Night's candles are burnt out.' Cf.
I. iv. 50, I. v. 50, *ante*.

that] i.e. shield, targe, cloak, dag-

ger, or 'belt with dagger' (Wilson).

6. *summons*] i.e. to sleep.

7–9. *merciful . . . repose*] 'Banquo . . .
cannot help dreaming of the three
Weird Sisters. . . In his extremity he
importunes precisely that order of
angels which God, in his providence,
has deputed to be concerned especially
with the restraint and coercion of
demons, namely, Powers' (Curry,
Shakespeare's Philosophical Patterns, p.
81). Kolbe suggests that Shakespeare
echoes the Hymn of Compline, i.e.
presumably, 'Procul recedant somnia /
Et noctium phantasmata.'

45

Macb. A friend.

Ban. What, Sir! not yet at rest? The King's a-bed:
He hath been in unusual pleasure, and
Sent forth great largess to your offices.
This diamond he greets your wife withal,					15
By the name of most kind hostess, and shut up
In measureless content.

Macb.					Being unprepar'd,
Our will became the servant to defect,
Which else should free have wrought.

Ban.					All's well.
I dreamt last night of the three Weïrd Sisters:					20
To you they have show'd some truth.

Macb.					I think not of them:
Yet, when we can entreat an hour to serve,
We would spend it in some words upon that business,
If you would grant the time.

Ban.					At your kind'st leisure.

Macb. If you shall cleave to my consent, when 'tis,					25

---

13. and] *so Jennens; begins line 14, F.*		14. offices] *F;* officers *Rowe.*		16. and shut up] *begins next line* And shut up *F1;* And shut it up *F2–3;* and 's shut up *Hanmer;* and shut him up *conj. Kinnear.*		19. All's well] Sir, all is well *conj. Steevens.*		20. Weïrd] *Theobald;* wayward *F.*		24. kind'st] *F1–2;* kind *F3–4.*		25–6. when 'tis . . . you.] *so Rowe;* one line, *F.*

---

14. *offices*] i.e. servants' quarters, though Malone and others have supported Rowe's emendation, *officers.* Chambers suggests 'a case of the use of the abstract for the concrete'.

15. *diamond*] Holinshed mentions that Donwald was presented with an honourable gift by King Duff on the night of the murder. See Appendix, p. 165.

16. *shut up*] This means either 'wrapped in' (Chambers) or 'concluded' (Steevens). Duncan has ended his day in measureless content. Cf. Spenser, *Faerie Queene*, IV. ix. 15: 'And for to shut vp all in friendly loue'; *All's W.*, I. i. 197: 'Whose baser stars do shut us up in wishes'; and *Troil.*, I. iii. 57–8: 'In whom the tempers and the minds of all / Should be shut up'.

17–19. *Being . . . wrought*] i.e. As we were unprepared, our desire to give liberal hospitality to the king could not be fulfilled.

20–1. *I . . . truth*] Cuningham thought these words were a 'veiled incitement to Macbeth'; but they are perfectly compatible with innocence.

22. *we*] 'Now that the crown is within his grasp, he seems to adopt the royal "we" by anticipation' (Clarendon). But, as Chambers argues, Macbeth is too good an actor to use the kingly 'we'. It probably means 'you and I' and 'would' (23) = should.

25. *cleave . . . 'tis*] i.e. become or remain an adherent of my party when it exists, *or,* follow my advice when the time comes. Macbeth is purposely ambiguous. His words can mean that

　　　It shall make honour for you.

Ban.   So I lose none
　　In seeking to augment it, but still keep
　　My bosom franchis'd, and allegiance clear,
　　I shall be counsell'd.

Macb.   Good repose, the while!

Ban. Thanks, Sir: the like to you.   30

　　　　　　　　　　　　　[*Exeunt Banquo and Fleance.*

Macb. Go, bid thy mistress, when my drink is ready,
　　She strike upon the bell. Get thee to bed.—

　　　　　　　　　　　　　　　　[*Exit Servant.*

　　Is this a dagger, which I see before me,

he wants Banquo to support his claim to the crown in the event of Duncan's natural death, or they can be regarded as a bribe. Case suggests 'when 'tis' means 'when we have our talk'. The phrase *to be of consent* meant *to be accessory.* Cf. *AYL.,* II. ii. 3: 'Some villains . . . Are of consent and sufferance in this.' *Consent* also meant a party united by common agreement, or adherence to an opinion. *O.E.D.* quotes Florio's *Montaigne*: 'Even those which are not of our consent, doe flattly inhibite . . . the use of the sacred name.' The word was often spelt *concent* down to the sixteenth century, and was thus liable to confusion with musical *concent,* when this latter word was introduced. In some passages, it is difficult to say which of the two was meant. For *consent,* meaning counsel or advice, Wilson refers to *Wint.,* v. iii. 136.

26–8. *honour . . . clear*] Bradley, *Shakespearean Tragedy,* pp. 383–4, thinks that 'Banquo fears a treasonable proposal.' Wilson thinks that Banquo supposes Macbeth to refer only to Duncan's death in the course of nature. Liddell believes that Banquo means by *honour,* its feudal sense of *lordship*; i.e. that his honours must be of 'free tenure' as far as Macbeth is concerned. He carries the notion further in *allegiance clear,* i.e. such fealty as no man may owe to more than one lord.

It seems to me that Bradley is right, and that we must interpret *franchis'd* as *free from guilt,* and *clear* as *innocent.* Banquo is telling Macbeth that he will only join his party if there is to be no foul play. As Grierson points out, there is a play on the two senses of 'honour' which can either mean the distinction accorded to worth or the honourableness that merits such distinction. Some honours are bought only with the loss of honour.

30.] See note on II. ii. 12–13 *post.*

31. *drink*] i.e. the posset. Cf. note on II. ii. 6 *post.*

33. *Is . . . dagger*] 'the dagger should not be in the air, but on a table; he thinks it real at first' (Chambers). 'Macbeth is to wait for the bell; and to wait is to sit' (Wilson). But if the scene is laid in the courtyard, would there be a table? And would it not be impossible for a man like Macbeth to sit at such a moment? The speech is not realistic; but in answer to Chambers it may be said that if Macbeth indeed thought the dagger a real one he would not begin with a question, and such a question. Seymour, *Remarks,* etc., 1805, I. 196, argues that the actor should not express terror, but confidence and animation. But there is surely an undertone of horror in the speech (59). Curry, *Shakespeare's Philosophical Patterns,* p. 84, suggests that the dagger 'is an hallucination caused

The handle toward my hand? Come, let me clutch
    thee:—
I have thee not, and yet I see thee still.   35
Art thou not, fatal vision, sensible
To feeling, as to sight? or art thou but
A dagger of the mind, a false creation,
Proceeding from the heat-oppressed brain?
I see thee yet, in form as palpable   40
As this which now I draw.
Thou marshall'st me the way that I was going;
And such an instrument I was to use.—
Mine eyes are made the fools o'th'other senses,
Or else worth all the rest: I see thee still;   45
And on thy blade, and dudgeon, gouts of blood,
Which was not so before.—There's no such thing.
It is the bloody business which informs
Thus to mine eyes.—Now o'er the one half-world

34. thee:—] thee: *F;* thee— *Rowe.*   41. As . . . draw.] *Walker and Keightley*
end line at me *(42) with subsequent re-arrangement.*

immediately, indeed, by disturbed
bodily humours and spirits but ultimately by demonic powers, who have
so controlled and manipulated these
bodily forces as to produce the effect
they desire'.

36. *sensible*] i.e. capable of being
perceived by the senses, perceptible.
Florio, *Worlde of Wordes:* 'Percettible,
perceivable, sensible'. Johnson quotes
Hooker, *Ecclesiastical Polity,* i. vii. 1:
'By reason man attaineth unto the
knowledge of things that are and are
not *sensible.'*

39. *heat-oppressed*] fevered (Wilson).

41.] The short line is filled out by
the action of drawing the dagger
(Chambers).

42. *marshall'st me*] The dagger seems
to move towards the room where
Duncan sleeps.

44. *Mine . . . senses*] This conflict
between the senses is mentioned several
times in the course of the play. See
Introduction, p. xxvii.

46. *dudgeon*] haft, handle. Originally
the word meant a kind of wood used

for the handles of knives and daggers,
and thus came to mean the hilt of a
dagger made from this wood. Gerard,
Herball, speaking of the root of the box-
tree, says: 'Turners and cutlers, if I
mistake not the matter, do calle this
woode *dudgeon,* whence they make
dudgeon hafted daggers'. And Cotgrave, *Dict.,* 1611, has 'Dague à
roëlles: *A Scottish dagger; or Dudgeon
haft dagger';* i.e. one turned with little
spiral rings to give a better grip.

gouts] drops, Fr. *goutte.*

48. *informs*] takes shape (*O.E.D.*);
gives false impression (Kittredge).

49–50. *o'er . . . dead*] 'over our hemi-
sphere all action and motion seem to
have ceased' (Johnson). Malone compares a passage from the opening
scene of the second part of Marston,
Antonio and Mellida, 1602, i. i. 3–8:
' 'Tis yet dead night, yet al the earth
is cloucht / In the dull leaden hand of
snoring sleepe: / No breath disturbs
the quiet of the ayre. / No spirit moves
upon the breast of earth, / Save howl-
ing dogs, night-crowes, and screeching

Nature seems dead, and wicked dreams abuse   50
The curtain'd sleep: Witchcraft celebrates
Pale Hecate's off'rings; and wither'd Murther,
Alarum'd by his sentinel, the wolf,
Whose howl's his watch, thus with his stealthy pace,
With Tarquin's ravishing strides, towards his design   55
Moves like a ghost.—Thou sure and firm-set earth,
Hear not my steps, which way they walk, for fear

51. sleep:] sleeper *conj. Steevens.*   Witchcraft] Now witchcraft *D'Avenant,*
Rowe, Kittredge.   55. strides] *Pope;* sides *F.*   56. sure] *Capell (conj. Pope);*
sowre *F;* sound *Pope.*   57. which way they] *Rowe;* which they may *F.*

owls, / Save meager ghosts, *Piero,* and
black thoughts.'
  50. *wicked dreams*] Cf. 7–9 *ante.*
abuse] deceive.
  51. *sleep: Witchcraft*] Various attempts have been made to regularize
the line, by inserting 'now' between
these two words (D'Avenant), or by
changing 'sleep' to 'sleeper'. But the
pause was probably deliberate.
  52. *Hecate's*] Cf. note on III. ii. 41
post. Hecate was the goddess of classical
and medieval witchcraft. Jonson,
Masque of Queenes (1609) says, 'She
was belleeu'd to gouerne in witchcraft;
and is remembered in all theyr inuo-
cations.' Baldwin, *Shakespeare's Small
Latine,* II. 437, quotes Golding's ex-
planatory interpolation in *Metam.,*
vii. 74–5: 'Of whom the witches holde
/ As of their goddesse'. The word is a
dissyllable here. Cf. *Lr.,* I. i. 112: 'The
mysteries of Hecate and the night'.
off'rings] rituals (Wilson) or 'mysteries'.
  54. *Whose...watch*] Craig interprets.
'His (the murderer's) way of knowing
the passage of the night'. Cf. *Lucr.,* 370:
'Which gives the watch-word to his
hand full soon'. But 'his' probably
refers to 'wolf', who howls at regular
intervals, as the sentinel calls out, and
'watch' = watchword. Wilson gives
'timepiece' as an alternative meaning.
  55. *Tarquin's*] Warburton compares
Lucr., 162–8: 'Now stole upon the time
the dead of night, / When heavy sleep

had clos'd up mortal eyes, / No com-
fortable star did lend his light, / No
noise but owls' and wolves' death-
boding cries: / Now serves the season
that they may surprise / The silly
lambs, pure thoughts are dead and
still, / While Lust and Murder wakes
to stain and kill.' Cf. II. i. 5, 52, 53, and
II. ii. 3.
  ravishing] transferred epithet.
  strides] Pope's emendation is certain,
though Johnson and Knight object to
'stride' as implying violence or impetuosity. Yet the word is coupled
with 'tedious' in *R2,* I. iii. 268, and
with 'soft' in *Faerie Queene,* IV. viii. 37.
Tarquin *stalks* to the chamber of
Lucrece (*Lucr.,* 365). Case refers to
'the long tip-toe stealing steps one
takes in order to avoid sound by
planting the feet as seldom as possible'.
Liddell reads *slides* and quotes Coo-
per's *Thesaurus*; 'Lapsus serpentum,
the sliding, gliding, or creeping of a serpent'
and Cotgrave's *Dict.,* 'Griller: *to glide,
slip, slide, steal.*' In spite of *Lucr.,* 305
and 362 (*creeping* and *serpent*), few will
agree with this emendation.
  56. *sure*] Pope's conj. is now universally accepted. Wilson compares Ps.,
xciii. 2: 'He hath made the round
world so sure: that it cannot be
moved.'
  57. *which...walk*] R. Walker, *op. cit.,*
p. 59, points out that in the dedicatory
epistle to the Authorized Version, the
translators tell James I that on the

Thy very stones prate of my where-about,
And take the present horror from the time,
Which now suits with it.—Whiles I threat, he lives: 60
Words to the heat of deeds too cold breath gives.
                                                        [*A bell rings.*
I go, and it is done: the bell invites me.
Hear it not, Duncan; for it is a knell
That summons thee to Heaven, or to Hell.   [*Exit.*

death of Elizabeth, many illwishers expected 'some thick and palpable cloud of darkness would so have overshadowed this Land, that men should have been in doubt *which way they were to walk.*' The resemblance is probably accidental, though it is not impossible that the writer had seen a performance of *Macbeth*, or that the phrase had been used in a sermon or pamphlet written on the accession of King James.

58. *Thy . . . prate*] 'A reminiscence of Luke xix. 40' (Chambers): 'I tell you if these should hold their peace, the stones would cry' (Geneva). But I suggest the following passage, though less familiar, is closer: 'For the stone shall cry out of the wal, & the beame out of the timber shal aunswere it' (Hab., ii. 11). The neighbouring stanzas fit the *Macbeth* context: 'Thou hast consulted shame to thine owne house, by destroying many people, and hast sinned against thine owne soule... Woe vnto him that buildeth a towne with *blood*, and erecteth a citie by iniquitie. . . But the *Lord is in his holy Temple;* let all the earth *keepe silence* before him' (vv. 10, 12, 20). Cf. with v. 20 'The Lord's anointed Temple' (II. iii. 67 *post*).

where-about] i.e. whereabouts. Shakespeare uses 'where' as a substantive in *Lr.*, I. i. 264: 'a better where'.

59. *take . . . time*] 'Whether to *take horror from the time* means not rather to *catch it* as communicated, than to *deprive the time of horror*, deserves to be considered' (Johnson). 'Macbeth asks that the earth . . . shall not hear his steps, for if it does so the very stones

will speak and betray him—thereby breaking the silence and so lessening the horror. "Take" combines two constructions. On the one hand, "for fear they take the present horror from the time" expresses attraction, identification with the appropriate setting of his crime. But "take" is also an imperative, expressing anguish and repulsion. "Which now sutes with it" implies acceptance, either gloating or reluctant according to the two meanings of the previous line' (Knights, *Explorations*, p. 23). I do not think Johnson's first alternative is plausible. As Wilson says, Macbeth 'speaks as if watching himself in a dream'; and in this queer state of objectivity he wants the details of the scene to be in keeping with the deed.

61. *Words . . . gives*] Although this line has been regarded as an interpolation and a 'feeble tag' (Clarendon) it can be paralleled in many scenes in the canon. The opposition between words and deeds was a main theme in *Hamlet*, and it recurs in a different form in *Macbeth* (see Introduction, p. xxvii). The singular verb with a plural subject is common in Shakespeare. 'There is here a double reason for it . . . the exigency of the rhyme, and . . . the occurrence, between the nominative and verb, of two singular nouns, to which, as it were, the verb is attracted' (Clarendon).

63–4. *Hear . . . Hell*] Cf. III. i. 140 *post* and *R3*, I. i. 118–20: 'I do love thee so, / That I will shortly send thy soul to heaven, / If Heaven will take the present at our hands.' F. M. Smith,

SCENE II.—[*The same.*]

Enter LADY MACBETH.

Lady M. That which hath made them drunk hath made me
        bold:
    What hath quench'd them hath given me fire.—Hark!
        —Peace!
    It was the owl that shriek'd, the fatal bellman,
    Which gives the stern'st good-night. He is about it.
    The doors are open; and the surfeited grooms   5
    Do mock their charge with snores: I have drugg'd
        their possets,
    That Death and Nature do contend about them,
    Whether they live, or die.

Scene II

S.D. *The same.*] *Capell.*   2–6. What . . . possets,] *so Rowe; lines end* fire, /
shriek'd, / night. / open: / charge / Possets, *F; lines end* fire. / shriek'd / night /
open: / snores / possets, *Knight.*

P.M.L.A., 1945, compares *R3*, v. iii.
313–14.

Scene II

The scene follows on with hardly a
break; and there is no break between
scenes ii and iii. Liddell says that at
Kenilworth, with which Shakespeare
may have been familiar, there was 'a
large courtyard with a flight of steps in
one corner leading up to the sleeping-
rooms. . . In these quadrangular
houses the hall occupied one side of
the building, and out of this, at one
end, a flight of steps led to a lobby
which opened on the guest-chamber...
In the theatre this lobby would, of
course, be the usual gallery or balcony
at the back of the stage. Duncan and
his two grooms of the chamber would
naturally be lodged in the guest-
chamber; back of this would be the
"second chamber", occupied by
Donalbain and another. Such an arrangement would be familar to the
Elizabethan audience, and explains
clearly the action of the scene.'
    3. *the fatal bellman*] Cf. Webster,

Duchess of Malfi, IV. ii. 173: 'I am the
common Bellman, / That usually is
sent to condemn'd persons / The night
before they suffer'; and Spenser,
Faerie Queene, v. vi. 27, where the cock
is called 'the natiue Belman of the
night'. Liddell quotes from *Phraseologia
Generalis*, 1681, a reference to the
'bellman which goeth before a corps,
praeco feralis'. Thus 'the stern'st good-
night is the last good-night of death.'
Possibly a reference to Robert Dow's
gift in May 1605 to pay for visits of the
bellman to condemned prisoners in
Newgate (Paul).
    5. *grooms*] serving-men; menial
servants of any kind.
    6. *possets*] Malone quotes Randle
Holmes, *Academy of Armourie*, 1688, bk
III, p. 84: 'posset is hot milk poured on
ale or sack, having sugar, grated
bisket, eggs, with other ingredients
boiled in it, which goes all to a curd.'
Cf. note on II. i. 31 *ante*, and Middleton,
The Witch, IV. iii. 17: 'For the maide-
servants, and the girles o'the house, /
I spic'd them lately with a drowsie
posset.'

Macb.   [*Within.*] Who's there?—what, ho!
Lady M.   Alack! I am afraid they have awak'd,
        And 'tis not done:—th'attempt and not the deed   10
        Confounds us.—Hark!—I laid their daggers ready;
        He could not miss 'em.—Had he not resembled
        My father as he slept, I had done't.—My husband!

                        Enter MACBETH.

Macb.   I have done the deed.—Didst thou not hear a noise?
Lady M.   I heard the owl scream, and the crickets cry.   15
        Did not you speak?
Macb.   When?
Lady M.   Now.
Macb.   As I descended?

8. S.D.] *Johnson and Steevens (1773)*.   10. attempt . . . deed] *Camb.* (*conj.
Hunter*); attempt, and . . . deed, *F;* attempt, and . . . deed *Rowe, Pope, Hanmer;*
attempt and . . . deed, *Warburton, Johnson, Var. '73, Singer (ed. 2)*.   14. I . . .
noise?] *so Rowe; two lines, the first ending* deed. *F.*   16. Did . . . descended?]
Macb. Did . . . speak? *Lady M.* When? Now? *Macb.* As . . . descended. *conj.
Hunter; Macb.* Did . . . speak? *Lady M.* When? *Macb.* Now, as I descended.
conj. Fleay (Shakespeariana, Dec. 1884, apud Camb.).

8. *Who's there?*] Macbeth loses control over himself, and breaks out into
an exclamation, fancying he hears a
noise (see l. 14). The S.D. was added
by Steevens in place of the Folio
'Enter'. Chambers makes Macbeth
enter above, for a moment; and Booth
thinks the line was spoken by one of the
drunken grooms. Wilson is doubtless
right when he says that the Folio S.D.
merely means that the player is to
speak, and that it is far more effective
for Macbeth to be unseen here than
seen.

10. *attempt . . . deed*] Critics have
quarrelled about the punctuation of
this line—unnecessarily, as the Folio
commas emphasize the words *attempt*
and *deed*, and the meaning is brought
out in modern punctuation by the
omission of the commas. Lady Macbeth discovers later that the attempt *with* the deed also confounds
them.

12–13. *Had . . . done't*] Wilson links

these lines with his theory that there
was an earlier version of the play. See
Introduction, p. xx. Adams believes
that at II. i. 30 two scenes, separated in
time, have been run together and,
possibly, that an intervening scene has
been omitted. This omitted scene, he
thinks, represented Lady Macbeth in
her attempt to kill Duncan without
assistance. But neither the alleged
break in the metre, nor the fact that
several hours are supposed to pass in
200 lines, can be regarded as strong
arguments for this fantastic theory.
Faustus' last soliloquy takes only five
minutes to deliver, though an hour is
supposed to pass.

13. *husband*] Only here does she call
him that.

15. *crickets*] According to Grimm the
cricket foretold death.

16–20.] Murry comments, *Shakespeare*, p. 329, that we can almost hear
'the snapping of the strings'—referring
back to I. vii. 61.

Lady M. Ay.
Macb. Hark!
     Who lies i'th'second chamber?
Lady M.   Donalbain.
Macb. This is a sorry sight.   20
Lady M. A foolish thought to say a sorry sight.
Macb. There's one did laugh in's sleep, and one cried,
     'Murther!'
     That they did wake each other: I stood and heard them;
     But they did say their prayers, and address'd them
     Again to sleep.
Lady M.   There are two lodg'd together.   25
Macb. One cried, 'God bless us!' and, 'Amen,' the other,
     As they had seen me with these hangman's hands.
     List'ning their fear, I could not say, 'Amen,'
     When they did say, 'God bless us.'
Lady M.   Consider it not so deeply.
Macb. But wherefore could not I pronounce 'Amen'?   30
     I had most need of blessing, and 'Amen'
     Stuck in my throat.
Lady M.   These deeds must not be thought
     After these ways: so, it will make us mad.
Macb. Methought, I heard a voice cry, 'Sleep no more!
     Macbeth does murther Sleep,'—the innocent Sleep;   35

17. Ay] *Rowe; I F; I! Chambers.*   18–19. Hark! . . . chamber?] *so Steevens
(1793); one line, F.*   22–5. There's . . . sleep] *so Rowe; lines end* sleep, / other: /
Prayers, / sleepe. *F.*   27. hands.] hands: *F;* hands, *Rowe.*   31–2. I . . .
throat] *one line, F.*   32. thought] thought on *Hanmer.*   34–5.] *Johnson;
inverted commas not in F; quotation extends to* feast *(39), Hanmer.*

20. *sorry*] miserable, sad, pitiable.

24. *address'd them*] prepared themselves. Cf. *Mer.V.*, II. ix. 19: 'and so
have I address'd me'.

25. *two*] Malcolm and Donalbain,
not the two grooms. 'The picture of the
sons, half waking while their father
is murdered, adds to the horror of
the situation' (Chambers). But it is
curious, if the princes are in the same
room, that Lady Macbeth mentions
only the younger.

27. *As*] i.e. as if. Cf. *Lr.*, III. iv. 15:
'Is it not as this mouth should tear this
hand?'

hangman] The hangman had to draw
and quarter his victim, and the word
is sometimes used loosely for 'execu-
tioner'. Cf. *Mer.V.*, IV. i. 125: 'hangman's axe'.

28. *List'ning*] Cf. *Caes.*, IV. i. 41:
'Listen great things.'

32. *thought*] In support of Hanmer's
emendation, Cuningham cites III. ii.
11 *post* and *Tw.N.*, v. i. 324.

34–9. *Methought . . . feast*] perhaps
suggested by a passage in Holinshed's
account of King Kenneth. See Appendix, p. 166. It cannot be determined from the Folio where the voice

Sleep, that knits up the ravell'd sleave of care,
The death of each day's life, sore labour's bath,
Balm of hurt minds, great Nature's second course,
Chief nourisher in life's feast;—

Lady M.   What do you mean?

Macb. Still it cried, 'Sleep no more!' to all the house: 40
'Glamis hath murther'd Sleep, and therefore Cawdor
Shall sleep no more, Macbeth shall sleep no more!'

36. sleave] *Steevens (conj. Seward); Sleeue F.*   39. feast;—] feast.—*Theobald;*
Feast. *F.*   41–2.] *Hanmer; inverted commas not in F.*

is supposed to end, but Johnson's arrangement has been followed by nearly all subsequent editors. 'the innocent . . . feast' 'is a comment made by Macbeth upon the words he imagined he heard' (Clarendon).

34. *Sleep no more*] Cf. III. ii. 16–26, III. iv. 141, and v. i *passim.* Cf. also note on I. iii. 19–20. Kolbe analyses the sleep references in *Shakespeare's Way,* pp. 5–10, and Murry in his *Shakespeare,* pp. 332 ff. Cf. Knight, *The Wheel of Fire,* 1949, pp. 126–7. The whole passage is reminiscent of Ovid, *Metam.,* xi. 624: 'Pax animi, quem cura fugit, qui corpora duris / Fessa ministeriis mulces reparasque labori'; which is thus translated by Golding (ed. Rouse, xi. 723–6): 'O sleepe (quoth shee), the rest of things: O gentlest of the Goddes, / Sweete sleepe, the peace of mynd, with whom crookt care is aye at oddes: / Which cherrishest mennes weery limbes appalld with toyling sore, / And makest them as fresh to woork, and lustye as before'. Malone suggested there was an echo of Sidney's sonnet (No. 39): 'Come, Sleepe, O Sleepe, the certaine knot of peace, / The baiting place of wit, the balme of woe.' (Cf. *balm, feast, knits.* The 1591 ed. of *Astrophel and Stella* misprinted *baiting* as *bathing.* Cf. *bath.*) There is another close parallel in Seneca, *Her. Fur.* (1065–7): 'tuque O domitor / Somne malorum, requies animi, / Pars humanae melior vitae'. Jasper Heywood translates thus: 'And thou O tamer best / O sleepe of toyles,

the quietnesse of mynde, / Of all the lyfe of man the better parte'. It seems probable that 'balm of hurt minds' was suggested by the situation in *Hercules Furens,* where the Chorus invokes Sleep to cure the madness of the hero.

36. *sleave*] 'a slender filament of silk obtained by separating a thicker thread' (*O.E.D.*). But it seems also to mean 'coarse silk'. See Florio, *Worlde of Wordes:* 'Sfilazza: *any kinde of raveled stuffe, or sleaue silk* . . . Capitone, *a kinde of course silke called sleaue silke.*'

38–9. *second . . . nourisher*] Pudding appears anciently to have been the first course at dinner, the joint or roast being the 'second'—*the pièce de résistance.* Steevens quotes Chaucer, *Squire's Tale,* 347: 'The norice of digestioun, the slepe'. Wilson makes the admirable point that 'course' (meaning *race* or *career*) suggested to Shakespeare the other meaning of the word.

39. *Chief . . . feast*] This may also have been suggested by an alternative meaning of *ravell'd* (36). Ravel, or ravelled, bread was whole meal bread, and could be regarded as 'chief nourisher'. See Harrison, *England* (1877), I. 154: 'The raueled is a kind of cheat bread also.'

41–2. *Glamis . . . more*] Johnson thought the voice said only, 'Glamis hath murther'd sleep', the rest being Macbeth's comment; but it is difficult to distinguish between the voice of conscience speaking directly through

Lady M. Who was it that thus cried? Why, worthy Thane,
You do unbend your noble strength, to think
So brainsickly of things. Go, get some water,   45
And wash this filthy witness from your hand.—
Why did you bring these daggers from the place?
They must lie there: go, carry them, and smear
The sleepy grooms with blood.

Macb.   I'll go no more:
I am afraid to think what I have done;   50
Look on't again I dare not.

Lady M.   Infirm of purpose!
Give me the daggers. The sleeping, and the dead,
Are but as pictures; 'tis the eye of childhood
That fears a painted devil. If he do bleed,
I'll gild the faces of the grooms withal,   55
For it must seem their guilt.   [*Exit.—Knocking within.*

Macb.   Whence is that knocking?—
How is't with me, when every noise appals me?
What hands are here? Ha! they pluck out mine eyes.

Macbeth, and the same voice speaking (as he imagines) from outside him. Bradley comments that the voice 'denounced on him, as if his three names gave him three personalities to suffer in, the doom of sleeplessness'.

44. *unbend*] Cf. I. vii. 80 (Wilson).

45. *brainsickly*] Shakespeare uses the adj. 'brainsick' six times but not the adv. elsewhere.

46. *wash*] Cf. v. i. 58 *post*.

witness] evidence. Cf. *Mer.V.*, I. iii. 100.

47. *Why . . . place?*] It is difficult to perform the scene so as to make plausible Lady Macbeth's delay in noticing the daggers. Presumably at lines 20, 27, the daggers were in one hand, perhaps concealed behind Macbeth's back. In any case ll. 45–6 serve as a cue to draw them to her attention.

54. *painted devil*] Cf. Webster, *White Devil*, III. ii. 151: 'Terrify babes, my Lord, with painted devils.'

55–6. *gild . . . guilt*] Knowles points

out that these words are a 'taunt at Macbeth, reminding him of his own arrangement, and the imbecility that prevents him from carrying it into execution'. The grim pun is rather a sign of the immense effort of will needed by Lady Macbeth to visit the scene of the crime. Those who find it distasteful should read more genteel authors. Cf. 'golden blood' (II. iii. 110 *post*); *John*, II. i. 316: 'armours . . . gilt with Frenchmen's blood'; and *2H4*, IV. v. 129: 'England shall double gild his treble guilt.'

58. *hands . . . eyes*] See Introduction, p. xxix.

R. Walker, *op. cit.*, p. 72, quotes Matt., xviii. 9: 'And if thine eye cause thee to offend, plucke it out, and cast it from thee: it is better for thee to enter into life with one eie, then hauing two eyes to be cast into hell fire.' He links this verse with Luke, xi. 34–6, and the knocking at the gate with Luke, xi. 9–10. It may be added Beelzebub is mentioned three times in the same

Will all great Neptune's ocean wash this blood
Clean from my hand? No, this my hand will rather   60
The multitudinous seas incarnadine,
Making the green one red.

61. incarnadine,] *Rowe;* incarnardine, *F.*   62. green one red.] *F4;* Greene
one, Red *F1–3;* green, One red— *Johnson;* green—one red. *Steevens, 1778*
(*conj. Murphy*).

chapter, and by Shakespeare a few
lines later (II. iii. 4); and that the hell
fire of Matt., xviii reappears also in
the Porter scene.

59–62. *Will . . . red*] Upton, *Critical
Observations*, 1746, compares Sophocles
Oedip. Tyrannos, 1227; Steevens compares Catullus, *In Gellium;* but Shakespeare is more likely to have read
Seneca, *Phaedra*, 715–18 (cited by
Cunliffe): 'Quis eluet me Tanais? aut
quae barbaris / Maeotis undis Pontico
incumbens mari? / Non ipse toto
magnus Oceano pater / Tantum
expiarit sceleris.' Studley translates:
'What bathing lukewarme Tanais
may I defilde obtaine, / Whose clen-
sing watry Channell pure may washe
mee Cleane againe? / Or what Meotis
muddy meare, with rough Barbarian
wave / That boardes on Pontus roring
Sea? Not Neptune graundsire grave /
With all his Ocean foulding floud can
purge and wash away / This dunghill
foule of stane.' Cf. the following passage from Seneca, *Hercules Furens*,
1323–9 (1330–6): 'Quis Tanais aut
quis Nilus aut quis Persica / Violentus
unda Tigris aut Rhenus ferox /
Tagusve Hibera turbidus gaza fluens, /
Abluere dextram poterit? Arctoum
licet / Maeotis in me gelida trans-
fundat mare, / *Et tota Tethys per meas
currat manus,* / Haerebit altum facinus.'
C. B. Young (cited by Wilson) points
out that Shakespeare's echo is nearer
to the original than Heywood's version of the italicized line ('And al the
water thereof shoulde now pas by my
two handes'). Shakespeare might,
perhaps, have amalgamated the two
passages in translation. But, as Young
also points out, 'Haerebit' etc. is close

to v. ii. 17 *post;* and the latter is much
closer than the Heywood version ('Yet
wil the mischiefe deep remayne'). It is
therefore highly probable that Shakespeare knew the original. Chambers
compares what is probably an independent imitation of Seneca in
Marston, *The Insatiate Countess*, v. i:
'Although . . . the waves of all the
northerne sea, / Should flow for ever,
through these guiltie hands, / Yet the
sanguinolent staine would extant be.'

61. *multitudinous seas*] not referring
to the multitude of creatures in the
seas, nor the many-waved ocean, but
to the countless masses of waters on
the surface of the globe (Malone). Cf.
Munday and Chettle, *Death of Robert,
Earl of Huntingdon*, 1601, II. ii (Dodsley, ed. Hazlitt, VIII. 268), 'The mul-
titudes of seas dyed red with blood'.

incarnadine] The word was used in
Shakespeare's days as adj. and sb. but
he seems to have been the first to use it
as vb. Properly it would mean 'make
flesh-coloured', but Shakespeare obviously means 'turn blood-red'. He
may have been thinking of a crimson
blush.

62. *Making . . . red*] i.e. changing the
green sea into total red. Cf. Munday
and Chettle, *Downfall of Robert, Earl of
Huntington*, 1601, IV. i (Dodsley, ed.
Hazlitt, VIII. 173), 'And made the
greene sea red with Pagan blood'.
Chambers compares what is possibly a
Shakespearian passage in *Two Noble
Kinsmen*, v. i. 49–50: 'Thou mighty
one, that with thy power has turn'd /
Great Neptune into purple'. Simpson,
Shakespeare's Punctuation, shows that in
the Folio, a comma often follows a
stressed word.

Re-enter LADY MACBETH.

Lady M. My hands are of your colour; but I shame
　　To wear a heart so white. [*Knock.*] I hear a knocking
　　At the south entry:—retire we to our chamber.　　　65
　　A little water clears us of this deed:
　　How easy is it then! Your constancy
　　Hath left you unattended.—[*Knock.*] Hark! more
　　　　knocking.
　　Get on your night-gown, lest occasion call us,
　　And show us to be watchers.—Be not lost　　　70
　　So poorly in your thoughts.
Macb. To know my deed, 'twere best not know myself.
　　　　　　　　　　　　　　　　　　　　　　[*Knock.*

　　Wake Duncan with thy knocking: I would thou
　　　　couldst!　　　　　　　　　　　　　　[*Exeunt.*

64–8. To . . . knocking] *so Pope; seven lines, ending* white. / entry: / Chamber: /
deed. / Constancie / unattended. / knocking. *F.*　　67. then!] then? *F.*　　72–3.
To . . . couldst!] *so Pope; four lines, ending* deed, / selfe / knocking: / could'st. *F.*
72. To know] T'unknow *Hanmer.*　　73. Wake . . . thy] Wake, Duncan, with
this *D'Avenant, Theobald.*

64. S.D.] De Quincey, *Works,* ed.
Masson, x. 389, comments on the
knocking: 'Hence it is, that when the
deed is done, when the work of darkness is perfect, then the world of darkness passes away like a pageantry in
the clouds: the knocking at the gate is
heard, and it makes known audibly
that the reaction has commenced; the
human has made its reflux upon the
fiendish; the pulses of life are beginning to beat again; and the re-
establishment of the goings-on of the
world in which we live first makes us
profoundly sensible of the awful parenthesis that had suspended them.'
67–8. *Your . . . unattended*] 'Your firm-
ness has deserted you' (Chambers).
69. *night-gown*] dressing-gown or
robe de chambre. 'In Macbeth's time and
for centuries later, it was the custom
for both sexes to sleep without other

covering than that belonging to the
bed' (Grant White). If Macbeth and
his wife were found in ordinary
clothing, it would bring suspicion on
them.
72. *To know . . . myself*] 'If I must
look my deed in the face, it were better
for me to lose consciousness altogether'
(Clarendon). 'Better be lost in thought
than look my deed in the face' (Wilson). The latter brings out the connection between this line and Lady
Macbeth's remark, to which it is an
answer; but I think it means rather: 'It
were better for me to remain perma-
nently "lost" in thought, i.e. self-
alienated, than to be fully conscious
of the nature of my deed.' Ellis-Fermor
suggests the following (privately): 'If I
am to live on terms with this deed, I
must break with my real—my former
—self.'

SCENE III.—[*The same.*]

Enter a Porter.

[*Knocking within.*

Porter. Here's a knocking, indeed! If a man were Porter
of Hell Gate, he should have old turning the key.
[*Knocking.*] Knock, knock, knock. Who's there,
i'th'name of Belzebub?—Here's a farmer, that
hang'd himself on th'expectation of plenty: come in,   5
time-pleaser; have napkins enow about you; here

Scene III

S.D. *The same.*] *Capell.*   6. time-pleaser] *conj. Krabbe;* time-server *conj. Wilson;*
time *F etc.*   enow] *F1;* enough *F2–3.*

Capell in his *Notes*, p. 13, remarks:
'Without this scene Macbeth's dress
cannot be shifted nor his hands
washed. To give a rational space for
the discharge of these actions was this
scene thought of.' This may be true,
but it can be defended on other
grounds. See Introduction, pp. xxiii ff.
Pope relegated the first 40 lines of
this scene to the margin. Coleridge,
Shakespearean Criticism, I. 75–8, declares: 'This low soliloquy of the Porter, and his few speeches afterwards,
I believe to have been written for the
mob by some other hand, perhaps with
Shakespeare's consent; and that finding it take, he with the remaining ink
of a pen otherwise employed, just interpolated the words "I'll . . . bonfire"
(19–21). Of the rest not one syllable
has the ever-present being of Shakespeare.' Hales, *Notes and Essays on
Shakespeare*, pp. 273–90, argues that the
Porter is inseparably associated with
the knocking, which is an integral part
of the play; that some relief is necessary at this point in the play; that the
whole speech is a powerful piece of
irony, because the man *is* Porter of
hell-gate as in the Mystery plays, and
that the style and language are
Shakespearian. The links with medieval drama are discussed by Glynne
Wickham in 'Hell-Castle and its Door-
Keeper' (*S.S.*, xix. 68–74). N.

2. *old*] frequently used as a collo-
quial augmentative, meaning plenti-
ful, great, abundant or, as Steevens
says, '*frequent*, more than enough'.
5. *th'expectation of plenty*] which
would, of course, bring low prices.
Malone compares Hall, *Satires*, IV. 6
(ed. 1597): 'Ech Muck-worme wil be
riche with lawlesse gaine, / Altho he
smother vp mowes of seuen yeares
graine, / And hang'd himself when
corne growes cheap again.' The passage
has been used to fix the date of the play
by Malone and others. See Introduction, p. xxii.
6. *time-pleaser*] This conjecture by
H. Krabbe (in a private communication) seems preferable to Wilson's
'time-server' (*Edin. Bib. Soc. Trans.*,
1946, ii, pt 4, pp. 413–16). The twice-
repeated 'Come in' strongly suggests
that the Porter also says 'Come in' to the
farmer, with some word relating to his
miscalculating time (Darmesteter).
But although 'time-server' is appropriate to farmers, who must serve time
in its changes of seasons, and server (in
the sense of waiter) provides a link with
napkins, Shakespeare does not use
either 'server' or 'time-server'. He
does, however, twice use the expression
'time-pleaser' and in *Cor.*, III. i. 45 (as
Krabbe points out), it comes just after
a mention of 'corn' (43).
napkins] handkerchiefs.

you'll sweat for't. [*Knocking*.] Knock, knock. Who's
there, i'th'other devil's name?—Faith, here's an
equivocator, that could swear in both the scales
against either scale; who committed treason enough   10
for God's sake, yet could not equivocate to heaven:
O! come in, equivocator. [*Knocking*.] Knock, knock,
knock. Who's there?—Faith, here's an English tailor
come hither for stealing out of a French hose: come
in, tailor; here you may roast your goose. [*Knocking*.]   15

8. *other*] The Porter cannot remember the name of another devil.

9. *equivocator*] i.e. a Jesuit (Warburton). See Introduction, pp. xv ff., for the connection between this passage and the trial of Garnet, who went under the name of 'Farmer', so that, as Kellett, *Suggestions*, p. 64, points out, there is a punning link between farmer and equivocator. Cf. *New Variorum*, 1903, p. 355. Dowden, *New Shakes. Soc. Trans.*, 1874, p. 275, thinks we 'should ask whether Shakespeare did not make the porter use this word . . . with unconscious reference to Macbeth, who even then had begun to find that he could not "equivocate to heaven" '.

14. *stealing . . . hose*] The joke against tailors was a very old one. Scot, *Discouerie of Witchcraft*, VII. 12, says of Samuel's apparition: 'Belike he had a new mantell, made him in heaven: and yet they saie Tailors are skantie there, for that their consciences are so large here.' Stubbes, *Anatomie of Abuses*, 1585, fol. 23*b*: 'The Frenche hose are of two diuers makinges, for the common Frenche hose (as they list to call them) containeth length, breadth, and sidenesse sufficient, and is made very rounde. The other contayneth neyther length, breadth, nor sidenesse (being not past a quarter of a yarde side), whereof some be paned, cut, and drawen out with costly ornamentes, with Canions annexed, reaching downe beneath their knees.' This passage is cited by the Clar. Edd. who say that in *Mer.V.*, I. ii. 80, 'Shakespeare clearly speaks of the larger kind,

the "round hose" which the Englishman borrows from France, and it is enough to suppose that the tailor merely followed the practice of his trade without exhibiting any special dexterity in stealing.' But Warburton thought that the Porter referred to the latter kind of hose, for 'a tailor must be a master of his trade who could steal anything from thence.' I agree with Wilson that the context implies that the tailor 'had tried the trick once too often' and had been caught when the fashion changed and French hose became tight-fitting. The implication with farmer, equivocator, and tailor is not merely that they go to hell for their sins, but that they are caught out by overreaching themselves. N.

15. *goose*] smoothing iron. But the word also means a swelling caused by venereal disease, and it may therefore have been suggested by 'sweat' (7) *via* 'French' (14), and it in turn suggests 'lechery' (28). As Wilson observes, the *O.E.D.* gives no instance of 'cook one's goose' (= do for oneself) earlier than 1851; but in the phrase 'roast your goose' there may be a reference to killing the goose that laid the golden eggs, just as the tailor ruined himself in the attempt to get rich quickly. E. A. Armstrong, *Shakespeare's Imagination*, pp. 57–65, 187–8, has some interesting remarks on the image 'cluster' in Shakespeare relating to the goose, and he proves the authenticity of the Porter scene by showing its relations with other scenes in Shakespeare. Cf. in particular Launce's

Knock, knock. Never at quiet! What are you?—But
this place is too cold for Hell. I'll devil-porter it no
further: I had thought to have let in some of all
professions, that go the primrose way to th'everlasting bonfire. [*Knocking.*] Anon, anon: I pray you,   20
remember the Porter.   [*Opens the gate.*

Enter MACDUFF *and* LENOX.

Macd. Was it so late, friend, ere you went to bed,
   That you do lie so late?
Port. Faith, Sir, we were carousing till the second cock;
   and drink, Sir, is a great provoker of three things.   25
Macd. What three things does drink especially provoke?
Port. Marry, Sir, nose-painting, sleep, and urine.
   Lechery, Sir, it provokes, and unprovokes: it provokes the desire, but it takes away the performance.
   Therefore, much drink may be said to be an equi-   30
   vocator with lechery: it makes him, and it mars him;
   it sets him on, and it takes him off; it persuades him,
   and disheartens him; makes him stand to, and not
   stand to: in conclusion, equivocates him in a sleep,
   and, giving him the lie, leaves him.   35

24-5. Faith . . . things] *prose, Johnson; verse,* F.

soliloquy (*Gent.*, IV. iv) where we have
'steals her capon's leg . . . hanged for't
. . . a pissing while . . . geese . . . heave
up my leg'. There are close parallels
with all these phrases and words in the
present scene.

17. *too . . . Hell*] Shakespeare may
not have been aware that in Dante's
Inferno, XXXII–XXXIV, those who were
traitors to their kin, to their country,
to their friends and guests, and to their
lords and benefactors are tortured
together in the Ninth, or *frozen* Circle
of Hell. Macbeth might be regarded
as a traitor to his kinsman, Duncan, to
his country, Scotland, to his friend,
Banquo, to his guest, lord, and bene-
factor, Duncan. R. Walker, p. 74,
noted this independently.

19. *primrose way*] Cf. *All's W.*, IV. v.
56: 'the flowery way that leads to the

broad gate and the great fire'; and
Ham., I. iii. 50; 'the primrose path of
dalliance'.

20-1. *I . . . Porter*] addressed to the
audience (Wilson). Perhaps it was,
though I doubt whether Shakespeare
intended this.

24. *the second cock*] i.e. 3 a.m. Cf.
Rom., IV. iv. 3: 'the second cock hath
crow'd, / The curfew bell hath rung,
'tis three o'clock.'

27-35. *Marry . . . him*] See Introduction, p. xxviii. Rabelais also thought
that 'Carnal concupiscence is cooled
and quelled . . . by the means of wine'
(III. xxxi).

34. *in a sleep*] a quibble: 'tricks him
into a sleep' and 'tricks him in a sleep',
i.e. by a dream (Elwin).

35. *giving . . . lie*] laying him out, as
in wrestling.

Macd. I believe, drink gave thee the lie last night.

Port. That it did, Sir, i'the very throat on me: but I
　　requited him for his lie; and (I think) being too
　　strong for him, though he took up my legs sometime,
　　yet I made a shift to cast him.　　　　　　　　　40

Macd. Is thy master stirring?

Enter MACBETH.

　　Our knocking has awak'd him; here he comes.

Len. Good morrow, noble Sir!

Macb.　　　　　　　　Good morrow, both!

Macd. Is the King stirring, worthy Thane?

Macb.　　　　　　　　　　　　Not yet.

Macd. He did command me to call timely on him:　　45
　　I have almost slipp'd the hour.

Macb.　　　　　　　　I'll bring you to him.

Macd. I know, this is a joyful trouble to you;
　　But yet 'tis one.

Macb. The labour we delight in physics pain.
　　This is the door.

Macd.　　　　　　　I'll make so bold to call,　　50
　　For 'tis my limited service.　　　　　　　　[*Exit.*

Len. Goes the King hence to-day?

Macb.　　　　　　　　He does:—he did appoint so.

Len. The night has been unruly: where we lay,
　　Our chimneys were blown down; and, as they say,
　　Lamentings heard i'th'air; strange screams of death,　55

---

37. on] *F*; o' *Theobald.*　　50-1. I'll . . . service] *one line, F.*　　51-2.] *Steevens
ends lines at* king / so *and begins 52* From hence.　　53-5. The . . . death,] *so
Rowe; four lines, ending* vnruly: / downe, / Ayre / Death, *F.*

39. *took . . . legs*] a quibble on the
effect of drink, and a wrestling action.
Perhaps also an echo of 'heave up my
leg' (i.e. like a dog = urinate).

40. *made a shift*] managed.

cast] quibble on cast (= throw in
wrestling) and cast = vomit (Wilson).
But 'cast' can also mean 'emit', not
necessarily through the *mouth*. And cf.
v. iii. 50 *post.*

49. *The . . . pain*] Cf. *Cym.*, III. ii. 34,
and *Tp.*, III. i. 1-2.

51. *limited*] appointed. Cf. *Meas.*,
IV. ii. 176.

52. *he . . . so*] 'guilty self-correction'
(Grierson).

53. *The . . . unruly*] Curry, *Shakespeare's Philosophical Patterns*, p. 80,
says that 'the storm which rages over
Macbeth's castle . . . is no ordinary
tempest caused by the regular movements of the heavenly bodies, but
rather a manifestation of demonic
power over the elements of nature.

And, prophesying with accents terrible
Of dire combustion, and confus'd events,
New hatch'd to th'woeful time, the obscure bird
Clamour'd the livelong night: some say, the earth
Was feverous, and did shake.

Macb.   'Twas a rough night.   60

57. combustion] combustions *F2–4.*   57–8. events, New . . . time, the] *Knight,*
Hudson; Events, New . . . time. The *F;* events. New . . . time, the *conj. Johnson.*
58–60. New . . . night] *so Hanmer; four lines, ending* time. / Night. / feuorous, /
Night. *F; lines end* time. / Night, / shake. / Night. *Rowe.*

Indeed, natural forces seem to be partly in abeyance . . . the firm-set earth is so sensitized by the all-pervading demonic energy that it is feverous and shakes. Macbeth senses this magnetization (cf. II. i. 58). . . . As the drunken Porter feels, Macbeth's castle is literally the mouth of hell through which evil spirits emerge in this darkness to cause upheavals in nature.' Cf. Masefield, *Recent Prose,* pp. 270–1. James I, *Workes,* p. 117, says that witches 'can raise stormes and tempests in the aire, either vpon Sea or Land, though not vniuersally, but in such a particular place and prescribed bounds, as God will permit them so to trouble.' There was a hurricane on the night of 29 March 1606 (Paul).

56–8. *And . . . bird*] I have adopted the Knight-Hudson punctuation which connects 'prophesying' with 'bird'. Wilson Knight suggests (privately) that the owl in *Caes.* (I. iii. 28) 'hooting and shrieking in the market-place' and prophesying doom may be compared with 'the obscure bird'; that 'new-hatch'd' suits the bird (as it must otherwise have suggested it—cf. Kellett, *Suggestions,* p. 65); that Shakespeare does not elsewhere use 'prophesying' as a gerund; and that the build-up for four lines to a climax, with a quiet and reserved conclusion after 'night' is typically Shakespearian. I agree and add only that with the usual punctuation there are two short sentences at the end of the speech, which prevents the actor from doing

much with it; and that all editors emend Folio punctuation and lineation of this speech in one way or another. Cf. Ovid, *Metam.,* xv. 791: 'Tristis mille locis stygius dedit omina bubo.' Pliny (tr. Holland, 1634, x. xii. 276) says: 'The Scritch-Owle alwaies betokeneth some heauie newes and is most execrable and accursed, and namely, in the presages of publick affaires: he keepeth euer in desarts: and loueth not only such vnpeopled places, but also that are horrible and hard of accesse. In summe, he is the very monster of the night, neither crying nor singing out cleare, but vttering a certaine heauy groane of dolefull mourning. And therefore if he be seen to fly either within cities, or otherwise abroad in any place, it is not good, but prognosticates some fearfull misfortune.'

57. *combustion*] tumult, confusion, especially of a political kind. Cf. *H8,* v. iv. 51. Hotson suspects a reference to the Gunpowder Plot.

58. *hatch'd . . . time*] Malone thought *new hatch'd* should be referred to *events,* though the events were yet to come, and he compared *2H4,* III. i. 86, 'Such things become the hatch and brood of time.' He therefore argued that *hatch'd* = hatching, and that 'to' meant 'to suit', or perhaps 'born to'. Cf. *Ham.,* III. i. 173–5.

60. *feverous*] referring perhaps to the fever of the ague, which was very common in Shakespeare's day, but implying, of course, an earthquake.

Len. My young remembrance cannot parallel
　　A fellow to it.

　　　　　　　Re-enter MACDUFF.

Macd.　　　　　O horror! horror! horror!
　　Tongue nor heart cannot conceive, nor name thee!
Macb., Len. What's the matter?
Macd. Confusion now hath made his masterpiece!　　65
　　Most sacrilegious Murther hath broke ope
　　The Lord's anointed Temple, and stole thence
　　The life o'th'building!
Macb.　　　　　　　What is't you say? the life?
Len.　　　　　　　Mean you his Majesty?
Macd. Approach the chamber, and destroy your sight　　70
　　With a new Gorgon.—Do not bid me speak:
　　See, and then speak yourselves.—
　　　　　　　　[*Exeunt Macbeth and Lenox.*
　　　　　　　　　　Awake! awake!—
　　Ring the alarum-bell.—Murther, and treason!
　　Banquo, and Donalbain! Malcolm, awake!
　　Shake off this downy sleep, death's counterfeit,　　75

62–4. *O . . . matter?*] *so* F; *two lines, ending* heart, / matter? *Capell, etc.*　　72.
S.D.] *so Dyce; after* awake! F.

62–4. *O . . . matter?*] This lineation is in accordance with the Folio. But according to Flatter, *op. cit.*, p. 23, a character, entering, begins a new line, unless he is supposed to overhear the previous conversation. Here Macduff rushes in with his tidings, and he can be heard before he actually appears. His opening words should not, therefore, be regarded as the completion of Lenox's line. Perhaps Macduff's opening words should be heard before Lenox has completed his sentence, while 'What's the matter?' is an extra-metrical interjection. The usual lineation, following Capell, has the effect of making the horror too orderly and metrical; but, of course, in this scene, the lineation of which even the most conservative editors are forced to emend, it would be easy to fall into the error of finding subtleties in textual corruptions.

67. *The Lord's anointed Temple*] Cf. 1 Sam., xxiv. 10: 'The Lord's anointed' and 2 Cor., vi. 16: 'Ye are the Temple of the living God.' Though the metaphor is mixed, it can be regarded as shorthand for 'the temple of the Lord's anointed'; and by putting it in this form, Shakespeare is able to recall both texts and to glance at the heinous sin of regicide—David in the context protests that he could not put forth his hand against King Saul. Draper, *Eng. Stud.*, lxxii, regards the passage as a reference to James I's favourite theory of Divine Right. Cf. II. i. 58 *ante*.

68–9. *What . . . Majesty?*] Macbeth and Lenox possibly speak together.

75–81. *Shake . . . house?*] David E. Jones, *The Plays of T. S. Eliot* (1960),

And look on death itself!—up, up, and see
The great doom's image!—Malcolm! Banquo!
As from your graves rise up, and walk like sprites,
To countenance this horror!   [*Bell rings.*

Enter LADY MACBETH.

Lady M.   What's the business,
That such a hideous trumpet calls to parley   80
The sleepers of the house? speak, speak!
Macd.   O gentle lady,
'Tis not for you to hear what I can speak:
The repetition, in a woman's ear,
Would murther as it fell.

Enter BANQUO.

                    O Banquo! Banquo!
Our royal master's murther'd!
Lady M.   Woe, alas!   85
What! in our house?

79. horror!] *Theobald;* horror. Ring the Bell. *F.*   84–6. O . . . anywhere]
Theobald; one line, O Banquo . . . murther'd. *followed by three lines, ending* alas: /
House? / where *F.*

p. 17, comments: 'Standing probably, in the Elizabethan theatre, upon
the upper stage, Macduff calls up
"the sleepers of the house" to witness
the "great doom's image", the Last
Judgment. Rising in their night-
shirts and flocking on to the stage by
every entrance . . . they present a
visual resemblance to the spirits rising
from their graves on the Last Day, and
the theatrical image complements the
verbal image.' He adds that Lady
Macbeth calls the bell a trumpet to
remind the audience once again of the
Last Judgment.
    75. *sleep . . . counterfeit*] Cf. *Lucr.*, 402,
where sleep is called 'the map of
death', and *MND.*, III. ii. 364: 'death-
counterfeiting sleep'. Baldwin, *Shakespeare's Small Latine*, I. 591, thinks that
Shakespeare may have read at school
in *Sententiae Pueriles* the phrase 'Somnus

mortis imago'. Cf. Anders, *Shakespeare's Books*, p. 48.
    77. *doom's image*] Cf. *Lr.*, v. iii.
264: 'Is this the promised end?' 'Or
image of that *horror*?' The idea of
doomsday is continued in 78–9, and
the word 'horror' is used there too.
    79. *countenance*] 'suit' or 'behold', or
both.
    Bell rings] Theobald suggested
that the words which complete the
line in the Folio were a stage direction,
accidentally repeated as 'Bell rings'.
Stage directions often appear as im-
peratives (e.g. *Knock*, II. ii. 64 *ante*).
Lady Macbeth's opening words complete the line if Theobald's suggestion
is adopted. Cuningham, however,
agrees with Keightley that Macduff,
in his impatience, reiterates the
order.
    86. *in our house?*] Warburton thought

Ban.   Too cruel, anywhere.
Dear Duff, I pr'ythee, contradict thyself,
And say, it is not so.

Re-enter MACBETH *and* LENOX.

Macb. Had I but died an hour before this chance,
I had liv'd a blessed time; for, from this instant,   90
There's nothing serious in mortality;
All is but toys: renown, and grace, is dead;
The wine of life is drawn, and the mere lees
Is left this vault to brag of.

Enter MALCOLM *and* DONALBAIN.

Don. What is amiss?
Macb.   You are, and do not know't: 95
The spring, the head, the fountain of your blood
Is stopp'd; the very source of it is stopp'd.
Macd. Your royal father's murther'd.
Mal.   O! by whom?
Len. Those of his chamber, as it seem'd, had done't:
Their hands and faces were all badg'd with blood;   100
So were their daggers, which, unwip'd, we found

---

87. contradict| *F1*; contract *F2–4.*   88. S.D.| *Capell;* Enter Macbeth, Lenox,
and Rosse *F.*

that Lady Macbeth blundered with
these words, and that Banquo accordingly reproved her; but Kittredge
thinks it 'a natural expression from an
innocent hostess'.

89–94. *Had . . . brag of*] Bradley
points out, *Shakespearean Tragedy*, p.
359, that 'this is meant to deceive, but
it utters at the same time his pro-
foundest feelings.' I would add that
Macbeth was unconscious of the
truth of his words, though Murry,
Shakespeare, p. 332, thinks otherwise:
'The irony is appalling: for Macbeth
must needs be conscious of the im-
port of the words that come from
him. He intends the monstrous hypocrisy of a conventional lament for

Duncan; but as the words leave his lips
they change their nature, and become
a doom upon himself. He is become the
instrument of "the equivocation of the
fiend That lies like truth".'

91. *mortality*] 'human destiny'
(Grierson).

94. *vault*] 'A metaphorical comparison of this world vaulted by the sky and
robbed of its spirit and grace, with a
vault or cellar from which the wine has
been taken and the dregs only left'
(Elwin). In Case's view, Macbeth is
thinking of the earth as a burial vault,
and so proceeds to the idea of a wine
vault.

100. *badg'd*] Cf. *2H6*, III. ii. 200:
'murder's crimson badge'.

Upon their pillows: they star'd, and were distracted;
No man's life was to be trusted with them.
Macb. O! yet I do repent me of my fury,
   That I did kill them.
Macd.   Wherefore did you so?   105
Macb. Who can be wise, amaz'd, temperate and furious,
   Loyal and neutral, in a moment? No man:
   Th'expedition of my violent love
   Outrun the pauser, reason.—Here lay Duncan,
   His silver skin lac'd with his golden blood;   110
   And his gash'd stabs look'd like a breach in nature
   For ruin's wasteful entrance: there, the murtherers.
   Steep'd in the colours of their trade, their daggers
   Unmannerly breech'd with gore. Who could refrain,
   That had a heart to love, and in that heart   115
   Courage, to make's love known?
Lady M.   Help me hence, ho!
Macd. Look to the Lady.

102–3. Upon . . . them] *so F; three lines, ending* pillows: / life / them. *Steevens (1793).*

102–3. *Upon . . . them*] Many editors
have departed from the Folio arrangement of these lines, but with insufficient justification. Cuningham's conj.
'That no man's . . .' is attractive, but
not essential. The break in the metre
after *pillows* and the rhythm of 103
well express the breathless haste and
horror of the speaker.

109. *pauser*] i.e. delayer.

110. *lac'd*] interlaced, in reticulate
fashion. Cf. *Rom.*, III. v. 8: 'What
envious streaks / Do lace the severing
clouds in yonder East'. And *Cym.*,
II. ii. 22: 'white and azure laced / With
blue of heaven's own tint'. 'It is not
improbable that Shakespeare put
these forced and unnatural metaphors
into the mouth of Macbeth, as a mark
of artifice and dissimulation, to show
the difference between the studied
language of hypocrisy and the natural
outcries of sudden passion. The whole
speech, so considered, is a remarkable
instance of judgment, as it consists
entirely of antithesis and metaphor'
(Johnson).

112. *wasteful*] destructive. The
attackers enter through the breech to
lay waste the town (Kittredge).

114. *breech'd*] doubtless suggested by
'breach' (111) and meaning 'covered
as with breeches, covered with gore up
to the hilts'; and this of course would
be 'unmannerly' as contrasted with
'mannerly' breeches, i.e. the sheaths.
Harris, *M.L.N.*, xxi. 12, quotes from
Guazzo, *The Ciuile Conversation*, tr. G.
Pettie, 1586: 'you meane by your
wordes to include mee in the number
of the melancholike, which have *their
wit so breeched*, that they cannot discerne sweete from sowre.' The italicized words translated 'le cerveau
obfusqué'. Harris thinks that '*breech*'
was more or less current (perhaps
current only as an affectation) in the
sense of 'cover over' (of the mind,
'becloud'), the original sense being, no
doubt, 'cover as with breeches'. But,
though affected, the image fits in with
the clothing imagery of the play.

117–23. *Look . . . motion*] These
asides are spoken while Lady Macbeth

Mal. [*Aside to Don.*] Why do we hold our tongues, that
    most may claim
    This argument for ours?
Don. [*Aside to Mal.*]   What should be spoken
    Here, where our fate, hid in an auger-hole,   120
    May rush, and seize us? Let's away:
    Our tears are not yet brew'd.
Mal. [*Aside to Don.*]   Nor our strong sorrow
    Upon the foot of motion.
Ban.   Look to the Lady:—
                  [*Lady Macbeth is carried out.*
    And when we have our naked frailties hid,
    That suffer in exposure, let us meet,   125
    And question this most bloody piece of work,
    To know it further. Fears and scruples shake us:

118, 119, 122. S.D.] *Staunton; not in F.*
tongues, / ours? / here, / hole, / away, /
arrangements.   120. in] within *F3–4.*
hole, *F1.*   123. S.D.] *Rowe; not in F.*

118–22. Why . . . sorrow] *lines end*
brew'd. / Sorrow *F; various alternative*
auger-hole,] awger-hole, *F3;* augure
125. exposure,] exposure; *F.*

is being revived from her fainting-fit—
which may be real or pretended. I
believe the arrangement of these lines
is new, though all editors make some
change in the Folio arrangement. It is
better to have the metrical pause
between 'Look to the lady' and the
asides, than between Malcolm's and
Donalbain's speeches. Similarly, by
preserving the Folio arrangement
(121–2) a metrical gap is avoided
between the speeches of Donalbain
and Malcolm, and the *our,* by coming
at the beginning of the line, has its
proper emphasis. Donalbain is contrasting the attitude of himself and his
brother with the suspiciously glib
emotion displayed by the Macbeths.

119. *argument*] subject or theme. Cf.
Tim., III. iii. 20: 'So it may prove an
argument of laughter.'

120. *where . . . auger-hole*] Cuningham
proposes to begin the line with 'where-
out' and assumes that Donalbain
means that their fate may be 'lurking
in any minute spot', ready to rush and
seize them. Cf. *Cor.,* IV. vi. 87: 'Confined / Into an auger's bore'. Bradley

quoted Scot, *The Discouerie of Witchcraft,* I. 4: 'they (witches) can go in and
out at awger holes.' I suppose this
passage may have suggested the image
to Shakespeare; but, as Chambers
points out, he may have been thinking
primarily of 'a hole made with a
sharp point, as of an auger—or a
dagger'.

123. *Upon . . . motion*] 'yet begun to
express itself'.

Look . . . Lady] Flatter, *op. cit.,* p. 12,
believes that a character never completes the line of another's aside; so
that we should perhaps assume that
these words begin a fresh line, the
metrical gap being filled by stage
business. It is more likely, I think, that
a cut has here obscured Shakespeare's
intentions.

124, 131.] The circumlocutions may
be explained by the clothing imagery
of the play; Shakespeare calls so many
other things *clothes,* that he must call
clothes something else; 'naked frailties'
= unclothed, and therefore weak,
bodies.

127. *scruples*] doubts.

In the great hand of God I stand; and thence
Against the undivulg'd pretence I fight
Of treasonous malice.
Macd.   And so do I.
All.   So all.   130
Macb. Let's briefly put on manly readiness,
And meet i'th'hall together.
All.   Well contented.
                    [*Exeunt all but Malcolm and Donalbain.*
Mal. What will you do? Let's not consort with them:
To show an unfelt sorrow is an office
Which the false man does easy. I'll to England.   135
Don. To Ireland, I: our separated fortune
Shall keep us both the safer; where we are,
There's daggers in men's smiles: the near in blood,
The nearer bloody.
Mal.   This murtherous shaft that's shot
Hath not yet lighted, and our safest way   140
Is to avoid the aim: therefore, to horse;
And let us not be dainty of leave-taking,
But shift away. There's warrant in that theft
Which steals itself, when there's no mercy left.   [*Exeunt.*

133–9. What . . . bloody] *so Rowe; nine lines, ending* doe? / them: / Office / easie. /
England. / I: / safer: / Smiles; / bloody. *F.*   141. horse;] house, *F2–4.*

128–9. hand . . . stand; thence . . . pre-
tence] Note rhymes. Perhaps two coup-
lets have been rewritten as blank verse.

129. pretence] design. Cf. II. iv. 24 post
and *Lr.*, I. iv. 75: 'a very pretence and
purpose of unkindness'. Banquo presumably fears that Macbeth will kill
Malcolm.

131. manly readiness] Cuningham
said this meant merely 'men's clothes'.
But it surely implies 'warlike equip-
ment or temper' (New Clarendon).
'Ready' frequently means *dressed*, and
'unready' *undressed*. Cf. *Cym.*, II. iii. 87.
Case prefers the straightforward abstract meaning.

135. easy] i.e. easily.

138. the near] i.e. the nearer. Cf. *R2*,
v. i. 88: 'Better far off than near, be
ne'er the near'. Donalbain means
Macbeth, Duncan's kinsman. Cf. *R3*,
II. i. 92: 'Nearer in bloody thoughts,
but not in blood'. The phrase means,
'The closer our relationship, the more
likely he is to murder us.'

142. dainty] particular.

143. shift away] slip off.
warrant] justification.

143–4. theft . . . steals] Cf. *All's W.*,
II. i. 33: '*Bert.* I'll steal away. *First Lord.*
There's honour in the theft.'

SCENE IV.—[*Without the castle.*]

Enter ROSSE *and an Old Man.*

Old M. Threescore and ten I can remember well;
Within the volume of which time I have seen
Hours dreadful, and things strange, but this sore night
Hath trifled former knowings.

Rosse.   Ha, good Father,
Thou seest the heavens, as troubled with man's act,   5
Threatens his bloody stage: by th'clock 'tis day,
And yet dark night strangles the travelling lamp.
Is't night's predominance, or the day's shame,
That darkness does the face of earth entomb,
When living light should kiss it?

Old M.   'Tis unnatural,   10
Even like the deed that's done. On Tuesday last,
A falcon, towering in her pride of place,

S.D. *Without the castle.*] *Hanmer.*   4. Ha] Ah *Rowe.*   6. Threatens] Threaten
Rowe.   his] this *Theobald.*   7. travelling] *F3–4;* trauailing *F1–2.*   10.
should] shall *F2.*

This scene, as Liddell remarks, serves as a chorus; but by means of the portents it underlines the unnaturalness of Duncan's murder, it reports the success of Macbeth's schemes, and it gives us a taste of Macduff's integrity.

S.D. Without the castle] Theobald's localizing of the scene has been followed by all editors, presumably on the ground that Macduff arrives with the latest news from the castle.

3. *sore*] dreadful, grievous. Cf. Scottish *sair.*

4. *trifled . . . knowings*] i.e. made former experience seem trifling.

Ha] All editors have followed Rowe's emendation to 'Ah'; but there seems to be no point in the change.

6. *Threatens*] a common use of singular verb with plural subject.

stage] Whiter, *Specimen of a Commentary*, pp. 160–1, shows that this word was suggested by the theatrical

meaning of 'heavens', i.e. roof of the stage.

7. *travelling*] The word was spelt indifferently 'travel' and 'travail', and both meanings may be intended.

lamp] i.e. the sun.

8. *Is't . . . shame*] 'Is night triumphant in the deed of darkness . . . or is day ashamed to look upon it?' (Clarendon).

predominance] astrological influence. Cf. *Troil.*, II. iii. 138: 'his humorous predominance', and *Lr.*, I. ii. 134: 'spherical predominance'.

12. *towering . . . place*] terms of falconry. 'Towering' means mounting higher and higher in wide circles, and 'place' is the highest 'pitch' or flight attained by the hawk before stooping. Cf. *John*, v. ii. 149. Turberville, *Book of Falconrie*, ed. 1611, p. 53, writes of 'the number of those Hawkes that are hie flying and towre Hawks'.

Was by a mousing owl hawk'd at, and kill'd.
Rosse. And Duncan's horses (a thing most strange and
    certain)
    Beauteous and swift, the minions of their race,   15
    Turn'd wild in nature, broke their stalls, flung out,
    Contending 'gainst obedience, as they would make
    War with mankind.
Old M.   'Tis said, they eat each other.
Rosse. They did so; to th'amazement of mine eyes,
    That look'd upon't.

Enter MACDUFF.

              Here comes the good Macduff.   20
    How goes the world, Sir, now?
Macd.   Why, see you not?
Rosse. Is't known, who did this more than bloody deed?
Macd. Those that Macbeth hath slain.
Rosse.   Alas, the day!
    What good could they pretend?
Macd.   They were suborn'd.
    Malcolm, and Donalbain, the King's two sons,   25
    Are stol'n away and fled; which puts upon them
    Suspicion of the deed.
Rosse.   'Gainst nature still:
    Thriftless Ambition, that will ravin up

---

14. And . . . certain)] *so Pope; two lines, the first ending* horses *F.*   17–18. would
make War *so Steevens (1793); line 17 ends* would *F.*   18. eat] ate *Singer.*
19–20. They . . . Macduff] *so Pope; three lines, ending* so: / upon't. / Macduffe. *F.*
28. will] *F;* wilt *Warburton.*   ravin up] *Theobald;* rauen up *F1;* raven upon
F2–4.

14. *horses*] Walker conj. 'horse', the
old collective plural. Cf. IV. i. 140:
'the galloping of horse'.

15. *minions*] darlings, favourites, i.e.
best of their breed. According to
Chambers the owl and the horses
symbolize the traitor who struck the
king. But it may be an exhibition of
demonic power over the elements of
nature (cf. note on II. iii. 53) or a reflection of the violation of the natural
order which the murder involves.

17. *as*] as if. Cf. II. ii. 27 *ante.*

24. *pretend*] intend. Cf. 'pretence'
(II. iii. 129 *ante*).

suborn'd] instigated to commit any
evil action.

27–9. *'Gainst . . . means*] R. Walker,
op. cit., p. 79, comments: 'Ostensibly the words relate to Malcolm and
Donalbain. . . But how much better
the words describe Macbeth!'

28. *will*] No emendation is required
as this use was common in Elizabethan
English.

ravin up] swallow greedily. Cf. IV. i.

> Thine own life's means!—Then 'tis most like
> The sovereignty will fall upon Macbeth.　　　　30
>
> *Macd.* He is already nam'd, and gone to Scone
> 　To be invested.
>
> *Rosse.* 　　　　　　　Where is Duncan's body?
>
> *Macd.* Carried to Colme-kill,
> 　The sacred storehouse of his predecessors,
> 　And guardian of their bones.
>
> *Rosse.* 　　　　　　　Will you to Scone? 　35
>
> *Macd.* No cousin; I'll to Fife.
>
> *Rosse.* 　　　　　　　Well, I will thither.
>
> *Macd.* Well, may you see things well done there:—adieu!—
> 　Lest our old robes sit easier than our new!
>
> *Rosse.* Farewell, Father.
>
> *Old M.* God's benison go with you; and with those 　40
> 　That would make good of bad, and friends of foes!
>
> 　　　　　　　　　　　　　　[*Exeunt.*

---

29. Thine] Its *Hanmer.* 　　life's] *Pope;* liues *F.* 　　33. Colme-kill,] Colmeshill, *Rowe;* Colmeskill, *Johnson.* 　　37. Well, may] *Theobald;* Well may *F.* 　　40. you;] you Sir, *F2–4.*

---

24 *post*; *Meas.*, I. ii. 133: 'Like rats that ravin down their proper bane'; and Jonson, *Every Man in His Humour*, III. iv. 42: 'I am sure on't; for they rauen vp more butter, then all the dayes of the weeke beside.'

31. *nam'd*] chosen.

Scone] The ancient royal city, probably the capital of the old Pictish kingdom, about two miles north of Perth. The Stone of Destiny, on which the Scottish kings were crowned, was thought to have been Jacob's pillow: it was purloined by Edward I in 1296 and taken to Westminster Abbey.

33. *Colme-kill*] Iona. See note on I.

ii. 63 *ante* and Appendix, p. 172.

36. *I will thither*] The verb of motion is sometimes omitted. Cf. *R2*, I. ii. 73: 'desolate will I hence and die.'

37. *Well . . . well*] ironical repetition of Rosse's 'well'.

40–1. *and with . . . foes*] Fleay and Wilson suspect an interpolation, but the couplet contains the antitheses so common through the play. 'The Old Man rightly judges Rosse as a mere time-server' (Chambers). The blessing, however, is more likely to be sincere. 'The Old Man blesses those who would transform bad into good and foes into friends' (Flatter).

ACT III

SCENE I.—[*Forres. A room in the palace.*]

Enter BANQUO.

Ban. Thou hast it now, King, Cawdor, Glamis, all,
  As the Weïrd Women promis'd; and, I fear,
  Thou play'dst most foully for't; yet it was said,
  It should not stand in thy posterity;
  But that myself should be the root and father   5
  Of many kings. If there come truth from them
  (As upon thee, Macbeth, their speeches shine),
  Why, by the verities on thee made good,
  May they not be my oracles as well,
  And set me up in hope? But, hush; no more.   10

Sennet sounded. Enter MACBETH *as King;* LADY MACBETH, *as Queen;* LENOX, ROSSE, *Lords and Attendants.*

ACT III

Scene 1

S.D. *Forres . . . palace.*] *Capell.*   10. *Lady . . . Lenox*] *Rowe;* Lady Lenox F.

1–10. *Thou . . . more*] In Holinshed, Banquo is Macbeth's accomplice in the murder of Duncan; but as he was James I's ancestor he had to be treated with some respect. For purely dramatic reasons it was obviously desirable to contrast Macbeth and Banquo, and to give Macbeth and his wife no accomplices. Bradley, *Shakespearean Tragedy*, pp. 384–5, thinks that this speech proves that Banquo has become an accessory to the murder because, out of ambition, he has kept silent about the witches and thus refrained from exposing Macbeth. Wilson argues that Shakespeare could not have depicted James I's ancestor as a cowardly time-server, and refers to Macbeth's oblique compliments later in the scene (49–52 'royalty of nature', 'dauntless temper', 'wisdom'). He suggests further, and rather weakly, that in the un-cut *Macbeth*, Banquo may have been working with Macduff on behalf of Malcolm. If so, the cut (which on Wilson's theory was made by Shakespeare himself) was a very queer one. Cf. Introduction, p. xxv.

3. *play'dst*] Cf. I. v. 21.

4. *stand*] Cf. *MND.*, v. i. 417.

5. *root*] possibly suggested by the Banquo tree in Leslie (Paul).

10. S.D. Sennet] 'A word chiefly oc-

Macb. Here's our chief guest.

Lady M.   If he had been forgotten,
    It had been as a gap in our great feast,
    And all-thing unbecoming.

Macb. To-night we hold a solemn supper, Sir,
    And I'll request your presence.

Ban.   Let your Highness   15
    Command upon me, to the which my duties
    Are with a most indissoluble tie
    For ever knit.

Macb. Ride you this afternoon?

Ban.   Ay, my good Lord.

Macb. We should have else desir'd your good advice   20
    (Which still hath been both grave and prosperous)
    In this day's council; but we'll take to-morrow.
    Is't far you ride?

Ban. As far, my Lord, as will fill up the time
    'Twixt this and supper: go not my horse the better,   25
    I must become a borrower of the night,
    For a dark hour, or twain.

Macb.   Fail not our feast.

Ban. My Lord, I will not.

Macb. We hear, our bloody cousins are bestow'd
    In England, and in Ireland; not confessing   30
    Their cruel parricide, filling their hearers
    With strange invention. But of that to-morrow,
    When, therewithal, we shall have cause of State,

---

13. all-thing] *F1*; all-things *F2*; all things *F3–4*.   15. Let your Highness] Lay
your Highness's *D'Avenant, Rowe*; Set your highness' *conj. Mason.*   16. upon]
be upon *Keightley.*   20–3. We . . . ride?] *lines end* desir'd / grave, / but / ride?
Pope.   22. take] talk *Malone;* take't *Warburton* (*MS.*) *and Keightley* (*apud Camb.*).

curring in the stage-directions of old
plays, and seeming to indicate a particular set of notes on the trumpet or
cornet, different from a flourish'
(Nares).

  13. *all-thing*] wholly; or everything.

  14. *solemn*] formal or ceremonious.
Cf. *MND.*, IV. i. 191: 'We'll hold a
feast in great solemnity.'

  15–16. *Let . . . which*] 'Command
upon' is an unusual phrase for 'lay
your command upon', but such tele-

scoping is not unique in Shakespeare.
Cuningham thought that the antecedent of 'which' was 'Command', the
Clar. Edd. thought it was 'the idea
contained in the preceding clause',
and Case that it was 'your highness'.

  21. *still . . . prosperous*] always . . .
profitable.

  25. *go . . . horse*] i.e. if my horse go not.
Cf. *R2*, II. i. 300: 'Hold out my horse,
and I will first be there.'

  33. *cause*] subject, matter of debate;

Craving us jointly. Hie you to horse: adieu,
Till you return at night. Goes Fleance with you?   35
Ban. Ay, my good Lord: our time does call upon's.
Macb. I wish your horses swift, and sure of foot;
And so I do commend you to their backs.
Farewell.—   [*Exit Banquo.*
Let every man be master of his time   40
Till seven at night;
To make society the sweeter welcome,
We will keep ourself till supper-time alone:
While then, God be with you.
                    [*Exeunt all except Macbeth and a Servant.*
                              Sirrah, a word with you.
Attend those men our pleasure?
Serv.   They are, my Lord,   45
Without the palace gate.
Macb.   Bring them before us.
                                                  [*Exit Servant.*
To be thus is nothing, but to be safely thus:
Our fears in Banquo
Stick deep, and in his royalty of nature
Reigns that which would be fear'd: 'tis much he
          dares;   50

34-5. Craving . . . you?] *so Pope; three lines, ending* Horse: / Night. / you? F.
38. I do] do I *F3-4*.   41-7. Till . . . safely thus:] *lines end* societie / welcome: /
alone: / you. / men / pleasure? / Gate. / us. / safely thus: F.   41-2. night; To
. . . welcome,] *Theobald;* Night, to . . . welcome: F.   48-50. Our . . . dares;]
lines end deepe, / that / dares, F.

cf. IV. iii. 196 *post*, where the 'general
cause' means the public interest.
   41-8.] The Folio arrangement of
these lines cannot be right, and all
editors have made some changes. But
no editor since Rowe has kept 47
intact and the rhythm of 41-6, as
usually printed, is dreadfully flabby.
The Folio printers made the mistake
of adding 'to make societie' to the
short line 41, but they realized that 43
was a complete line. The shortness of
line 48 enables a dramatic pause to be
made after the key line, 47.
   44. *While*] until. Cf. *R2*, IV. i. 269:
'Read o'er the paper while the glass

doth come.' This usage is still common
in the North of England.
   God . . . you] i.e. God b'wi'you
(= good-bye), and so scanned.
   47. *To be thus . . . thus*] i.e. to be a king
in name is nothing, but to reign in
safety is the thing. Cf. III. ii. 6, 13-26,
32.
   49. *Stick deep*] like thorns (Wilson).
   49-53. *royalty . . . safety*] Stewart,
M.L.R., 1945, p. 172, claims rightly
that 'the ungrudging recognition and
boundless admiration' expressed in
this speech are not, as some critics
believe, psychologically unconvincing.
'It is surely natural enough for Mac-

And, to that dauntless temper of his mind,
He hath a wisdom that doth guide his valour
To act in safety. There is none but he
Whose being I do fear: and under him
My Genius is rebuk'd; as, it is said,   55
Mark Antony's was by Cæsar. He chid the Sisters,
When first they put the name of King upon me,
And bade them speak to him; then, prophet-like,
They hail'd him father to a line of kings:
Upon my head they plac'd a fruitless crown,   60
And put a barren sceptre in my gripe,
Thence to be wrench'd with an unlineal hand,
No son of mine succeeding. If't be so,
For Banquo's issue have I fil'd my mind;
For them the gracious Duncan have I murther'd;   65
Put rancours in the vessel of my peace,
Only for them; and mine eternal jewel
Given to the common Enemy of man,
To make them kings, the seed of Banquo kings!
Rather than so, come, fate, into the list,   70
And champion me to th'utterance!—Who's there?—

---

69. seed] *Pope;* Seedes *F.*   71. And . . . there] *so Pope; two lines, the first ending*
utterance. F.

---

beth to assert that the enemy he fears
and proposes to have assassinated is a
formidable enemy, of regal temper, at
once daring and prudent. Anyone who
doubts this should try writing a speech
for Macbeth in which Banquo is
represented as timid, foolish, and
generally negligible.' See Introduction
p. lvi.

55–6. *My Genius . . . Cæsar*] Cf. *Ant.,*
II. iii. 19, and North's *Plutarch* (Temple
ed. IX, pp. 43–4): 'For thy demon, sàid
he (that is to say, the good angell and
spirit that keepeth thee), is afraid of
his: and being couragious and high
when he is alone, becometh fearfull
and timorous when he cometh neare
vnto the other.'

60–3. *Upon . . . succeeding*] This part
of the prophecy had not been mentioned earlier as it was necessary in
I. iii for the prospect of kingship to

appear 'entirely unclouded' (Schanzer).

62. *with*] i.e. by. Cf. e.g. *Wint.,*
v. ii. 68.

64. *fil'd*] defiled. The word is used
by Spenser, *Faerie Queene,* III. i. 62, and
Wilkins, *Miseries of Inforc'd Marriage*
(Dodsley, ed. Hazlitt, IX. 511).

66. *Put . . . peace*] Wilson compares
Ps., xi. 6, and Isa., li. 17. Grierson
suggests the image is drawn from the
sacramental cup.

67. *eternal jewel*] immortal soul. Cf.
Oth., III. iii. 361 : 'eternal soul'.

69. *seed*] Possibly F is correct (Paul).

71. *champion me*] Cuningham thought
this 'must mean that Fate is called in to
be Macbeth's champion to defend his
royal title'; but Macbeth is rather
challenging Fate to the combat
(*O.E.D.*).

to th'utterance] Holinshed, III. 560*a,*

Re-enter Servant, with two Murderers.

Now, go to the door, and stay there till we call.

                        [Exit Servant.

Was it not yesterday we spoke together?

1 *Mur.* It was, so please your Highness.

Macb.   Well then, now

Have you consider'd of my speeches?—know   75

That it was he, in the times past, which held you

So under fortune, which you thought had been

Our innocent self? This I made good to you

In our last conference; pass'd in probation with you,

How you were borne in hand; how cross'd; the

    instruments;   80

Who wrought with them; and all things else, that

    might,

To half a soul, and to a notion craz'd,

Say, 'Thus did Banquo.'

1 *Mur.*   You made it known to us.

Macb. I did so; and went further, which is now

Our point of second meeting. Do you find   85

Your patience so predominant in your nature,

74–81. It . . . might,] *so Rowe; lines end* then, / speeches: / past, / fortune, / selfe. / conference, / you: / crost: / them: / might *F.*   75. Have you] You have *F3.* speeches?—know] *Muir;* speeches: Know *F;* speeches? Know. *Rowe.*   78. self?] selfe. *F, etc.*   84–90. I . . . ever?] *so Rowe; lines end* so: / now / meeting, / predominant, / goe? / man, / hand / begger'd / euer? *F.*

---

has: 'the lord Mountainie . . . would not yeeld, but made semblance, as though he meant to defend the place, *to the utterance.*' Cotgrave defines 'Combatre à oultrance' as '. . . to *fight it out, or to the uttermost*'.

S.D. two Murderers] Granville-Barker says that 'the text's implication is surely that they were officers, cast perhaps for some misdemeanour and out of luck.' N.

75–8. *Have . . . self*] The F punctuation is possible; but editors usually insert a question-mark at 75, and as Macbeth informs the murderers that he has already told them about Banquo's villainy at a previous

conference, I believe the meaning is: 'Have you considered my speeches and [do you] know that it was he, etc.'

77. *under fortune*] beneath your deserts.

79. *pass'd in probation*] went over the proof.

80. *borne in hand*] i.e. deceived. Cf. *Ham.,* II. ii. 67: 'That so his sickness, age and impotence / Was falsely borne in hand'. Cf. also *Meas.,* I. ii. 51–2, and Wyatt, *Poems,* ed. Muir, p. 15: 'For he that beleveth bering in hand / Plowithe in water and soweth in the sand.'

82. *notion*] mind.

That you can let this go? Are you so gospell'd,
To pray for this good man, and for his issue,
Whose heavy hand hath bow'd you to the grave,
And beggar'd yours for ever?
1 *Mur.*   We are men, my Liege. 90
Macb. Ay, in the catalogue ye go for men;
    As hounds, and greyhounds, mongrels, spaniels, curs,
    Shoughs, water-rugs, and demi-wolves, are clept
    All by the name of dogs: the valu'd file
    Distinguishes the swift, the slow, the subtle,   95
    The housekeeper, the hunter, every one
    According to the gift which bounteous Nature

93. clept] *Capell;* clipt *F;* cleped *Theobald;* clep'd *Hanmer.*

87-8. *gospell'd . . . man*] Cf. Matt., v. 44 (Geneva): 'Loue your enemies: blesse them that curse you: doe good to them that hate you, and pray for them which hurt you, and persecute you.' In the scenes relating to the murder of Banquo there seem to be several echoes from verses in the same chapter. Cf. 107 'perfect' and v. 48; 127 'shine' and v. 16; III. iii. 16 'rain . . . come down' and v. 45; III. iii. 11–12 'go . . . mile' and v. 41; and perhaps III. i. 108 'vile blows and buffets' and v. 39; and III. i. 141, 'If . . . to-night' and v. 10—implying that Banquo is persecuted for righteousness' sake.

90. *men*] Gervinus notes that Macbeth uses the very means which had wrought most effectually upon himself: he appeals to the manliness of the murderers.

91–100. *Ay . . . men*] 'an image of order' (Knights).

93. *Shoughs*] 'what we now call *shocks*' (Johnson); a shag-haired dog. Steevens quotes Nash, *Lenten Stuffe,* ed. McKerrow, III. 182: 'they are for *Vltima Theule,* the north-seas, or *Island* [Iceland], and thence yerke ouer . . . a trundle-taile tike or *shaugh* or two.'

water-rugs] rough-haired water dog.

demi-wolves] 'dogs bred between wolves and dogs, like the Latin *lycisci*' (Johnson).

clept] called. The word was becoming obsolete in Shakespeare's day. Cf. *LLL.,* v. i. 23, and *Ham.,* I. iv. 19.

94. *the valu'd file*] 'The file or list where the value and peculiar qualities of everything are set down, in contradistinction to what he immediately mentions, "the bill that writes them all alike"' (Steevens). Cf. 101 *post* and v. ii. 8. See also *Meas.,* III. ii. 144: 'The greater file of the subject held the Duke to be wise.' It should be noted that *valu'd* is an adj. from the noun *value,* not the participle of the vb.

96. *housekeeper*] In Topsell, *History of Four-Footed Beasts,* 1608, pp. 160, the *housekeeper* is enumerated among the different kinds of dogs (Clarendon).

97. *According . . . gift*] Noble compares Eph., iv. 7, and Matt., xxv. 15.

bounteous Nature] *naturae benignitas.* The phrase is used by Erasmus in his *Colloquia* (ed. 1664, p. 662). Rea pointed out (*M.L.N.,* xxxv) that in the same colloquy there is a comparison between dogs and men, similar to Macbeth's. Shakespeare may have read the passage at school. For convenience I give H.M.'s translation, 1671, pp. 482–3: '*Sy.* All Dogs are contained under one *species,* but into how innumerable shapes is this special kind divided, so that thou wouldest say that they are distinguished in the *genus,* and not in the *species.* Now how

Hath in him clos'd; whereby he does receive
Particular addition, from the bill
That writes them all alike; and so of men.   100
Now, if you have a station in the file,
Not i'th'worst rank of manhood, say't;
And I will put that business in your bosoms,
Whose execution takes your enemy off,
Grapples you to the heart and love of us,   105
Who wear our health but sickly in his life,
Which in his death were perfect.

2 *Mur.*   I am one, my Liege,
Whom the vile blows and buffets of the world
Hath so incens'd, that I am reckless what
I do, to spite the world.

1 *Mur.*   And I another,   110
So weary with disasters, tugg'd with fortune,
That I would set my life on any chance,
To mend it, or be rid on't.

Macb.   Both of you
Know, Banquo was your enemy.

---

102. Not] And not *Rowe.*   say't] *F;* say it *Rowe.*   103. that] the *F3-4.*
105. heart] heart; *F.*   109. Hath] *F;* Have *most Edd.*   109-10. what I do]
line ends with doe *F.*   111. weary] weary'd *Capell.*   113-14. Both . . . enemy]
so Rowe ; one line *F.*

different are the manners and dis-
positions of Dogs even altogether of the
same special kind? *Ph.* There is a very
great variety. *Sy.* Suppose that which
is spoken of dogs, to be spoken of all the
several kinds of living creatures, but
the difference appeareth in no kind
more than in Horses. *Ph.* Thou sayest
true, but to what purpose dost thou
speak these things? *Sy.* Whatsoever
variety there is in the general kinds, or
in the shapes of living creatures, or in
every several creature, imagine all this
to be in man: Thou shalt find there
diverse Wolves, Dogs of an unspeak-
able variety.' This passage may have
been recalled to Shakespeare's mind
by the reference to *Genius* (55) for
Erasmus also mentions *Genius* (*op. cit.*,
p. 661).

98. *clos'd*] set, like a jewel (Wilson),
or just 'enclosed'.

99. *addition*] Cf. I. iii. 106 *ante.*

101. *file*] a pun on the two meanings
of 'file'—as in 94, and in the military
sense.

105. *Grapples*] Cf. *Ham.*, I. iii. 63:
'Grapple them to thy soul with hoops
of steel.'

111. *tugg'd*] scuffled. Cf. *Wint..*
IV. iv. 508: 'let myself and fortune /
Tug for the time to come.' The metaphor is apparently from a rough-and-
tumble at wrestling. Drayton, *Mortimeriados*, 2725, uses the same expression: 'Fortune and I have tugg'd
together so.' Cf. Daniel's *Epistle to
Southampton*, 1-2: 'He who hath neuer
warr'd with miserie, / Nor euer tugg'd
with Fortune and distresse'.

2 *Mur.*   True, my Lord.

Macb. So is he mine; and in such bloody distance,   115
　　That every minute of his being thrusts
　　Against my near'st of life: and though I could
　　With bare-fac'd power sweep him from my sight,
　　And bid my will avouch it, yet I must not,
　　For certain friends that are both his and mine,   120
　　Whose loves I may not drop, but wail his fall
　　Who I myself struck down: and thence it is
　　That I to your assistance do make love,
　　Masking the business from the common eye,
　　For sundry weighty reasons.

2 *Mur.*   We shall, my Lord,   125
　　Perform what you command us.

1 *Mur.*   Though our lives—

Macb. Your spirits shine through you. Within this hour,
　　at most,
　　I will advise you where to plant yourselves,
　　Acquaint you with the perfect spy o'th'time,

---

127. Your . . . most] *so Pope; two lines, the first ending* you. *F.*   129. the . . .
time] *F;* the perfect spot, the time *conj. Tyrwhitt;* a . . . time *conj. Johnson;* the
perfectry o' the time *conj. Beckett;* a perfect spy, o' the time *Collier MS.*

---

115. *distance*] in fencing, definite
interval of space to be kept between
the combatants (Onions); hence
enmity. Cf. Bacon, *Essays*, xv. *Of
Seditions and Troubles*: 'the Dividing
and Breaking of all Factions, and
setting them at distance, or at least
distrust amongst themselves'.

117. *near'st of life*] i.e. vital parts.
For the construction, cf. v. ii. 11 *post*
and *Meas.*, III. i. 17: 'best of rest'.

119. *avouch*] warrant, justify. Cf.
v. v. 47 *post*.

120. *For*] on account of, because of.
Cf. Abbott, *Shakes. Gram.*, § 150, and
Ven., 114.

121. *but*] Abbott, *Shakes. Gram.*, §
385, considers that the finite verb is to
be supplied here *without* the negative,
i.e. 'but (I must) wail his fall', etc.;
and compares 47 *ante*. Cuningham,
however, suggested 'but' was a corruption of 'would'.

122. *Who*] i.e. whom—frequent in
Shakespeare.

129. *the perfect . . . time*] The meaning
of this is much disputed: (i) the third
murderer (Johnson, who emends *the*
to *a*); (ii) *espyal* = exact intimation of
precise time (Heath); (iii) the exact
time most favourable to your purposes
(Steevens, who proposes a full-stop at
the end of 128). There are numerous
variations of these explanations
and many conjectural emendations.
If Johnson's explanation is correct, it is curious that Macbeth did
not introduce the two murderers
to the third. In Sc. iii they seem
surprised to see him. Wilson thinks
there has been a cut. Perhaps
for 'spy' we should read 'spial'
(= observation, watch—*O.E.D.*).
Flatter suggests that *perfect* is the
theatrical term, and that it relates to
time.

The moment on't; for't must be done to-night,   130
And something from the palace; always thought,
That I require a clearness: and with him
(To leave no rubs nor botches in the work),
Fleance his son, that keeps him company,
Whose absence is no less material to me   135
Than is his father's, must embrace the fate
Of that dark hour. Resolve yourselves apart;
I'll come to you anon.
2 *Mur.*   We are resolv'd, my Lord.
Macb. I'll call upon you straight: abide within.—
                              [*Exeunt Murderers.*
It is concluded: Banquo, thy soul's flight,   140
If it find Heaven, must find it out to-night.   [*Exit.*

SCENE II.—[*The same. Another room.*]

Enter LADY MACBETH *and a Servant.*

Lady M. Is Banquo gone from court?
Serv. Ay, Madam, but returns again to-night.

133. (*To . . . work*),] To . . . Worke: *F.*   139. S.D.] *Theobald;* Exeunt (*after 141*) *F.*

Scene II

S.D. *The same. Another room.*] *Capell.*

131. *something*] used adverbially, like 'somewhat'. Cf. *2H4*, I. ii. 212: 'a white head and something a round belly'.

thought] i.e. it being thought. Liddell quotes a similar idiom from Florio's *Montaigne*, I. xxv: 'Always conditioned the master bethinke himselfe where to his charge tendeth'.

132. *clearness*] 'So that he . . . might cleare himselfe' (Holinshed). Cf. Appendix, p. 173. The word also implies 'completeness'. Cf. l. 133.

133. *rubs*] Editors assume that the metaphor is from the bowling-green, a 'rub' being an impediment. Cf. *Ham.*,

III. i. 65, and *John*, III. iv. 128. But I doubt whether Shakespeare was thinking of bowls here. The word means 'a roughness; an unevenness or inequality' (*O.E.D.*) in a piece of work, as well as on a green. This interpretation is supported by 'botches', which means 'parts spoiled by clumsy work'.

Scene II

1. *Is . . . court?*] 'May not Lady Macbeth's suspicions have been aroused by the particularity with which she had heard her husband ask concerning Banquo's movements in III. i?' (Furness).

Lady M. Say to the King, I would attend his leisure
     For a few words.
Serv.   Madam, I will.   [*Exit.*
Lady M.   Nought's had, all's spent,
     Where our desire is got without content: 5
     'Tis safer to be that which we destroy,
     Than by destruction dwell in doubtful joy.

Enter MACBETH.

How now, my Lord? why do you keep alone,
Of sorriest fancies your companions making,
Using those thoughts, which should indeed have died 10
With them they think on? Things without all remedy
Should be without regard: what's done is done.
Macb. We have scorch'd the snake, not kill'd it:
She'll close, and be herself; whilst our poor malice
Remains in danger of her former tooth.   15
     But let the frame of things disjoint, both the worlds
          suffer,

---

11. all] *not in Hanmer.*   13. scorch'd] *F, Grierson, Wilson;* scotch'd *Theobald, etc.*   16. But . . . suffer] *so Theobald; two lines, the first ending* dis-joynt, *F.* disjoint] become disjoint *conj. Bailey.*   suffer] suffer dissolution *conj. Bailey.* But let the frame of things disjoint itself, *followed by Bailey's second conj.— conj. Cuningham.*

C y. ‖T⸓ ⸓⸓jʊ] ⸓f. ⸓⸓ ⸓. ⸓⸓ ⸓⸓⸓ ⸓ ⸓⸓⸓⸓⸓⸓⸓⸓ ⸓⸓ ⸓⸓⸓⸓⸓⸓⸓⸓ ⸓f. ⸓⸓⸓,
19–22 *post.*   I. ii. 3–7.

7. *doubtful*] full of doubt, suspicious, apprehensive. W. D. Sargeaunt, *Macbeth: The Play as Shakespeare Wrote It,* 1916, thinks the line means 'Than to dwell near destruction in joy doubtful (fearful) of destruction'; but the title of the book is somewhat misleading.

8–45.] 'One of the few strokes of pathos that are let soften the grimness of the tragedy is Lady Macbeth's wan effort to get near enough to the tortured man to comfort him. But the royal robes, stiff on their bodies—stiff as with caked blood—seem to keep them apart' (Granville-Barker, *op. cit.,* p. xli).

9. *sorriest*] Cf. II. ii. 20 *ante.*

10. *Using*] keeping company with,

entertaining as companions Cf. *Rom.,* I. ii. 3–7.

11. *without all remedy*] i.e. beyond all remedy. Cf. *MND.,* IV. i. 158: 'without the peril of the Athenian law', and *Wint.,* III. ii. 223: 'What's gone and what's past help / Should be past grief.'

12. *what's done is done*] Cf. I. vii. 1; v. i. 64.

13. *scorch'd*] slashed, as with a knife (*O.E.D.*). Theobald's emendation is unnecessary.

snake] possibly suggested by the serpentine trunk of the Banquo tree in Leslie's book. Cf. III. iv. 28 (Paul).

15. *her former tooth*] i.e. her tooth as formerly, before she was 'scorch'd'.

16. *But . . . suffer*] This line, unwieldy as it is, consists of two lines, both imperfect in the Folio. Shakespeare made

Ere we will eat our meal in fear, and sleep
In the affliction of these terrible dreams,
That shake us nightly. Better be with the dead,
Whom we, to gain our peace, have sent to peace,   20
Than on the torture of the mind to lie
In restless ecstasy. Duncan is in his grave;
After life's fitful fever he sleeps well;
Treason has done his worst: nor steel, nor poison,
Malice domestic, foreign levy, nothing   25
Can touch him further!
Lady M.   Come on:
Gentle my Lord, sleek o'er your rugged looks;
Be bright and jovial among your guests to-night.
Macb. So shall I, Love; and so, I pray, be you.
Let your remembrance apply to Banquo: 30
Present him eminence, both with eye and tongue:

20. peace] *F1; place F2–4.*   22. In . . . grave] *so Rowe; two lines, the first
ending* extasie. *F.*   28. among] *F1;* 'mong *F2–4.*   30. apply] still apply
F2–4.

frequent use of short lines, but he did
not have two together in the middle of
a speech. Bailey's conj. given above
seems to be unlike the style of the play,
and Cuningham's 'disjoint itself' is
flat. I suspect we should keep the
Folio lines, but emend the first to 'But
let the very frame of things disjoint'.
Cuningham compares *Ham.*, I. ii. 20:
'Our state to be disjoint and out of
frame'. In support of Bailey's conj. 'dissolution', Cuningham quotes *Troil.*,
v. ii. 156: 'The bonds of heaven are
slipp'd, dissolved, and loosed,' and
Tp., IV. i. 154: 'The great globe itself
. . . shall dissolve.' Wilson compares
1H4, III. i. 16. The metaphor is from
carpentry or house-building. Macbeth
would rather have the universe fall to
pieces than suffer from bad dreams.
Nashe, *Lenten Stuffe* (ed. McKerrow,
III. 214), uses 'disioynt' in an active
sense.

frame of things] i.e. the universe, both
the worlds, celestial and terrestrial.

18. *dreams*] Wilson says that the context (24–6 *post*) shows that he dreams

he is being murdered, apparently by
Banquo. This may be; but perhaps he
dreams, more terribly, of murdering
Duncan or Banquo—as Lady Macbeth was to do. His feeling of guilt
would make him fear Banquo.

20. *gain . . . to peace*] i.e. to gain the
peace of satisfied ambition have sent
to the peace of the grave. F2 ruins a
nice point. The critics who defend
'place' on the ground that Macbeth
did not gain 'peace' confuse fact and
intention.

21. *on . . . lie*] The metaphor is from
the rack.

22. *ecstasy*] 'Every species of alienation of mind, whether temporary or
permanent, proceeding from joy,
sorrow, wonder, or any other exciting
cause' (Nares, *Glossary*). Cf. *Err.*,
IV. iv. 50.

23. *fitful*] Shakespearian coinage.

30. *remembrance*] a quadrisyllable.
Cf. Abbott, *Shakes. Gram.*, § 477.

apply] be given.

31. *Present him eminence*] i.e. assign to
him the highest rank.

Unsafe the while, that we
Must lave our honours in these flattering streams,
And make our faces vizards to our hearts,
Disguising what they are.

Lady M.   You must leave this.   35

Macb. O! full of scorpions is my mind, dear wife!
    Thou know'st that Banquo, and his Fleance, lives.

Lady M. But in them Nature's copy's not eterne.

Macb. There's comfort yet; they are assailable:

32-3. Unsafe . . . streams,] *lines end* laue / streames, *F.*

32. *Unsafe . . . we*] The Folio line-division is wrong here, and something may be missing; but the general meaning is, 'For the time being we are unsafe, so that we must keep our honours clean by flattering Banquo and disguising our hatred.' Wilson comments that Macbeth fears exposure as well as assassination from Banquo. Grierson points out that 'flattering' has the force of a defining genitive. N.

36. *full . . . mind*] It has been suggested (*M.L.N.*, LX) that there is a reference to the superstition that basil propagated scorpions. Topsell, *Historie of Serpents*, p. 225, says that '*Hollerius* . . . writeth that in Italy in his dayes, there was a man that had a Scorpion bredde in his braine, by continuall smelling to this herbe Basill, and *Gesner* by relation of an Apothecary in Fraunce, writeth likewise a storie of a young mayde, who by smelling to Basill, fell into an exceeding head-ach, whereof she dyed without cure, and after her death beeing opened, there were found little Scorpions in her braine.' Cf. Browne, *Vulgar Errors*, II. vii. 9 (ed. Keynes, II. 176) and the note on v. iii. 55.

38. *Nature's . . . eterne*] usually explained as 'their holding by "copy" from nature is not for ever'. Copy, or copyhold, is the tenure of lands 'at the will of the lord according to the custom of the manor', by copy of the manorial court-roll. Coke on Littleton (ed. 1670) c. ix, § 73: 'Tenant by copy of court roll is as if a man be seised of a manor within which manor there is a custom which hath been used to have lands and tenements, to hold to them and their heirs in fee simple, or fee tail, or for term of life, at the will of the lord according to the custom of the same manor.' Just as, in the case of the tenure of the estate being only for the life of the tenant, the estate would revert to the lord on the former's death, so the tenure of their lives by Banquo and Fleance under Nature as 'lady of the manor' would cease with their deaths. But Clarkson and Warren in an exhaustive discussion of the passage (*M.L.N.*, LV. 483-93) argue that copyholds were not subject to arbitrary termination; that Shakespeare does not specifically refer to copy of court-roll; and that elsewhere he never uses the terms copyhold or copy of court roll at all; and that by *copy* he invariably means (i) a thing to be copied, or (ii) the result of imitation, or some variation thereof. Shakespeare, perhaps, used the legal term inaccurately; and there is another legal metaphor, 49 *post*; but I agree in the main with Clarkson and Warren, and only add that the *legal* sense of *copy* may be an undertone of the passage. Kittredge compares Massinger, *Fatal Dowry*, IV. i, 'Nature's copy that she works form by', and *Oth.*, v. ii. 11.

39. *There's*] i.e. in that there is.
comfort] Cf. I. ii. 27 *ante*.

Then be thou jocund. Ere the bat hath flown   40
His cloister'd flight; ere to black Hecate's summons
The shard-born beetle, with his drowsy hums,
Hath rung Night's yawning peal, there shall be done
A deed of dreadful note.
Lady M.   What's to be done?
Macb. Be innocent of the knowledge, dearest chuck,   45
Till thou applaud the deed. Come, seeling Night,

42. shard-born] *F3;* shard-borne *F1-2.*   43-4. Hath . . . note] *so Rowe;*
lines end Peale, / note. *F.*   46. seeling] *F;* sealing *Rowe.*

40. *jocund*] a revealing adjective.
41. *cloister'd*] It may be used either
literally or metaphorically.
black Hecate] As Shakespeare was
aware (cf. *AYL.*, iii. ii. 2) Hecate is
properly another name for Diana and
Luna, so that 'black' might seem to be
an inappropriate epithet. Cf. 'pale'
(ii. i. 52). But already in *MND.* (v. i.
391) Shakespeare had described
Hecate almost as a personification of
Night, and 'black' also suggests *evil* as
well as *dark.*
42. *shard-born*] i.e. dung-bred
(*O.E.D.*) though most editors still
interpret as 'borne on scaly wings'.
Either meaning would suit *Ant.*, iii. ii.
20, though the latter is more appropriate to *Cym.*, iii. iii. 20, and, perhaps,
to the present context. It may be
another quibble. Baldwin, *Shakespeare's
Small Latine*, i. 635, supports *O.E.D.*
Cuningham quotes a passage from
Mouffet, *The Theater of Insects*, on the
tree-beetle: 'Some there are which fly
about with a little *humming*; some with
a terrible & with a formidable noise . . .
but their breeding in *dung*, their feeding, life, and delight in the same, this
is common to them all . . . especially in
the moneths of *July* and *August*, after
Sun-set, for then it flyeth giddily in
men's faces with a great *humming*. . .
We call them *Dorrs* in English. . . The
sheaths of their wings are of a light
red colour . . . in . . . 1574 . . . there fell
such a multitude of them into the
River *Severn*, that they stopt and clog'd
the wheels of the Water-mils.'

beetle] Armstrong, *Shakespeare's Imagination*, pp. 18–24, shows that the
word belongs to an image cluster including *crow* (50), *bat* (40), *night* (43),
and *deed* (44). Cf. *Lr.*, iv. vi. 13–38.
hums] Armstrong, *op. cit.*, pp. 44–5,
shows that after *c.* 1600 this word
appears in close proximity to death—
Banquo's death being the subject of
this speech. Cf. iii. vi. 42 and iv. iii. 203
post, which are linked to the threat to
Macduff and the murder of his family.
Also *H5*, i. ii. 202–4, where 'yawning'
is used: 'The sad-eyed justice, with his
surly hum, / Delivering o'er to executors pale / The lazy yawning drone'.
Armstrong might have added that
'executors pale' may be compared with
'that great bond which keeps me pale'
(49–50 *post*).
43–4.] Few editors have kept the
Folio arrangement of these lines.
45. *dearest chuck*] a familiar term of
endearment, in grim contrast to the
intended murder of Banquo.
46. *seeling*] In the language of
falconry to 'seel' was to sew up the
eyelids of a hawk by running a fine
thread through them, in order to make
her tractable. Cotgrave has: 'Siller les
yeux. *To seele, or sow vp, the eyelids; (and
thence also) to hoodwinke, blinde, keepe in
darknesse, depriue of sight.*' Cf. *Oth.*, iii.
iii. 210, and *Ant.*, iii. xiii. 112. R.
Walker, *op. cit.*, p. 104, remarks:
'Macbeth is simultaneously seeling up
the eye of nature and filling his whole
body with darkness.' The phrase 'is the
precise evil counterpart of the super-

Scarf up the tender eye of pitiful Day,
And, with thy bloody and invisible hand,
Cancel, and tear to pieces, that great bond
Which keeps me pale!—Light thickens; and the
    crow   50
Makes wing to th'rooky wood;

50–1. Which ... wood;] *so Rowe; lines end* thickens, / Wood: *F.*   50. pale] *F;*
paled *Hudson (conj. Staunton).*

ficially similar injunction, if thine eye
offend thee, pluck it out'.

49–50. *Cancel ... pale*] Seronsy compares Daniel, *The Queenes Arcadia,*
2564–7: 'Custome, who takes from vs
our priuiledge / To be our selues,
rendes that great charter too / Of
nature and would likewise cancell
man.' It may be added that six lines
earlier Daniel uses the phrase 'bonds
of mischiefe' which may have linked
up with 'that great charter' to form
Shakespeare's 'that great bond'. There
is, however, an even closer parallel (as
G. K. Hunter points out) in the episode
in Montemayor's *Diana* which was the
probable source of *The Two Gentlemen
of Verona,* as translated by B. Yonge
(1598). See Bullough, *Narrative and
Dramatic Sources of Shakespeare,* I. 252:
'How small account would I make of
my life (my deerest *Felismena*) for
cancelling that great bond, wherein
(with more then life) I am for ever
bound unto thee.' Shortly before this
Montemayor speaks of the knight's
'pale visage'.

49. *Cancel ... bond*] The legal metaphor was probably suggested by a
concealed pun on *seeling/sealing* (46)
and also by *copy* (38). Steevens compares *R3,* IV. iv. 77: 'Cancel his bond
of life, dear God, I pray', and *Cym.,*
v. iv. 27: 'Take this life, / And cancel
these cold bonds.' Macbeth means
'Cancel the bond by which Banquo
and Fleance hold their lives from
Nature' (New Clarendon). Some
think he refers to the promise of the
Weird Sisters to Banquo, but this, in
view of the above quotations and 38, is
unlikely. Keightley thought 'bond'

should be printed 'band' to rhyme
with 'hand'. Cf. 'The bands of life'
(*R2,* II. ii. 71). I am inclined to agree.

50. *pale*] Staunton's impression was
that this should be *paled,* on the ground
that the context required a word implying *restraint, abridgement of freedom,*
etc., rather than *dread;* and there is
something to be said for this view. Cf.
III. iv. 23 *post.* Wilson points out that
'paled' would develop another aspect
of 'bond' and 'only involves a simple
e:d misprint'. Shakespeare used the
word in *Cym.,* III. i. 19. But, on the other
hand, the word 'pale' may have been
suggested by the parchment. Cf. IV.
i. 84–5 ('bond of fate ... pale-hearted
fear') and note on 42 *ante.* Curry,
Shakespeare's Philosophical Patterns, p.
127, says that Macbeth 'recognizes
that the acts of conscience which
torture him are really expressions of
that outraged natural law, which inevitably reduces him as individual
to the essentially human. This is the
inescapable bond that keeps him pale.'

thickens] Malone compares Spenser,
Shep. Cal., March, 115: 'the welkin
thicks apace.'

crow] i.e. the rook: the carrion crow
is not gregarious.

51. *Makes ... wood*] Cuningham
thought that 'some words, the last
rhyming with *crow,* have been care-
lessly omitted ... either "all on a row"
or "in due arow" .' Few would agree.

rooky] i.e. black and filled with
rooks. There have, however, been
many attempts to save Shakespeare
from writing this excellent line, which
is regarded as tautological—'murky'
(Roderick), 'roky' = misty (various),

Good things of Day begin to droop and drowse,
Whiles Night's black agents to their preys do rouse.
Thou marvell'st at my words: but hold thee still;
Things bad begun make strong themselves by ill.   55
So, pr'ythee, go with me.   [*Exeunt.*

SCENE III.—[*The same. A park, with a road leading to the palace.*]

Enter three Murderers.

1 *Mur.* But who did bid thee join with us?
3 *Mur.*   Macbeth.

Scene III

S.D. *The same . . . palace.*] *Rowe. subst.*

'rouky' = perching, i.e. where the crow settles for the night (Cuningham), 'reeky' = steamy (Wilson), 'rooky' = foggy, misty (Scots and northern dial.), 'rouky' = chattering (from 'rouk', talk privately), 'rucky' (from 'ruck') = multitudinous. With the last two suggestions, cf. Meredith, *Modern Love*, 'multitudinous chatterings'.

52. *Good . . . drowse*] 'the motto of the entire tragedy' (Dowden).

53. *Night's . . . rouse*] Steevens quotes Sidney, *Astrophel and Stella*, xcvi. 10: 'In night, of Sprites the ghastly powers do stir'; and Ascham, *Toxophilus* (ed. Arber, p. 52): 'For on the nighte tyme & in corners, Sprites and theues, rattes and mise, toodes and oules . . . and noysome beastes, vse mooste styrringe, when in the dayelyght, and in open places whiche he ordenyed of God for honeste thynges, they darre not ones come, which thinge Euripides noted verye well, sayenge, *Il thinges the night, good thinges the daye doth haunt & vse.*' The quotation is from *Iphig. in Taur.*, 1027.

55. *Things . . . ill*] Wilson compares Seneca, *Agam.*, 115: 'per scelera semper sceleribus tutum est iter' ('The

safest path to mischiefe is by mischiefe open still'—Studley).

56. *So . . . me*] either 'consent to my design' or 'a mere exit note' (Chambers). But cf. 45 *ante*, which implies that Macbeth is not asking his wife's advice. See on this speech Empson, *op. cit.*, pp. 23–5.

Scene III

S.D. Enter three Murderers] Johnson here remarks: 'The *perfect* spy mentioned by Macbeth in the foregoing scene has, before they enter upon the stage, given them the directions which were promised at the time of their agreement; yet one of the murderers suborned, suspects him of intending to betray them; the other observes that, by his exact knowledge of *what they were to do* he appears to be employed by Macbeth, and needs not to be mistrusted.' It has been argued that the Third Murderer was Macbeth himself (*N.Q.*, 1869). Irving thought he was the attendant or servant mentioned in III. i (*Nineteenth Century*, 1877). Libby thought he was Rosse (*New Notes on Macbeth*). Another critic thought he was Destiny. These theories are all fantastic. Macbeth's agita-

2 *Mur.* He needs not our mistrust; since he delivers
    Our offices, and what we have to do,
    To the direction just.
1 *Mur.*   Then stand with us.
    The west yet glimmers with some streaks of day;   5
    Now spurs the lated traveller apace,
    To gain the timely inn; and near approaches
    The subject of our watch.
3 *Mur.*   Hark! I hear horses.
Ban. [*Within.*] Give us a light there, ho!
2 *Mur.*   Then 'tis he: the rest
    That are within the note of expectation,   10
    Already are i'th'court.
1 *Mur.*   His horses go about.
3 *Mur.* Almost a mile; but he does usually,
    So all men do, from hence to the palace gate
    Make it their walk.

Enter BANQUO, *and* FLEANCE, *with a torch.*

2 *Mur.*   A light, a light!
3 *Mur.*   'Tis he.
1 *Mur.* Stand to't.   15
Ban. It will be rain to-night.
1 *Mur.*   Let it come down.
    [*The First Murderer strikes out the light,
    while the others assault Banquo.*

---

6. lated] latest *F2–4*.   7. and] *F2;* end *F1*.   9–10. Give . . . expectation,]
lines end hee: / expectation, *F*.   9. 'tis] *F; it is Pope, Arden (ed. 1)*.   16. S.D.]
Wilson, subst.

tion in III. iv when he hears that
Fleance has escaped is proof that he
cannot have been present at the murder of Banquo. Shakespeare, as Wilson
suggests, introduces the Third Murderer to show that Macbeth, 'tyrantlike, feels he must spy even upon his
chosen instruments'.

    2. *He . . . mistrust*] i.e. we need not
distrust him.

    4. *To . . . just*] exactly according to
Macbeth's instructions.

4–8.] 'The lovely lines . . . are not
gutter-bred' (Granville-Barker, *op.
cit.*, p. 85). But 'it is . . . dangerous to
speak of certain characters as being
more "poetic" than others: in poetic
drama every one necessarily speaks
poetry' (Bethell, *Shakespeare and the
Popular Dramatic Tradition*, p. 65).

    6. *lated*] belated.

    7: *timely*] in good time.

    10. *note of expectation*] list of expected
guests.

Ban. O, treachery! Fly, good Fleance, fly, fly, fly!
    Thou may'st revenge—O slave!   [*Dies. Fleance escapes.*
3 *Mur.* Who did strike out the light?
1 *Mur.*   Was't not the way?
3 *Mur.* There's but one down: the son is fled.
2 *Mur.*   We have lost
    Best half of our affair.
1 *Mur.*   Well, let's away,   21
    And say how much is done.   [*Exeunt.*

SCENE IV.—[*A room of state in the palace.*]

A banquet prepared. Enter MACBETH, LADY MACBETH,
ROSSE, LENOX, *Lords, and Attendants.*

Macb. You know your own degrees, sit down: at first
    And last, the hearty welcome.
Lords.   Thanks to your Majesty.
Macb. Ourself will mingle with society,
    And play the humble host.
    Our hostess keeps her state; but, in best time,   5
    We will require her welcome.
Lady M. Pronounce it for me, Sir, to all our friends;
    For my heart speaks, they are welcome.

Enter first Murderer, to the door.

17. O . . . fly] *so Hanmer; two lines, the first ending* Trecherie *F.*   good] godd *F2.*
18. S.D.] *Pope; not in F.*   21–2. Well . . . done] *one line, F.*

Scene IV

S.D. *A room . . . palace.*] Capell, *subst.*   1–2. You . . . welcome] *so Capell (conj.
Johnson); lines end* downe: / welcome. *F; lines end* last / welcome. *Delius, Arden
(ed. 1).*   1. down: at first] down at first *conj. Johnson.*   at] to *conj. Johnson.*
5. best] *F1;* the best *F2–4.*

18. Fleance escapes] the turning
point of the play.

Scene IV

1–2. *at . . . last*] i.e. from beginning
to end. Cf. *1H6,* v. v. 102, and *Cym.,*
I. iv. 102.
    5. *state*] originally the canopy, then
the chair of state with a canopy.
Cotgrave has 'Dais or Daiz. *A cloth of
Estate, Canopie, or Heauen, that stands
ouer the heads of Princes thrones; also, the
whole State, or seat of Estate.*'
    6. *require*] request, not with the
modern meaning of demanding as of
right.

Macb. See, they encounter thee with their hearts' thanks.
Both sides are even: here I'll sit i'th'midst.   10
Be large in mirth; anon, we'll drink a measure
The table round.   [*Goes to door.*
There's blood upon thy face.
Mur.   'Tis Banquo's then.
Macb. 'Tis better thee without, than he within.
Is he dispatch'd?
Mur.   My Lord, his throat is cut;   15
That I did for him.
Macb.   Thou art the best o'th'cut-throats;
Yet he's good that did the like for Fleance:
If thou didst it, thou art the nonpareil.
Mur. Most royal Sir . . . Fleance is scap'd.
Macb. Then comes my fit again: I had else been perfect;   20
Whole as the marble, founded as the rock,

12–13. The table . . . then] *lines end* face. / then. *F, etc.*   14. he] him *Hanmer*.
15–19. Is . . . scap'd] *lines end* dispatch'd? / him. / Cut-throats, / Fleans: /
Nonpareill. / Sir / scap'd *F; lines end* dispatch'd? / him. / good, / it, / Sir, /
scap'd. *Rowe.*   20. Then . . . perfect] *so Pope; two lines, the first ending* againe: *F.*

10. *Both . . . even*] i.e. there are equal
numbers on both sides of the table.
But it has been suggested that the
phrase might mean, 'Lady Macbeth's welcome has now been answered by the guests' thanks, so
that both parties are now on a level,
quits.'
11. *large*] liberal, free. Cf. *Ant.*, III.
vi. 93: 'most large / In his abomina-
tions'.
13. *There's . . . face*] absurd from a
naturalistic point of view, but proper
to a murderer in a poetic play. In previous editions these words are printed
as part of the previous line; but it is
better to have the metrical gap before
these words than after. A pause is
necessary while Macbeth goes to the
door, and one is undesirable either
before or after the speech of the
murderer.
14. *'Tis . . . within*] 'I am more
pleased that the blood of Banquo
should be on thy face than in his body'
(Johnson). Hunter thinks the words

are an aside, meaning, 'It is better that
the murderer should be without the
banquet than that Banquo should be
inside as a guest'; but there is no
effective antithesis unless we construe:
'the blood is better outside thee than
inside him.'
15–19. *Is . . . 'scap'd*] This arrangement of the lines eliminates the superfluous break after *dispatch'd*, preserves
the Folio lineation in Macbeth's
speech (16–18) which Rowe and later
editors have abandoned, emphasizes
I (16), *he* (17), and *thou* (18), and provides an effective pause of embarrass-
ment before the murderer can bring
out his confession of failure (19). This
is suggested in the Folio by printing
the line as two. But Flatter, *op. cit.*,
p. 104, ends the lines with *nonpareil,*
Sir, again.
18. *nonpareil*] paragon. Cf. *Tw.N.*,
I. v. 273.
20. *perfect*] Cf. III. i. 107.
21. *founded*] immovable. Cf. Matt.,
vii. 25.

As broad and general as the casing air:
But now, I am cabin'd, cribb'd, confin'd, bound in
To saucy doubts and fears.—But Banquo's safe?
Mur. Ay, my good Lord, safe in a ditch he bides,   25
With twenty trenched gashes on his head;
The least a death to nature.
Macb.   Thanks for that.—
There the grown serpent lies; the worm, that's fled,
Hath nature that in time will venom breed,
No teeth for th'present.—Get thee gone; to-morrow   30
We'll hear ourselves again.   [*Exit Murderer.*
Lady M.   My royal Lord,
You do not give the cheer: the feast is sold,
That is not often vouch'd, while 'tis a-making,
'Tis given with welcome: to feed were best at home;
From thence, the sauce to meat is ceremony;   35
Meeting were bare without it.
Macb.   Sweet remembrancer!—

---

31. We'll] Well *F3*.   31. hear ourselves] *F;* hear't, ourselves, *Theobald;* hear,
ourselves *Steevens;* hear, ourselves, *Dyce*.   32. sold] cold *Pope*.   33. vouch'd]
vouched *Rowe*.   a-making,] *Hudson;* a making: *F1;* making *F2–4*.

---

22. *broad and general*] free and unrestrained.
   casing] surrounding.
23. *cribb'd*] shut in a hovel.
24. *saucy*] insolent, importunate.
24, 25. *safe*] Cf. III. v. 32–3.
26. *trenched*] cut.
27. *a death to nature*] enough to kill a
man (New Clarendon).
28. *worm*] serpent. Cf. *Ant.*, v. ii. 243.
31. *hear . . . again*] i.e. hear each other
again, when I shall receive a more
detailed account of the affair, and you
will get your promised reward. R.
Walker, *op. cit.*, p. 111, says, 'this
plural royalty will hear himself when
he hears the murderers again; murderers and "ourselves" are one.'
32–4. *the feast . . . welcome*] That feast
can only be considered as sold, not
given, during which the entertainers
omit such courtesies as may assure
their guests that it is given with
welcome (Dyce).

33. *vouch'd*] 'warranted', 'recom-
mended by words of welcome'. Cf.
III. i. 119.
35. *From thence*] i.e. away from
home.
   ceremony] a trisyllable, as frequently
in Shakespeare. Marston, *Sophonisba*,
I. ii. 5–27, has a discussion on the
value of ceremony, which may either
have suggested this passage or been
suggested by it.
36. *remembrancer!*] Perhaps, as Cuningham suggests, a playful reference
to the Remembrancers, officers of the
Exchequer, of whom there were three,
i.e. The King's Remembrancer, the
Lord Treasurer's Remembrancer, and
the Remembrancer of First Fruits. But
I can see little resemblance between
these functionaries and Lady Macbeth
who reminds Macbeth of his duties as
host, and 'remembrancer' probably
means simply 'one engaged or appointed to remind another'.

Now, good digestion wait on appetite,
And health on both!

Len.　　　　　　　　　May it please your Highness sit?

Macb. Here had we now our country's honour roof'd,
Were the grac'd person of our Banquo present;　　40

The Ghost of BANQUO *enters, and sits in* MACBETH's *place.*

Who may I rather challenge for unkindness,
Than pity for mischance!

Rosse.　　　　　　　　　His absence, Sir,
Lays blame upon his promise. Please't your Highness
To grace us with your royal company?

Macb. The table's full.

Len.　　　　　　　　Here is a place reserv'd, Sir.　　45

Macb. Where?

Len. Here, my good Lord. What is't that moves your
Highness?

Macb. Which of you have done this?

Lords.　　　　　　　　What, my good Lord?

Macb. Thou canst not say, I did it: never shake

---

40. S.D.] *See note below; after* without it *(36) F.*　　42. mischance!] *Pope;*
Mischance. *F.*　　43. Please't] *F;* Please it *Steevens.*　　47. Here . . . Highness]
so Capell; two lines, the first ending Lord. *F.*

---

39. *our . . . honour*] not, as Wilson suggests, 'all the rank and distinction of Scotland', but Banquo.

40. *grac'd*] gracious, gracing, or full of grace. Cf. *Lr.*, I. iv. 267: 'a graced palace'.

S.D.] The Folio marks the entrance of the Ghost after Lady Macbeth's last speech. This may be either a premature direction to give plenty of warning to the actor, or it may merely indicate that on the Elizabethan stage the ghost would have some distance to walk. According to Forman's account the Ghost entered as Macbeth began to speak of Banquo. I have marked the entrance accordingly. Wilson adheres to the Folio entrance, other editors have marked it at 43 and 45, but the favourite place is after 39. The Ghost appears when summoned. In De Loier's *Treatise of*

Spectres (1605), p. 113, King Thierry 'on an evening as he sat at supper' is haunted by the ghost of a man he has slain (Paul).

47. *Here . . . Highness?*] Wilson argues that F prints this line as two, to mark the pause as Macbeth recognizes the figure. Flatter, *op. cit.*, pp. 106–8, argues for the F lineation, and remarks that by printing 'Where?' in a line by itself, the pause comes here, thereby obliterating the essential pause after 'Here, my good Lord'— which, in a modern edition, should be printed as part of line 46. There is another pause after 'Highness?'

48. *done this*] i.e. killed Banquo.

49. *Thou . . . it*] 'He has had some strange childish notion that the second murder would not afflict his conscience if he did not wet his own hands in Banquo's blood' (Grierson).

Thy gory locks at me.   50
Rosse. Gentlemen, rise; his Highness is not well.
Lady M. Sit, worthy friends. My Lord is often thus,
    And hath been from his youth: pray you, keep seat;
    The fit is momentary; upon a thought
    He will again be well. If much you note him,   55
    You shall offend him, and extend his passion;
    Feed, and regard him not.—Are you a man?
Macb. Ay, and a bold one, that dare look on that
    Which might appal the Devil.
Lady M.   O proper stuff!
    This is the very painting of your fear: 60
    This is the air-drawn dagger, which, you said,
    Led you to Duncan. O! these flaws and starts
    (Impostors to true fear), would well become
    A woman's story at a winter's fire,
    Authoris'd by her grandam. Shame itself!   65
    Why do you make such faces? When all's done,
    You look but on a stool.
Macb.   Pr'ythee, see there!
    Behold! look! lo! how say you?
    Why, what care I? If thou canst nod, speak too.—
    If charnel-houses and our graves must send   70
    Those that we bury, back, our monuments
    Shall be the maws of kites.   [*Ghost disappears.*

---

63. Impostors to true] *F;* Impostors of true *Hanmer;* Impostures true to *conj.*
Johnson; Impostures of true *Capell.*   67–8. Pr'ythee . . . you?] *so F; one*
line, Capell.

54. *upon a thought*] in a moment. Cf.
Tp., IV. i. 164.
    56. *extend his passion*] i.e. prolong his
suffering or emotion.
    59. *stuff!*] Curry, *Shakespeare's Philo-
sophical Patterns*, p. 85, thinks 'Banquo's
ghost is an infernal illusion created out
of air by demonic forces and presented
to Macbeth's sight at the banquet in
order that the murderer may be confused and utterly confounded.' But
this is questionable. See Introduction,
p. lx.
    61. *air-drawn*] drawn on the air, or

drawn through the air, or both
(Wilson).
    62. *flaws*] sudden squalls or gusts of
wind, hence bursts of passion. Cf. *Ham.,*
v. i. 239, and *2H6,* III. i. 354.
    63. *to*] i.e. compared with.
    65. *Authoris'd*] sanctioned, warran-
ted, given on the authority of. The
accent is on the second syllable. Cf.
Sonn., xxxv. 6.
    67–8. *You . . . you?*] There seems to
be no point in altering the Folio division of these lines.
    71–2. *monuments . . . kites*] Wilson

Lady M.   What! quite unmann'd in folly?
Macb. If I stand here, I saw him.
Lady M.   Fie! for shame!
Macb. Blood hath been shed ere now, i' th' olden time,
    Ere humane statute purg'd the gentle weal;   75

75. humane] *F;* human *Theobald (ed. 2), etc.*

quotes Scot, *The Discouerie of Witch-craft,* v. vi: 'Some write that after the death of Nabuchadnezzar his sonne Eilusmorodath gave his bodie to the ravens to be devoured, least after-wards his father should arise from death.' The meaning would thus be: 'To prevent bodies from returning from the grave, we shall have to give them to the ravens to be devoured' (cf. Nashe, ed. McKerrow, III. 281).

There seems to be no substance in Harry Rowe's explanation that the food of carnivorous birds was vulgarly supposed to pass their stomachs undigested, the clause therefore meaning: 'Our monuments will be like the maws of kites in that they send back those that we bury *undigested.*' But Harting, *Ornithology of Shakespeare,* p. 46, mentions the kite's habit of disgorging the undigested portions of food; and Miss Dorothy Sasse calls my attention to Whitney, *Choice of Emblems,* 1586, p. 170, where the emblem represents two kites, one of which is disgorging 'what appears to be a knotted snake'. Underneath are the following verses: 'The greedie kyte, so full his gorge had cloy'de, / He could not brooke his late deuoured praie: / Wherefore with griefe, vnto his damme he cry'de, / My bowelles lo, alas, doe waste awaie. / With that quoth shee, why doste thou make thy mone, / This losse thou haste is nothinge of thy owne. / By which is mente, that they who liue by spoile, / By rapine, thefte, or griping goodes by mighte, / If that with losse they suffer anie foile, / They loose but that, where in they had no right! / Hereof, at firste the prouerbe oulde did growe: / *That goodes ill got, awaie as ill will goe.*'

Shakespeare may have unconsciously remembered these verses about ill-gotten gains, though I believe Wilson's explanation is correct. For the idea of a grave as a maw, compare *Rom.,* v. iii. 45 ff.: 'Thou detestable maw ... / Gorg'd with the dearest morsel of the earth, / Thus I enforce thy rotten jaws to open; / And, in despite, I'll cram thee with more food.' Armstrong, *Shakespeare's Imagination,* pp. 11–17, shows that 'kite' belonged to a cluster of ideas in the poet's mind, and that *bed, death, spirits, birds,* and *food* were likely to be mentioned in the same context. Cf. *Ham.,* II. ii. 595–620, and *Wint.,* IV. iii. 5–57. In the present context we have *sleep* (141), *monuments* (71), *ghost* (72), *birds* (124), *feed* (57), and *maws* (72). Steevens compares Spenser, *Faerie Queene,* II. viii. 16: 'But be entombed in the rauen or the Kight'; and Malone cites Kyd, *Cornelia,* v. i. 33–6: 'Where are our Legions? . . . the vultures and the Crowes, / Lyons and Beares, are theyr best Sepulchers.'

75. *humane*] not distinguished in Shakespeare's day from *human,* and as the word may here imply both meanings, it is better to retain F spelling. Cf. *Cor.,* III. i. 327: 'It is the humane way; the other course / Will prove too bloody.' See Empson, *op. cit.,* p. 258.

purg'd] This and other images of purging may have been suggested by James I's *Counter-Blaste to Tobacco*: 'For remedie whereof, it is the kings part (as the proper Phisician of his politicke-bodie) to purge it of all those diseases, by Medicines meete for the same' (Paul).

gentle weal] 'The *peaceable community,*

Ay, and since too, murthers have been perform'd
Too terrible for the ear: the time has been,
That, when the brains were out, the man would die,
And there an end; but now, they rise again,
With twenty mortal murthers on their crowns,   80
And push us from our stools. This is more strange
Than such a murther is.
Lady M.   My worthy Lord,
Your noble friends do lack you.
Macb.   I do forget.—
Do not muse at me, my most worthy friends,
I have a strange infirmity, which is nothing   85
To those that know me. Come, love and health to all;
Then, I'll sit down.—Give me some wine: fill full:—
I drink to th'general joy o'th'whole table,
And to our dear friend Banquo, whom we miss;
Would he were here!

Re-enter Ghost.

                    To all, and him, we thirst,   90
And all to all.
Lords.   Our duties, and the pledge.
Macb. Avaunt! and quit my sight! let the earth hide thee!
Thy bones are marrowless, thy blood is cold;
Thou hast no speculation in those eyes,

---

76. have] hath *Johnson.*   77. time has] *Grant White;* times has *F1;* time have
F2–4.

the state made quiet and safe by
human statutes' (Johnson). A proleptic use of the adjective, with the
meaning 'purged the commonwealth
and thus made it gentle'.
    80. *mortal murthers*] i.e. deadly
wounds, each of itself sufficient to
effect murder. Cf. 26–7 *ante.*
    90. S.D.] Grierson marks the
Ghost's re-entry here. 'He comes again
when summoned.' In the Folio the
entrance is marked after 88, but cf.
note on 40 *ante.*
    91. *all to all*] i.e. all good wishes to
all. Cf. *Tim.,* i. ii. 234: 'All to you.'
Wilson suggests that the phrase means,

'Let everybody drink to everybody.'
    94. *speculation*] i.e. the intelligence
arising in the brain but seen in the eye,
of which the eye is only the medium,
'intelligent or comprehending vision'
(*O.E.D.*). Cf. *Troil.,* iii. iii. 107–11:
'but eye to eye opposed / Salutes each
other with each other's form; / For
speculation turns not to itself, / Till it
hath travell'd and is mirror'd there /
Where it may see itself.' See also *Oth.,*
i. iii. 271: 'speculative . . . instruments'; and Bullokar, *Expositor,* 1616:
'Speculation: the inward knowledge
or beholding of a thing.'

Which thou dost glare with.

Lady M.   Think of this, good Peers, 95
But as a thing of custom: 'tis no other;
Only it spoils the pleasure of the time.

Macb. What man dare, I dare:
Approach thou like the rugged Russian bear,
The arm'd rhinoceros, or th'Hyrcan tiger;   100
Take any shape but that, and my firm nerves
Shall never tremble: or, be alive again,
And dare me to the desert with thy sword;
If trembling I inhabit then, protest me
The baby of a girl. Hence, horrible shadow!   105
Unreal mock'ry, hence!—   [*Ghost disappears.*
                          Why, so;—being gone,
I am a man again.—Pray you, sit still.

Lady M. You have displac'd the mirth, broke the good
      meeting
With most admir'd disorder.

Macb.   Can such things be,

104. I inhabit then,] *F1; I* inhabit, then *F2–4;* I inhibit, then *Pope, Theobald, Hanmer, Warburton, Halliwell;* I evade it, then *conj. Johnson;* I inhibit then, *Capell;* I inhibit thee, *Malone (conj. Steevens), Dyce;* I exhibit, then *A. Hunter (conj. Robinson);* I inhabit here *conj. Camb.;* I inherit then, *conj. Kinnear;* I, in habit then *conj. Jennens.*   protest] protect *F4.*   105. horrible] terrible *Theobald (ed. 2), Warburton, Johnson*   106 being gone,] he gone *F2–4*   108–9. broke ... disorder] *so Rowe; one line, F.*

98 *What ... dare*] This line would seem to be merely a continuation of Macbeth's last speech, Lady Macbeth's speech coming by way of parenthesis. Flatter, *op. cit.*, p. 110, suggests that the Macbeths speak simultaneously. This is improbable.

99-100. *bear ... tiger*] Cf. *H5*, III. vii. 154: 'Russian bear'; *3H6*, I. iv. 155: 'tigers of Hyrcania'. The Hircanian tiger and the rhinoceros are mentioned on adjacent pages of Holland's *Pliny*. N.

103. *dare*] Cf. *R2*, IV. i. 74: 'I dare meet Surrey in a wilderness'; i.e. for a fight to the death, with none to interrupt. See also *Cor.*, IV. ii. 23, and *Cym.*, I. i. 167.

desert] Cf. *Mor.V.*, II. vii. 41: 'Hyrcanian deserts'.

104. *If ... then*] three possible meanings: (i) If I inhabit, or house, trembling (Wilson); (ii) if I trembling stay at home (Henley); (iii) if I wear (inhabit) trembling (Maxwell).

105. *baby of a girl*] Not 'baby of an immature mother' (Clarendon), but 'girl's doll' (cf. Bald. *S.A.B.*, 1949, pp. 220–2), or 'baby girl' (Harrison *apud* Hudson). Cf. such a phrase as 'fool of a commentator'.

109. *admir'd*] wonderful, amazing.

disorder] 'lack of self-control' (Wilson); but there is an implied reference to the overthrowing of *order*—one of the main themes of the play.

And overcome us like a summer's cloud,   110
Without our special wonder? You make me strange
Even to the disposition that I owe,
When now I think you can behold such sights,
And keep the natural ruby of your cheeks,   114
When mine is blanch'd with fear.

Rosse.   What sights, my Lord?

Lady M. I pray you, speak not; he grows worse and worse;
    Question enrages him. At once, good night:—
    Stand not upon the order of your going,
    But go at once.

Len.   Good night, and better health
    Attend his Majesty!

Lady M.   A kind good night to all!   120
                [*Exeunt Lords and Attendants.*

Macb. It will have blood, they say: blood will have blood:
    Stones have been known to move, and trees to speak;

115. is] are *Malone.*   sights,] *F1;* signes *F2-4.*   121. It ... blood:] *so Rowe;*
two lines, the first ending say *F.*   blood, they say:] *F;* blood: they say, *Rowe;*
blood, they say *Pope;* blood.—They say, *Johnson.*

110. *overcome*] i.e. pass over.

111-12. *strange . . . owe*] i.e. self-
alienated or, perhaps, amazed at my
own nature. 'He had thought himself
brave; now, when he sees her un-
moved at sights which appal him, he
is staggered in his estimate of himself'
(Grierson).

112. *owe*] own, as often.

115. *mine*] the natural ruby of my
cheeks.

121. *It*] i.e. the murder of Banquo.
blood, they say: blood] As Simpson,
Shakespeare's Punctuation, p. 78, points
out, a colon often introduced a noun
clause, so that the Folio punctuation is
best represented by that of the text
(Wilson). But A. P. Rossiter argues
convincingly for the retention of F
punctuation, to preserve 'the rhythm
of terror'. Noble refers to Gen., ix. 6,
and Wilson to *Mirror for Magistrates,*
ed. Campbell, p. 99: 'Bloud wyll haue
bloud, eyther [at] fyrst or last.'

122. *Stones*] Two possible explanations: (i) covering the corpse of the

murdered man (Clarendon, Wilson);
(ii) Paton, *N.Q.,* 1869, argues that this
would only reveal the victim and not
the murderer. (But the discovery of
the corpse is the first step towards the
detection of the murderer.) He suggests that the allusion may be to the
rocking stones, or 'stones of judgment',
by which the Druids tested the guilt or
innocence of accused persons. There is
one near Glamis Castle, though there
is no reason to believe that Shakespeare had heard of it.

trees to speak] possibly a reminiscence of Scot, *Discouerie of Witchcraft*
(1930), VIII. vi. 94: 'This practice
began in the Okes of Dodona, in the
which was a wood, the trees thereof
(they saie) could speake.' Furness also
quotes from the same work, XI. xviii.
119: 'Divine auguries were such, as
men were made beleeve were done
miraculouslie, as when dogs spake; as
at the expulsion of Tarquinius out of
his kingdome; or when trees spake;
as before the death of *Caesar.*' Furness

Augures, and understood relations, have
By magot-pies, and choughs, and rooks, brought
   forth
The secret'st man of blood.—What is the night?   125
Lady M. Almost at odds with morning, which is which.
Macb. How say'st thou, that Macduff denies his person,
   At our great bidding?
Lady M.   Did you send to him, Sir?
Macb. I heard it by the way; but I will send.
There's not a one of them, but in his house   130

---

123. Augures] *F;* Augurs *Theobald;* Auguries *Rann (conj. Steevens).*   and
understood] that understood *Rowe;* that understand *Warburton.*

adds a reference to *Georgics,* I. 476-7, where Virgil, speaking of the portents before that event, says: 'Vox quoque per lucos vulgo exaudita silentes Ingens'. Most editors, however, follow Steevens in assuming that there is a reference to *Aen.,* III. 22-68, the story of the ghost of Polydorus speaking from a tree.

123. *Augures*] i.e. auguries. In Florio's *Worlde of Wordes,* 1598, *augure* is given as an equivalent of *soothsaying, prediction.* In the 1611 edition, the word is also given as an equivalent of *soothsayer.* Shakespeare uses the word *augury* twice, and *augurer* five times; but he also uses *augur (Sonn.,* 107, and *Phoenix and the Turtle,* where it may mean either *soothsayer* or *omen*). Wilson thinks that *Augures* here may be a misprint for *Auguries,* but the metre is better without emendation.

understood relations] not 'reports properly comprehended' (Kittredge) or 'overheard conversations' (*N.Q.,* 2 Dec. 1933). Johnson explained: 'the connection of effects with causes; to understand relations as an augur, is to know how those things relate to each other, which have no visible combination or dependence.' Schanzer compares *Per.,* IV. iii. 21-3, and interprets 'reports which could be understood' because the birds used human language. N.

124. *magot-pies*] i.e. magpies. (The Fr. *margot,* a familiar form of *Marguerite,* is also used to denote a magpie.)

choughs] The chough is a bird of the crow family, and the word formerly included all the smaller 'chattering' species, and esp. the jackdaw. See *MND.,* III. ii. 21 (note in Arden ed.), and *Tp.,* II. i. 265: 'a chough of as deep chat'.

125. *The . . . blood*] Wilson refers to a passage in James I's *Dæmonologie (Workes,* 1616, p. 136): 'for as in a secret murther, if the dead carkasse bee at any time thereafter handled by the murtherer, it will gush out of bloud, as if the bloud were crying to the heauen for reuenge of the murtherer, God hauing appoynted that secret supernaturall signe, for tryall of that secrete vnnaturall crime.' Furness refers to Florio's *Montaigne,* II. v. (Temple ed., III. 60).

126. *at odds with*] disputing with. Wilson comments: 'A symbolical timing of the central moment of the play; borne out by the immediate reference to Macduff, who is to usher in the dawn'.

127. *How say'st thou*] i.e. what do you say to this? Banquo being dead, Macbeth is driven towards the next murder.

130. *one*] Theobald conj. 'thane' and White 'man', but unnecessarily.

I keep a servant fee'd. I will to-morrow
(And betimes I will) to the Weïrd Sisters:
More shall they speak; for now I am bent to know,
By the worst means, the worst. For mine own good,
All causes shall give way: I am in blood   135
Stepp'd in so far, that, should I wade no more,
Returning were as tedious as go o'er.
Strange things I have in head, that will to hand,
Which must be acted, ere they may be scann'd.
Lady M. You lack the season of all natures, sleep.   140
Macb. Come, we'll to sleep. My strange and self-abuse
Is the initiate fear, that wants hard use:
We are yet but young in deed.   [*Exeunt.*

---

132. Weïrd] *Theobald;* weyard *F1;* wizard *F2-4;* wayward *Pope;* weird *Capell.*
134. worst. For . . . good] *Johnson;* worst, for . . . good, *F;* worst, for . . . good;
Rowe.   136. Stepp'd] (Stept) *F1;* Spent *F2-4.*   143. in deed] *Theobald;*
indeed *F.*

131. *fee'd*] Cf. Holinshed: 'in euerie
noble man's house one slie fellow or
other in fee with him'.

131-2. *I will . . . Sisters*] The Folio
has the phrase 'And betimes I will' in
brackets; but Shakespeare perhaps
intended the first 'I will' (131) to apply
to his sending to Macduff, and it
should be punctuated: 'I will to-
morrow: / And betimes I will to the
weird sisters.' Wheelock, *M.L.N.*, xv,
makes the same suggestion but since
betimes means *very early* we do not
remove the difficulty of the time
sequence in this and the following
scenes. But see Introduction, p. xxxiv.

135. *All . . . way*] i.e. everything else
must take second place.

I . . . blood] Cf. *MND.*, III. ii. 47:
'Being o'er shoes in blood, plunge in
knee deep, / And kill me too.' And,

closer, *R3,* IV. ii. 63-4: 'I am in / So
far in blood that sin will pluck on
sin.'

138-9. *Strange . . . scann'd*] Cf. IV. i.
145-8 *post.*

140. *season*] Whiter, *Specimen of a
Commentary,* p. 147, showed that
Shakespeare was thinking of the pre-
servative power of sleep. Cf. *Lucr.*, 796,
Ado., IV. i. 144, *Troil.*, I. ii. 278, and
Tw.N., I. i. 30. Macbeth, it will be
remembered, has murdered sleep.

141. *self-abuse*] deception, self-delu-
sion. Cf. II. i. 50.

142. *the initiate fear*] i.e. the fear of a
novice (Grierson).

hard use] practice that hardens one
(Kittredge).

143. *We . . . deed*] a 'line which
looks to nethermost hell' (Granville-
Barker).

SCENE V.—[*The heath.*]

Thunder. Enter the three Witches, meeting HECATE.

1 *Witch.* Why, how now, Hecate? you look angerly.
Hec. Have I not reason, beldams as you are,
 Saucy, and overbold? How did you dare
 To trade and traffic with Macbeth,
 In riddles, and affairs of death;   5
 And I, the mistress of your charms,
 The close contriver of all harms,
 Was never call'd to bear my part,
 Or show the glory of our art?
 And, which is worse, all you have done   10
 Hath been but for a wayward son,
 Spiteful, and wrathful; who, as others do,
 Loves for his own ends, not for you.
 But make amends now: get you gone,
 And at the pit of Acheron   15
 Meet me i'th'morning: thither he
 Will come to know his destiny.
 Your vessels, and your spells, provide,
 Your charms, and everything beside.
 I am for th'air; this night I'll spend   20
 Unto a dismal and a fatal end:
 Great business must be wrought ere noon.

Scene v

1. Hecate? . . . angerly.] Hecat, . . . angerly? *F.* 2. are,] are? *F.* 3.
overbold?] over-bold, *F.*

This scene is probably not Shake-speare's. See Introduction, p. xxx.

1. *Hecate*] The common pronuncia-tion of this name was dissyllabic, as in II. i. 52 and III. ii. 41 *ante*; and *MND.*, v. i. 391. Shakespeare was possibly not responsible for the trisyllable in *1H6*, III. ii. 64: 'I speak not to that railing Hecate.'

8–9.] Nosworthy, *R.E.S.*, Apr. 1948, argued that these lines were inserted to explain the interpolation and he ex-plains 'to bear my part' as 'to take part in a previous performance'.

11. *wayward son*] 'We do not need Hecate to tell us that he is but a way-ward son, who . . . loves for his own end. . . Whatever he does is inevitably in pursuance of some apparent good, even though that apparent good is only temporal or nothing more than escape from a present evil' (Curry, *Shake-speare's Philosophical Patterns*, p. 131).

21. *dismal*] disastrous.

Upon the corner of the moon
There hangs a vap'rous drop profound;
I'll catch it ere it come to ground: 25
And that, distill'd by magic sleights,
Shall raise such artificial sprites,
As, by the strength of their illusion,
Shall draw him on to his confusion.
He shall spurn fate, scorn death, and bear   30
His hopes 'bove wisdom, grace, and fear;
And you all know, security
Is mortals' chiefest enemy.
                    [*Song within:* 'Come away, come away,' etc.

26. sleights,] *Collier;* slights, *F.*   27. raise] *F1;* rise *F2.*   33. S.D.] *Musicke,
and a Song F. See 35.*

23–9. *Upon . . . confusion*] These lines
can mean that 'with the aid of her
magic potion Hecate will fashion
phantom figures' or else that she will
'use her magic potion to call up powerful demons, just as is done with the
magic ingredients of the witches'
cauldron'. 'Artificial' would then
mean (*N.E.D.*, II. 9) 'displaying artifice; artful, cunning, deceitful'. The
second explanation is the more likely
one (Schanzer).

24. *vap'rous drop profound*] 'This
vaporous drop seems to have been
meant for the same as the *virus lunare* of
the ancients, being a foam which the
moon was supposed to shed on particular herbs, or other objects, when
strongly solicited by enchantment'
(Steevens). Cf. Lucan, *Pharsalia*, VI.
669. profound = with deep or hidden
qualities (Johnson), rather than 'deep,
and therefore ready to fall' (Clarendon). James O. Wood (*N.Q.*, 1964,
pp. 262–4) suggests that 'profound'
means 'profounded' (i.e. poured out)
and is derived from Leslie's *De origine*,
p. 193, 'instillato perfundere'.

32. *security*] i.e. over-confidence.

33. S.D.] The song is to be found in
Middleton, *The Witch*, III. iii, though
this does not necessarily mean that
he wrote the whole of this scene:

'Come away, come away,
  Hecate, Hecate, come away!
Hec. I come, I come, I come, I come,
    With all the speed I may,
    With all the speed I may.
    Where's Stadlin?
Voice. Here.
Hec. Where's Puckle?
Voice. Here;
    And Hoppo too, and Hellwain
      too;
    We lack but you, we lack but
      you;
    Come away, make up the count.
Hec. I will but 'noint, and then I
    mount.
        (*A Spirit like a cat descends.*
Voice. There's one comes down to
    fetch his dues,
    A kiss, a coll, a sip of blood;
    And why thou stay'st so long,
      I muse, I muse,
    Since the air's so sweet and good.
Hec. O, art thou come?
    What news, what news?
Spirit. All goes still to our delight:
    Either come, or else
      Refuse, refuse.
Hec. Now I'm furnish'd for the flight.
Fire. Hark, hark, the cat sings a brave
    treble in her own language!
Hec. (*going up*) Now I go, now I fly,
    Malkin my sweet spirit and I.

Hark! I am call'd: my little spirit, see,
Sits in a foggy cloud, and stays for me.   [*Exit.*   35
1 *Witch.* Come, let's make haste: she'll soon be back again.
                                                      [*Exeunt.*]

SCENE VI.—[*Somewhere in Scotland.*]

Enter LENOX *and another Lord.*

Len. My former speeches have but hit your thoughts,
     Which can interpret farther: only, I say,
     Things have been strangely borne. The gracious Duncan
     Was pitied of Macbeth:—marry, he was dead:—
     And the right-valiant Banquo walk'd too late;   5
     Whom, you may say (if't please you) Fleance kill'd,
     For Fleance fled. Men must not walk too late.

35.] S.D. *Sing within . . . etc. F. See 33.*   36. Come . . . again] *two lines, the first ending* be *F.*

Scene VI

1. My . . . thoughts] *so Rowe; two lines, the first ending* Speeches, *F.*   5. right-valiant] *so Theobald;* right valiant *F.*

O what a dainty pleasure 'tis
To ride in the air
When the moon shines fair,
And sing and dance, and toy and
     kiss!
Over woods, high rocks, and
     mountains,
Over seas, our mistress' fountains,
Over steep towers and turrets,
We fly by night, 'mongst troops of
     spirits:
No ring of bells to our ears sounds,
No howls of wolves, no yelps of
     hounds;
No, not the noise of water's breach,
Or cannon's throat our height can
     reach.
(*Voices above*) No ring of bells, etc.'
35.] Hecate is taken up in the cloud, i.e. a stage car, drawn up on pulleys, and concealed by billowing draperies (Wilson, who refers to Adams, *The Globe Playhouse*, pp. 335–66).

Scene VI

The location of this scene seems to be quite immaterial, but the conversation is unlikely to have taken place in a room of the palace, which was Capell's suggestion. The scene may have come originally after IV. i. See Introduction, p. xxxiv.

S.D. another Lord] Johnson suggested that the abbreviation *An.* (for Angus) in the manuscript was erroneously expanded by a transcriber into 'another Lord'. But cf. the anonymity of the Old Man in II. iv *ante.*

3. *borne*] carried on. Cf. 17 *post,* and *Ado,* II. iii. 229: 'The conference was sadly borne,' i.e. seriously conducted.

5. *walk'd too late*] Cf. Kyd, *Spanish Tragedie,* III. iii. 39 (see *M.L.R.,* I. 54): 'Why hast thou thus vnkindely kild the man? / Why? because he walkt abroad so late.' Ellis-Fermor suggests, privately, that there is an undertone of meaning—'lived too long'.

Who cannot want the thought, how monstrous
It was for Malcolm, and for Donalbain,
To kill their gracious father? damned fact!   10
How it did grieve Macbeth! did he not straight,
In pious rage, the two delinquents tear,
That were the slaves of drink, and thralls of sleep?
Was not that nobly done? Ay, and wisely too;
For 'twould have anger'd any heart alive   15
To hear the men deny't. So that, I say,
He has borne all things well: and I do think,
That, had he Duncan's sons under his key
(As, and't please Heaven, he shall not), they should find
What 'twere to kill a father; so should Fleance.   20
But, peace!—for from broad words, and 'cause he fail'd
His presence at the tyrant's feast, I hear,

8. Who ... the] You cannot want the *Hanmer;* We cannot want the *Keightley;*
Who can but want the *Collier (ed. 3);* Who can now want the *Hudson (1879;*
conj. Cartwright).   11. Macbeth!] *Capell;* Macbeth? *F.*   14. not that] *F1–2;*
that not *F3–4.*   18. his key] the key *F2–4.*   19. and't] *F;* an't *Theobald*
(ed. 2).   should] *F1;* shall *F2–4.*   21. 'cause] *Pope;* cause *F.*

8. *want the thought*] i.e. help thinking.
Shakespeare must have meant 'can'
and not 'cannot'; but 'this construction arises from a confusion of thought
common enough when a negative is
expressed or implied' (Clarendon).
But perhaps an ambiguity was intended, as Empson suggests, *Seven
Types of Ambiguity,* 1930, p. 265: 'Who
can avoid thinking, is the meaning; but
the *not* breaks through the irony into
"Who must not feel that they have not
done anything monstrous at all?"
"Who must not avoid thinking altogether about so touchy a state matter?"
This is not heard as the meaning, however, the normal construction is too
strong, and the negative acts as a sly
touch of disorder.'
    monstrous] probably a trisyllable,
though the dissyllable is much more
common in Shakespeare. Cf. i. v. 39
and iii. ii. 30 *ante.*
    10. *fact*] act, deed. Invariably used
in Shakespeare in the sense of 'evil
deed', 'crime'.

12. *pious*] loyal.
    14. *Was ... done*] Lenox apparently
accepted Macbeth's story at the time
(cf. ii. iii. 99); but he may have
changed his mind on reflection, or
perhaps he has been substituted here
for another character (cf. Introduction, p. xxxi), or he may be regarded as
a chorus, rather than as a person of
distinct character. He is still serving
Macbeth in iv. i.
    17. *He ... well*] Cf. iii. vi. 3 and iii. i.
80. He has managed things successfully
and cunningly.
    19. *and't*] if it. See Abbott, *Shakes.
Gram.,* § 101. Theobald's emendation
to the more usual form *an't* was unnecessary.
    should] would be sure to.
    21. *broad*] open, plain. Cf. *Tim.,*
iii. iv. 64.
    fail'd] Cf. iii. iv. 127 *ante.*
    22. *tyrant's*] 'usurper's' (Clarendon);
'Not *usurper's* but a blood-thirsty
king's' (Wilson). I think both senses
are implied.

Macduff lives in disgrace. Sir, can you tell
Where he bestows himself?
Lord.   The son of Duncan,
From whom this tyrant holds the due of birth,   25
Lives in the English court; and is receiv'd
Of the most pious Edward with such grace,
That the malevolence of fortune nothing
Takes from his high respect. Thither Macduff
Is gone to pray the holy King, upon his aid   30
To wake Northumberland, and warlike Siward;
That, by the help of these (with Him above
To ratify the work), we may again
Give to our tables meat, sleep to our nights,
Free from our feasts and banquets bloody knives,   35
Do faithful homage, and receive free honours,
All which we pine for now. And this report
Hath so exasperate the King, that he
Prepares for some attempt of war.
Len.   Sent he to Macduff?
Lord. He did: and with an absolute 'Sir, not I,'   40
The cloudy messenger turns me his back,
And hums, as who should say, 'You'll rue the time
That clogs me with this answer.'
Len.   And that well might
Advise him to a caution, t'hold what distance

---

24. son] *Theobald;* Sonnes *F.*   26. Lives] Live *F2–4.*   31. Siward] *Theobald*
(*ed. 2*), *Hanmer;* Seyward *F.*   38. the] *Hanmer;* their *F.*   44. caution, t'hold]
F; caution, to hold *Camb.*

27. *Of*] by. Cf. III. vi. 4 *ante.*

30. *Is gone*] Perhaps, as Cuningham
and others suggest, these words ought
to be printed at the end of the previous line.

31. *Northumberland*] N.

35. *Free . . . knives*] i.e. free our feasts
and banquets from bloody knives. Cf.
Tp., Epil. 18: 'frees all faults', i.e. frees
me from all faults.

36. *free*] not bought by servility and
crime, but enjoyed in freedom.

38. *exasperate*] Cf. *Troil.,* v. i. 34:
'Why art thou then exasperate?' See
Abbott, *Shakes. Gram.,* §§ 341–2.

the] their—F. Presumably the
printer thought the king referred to
was Edward the Confessor.

40. *absolute*] curt, peremptory. Cf.
Cor., III. i. 90. N.

41. *cloudy*] cloudy-visaged, sullen.
Cf. *1H4,* III. ii. 83. N.

42. *hums*] Cf. note on III. ii. 42.

43. *clogs*] The messenger knows he
will suffer for the bad tidings. Cf. the
reception of the messengers later in the
play, v. iii. 11 and v. v. 35.

44. *Advise . . . t'hold*] Cf. *Lr.,* I. ii.
188: 'I advise you to the best' and *ib.,*
III. vii. 9.

His wisdom can provide. Some holy Angel   45
Fly to the court of England, and unfold
His message ere he come, that a swift blessing
May soon return to this our suffering country
Under a hand accurs'd!

Lord.   I'll send my prayers with him.

                                                    [*Exeunt.*

48-9. *suffering ... Under*] i.e. country suffering under. Cf. *R2*, III. ii. 8: 'As a long-parted mother with her child'.

Or 'Under a hand accurs'd' may be a kind of relative clause, with 'which is' understood.

ACT IV

SCENE I.— [*A house in Forres. In the middle, a boiling cauldron.*]

Thunder. Enter the three WITCHES.

1 *Witch.* Thrice the brinded cat hath mew'd.
2 *Witch.* Thrice, and once the hedge-pig whin'd.
3 *Witch.* Harpier cries:—'Tis time, 'tis time.

ACT IV
Scene I

S.D. *A . . . Forres*] Paul.   *In . . . cauldron*] Rowe.   *Thunder . . . Witches*] F.
2. hedge-pig] Hedges Pigge *F2–4.*

S.D.] Paul points out that the cave setting, suggested by Rowe and followed by nearly all editors, conflicts with the locks mentioned later (46). Holinshed speaks of a house in Forres where the witches met.

1. *the brinded cat*] the first sister's familiar. Cf. 'Graymalkin', I. i. 8 *ante.* 'Brinded', i.e. branded, as if with fire, streaked, is the Elizabethan form of 'brindled'. Milton, *Paradise Lost*, VII. 466, speaks of the lion's 'brinded mane'.

2. *Thrice, and once*] 'The Second Witch only repeats the number which the First had mentioned, in order to confirm what she had said; and then adds, that the *hedge-pig* had likewise cried, though but once. Or what seems more easy, the hedge-pig had whined *thrice*, and after an interval had whined once again' (Steevens). Theobald quotes Virgil, *Ecl.*, viii. 75, 'Numero deus impare gaudet,' and Elwin says that 'as even numbers were considered inappropriate to magical operations, the Second Witch makes the *fourth* cry of the hedge-pig an odd number by her method of counting.

She tells three, and then begins a new reckoning.' Jonson, however, used even numbers in his *Masque of Queenes*, ed. Herford and Simpson, VII. 300: 'Thou shalt haue three, thou shalt haue foure, / Thou shalt haue ten, thou shalt haue a score.'

3. *Harpier*] the third sister's familiar. Steevens suggested it was a corruption of 'Harpy' which appears in Marlowe, *I Tamb.*, II. vii. 50, as 'Harpyr' (1590), 'Harpye' (1592), and 'Harper' (1605). Cuningham thinks that Shakespeare took the word from Spenser, *Faerie Queene*, II. xii. 36: 'The hellish Harpyes prophets of sad destiny'. The suggestion that the word may be derived from the Hebrew *Habar*, mentioned in Scot, *Discouerie of Witchcraft*, XII. 1 (Clarendon), is over-ingenious. R. Walker cites *Aen.* III, which contains a description of harpies. Paul, however, thinks harpier is an owl. There are references to the owl before the three murders of Duncan, Banquo, and Lady Macduff.

'*Tis time*] Harpier cries, i.e. gives them the signal, and therefore it is time for them to begin.

1 *Witch.* Round about the cauldron go;
         In the poison'd entrails throw.—
         Toad, that under cold stone   5
         Days and nights has thirty-one
         Swelter'd venom, sleeping got,
         Boil thou first i'th'charmed pot.
All. Double, double toil and trouble: 10
         Fire, burn; and, cauldron, bubble.
2 *Witch.* Fillet of a fenny snake,
         In the cauldron boil and bake;
         Eye of newt, and toe of frog,
         Wool of bat, and tongue of dog,   15
         Adder's fork, and blind-worm's sting,
         Lizard's leg, and howlet's wing,
         For a charm of powerful trouble,
         Like a hell-broth boil and bubble.
All. Double, double toil and trouble: 20

5. throw.] *Rowe;* throw *F.*   6. cold] *F;* the cold *Rowe (ed. 2);* coldest *Steevens*
(*1793*); a cold *conj. Staunton.*   7. has] *F3–4;* ha's *F1–2;* hast *Capell.*   thirty-
one] *Capell;* thirty one: *F.*   10,20. Double, double] *Steevens;* Double, double, *F.*

6. *cold*] Various superfluous attempts
have been made to emend this line;
but it is not even desirable to regard
the word as a dissyllable. The juxtaposed stresses on *cold stone* make the
stone colder than Steevens's *coldest.*
8. *Swelter'd*] exuded, like sweat
(*O.E.D.*).
venom] Topsell, *History of Serpents* (ed.
1658, p. 730) says: 'All manner of
toads, both of the earth and of the
water, are venomous, although it be
held that the toads of the earth are
more poysonful than the toads of the
water. . . But the toads of the land,
which do descend into the marishes,
and so live in both elements, are most
venomous. . . The women-witches of
ancient time which killed by poyson-
ing, did much use Toads in their con-
fections.' The secretion of the skin-
glands of the toad contains a poisonous
substance (phrynin) acrid enough to
be felt on tongue or eyes, and serving
to protect the toad.
12. *Fillet . . . snake*] i.e. a slice of

snake from the fens. Furness thinks
there may also be a reference to the
other meaning of fillet, *headband,* and
he compares Lucan, *Pharsal.,* VI. 656:
'Et coma vipereis substringitur horrida
sertis.' The line comes in a passage
about a witch, only a few lines from the
quotation given in the note to III. v. 24
ante. Paul compares Ovid, *Metam.,* vii.
269, 272, with this line and l. 17 *post.*
16. *fork*] i.e. double tongue. Cf.
Meas., III. i. 16.
blind-worm's sting] Cf. *MND.,* II. ii.
11, and *Tim.,* IV. iii. 182: 'The eyeless
venom'd worm'. Drayton, *Noah's
Floud,* 481–4, ed. Hebel, III. 339,
mentions that 'The small-ey'd slowe-
worme held of many blinde . . . / Out of
its teeth shutes the invenom'd slime.'
Topsell, *History of Serpents,* p. 763, says,
'it receiveth name from the blindnesse
and deafness thereof. . . It is harmless
except being provoked . . . for the
poyson thereof is very strong.' It is
now known that both the slow-worm
and the newt are harmless.

Fire, burn; and, cauldron, bubble.
3 *Witch.*   Scale of dragon, tooth of wolf;
Witches' mummy; maw, and gulf,
Of the ravin'd salt-sea shark;
Root of hemlock, digg'd i'th'dark;   25
Liver of blaspheming Jew;
Gall of goat, and slips of yew,
Sliver'd in the moon's eclipse;
Nose of Turk, and Tartar's lips;
Finger of birth-strangled babe,   30
Ditch-deliver'd by a drab,
Make the gruel thick and slab:
Add thereto a tiger's chaudron,

---

23. Witches'] *Theobald (ed. 2)*; Witches *F*; Witch's *Singer*.   28. Sliver'd]
Silver'd *Rowe (ed. 3)*.

---

23. *mummy*] 'Egyptian mummy, or
what passed for it, was formerly a
regular part of the *Materia Medica*'
(Nares). Johnson mentions there were
two substances for medical use, which
went under the same name, 'the dried
flesh of human bodies embalmed with
myrrh and spice' and 'the liquor running from such mummies when newly
prepared, or when affected by great
heat'. Cf. *Oth.*, iii. iv. 74. Wilson has an
appropriate quotation from James I,
Dæmonologie, p. 43. The Devil 'causeth
them to joynt dead corpses, and to
make powders thereof, mixing such
other thinges there amongst, as he
giues vnto them' (*Workes*, 1616, p.
116).

gulf] stomach, voracious appetite.
Cf. *Cor.*, i. i. 101. *O.E.D.* quotes
Spenser, *Shepherd's Calendar*, Sept.
184-5: 'a wicked Wolfe / That with
many a Lambe had glutted his gulfe'.

24. *ravin'd*] 'glutted with prey'
(Steevens); the maw of a shark glutted
with human flesh has the right note of
horror. Other explanations: 'Used for
ravenous, the passive participle for the
adj.' (Malone, Chambers) and 'used
rather for the active participle raven-
ing' (Cuningham).

25. *dark*] The time when an herb

was gathered was supposed to affect
its potency (Kittredge).

27. *yew*] The yew, which grows
freely in churchyards, was regarded as
poisonous by the ancients, by writers
in the Middle Ages, and by Shakespeare's contemporaries. Douce quotes
Batman, *Uppon Bartholome*, xvii. 161:
'yew is altogether venomous, and
against man's nature. The birdes that
eate the redde berryes, eyther dye, or
cast theyr fethers.' Cf. *R2*, iii. ii. 117:
'double-fatal yew'.

28. *Sliver'd*] cut or sliced off. Cf. *Lr.*,
iv. ii. 34; and *Ham.*, iv. vii. 174. According to Craig the word is still used
in dialect and in America.

moon's eclipse] 'A most unlucky time
for lawful enterprises, and therefore
suitable for evil designs' (Clarendon).

29. *Nose . . . lips*] Turks and Tartars
were not only regarded as types of
cruelty, as in *Mer.V.*, iv. i. 32 (Craig),
but also like the Jew (26) and the
birth-strangled babe (30) they were
unchristened, and hence valued by the
witches (Wilson).

31. *drab*] prostitute.

32. *slab*] thick.

33. *chaudron*] entrails. Cf. Dekker,
Honest Whore, Part I, sc. vii: 'Sixpence
a meale, wench, as well as heart can

For th'ingredience of our cauldron.
All. Double, double toil and trouble: 35
      Fire, burn; and, cauldron, bubble.
2 *Witch.* Cool it with a baboon's blood:
      Then the charm is firm and good.

[*Enter* HECATE, *and the other three Witches.*]

Hec. O, well done! I commend your pains,
      And every one shall share i'th'gains.   40
      And now about the cauldron sing,
      Like elves and fairies in a ring,
      Enchanting all that you put in.
            [*Music and a song*, 'Black spirits,' etc.
            [*Exeunt Hecate and the three other Witches.*]

34. ingredience] *F;* ingredients *Rowe.*
Enter Hecate to the other three witches Globe.
retires Globe; Hecate goes Wilson; not in F.

38. S.D.] *F; Enter Hecate Ritson;*
43. *Exeunt . . . Witches*] *Hecate*

wish, with Calves chaldrons and
chitterlings'.

   34. *ingredience*] Cf. I. vii. II.

   37. *baboon*] with the accent on the
first syllable. Cf. *Per.*, IV. vi. 189.
Nosworthy suggests 'babione'.

   38. Enter Hecate, and the other
three Witches] Probably the appearance of Hecate with three additional
witches was a non-Shakespearian interpolation. Some have thought the
S.D. should read 'Enter Hecate *to* the
other three Witches.' Hecate was not a
witch, but might have been regarded
as such by book-keeper or printer. The
three spurious witches were needed for
the song and perhaps for the 'antic
round' (132 *post*).

   39–43. *O . . . put in*] The metre
changes and 'Like elves and fairies' is
manifestly spurious.

   43. song] It is given in *The Witch*,
v. ii:
'*Hec.* Black spirits and white, red
         spirits and gray,
    Mingle, mingle, mingle, you that
         mingle may!
      Titty, Tiffin,
      Keep it stiff in;

         Firedrake, Puckey,
         Make it lucky;
         Liard, Robin,
         You must bob in.
      Round, around, around, about
         about!
      All ill come running in, all good
         keep out!
   1 Witch. Here's the blood of a bat.
   Hec. Put in that, O put in that!
   2 Witch. Here's libbard's-bane.
   Hec. Put in again!
   1 Witch. The juice of toad, the oil of
      adder.
   2 Witch. Those will make the younker
      madder.
   Hec. Put in—there's all—and rid the
      stench.
   Fire. Nay, here's three ounces of the
      red-hair'd wench.
   All the Witches. Round, around,
      around, etc.'
It is to be hoped that this song was
altered for *Macbeth*, as some lines are
relevant only to the plot of Middleton's play. But the 1673 edition of
Macbeth prints them without alteration. No exit is marked for Hecate and
the spurious witches; but the sooner

2 *Witch.* By the pricking of my thumbs,
Something wicked this way comes.—   [*Knocking.*   45
Open, locks,
Whoever knocks.

Enter MACBETH.

Macb. How now, you secret, black, and midnight hags!
What is't you do?
All.   A deed without a name.
Macb. I conjure you, by that which you profess,   50
Howe'er you come to know it, answer me:
Though you untie the winds, and let them fight
Against the Churches; though the yesty waves
Confound and swallow navigation up;
Though bladed corn be lodg'd, and trees blown down;
Though castles topple on their warders' heads;   56
Though palaces, and pyramids, do slope

46–7. Open . . . knocks.] *so Dyce ; one line F.*

they depart the better. In the illustration of this scene in Rowe's edition,
there are only three witches remaining
at 112 *post,* though in D'Avenant's
version Hecate speaks 125–32.

44.] Shakespeare again.

pricking] 'It is a very ancient superstition that all sudden pains of the body
which could not naturally be ao
counted for, were presages of somewhat that was shortly to happen'
(Steevens).

48. *black . . . hags*] i.e. who practised
the Black Art.

50. *conjure*] here, as usually, with the
accent on the first syllable.

that . . . profess] i.e. the Black Art.

51. *Howe'er . . . it*] e.g. by making a
pact with the Devil.

52. *winds*] Scot, *The Discouerie of
Witchcraft,* 1930, p. 1, says: 'Such
faithlesse people (I saie) are also persuaded, that neither haile nor snowe,
thunder nor lightening, raine nor
tempestuous winds come from the
heauens at the commandement of
God; but are raised by the cunning

and power of witches and conjurors.'

53. *Against the Churches*] symbolically, as well as literally.

yesty] foaming, frothy, in a ferment.
Cf. *Ham.,* v. ii. 186; and *Wint.,* III. iii.
94.

55. *bladed corn*] Scot, *Discouerie of
Witchcraft,* p. 6, tells us that witches
were thought to be able to 'transferre
corne in the blade from one place to
another'. Comenius, *Janua Linguarum,*
1673, ch. 32 (cited by Staunton), says:
'As soon as standing corn shoots up to
a blade, it is in danger of scathe by a
tempest.'

lodg'd] laid, beaten down. Cf. *2H6,*
III. ii. 176, and *R2,* III. iii. 163.

56. *Though . . . heads*] Cf. Seneca,
Agam., tr. Studley, Chor. 1: 'What
castell strongly buylt, what bulwarke,
tower or towne, / Is not by mischyefes
meanes, brought topsy turuye downe?'
See note on v. iii. 45 *post.*

57. *slope*] i.e. bend. Not used elsewhere by Shakespeare. Capell conj.
'stoop', which, spelt 'stope', might
easily have been misread.

Their heads to their foundations; though the treasure
Of Nature's germens tumble all together,
Even till destruction sicken, answer me   60
To what I ask you.

1 *Witch.*   Speak.

2 *Witch.*   Demand.

3 *Witch.*   We'll answer.

1 *Witch.* Say, if thou'dst rather hear it from our mouths,
Or from our masters?

Macb.   Call 'em; let me see 'em.

1 *Witch.* Pour in sow's blood, that hath eaten
Her nine farrow; grease, that's sweaten   65
From the murderer's gibbet, throw
Into the flame.

---

59. germens] *Globe;* Germaine *F1–2;* germain *F3–4;* germen *Delius;* germains
Pope; germins *Theobald;* german *Elwin.*   all together] *Pope;* altogether *F.*
62. thou'dst] *Capell;* th' hadst *F.*   63. masters?] *Pope;* Masters. *F;* masters'?
Capell.

59. *germens*] The collective form, 'germen', may be correct; but cf. *Lr.,* III. ii. 8: 'Crack Nature's moulds, all germens spill at once'. For the idea cf. *Wint.,* IV. iv. 490: 'Let nature crush the sides o' th' earth together / And mar the seeds within.' Curry shows, *Shakespeare's Philosophical Patterns,* pp. 31 ff., that Nature's germens are the *rationes seminales,* 'the material essences which correspond to the exemplars in God's mind'. He quotes Augustine, *De Trinitate;* 'But in truth, some hidden seeds of all things that are born corporeally and visibly, are concealed in the corporeal elements of this world... For the Creator of these invisible seeds is the Creator of all things himself; since whatever comes forth to our sight by being born, receives the first beginnings of its course from hidden seeds, and takes the successive increments of its proper size and its distinctive forms from these as it were original rules.' Cf. note to I. iii. 58 *ante.* By being willing to tumble the germens all together in confusion, so that they became barren or produced only monstrosities, Macbeth shows how far he

has declined since the beginning of the play. Wilson (lxiii) thinks that Macbeth dwells on the prospect of such ultimate destruction with delight. It is rather the *reductio ad absurdum* of the principle that the end justifies the means, of which the equivocator in the Porter scene provides a mild example. Macbeth is willing to sacrifice the future of the universe to his own personal and temporary satisfaction. Cf. III. ii. 16 *ante,* and Knight, *The Wheel of Fire,* 1949, p. 154.

60. *sicken*] i.e. through surfeit.

61. *Speak*] N.

64. *sow's blood*] Steevens cites Holinshed, (1585), p. 133 (on the laws of Kenneth II): 'if a sow eate hir pigs, let hir be stoned to death, and buried, so that no man eate of hir fleshe.'

65. *farrow*] litter. Holland, *Pliny,* VIII. 51 (cited Clarendon) says: 'One sow may bring at one farrow twentie pigges.'

sweaten] irregularly formed, to rhyme with 'eaten'. Cf. Abbott, *Shakes. Gram.,* § 344.

All.   Come, high, or low;
Thyself and office deftly show.

Thunder. First Apparition, an armed head.

Macb. Tell me, thou unknown power,—
1 *Witch.*   He knows thy thought:
Hear his speech, but say thou nought.   70
1 *App.* Macbeth! Macbeth! Macbeth! beware Macduff;
Beware the Thane of Fife.—Dismiss me.—Enough.
                                        [*Descends.*
Macb. Whate'er thou art, for thy good caution, thanks:
Thou hast harp'd my fear aright.—But one word
        more:—
1 *Witch.* He will not be commanded. Here's another,   75
More potent than the first.

---

68. S.D.] *F; Wilson adds: like Macbeth's, rises from the cauldron.*   71. Macbeth
... Macduff.] *so Rowe; two lines, the second beginning* beware *F.*

68, 76, 86. an armed head, etc.]
Upton, *Crit. Obs.*, 1746, says: 'The
armed head represents symbolically
Macbeth's head cut off and brought to
Malcolm by Macduff. The bloody
child is Macduff untimely ripped from
his mother's womb. The child with a
crown on his head, and a bough in his
hand, is the royal Malcolm, who
ordered his soldiers to hew them down
a bough and bear it before them to
Dunsinane.'
Crawford, *M.L.N.*, XXXIX, and
Kittredge both think the 1st Apparition is Macduff. Knight, *The Imperial
Theme*, pp. 150–3, points out 'the
vivid destruction-birth sequence' in
this scene. 'The Armed Head, recalling Macdonwald's head (I. ii. 23) ...
blends with the "chaos" and "disorder" thought throughout ... and ...
suggests both the iron force of evil and
also its final destruction.' He suggests
that the order in which the apparitions appear is important: 'Violent
destruction, itself to be destroyed; the
blood-agony of birth that travails to
wrench into existence a force to right
the sickening evil; the future birth

splendid in crowned and accomplished royalty'.
69. *Tell ... thought*] Grierson calls
attention to the irony of these two
sentences, as the apparition is Macbeth's head.
70. *say ... nought*] Steevens quotes
Marlowe, *Faustus*, sc. x. (ed. Brooke,
p. 212): 'demand no questions ... /
But in dumbe silence let them come
and goe.'
72. *Enough*] He is in torment. Cf.
2H6, I. iv. 38.
74. *harp'd*] guessed. Cotgrave translates 'Parler à taston' by 'to speak by
ghesse or conjecture, onely to harpe at
the matter'.
76. *More potent*] This does not necessarily mean that Macduff is more
potent than Macbeth, but merely that
the apparition is more powerful than
the other. The First Witch has previously referred to them as their
'masters', which can only mean the
demons who assume the shape of the
apparitions. The phrase does not
therefore dispose of Kittredge's theory
(cf. note to 68 *ante*) as Wilson as-
serts.

Thunder. Second Apparition, a bloody child.

2 *App.* Macbeth! Macbeth! Macbeth!—
Macb. Had I three ears, I'd hear thee.
2 *App.* Be bloody, bold, and resolute: laugh to scorn
  The power of man, for none of woman born   80
  Shall harm Macbeth.   [*Descends.*
Macb. Then live, Macduff: what need I fear of thee?
  But yet I'll make assurance double sure,
  And take a bond of Fate: thou shalt not live;
  That I may tell pale-hearted fear it lies,   85
  And sleep in spite of thunder.—

Thunder. Third Apparition, a child crowned, with a tree in his hand.

            What is this,
  That rises like the issue of a king;
  And wears upon his baby brow the round
  And top of sovereignty?
All.   Listen, but speak not to't.
3 *App.* Be lion-mettled, proud, and take no care 90
  Who chafes, who frets, or where conspirers are:
  Macbeth shall never vanquish'd be, until
  Great Birnam wood to high Dunsinane hill

78–81. Had . . . Macbeth.] *three lines, Var. 1803, ending* bold / man, / Macbeth.
79. Be . . . scorn] *so Rowe; two lines, the first ending* resolute: *F.* 83. assurance
double] *Pope;* assurance: double *F1;* assurance, double *F2–4.* 86–7. What
. . . king] *so Rowe; one line, F.* 89. top] *type conj. Theobald.* 93. Birnam]
F4; Byrnam *F1–3.*

80–1. *for . . . Macbeth*] Cf. Holinshed (Appendix, p. 175).

83–4. *assurance . . . Fate*] Macbeth, unwitting that Macduff is not in the number of *woman born* is assured that Macduff cannot harm him. By killing him, Macbeth means to bind fate to perform the promise and make his own 'assurance double sure'. Rushton, *Shakespeare a Lawyer*, 1858, p. 20, says that the allusion is to 'a conditional bond, under or by virtue of which when forfeited, double the principal sum was recoverable'. Kittredge remarks that Fate has to break two of her fixed laws, produce a man never born, and bring back a man from the dead.

89. *top*] 'The crown not only completes (especially in the eye of Macbeth, the usurper) and rounds, as with the perfection of a circle, the claim to sovereignty, but it is figuratively the top, the summit, of ambitious hopes' (R. G. White).

93. *Birnam*] a high hill near Dunkeld, 12 miles W.N.W. of Dunsinnan, which is 7 miles N.E. of Perth.

Dunsinane] now Dunsinnan. The word here seems to be accented on the second syllable; but elsewhere in the play on the first syllable. Both pro-

Shall come against him.   [*Descends.*

Macb.   That will never be:
Who can impress the forest; bid the tree   95
Unfix his earth-bound root? Sweet bodements! good!
Rebellious dead, rise never, till the wood
Of Birnam rise; and our high-plac'd Macbeth
Shall live the lease of Nature, pay his breath
To time, and mortal custom.—Yet my heart   100
Throbs to know one thing: tell me (if your art
Can tell so much), shall Banquo's issue ever
Reign in this kingdom?

97. Rebellious dead] *F;* Rebellious head *Theobald (Warburton);* Rebellion's head *Hanmer (conj. Theobald).*   98. Birnam] *F2;* Byrnan *F1.*   our] your *conj. S. Walker.*

nunciations seem to have been employed by all Scottish writers. Wilson
suspects from the pronunciation of
'Dunsinane' here, the use of 'rise' (98),
and the rhythm of 105, the presence of
an interpolator. R. Walker, *op. cit.,*
p. 143, suggests that 'the unusual ac-
centuation . . . produced the startling
auditory sensation that the castle of
Macbeth is torn asunder by *sin,* and
therefore doomed to fall.' This is over-
ingenious.

94. *That*] Macbeth continues the
oracle in rhyme, and thus identifies
himself with the lying spirits (Kittredge).

97. *Rebellious dead*] Theobald's
emendation has been generally accepted, and Macbeth may be referring
to 'conspirers' (91 *ante*). Perhaps
'head' was suggested by the Armed
Head (Clarendon). For 'head' in the
sense of armed force, see *1H4,* III. ii.
167, and *Ham.,* IV. v. 101. Halliwell,
however, thought that the Folio 'dead'
referred to Banquo's ghost, which
would not stay buried (III. iv. 79–80
ante) and the original reading has been
defended by W. D. Sargeaunt, *Macbeth—a New Interpretation,* 1937, pp.
154–5, and by R. Walker, *op. cit.,* p.
143. The latter argues that the Folio
reading links up better with the reference to Banquo, 100–3 *post,* and that

Macbeth is afraid that the dead will
rise and drag him down into the grave,
or at least that Banquo's son will
avenge his father. Walker also compares v. ii. 3–5 *post.* On the whole there
would seem to be insufficient justification for emending the Folio reading;
cf. *T.L.S.,* 23 Sept. 1949.

98. *Birnam*] With Folio spelling, cf.
Holinshed: 'till the wood of Bernane
came to the castell of Dunsinane'.

rise] probably copied by mistake
from the previous line. Wilson conj.
'move'. The text seems to be corrupt
here. Cf. next note.

our . . . Macbeth] Even if 'our' is a
misprint for 'your', the phrase would
be queer in Macbeth's mouth. Cuningham interprets 'ourself, Macbeth,
the King'. Was Macbeth perhaps disguised, and here pretending that he
was not Macbeth? Or, as Fleay suggests, was this passage originally
spoken by one of the witches? Even as
the lines stand (96–100: 'Sweet . . .
custom') they might be given to the
First Witch, and we could then interpret the passage as another example
of 'the equivocation of the fiend / That
lies like truth'.

99. *the lease of Nature*] the term of
life.

100. *mortal custom*] the custom of
mortality, natural death.

All.   Seek to know no more.
Macb. I will be satisfied: deny me this,
    And an eternal curse fall on you! Let me know.—   105
    Why sinks that cauldron? and what noise is this?
                           [*Hautboys.*

1 *Witch.* Show!
2 *Witch.* Show!
3 *Witch.* Show!
All. Show his eyes, and grieve his heart;   110
    Come like shadows, so depart.

A show of eight Kings, the last with a glass in his hand;
               BANQUO *following.*

Macb. Thou art too like the spirit of Banquo: down!
    Thy crown does sear mine eye-balls:—and thy hair,
    Thou other gold-bound brow, is like the first:—
    A third is like the former:—filthy hags!   115
    Why do you show me this?—A fourth?—Start, eyes!
    What! will the line stretch out to th'crack of doom?
    Another yet?—A seventh?—I'll see no more:—
    And yet the eighth appears, who bears a glass,
    Which shows me many more; and some I see,   120
    That two-fold balls and treble sceptres carry.

105–6. know.—Why] know. Why *F;* know Why *conj. S. Walker.*   111. S.D.]
Hanmer subst. See note below.   113. hair,] haire *F;* air *Johnson;* heir *Jackson.*
116. eyes!] eye *F2–4.*   119. eighth] *F3;* eight *F1–2.*

106. *noise*] A concert or company of musicians, usually three in number, who attended taverns, etc., was called a 'noise'. Cf. *2H4,* II. iv. 12.

111. A show . . . following] The S.D. in Folio 'and Banquo last, with a glasse in his hand' is inconsistent with 119 *post.*

113. *hair*] Johnson's conj. 'air' is attractive. 'As Macbeth expected to see a train of kings, and was only inquiring from what race they would proceed, he could not be surprised that the hair of the second was bound with gold like that of the first; he was offended only that the second resembled the first, as the first resembled Banquo.' Steevens compares

Wint., v. i. 128: 'Your father's image is so hit in you, / His very air, that I should call you brother.' But *O.E.D.* gives five quotations, from 1387 to 1625, of 'hair' used in the sense 'of one colour and external quality; . . . stamp, character'.

119. *the eighth*] Shakespeare refers to kings only, omitting all mention of Mary, Queen of Scots. Perhaps we should retain the F reading. But cf. l. 118.

glass] not an ordinary mirror in which King James could see himself (cf. Flatter, *T.L.S.,* 23/3/51) but a prospective, or magic, glass.

121. *two-fold . . . sceptres*] The two-fold balls are usually taken to refer to

Horrible sight!—Now, I see, 'tis true;
For the blood-bolter'd Banquo smiles upon me,
And points at them for his.—What! is this so?

1 *Witch.* Ay, Sir, all this is so:—but why   125
Stands Macbeth thus amazedly?—
Come, sisters, cheer we up his sprites,
And show the best of our delights.
I'll charm the air to give a sound,
While you perform your antic round;   130
That this great King may kindly say,
Our duties did his welcome pay.

[*Music. The Witches dance, and vanish.*

Macb. Where are they? Gone?—Let this pernicious hour
Stand aye accursed in the calendar!—
Come in, without there!

Enter LENOX.

Len.   What's your Grace's will?   135
Macb. Saw you the Weïrd Sisters?
Len.   No, my Lord.
Macb. Came they not by you?
Len.   No, indeed, my Lord.

---

124. What! is] What? is *F1*; What is *F2–4*; What, is *Pope.*   133. Where . . .
hour] *so Rowe; two lines, the first ending* Gone? *F.*   136. Weïrd] *Theobald;*
Weyard *F1*; wizard *F2–3*; wizards *F4.*

the double coronation of James at
Scone and at Westminster. Chambers,
William Shakespeare, I. 473, interprets
'balls' to mean the 'mounds' borne on
the English and Scottish crowns; but
surely it is the orb, carried in the left
hand. The treble sceptres are the two
used for investment in the English
coronation, and the one used in the
Scottish coronation (Chambers). N.

123. *blood-bolter'd*] i.e. with the hair
in tangled knots, or clotted or matted
together in a coagulated mass. According to Malone the term was a pro-
vincialism, used in Warwickshire.
Other forms are *bolstred*, used in *Arden
of Fevershame*, III. i. 73, and *balter*, used
in Holland's *Pliny*, XII. xvii. 370 (cited
Steevens), referring to a goat's beard:

'it baltereth and cluttereth into knots
and balls.'

125–32. *Ay . . . pay*] possibly an interpolation. See Introduction, p. xxxii.

130. *antic round*] fantastic dance.
Wilson quotes Jonson's description in
The Masque of Queenes: 'a magicall
Daunce full of praeposterous change
and gesticulation . . . dauncing, back
to back, hip to hip, theyr handes
joyn'd, and making theyr *circles* backward to the left hand, with strange,
phantastique motions of theyr heads
and bodyes' (ed. Herford and Simpson, VII. 301).

131. *this . . . King*] If the speech is
interpolated, this line may be addressed to a King in the audience rather
than to Macbeth.

Macb. Infected be the air whereon they ride;
 And damn'd all those that trust them!—I did hear
 The galloping of horse: who was't came by?   140
Len. 'Tis two or three, my Lord, that bring you word,
 Macduff is fled to England.
Macb.   Fled to England?
Len. Ay, my good Lord.
Macb. [*Aside.*] Time, thou anticipat'st my dread exploits:
 The flighty purpose never is o'ertook,   145
 Unless the deed go with it. From this moment,
 The very firstlings of my heart shall be
 The firstlings of my hand. And even now,
 To crown my thoughts with acts, be it thought and done:
 The castle of Macduff I will surprise;   150
 Seize upon Fife; give to th'edge o'th'sword
 His wife, his babes, and all unfortunate souls
 That trace him in his line. No boasting like a fool;
 This deed I'll do, before this purpose cool:
 But no more sights!—Where are these gentlemen?   155
 Come, bring me where they are.   [*Exeunt.*

---

144. S.D.] *Johnson.*   147. firstlings] *F1;* firstling *F2–4.*   148. firstlings] *F;*
firstling *Rowe (ed. 2).*   155. sights!] flights *Singer (ed. 2).*

138. *air . . . ride*] Cf. Scot, *The Dis-*
couerie of Witchcraft, 1930, pp. 6, 19.
'These can passe from place to place in
the aire invisible . . . they ride and flie
in the aire.'

139. *damn'd . . . them*] as Macbeth
does.

142. *Macduff...fled*] Kittredge notes
that as in I. iii 'the predictions begin to
fulfil themselves instantly, and thus
their trustworthiness is established in
Macbeth's mind.'

143. *Ay . . . Lord*] Flatter, *op. cit.,*
p. 26, notes the significant pause before
Macbeth speaks.

144. *anticipat'st*] forestallest.

145–6. *The flighty . . . it*] Cf. II. iii.
28–35, 'flighty' = swift, fleet. *O.E.D.*

quotes Huloet (1552), 'Flighty, *pernix.*'
Cf. *All's W.,* v. iii. 40: 'on our quick'st
decrees, / The inaudible and noiseless
foot of Time / Steals ere we can effect
them.'

147–8. *firstlings . . . firstlings*] 'the
first conceptions of the heart and the
first acts of the hand' (Clarendon). Cf.
Troil., Prol. 27: 'the vaunt and firstlings of those broils'. *O.E.D.* quotes
Coverdale (1535), Prov., iii. 9, 'ye
firstlinges of all thine encrease'.

153. *trace*] in the sense of succeeding,
following in, another's tracks, as in
1H4, III. i. 47.

153–4. *No . . . cool*] Wilson, following
Fleay and others, thinks this rhyming
tag is spurious.

SCENE II.—[*Fife. A room in Macduff's castle.*]

Enter LADY MACDUFF, *her Son, and* ROSSE.

L. Macd. What had he done, to make him fly the land?
Rosse. You must have patience, Madam.
L. Macd.   He had none:
His flight was madness: when our actions do not,
Our fears do make us traitors.
Rosse.   You know not,
Whether it was his wisdom, or his fear.   5
L. Macd. Wisdom! to leave his wife, to leave his babes,
His mansion, and his titles, in a place
From whence himself does fly? He loves us not:
He wants the natural touch; for the poor wren,

S.D. *Fife . . . castle.*] *not in* F.   1. L. Macd.] Wife *F passim.*

Bradley says of this and the following scene, *Shakespearean Tragedy*, p. 391: 'They have a technical value in helping to give the last stage of the action the form of a conflict between Macbeth and Macduff. But their chief function is of another kind. It is to touch the heart with a sense of beauty and pathos, to open the springs of love and tears.' But Knights, *op. cit.*, pp. 26–7, points out that this scene 'echoes in different keys the theme of the false appearance, of doubt and confusion', and 'shows the spreading evil. . . There is much more in the death of young Macduff than "pathos"; the violation of the natural order is completed by the murder.' Macduff and his wife, says Fletcher, *Studies of Shakespeare*, p. 166 (*apud* Furness), 'are the chief representatives in the piece of the interests of loyalty and domestic affection, as opposed to those of the foulest treachery and . . . ambition'.

1. *What . . . land?*] Masefield, *Thanks before Going*, 1947, p. 172, argues that in the uncut *Macbeth*, Macduff 'debated with his wife the policy of going and had her full approval. Her outcry

against him to Rosse, in the beginning of this scene, is surely to divert suspicion from herself . . . she knows that spies are everywhere, and that Rosse may be one.' I think it more likely that Macduff did not discuss the matter with his wife, for fear of implicating her. There does not seem to be sufficient evidence for a cut here. Nor, although Rosse might well be suspect after his time-serving, can I see any evidence that Lady Macduff does suspect him; and it is apparently the murder of Lady Macduff which finally makes him desert Macbeth.

4. *traitors*] 'Our flight is considered as an evidence of our treason' (Steevens).

7. *titles*] This is usually explained to mean everything to which he was entitled, i.e. his possessions.

9. *natural touch*] the feeling of natural affection, 'natural sensibility' (Johnson). Cf. *Gent.*, II. vii. 18: 'the inly touch of love'; and *Tp.*, v. i. 21: 'Hast thou, which art but air, a touch, a feeling'.

wren] It need not worry us that the wren is not the smallest of birds, nor that it would not fight in defence of its

The most diminitive of birds, will fight,   10
Her young ones in her nest, against the owl.
All is the fear, and nothing is the love;
As little is the wisdom, where the flight
So runs against all reason.
Rosse.   My dearest coz,
I pray you, school yourself: but, for your husband,   15
He is noble, wise, judicious, and best knows
The fits o'th'season. I dare not speak much further:
But cruel are the times, when we are traitors,
And do not know ourselves; when we hold rumour
From what we fear, yet know not what we fear,   20
But float upon a wild and violent sea

---

10. diminitive] *F1*; diminutiue *F4*.   19. know] know't *Hanmer*.   19–20. we
hold rumour . . . we . . . wc] we bode ruin . . . we . . . we *or else* the bold running
. . . they . . . they *conj. Johnson*.   21. sea] *F;* sea, *Arden (ed. 1), Wilson, etc.*

---

young. See Harting, *The Ornithology of Shakespeare*, p. 91.

10. *diminitive*] variant of diminutive.

12. *All . . . love*] Noble, *Shakespeare's Biblical Knowledge*, compares 1 John, iv. 18: 'There is no feare in loue, but perfect loue casteth out feare: for feare hath painfulnesse: and he that feareth is not perfect in loue.'

13. *wisdom*] Cf. IV. iii. 15 *post.*

15. *school*] control.

17. *The fits o'th'season*] Steevens explains as *the violent disorders* of the season, its convulsions; and quotes *Cor.*, III. ii. 33: 'the violent fit o' the time'. The metaphor is from the fits of an intermittent fever. Cf. III. ii. 23 *ante*. Rosse is hinting at Macbeth's murderous fits.

19. *ourselves*] i.e. as such, 'without realizing it'. Cuningham suggests the word might mean 'one another'.

rumour] Paul thinks there may be an allusion to the rumour that James I had been stabbed on 22 March 1606.

19-20. *when . . . fear*] Cf. *John*, IV. ii. 144–6: 'I find the people strangely fantasied, / Possess'd with rumours, / full of idle dreams, / Not knowing what they fear, but full of fear.' Rosse means: 'When we entertain rumours, in-

spired by our fears, and those fears are themselves vague'.

21–2. *But . . . move*—] This passage is a field for much conjecture. Knights argues for the punctuation I have adopted: 'The substitution of a dash for the full stop after "move" is the only alteration that seems necessary in the Folio text. The other emendations . . . ruin both the rhythm and the idiom. Rosse is in a hurry and breaks off. . . That the tide is about to turn against Macbeth is suggested both by the rhythm and the imagery of Rosse's speech.' Wilson, however, argues that 'moue' is a simple minim error for 'none' and compares *Ant.*, I. iv. 44–7. One might also compare *Ant.*, III. ii. 49. But Taylor, *Shakespeare's Debt to Montaigne*, draws attention to a parallel with a passage in Florio, which seems to me decisive against the Camb. conj., accepted by Wilson: 'So are we drawne, as wood is shoved, / By others sinnewes, *each way moved*. / We goe not, but we are carried: as things that *flote*, now gliding gently, now hulling *violently*; according as the water is, either stormy or calme' (II. i, *Temple* III, p. 4). See Empson, *op. cit.*, pp. 128–9.

Each way, and move—I take my leave of you:
Shall not be long but I'll be here again.
Things at the worst will cease, or else climb upward
To what they were before.—My pretty cousin,   25
Blessing upon you!

L. Macd. Father'd he is, and yet he's fatherless.

Rosse. I am so much a fool, should I stay longer,
It would be my disgrace, and your discomfort:
I take my leave at once.   [*Exit.*

L. Macd.   Sirrah, your father's dead: 30
And what will you do now? How will you live?

Son. As birds do, mother.

L. Macd.   What, with worms and flies?

Son. With what I get, I mean; and so do they.

L. Macd. Poor bird! thou'dst never fear the net, nor lime,
The pit-fall, nor the gin.

Son.   Why should I, mother?   35
Poor birds they are not set for.
My father is not dead, for all your saying.

---

22. Each . . . move—] *conj. Johnson;* each way, and moue. *F;* Each way and
wave. *conj. Theobald;* And move each way. *Capell;* And each way move.
Keightley (conj. Steevens); Each sway and move *conj. Staunton;* Each way it moves
Hudson (conj. Daniel); Each day a new one *conj. Ingleby;* Each way and none.
Wilson (conj. Camb. subst.); Each wayward move *conj. Leighton;* Each way we
move *conj. Rolfe.*   26–9. Blessing . . . discomfort:] *lines end* yet / Foole, / disgrace, / discomfort. *Walker.*   27. Father'd . . . fatherless] *so Rowe; two lines,
the first ending is F.*   33. I mean] *not in F2–4.*   34. Poor . . . lime] *so Theobald;
two lines, the first ending* Bird, *F.*   lime] *F1;* line *F2–4.*   35–6. The pit-fall . . .
set for] *so F;* Why . . . for. *one line, Pope.*

---

23. *Shall not*] 'It', 'I', or 'And' understood; but Rosse is in a hurry, and
there are plenty of examples in Elizabethan English of the omission of the
subject.

24–5. *Things . . . before*] another
metaphor relating to the turn of the
tide.

29. *disgrace*] i.e. by weeping.

30. *Sirrah*] 'not always a term of reproach but sometimes used by masters
to servants, parents to children, etc.'
(Malone).

32. *As birds do*] The boy is thinking
of Matt., vi. 26. N.

with] i.e. on.

34. *lime*] bird lime.

35. *gin*] snare. N.

Why . . . mother?] All editors have
followed Pope in detaching these
words from this line, which they
complete.

36. *Poor . . . for*] 'In life traps are not
set for the poor but for the rich'
(Clarendon). 'Poor' is emphatic, and
'birds' is probably the object of 'set
for', 'they' referring to the traps. But
'they' may be in apposition to 'birds'.
The boy is referring, of course, to his
mother's epithet.

L. Macd. Yes, he is dead: how wilt thou do for a father?
Son. Nay, how will you do for a husband?
L. Macd. Why, I can buy me twenty at any market.   40
Son. Then you'll buy 'em to sell again.
L. Macd. Thou speak'st with all thy wit;
    And yet, i'faith, with wit enough for thee.
Son. Was my father a traitor, mother?
L. Macd. Ay, that he was.   45
Son. What is a traitor?
L. Macd. Why, one that swears and lies.
Son. And be all traitors that do so?
L. Macd. Every one that does so is a traitor, and must be
    hang'd.   50
Son. And must they all be hang'd that swear and lie?
L. Macd. Every one.
Son. Who must hang them?
L. Macd. Why, the honest men.
Son. Then the liars and swearers are fools; for there are   55
    liars and swearers enow to beat the honest men, an
    hang up them.
L. Macd. Now God help thee, poor monkey! But how
    wilt thou do for a father?
Son. If he were dead, you'ld weep for him: if you would   60
    not, it were a good sign that I should quickly have a
    new father.
L. Macd. Poor prattler, how thou talk'st!

Enter a Messenger.

Mess. Bless you, fair dame! I am not to you known,

38. Yes, . . . father?] *one line, Rowe; two lines, the first ending* dead *F.*   41. buy]
F3; by *F1-2.*   42-3. Thou . . . thee] *lines end* faith / thee. *Pope.*   42. with all]
F2; withall *F1.*   49-50. Every . . . hang'd] *prose, Pope; lines divided after*
Traitor *F.*   54. the] *not in F3-4.*   56. enow] *F;* enough *Hanmer.*   58-9.
Now . . . father] *so Pope; verse, divided after* Monkie: *F.*   58. Now] *not in F4.*

44-63.] Wilson thinks this passage
was added for a court performance
after the hanging of Henry Garnet.
    47. *one . . . lies*] Cf. II. iii. 10-12 *ante.*
    57. *hang up them*] Cf. *Rom.*, IV. ii. 41:
'deck up her'.

64-72. Messenger] He is a welcome
reminder that all have not been corrupted by Macbeth's tyranny. There
is no reason to believe, with Heath,
that he is one of the murderers; or,
with Paul, that he has been sent by
Lady Macbeth. Cf. v. i. 6n.

Though in your state of honour I am perfect.   65
I doubt, some danger does approach you nearly:
If you will take a homely man's advice,
Be not found here; hence, with your little ones.
To fright you thus, methinks, I am too savage;
To do worse to you were fell cruelty,   70
Which is too nigh your person. Heaven preserve you!
I dare abide no longer.   [*Exit.*

L. Macd.   Whither should I fly?
I have done no harm. But I remember now
I am in this earthly world, where, to do harm
Is often laudable; to do good, sometime   75
Accounted dangerous folly: why then, alas!
Do I put up that womanly defence,
To say, I have done no harm? What are these faces!

Enter Murderers.

Mur. Where is your husband?
L. Macd. I hope, in no place so unsanctified,   80
Where such as thou may'st find him.
Mur.   He's a traitor.
Son. Thou liest, thou shag-hair'd villain!

68–9. ones. To . . . thus,] *F2, subst.;* ones To . . . thus. *F1.*   70. worse to you]
less, to you *Hanmer;* less to you, *Capell.*   72. Whither] *F3–4;* Whether *F1–2.*
78. To . . . faces] *so Rowe; two lines, the first ending* harme? *F.*   I have] *F1;* I had
F2–4; I'd *Theobald;* I've *Dyce (ed. 2).*   82. shag-hair'd] *Singer (ed. 2), conj.*
Steevens; shagge-ear'd *F1–2;* shag-ear'd *F3–4, Camb.*

65. *state . . . perfect*] perfectly acquainted with your rank. Cf. *R3,* III.
vii. 120: 'Your state of fortune, and
your due of birth'.
  66. *doubt*] i.e. fear; a common usage.
Cf. *R2,* III. iv. 69; and Bacon, *Essays,*
Of Vicissitude of things: 'You may doubt
the springing up of a *New Sect.*'
  68. *little ones*] Cf. Matt., xviii. 6: 'But
whosoeuer shall offend one of these
little ones which beleeue in mee, it
were better for him, that a millstone
were hanged about his necke, and that
he were drowned in the depth of the
sea.'
  70. *To . . . cruelty*] three explanations,
of which I incline to the third: (i) 'to

fright you more, by relating all the
circumstances of your dangers; which
would detain you so long, that you
could not avoid it' (Edwards); (ii) 'to
let her and her children be destroyed
without warning' (Johnson); (iii) 'It
is too savage of me even to frighten you
like this: to harm you would be the act
of a monster—and such monsters, alas,
are on your track' (Grierson).
  80. *unsanctified*] 'We recall the associations set up in III. vi, a scene of
choric commentary upon Macduff's
flight . . . to the "pious Edward"'
(Knights, *Explorations,* p. 27).
  82. *shag-hair'd*] Steevens's conj. has
been generally adopted. The epithet

Mur.   What, you egg!
                                          [*Stabbing him.*
          Young fry of treachery!
Son.   He has kill'd me, mother:
          Run away, I pray you!   [*Dies.*
[*Exit Lady Macduff, crying 'Murther!' and pursued by the Murderers.*

SCENE III.—[*England. A room in the King's palace.*]

          Enter MALCOLM *and* MACDUFF.

Mal. Let us seek out some desolate shade, and there
          Weep our sad bosoms empty.
Macd.   Let us rather
          Hold fast the mortal sword, and like good men
          Bestride our downfall birthdom. Each new morn,
          New widows howl, new orphans cry; new sorrows   5
          Strike heaven on the face, that it resounds
          As if it felt with Scotland, and yell'd out
          Like syllable of dolour.

82. S.D.] *Rowe; not in F.*

                          Scene III
S.D.] *England . . . palace*] *Rowe subst.*   4. downfall] *F;* down-fall'n *Johnson.*

occurs in *2H6*, III. i. 367, and *Sir Thomas More*, Add. IVc. The spelling *heare* is common in Shakespeare, and Wilson points out that in his hand *g* and *h* are similar, so that 'shagheard' might be misread 'shaggeard'.
     egg] Cf. *LLL.*, v. i. 78: 'thou pigeon-egg of discretion'.

                    Scene III
     This scene is based on Holinshed (see Appendix, pp. 176 ff.) and it is the only considerable passage of dialogue in the *Chronicle* relating to Macbeth's reign. The dialogue is also given prominence in Bellenden and Stewart. Knights remarks of this scene that 'Malcolm's suspicion and the long testing of Macduff emphasize the mistrust which has spread from the

central evil of the play. But the main purpose of the scene is obscured unless we realize its function as choric commentary. In alternating speeches the evil which Macbeth has caused is explicitly stated, without extenuation. And it is stated impersonally' (*op. cit.*, p. 28). Chambers, more representatively, regards the scene as tedious. It does not seem tedious today, perhaps, as Masefield suggests, because of the events of recent years.
     3. *mortal*] deadly. Cf. 1. v. 41 *ante.*
     4. *downfall*] i.e. downfallen.
     birthdom] i.e. native land. The phrase means 'defend our fatherland, as we would the body of a fallen comrade'.
     6. *that*] so that. Cf. 1. ii. 60 *ante.*
     8. *Like . . . dolour*] Baldwin, *Shake-*

Mal.   What I believe, I'll wail;
      What know, believe; and what I can redress,
      As I shall find the time to friend, I will.   10
      What you have spoke, it may be so, perchance.
      This tyrant, whose sole name blisters our tongues,
      Was once thought honest: you have lov'd him well;
      He hath not touch'd you yet. I am young; but something
      You may deserve of him through me, and wisdom   15
      To offer up a weak, poor, innocent lamb,
      T'appease an angry god.
Macd. I am not treacherous.
Mal.   But Macbeth is.
      A good and virtuous nature may recoil,
      In an imperial charge. But I shall crave your pardon:
      That which you are my thoughts cannot transpose: 21
      Angels are bright still, though the brightest fell:
      Though all things foul would wear the brows of grace,

---

11. What] *When Chambers.*   15. deserve] *Theobald* (*Warburton*)*; discerne F.*
of him] *not in, conj. Steevens.*   and wisdom] *F;* 'tis wisdom *Hanmer;* and wisdom
is it *conj. Steevens;* and 'tis wisdom *conj. Collier;* and wisdom bids *conj. Staunton;*
and wisdom 'twere *Keightley;* and wisdom / Bids me remember it may be your
wisdom *conj. Grierson;* And wisdom 'tis *conj. Cuningham* (*lines 14–17 end* but / me, /
weak / god). 16. To offer] 'Tis t'offer *Nicholson* (*apud Camb.*). 17. T'
appease] *F,* To appease *many Edd.* 23. wear] bear *F4.*

---

speare's Small Latine, i. 570, shows that
Shakespeare might have read in his
Accidence of Interjections: 'Some are of . . .
Sorowe: as *Heu, hei.*'

10. *to friend*] i.e. for friend, to be-
friend me. Cf. *All's W.*, v. iii. 182, and
Caes., iii. i. 143.

12. *whose sole name*] the mere mention
of whose name (Chambers).

14–17. *He hath . . . god*] Cuningham
wished to alter the lineation of these
lines and to insert '*tis* after *wisdom*. But
'*tis* or '*twere* may be understood, and
need not be inserted.

15. *deserve*] Theobald's emendation
is almost universally accepted, but
Upton's explanation of the Folio 'discerne' ('You may see something to
your advantage by betraying me') is
not impossible.

19–20. *recoil . . . charge*] give way
under pressure of a royal command.
For this use of 'recoil' cf. v. ii. 23 and
Cym., i. vi. 128.

20. *imperial*] royal. Cf. *MND.*, ii. i.
163.

charge] command; but the word was
suggested by 'recoil', by a quibble.

21. *transpose*] change. Cf. *MND.*,
i. i. 233: 'Love can transpose to form
and dignity.' The line means: 'my
thoughts cannot alter what you really
are.'

23–4. *Though . . . so*] 'I do not say
that your virtuous appearance proves
you a traitor; for virtue must wear its
proper form, though that form be
counterfeited by villainy' (Johnson).

23. *would*] should. Cf. i. vii. 34,
etc.

Yet Grace must still look so.
Macd.   I have lost my hopes.
Mal. Perchance even there where I did find my doubts.   25
Why in that rawness left you wife and child
(Those precious motives, those strong knots of love),
Without leave-taking?—I pray you,
Let not my jealousies be your dishonours,
But mine own safeties: you may be rightly just,   30
Whatever I shall think.
Macd.   Bleed, bleed, poor country!
Great tyranny, lay thou thy basis sure,
For goodness dare not check thee! wear thou thy
          wrongs;
The title is affeer'd!—Fare thee well, Lord:
I would not be the villain that thou think'st   35
For the whole space that's in the tyrant's grasp,
And the rich East to boot.
Mal.   Be not offended:

---

25. Perchance . . . doubts] *so Rowe; two lines, the first ending* there *F.*   26. child]
Childe? *F;* children *F2–4.*   33. dare] *F1–2;* dares *F3–4, Wilson.*   34. The]
Thy *Malone.*   affeer'd] *Hanmer;* affear'd *F.*   35. think'st] think'st me
Keightley.

24–5. *hopes . . . doubts*] Macduff is
thinking of an expedition against
Macbeth; Malcolm is suspicious of
Macduff's conduct in leaving his wife
and children.

26. *rawness*] unprotected condition.
He suspects Macduff of having an
understanding with Macbeth, or he
would not have left his family to the
tyrant's mercies. Cf. *H5*, IV. i. 147:
'children rawly left'.

27. *motives*] persons inspiring love or
devotion, as well as incentives. Cf.
All's W., IV. iv. 20, and *Tim.*, v. iv.
27.

28. *Without . . . you*] Some editors
assume that something is missing. But,
as Abbott suggests, the pause after
'leave-taking' may be 'explained by
the indignation of Macduff, which
Malcolm observes and digresses to
appease'. Not that it is necessary to
explain every irregularity in the metre.

29. *jealousies*] suspicions.

33. *goodness . . . thee*] a criticism of
Malcolm's nervousness. Check = hold
in check, or call to account.

wrongs] ill-gotten gains.

34. *The . . . affeer'd*!] i.e. assured or
confirmed. '*Affeerers* . . . signifies in the
common law such as are appointed in
Court-Leets, upon oath, to set the fines
on such as have committed faults
arbitrarily punishable, and have no
express penalty appointed by statute'
(Cowell, *Interpreter*, cited Clarendon).
Ritson says: 'To *affeer* is to assess, or
reduce to certainty. All amerciaments
are by Magna Charta to be *affeered* by
lawful men, sworn to be impartial.'
Originally a commercial term, meaning 'fix the market-price'. Elwin suggests that there is a pun, the phrase
meaning also 'Malcolm is afraid of
asserting his title to the throne.'

37. *to boot*] in addition.

I speak not as in absolute fear of you.
I think our country sinks beneath the yoke;
It weeps, it bleeds; and each new day a gash   40
Is added to her wounds: I think, withal,
There would be hands uplifted in my right;
And here, from gracious England, have I offer
Of goodly thousands: but, for all this,
When I shall tread upon the tyrant's head,   45
Or wear it on my sword, yet my poor country
Shall have more vices than it had before,
More suffer, and more sundry ways than ever,
By him that shall succeed.

Macd.   What should he be?

Mal. It is myself I mean; in whom I know   50
All the particulars of vice so grafted,
That, when they shall be open'd, black Macbeth
Will seem as pure as snow; and the poor State
Esteem him as a lamb, being compar'd
With my confineless harms.

Macd.   Not in the legions   55
Of horrid Hell can come a devil more damn'd
In evils, to top Macbeth.

Mal.   I grant him bloody,
Luxurious, avaricious, false, deceitful,
Sudden, malicious, smacking of every sin

---

44. thousands] thousands ten *conj. Cuningham.*   but] but yet *Hanmer.*   59.
smacking] *F1;* smoaking *F2-4.*

42. *my right*] *mon droit.*
43. *gracious England*] i.e. Edward the
Confessor.
50-102. *It . . . spoken*] Knights,
Explorations, p. 28, argues that Malcolm here 'has ceased to be a person.
His lines repeat and magnify the evils
which have already been attributed to
Macbeth, acting as a mirror wherein
the ills of Scotland are reflected. And
the statement of evil is strengthened by
contrast with the opposite virtues.'
52. *open'd*] i.e. like buds—suggested
by 'grafted'.
55. *confineless*] boundless. Not used
elsewhere by Shakespeare.

56-7. *devil . . . evils*] pronounced as
monosyllables.
58. *Luxurious*] in the now obsolete sense of 'lascivious', 'lustful',
as always in Shakespeare. Lust, avarice, and deceit are the three vices
which Malcolm, as in Holinshed,
proceeds to charge himself with. He
only grants that Macbeth has
these vices for the sake of argument. Shakespeare is showing the
nature of royalty by describing its
opposite.
59. *Sudden*] hasty, passionate, violent. Cf. *AYL.,* ii. vii. 151: 'sudden and
quick in quarrel'.

That has a name; but there's no bottom, none,   60
In my voluptuousness: your wives, your daughters,
Your matrons, and your maids, could not fill up
The cistern of my lust; and my desire
All continent impediments would o'erbear,
That did oppose my will: better Macbeth,   65
Than such an one to reign.

Macd.   Boundless intemperance
In nature is a tyranny; it hath been
Th'untimely emptying of the happy throne,
And fall of many kings. But fear not yet
To take upon you what is yours: you may   70
Convey your pleasures in a spacious plenty,
And yet seem cold—the time you may so hoodwink:
We have willing dames enough; there cannot be
That vulture in you, to devour so many
As will to greatness dedicate themselves,   75
Finding it so inclin'd.

Mal.   With this, there grows
In my most ill-compos'd affection such
A staunchless avarice, that, were I King,
I should cut off the nobles for their lands;
Desire his jewels, and this other's house: 80

---

66. an] a *Capell.*   Boundless] *not in, conj. Steevens.*   72. cold—] cold,
Theobald (Johnson); cold. *F.*

63. *cistern*] Cf. *Oth.*, iv. ii. 61, where
also the word is used in connection with
lust. Holinshed here speaks of 'the
abhominable founteine of all vices'.

64. *continent*] restraining and chaste,
a quibble on the two meanings. Cf.
Lr., i. ii. 182, 'continent forbearance',
LLL., i. i. 262, 'continent canon', and
Wint., iii. ii. 35, 'as continent, as
chaste'.

65. *will*] desire, lust.

66–7. *Boundless ... tyranny*] i.e. want
of control over the natural appetites
constitutes a tyranny or usurpation
in the 'little kingdom' of man's nature.

71. *Convey*] The word is used in the
corresponding passage in Holinshed
(see Appendix, p. 176). It means

'arrange, manage secretly'; cf. 'hoodwink' (72). Staunton quotes *The Plain
Man's Pathway to Heaven* (1599): 'But
verily, verily, though the adulterer do
never so closely and cunningly *convey*
his sin under a canopy, yet . . .' etc.
'Convey' and 'Conveyers' were eu-
phemisms for *theft* and *thieves,* as in
Wiv., i. iii. 32: ' "Convey" the wise it
call', and *R2*, iv. i. 317: 'Conveyers are
you all.'

75. *dedicate*] See Murry, *Countries of
the Mind,* ii, for an interesting essay on
Shakespeare's use of this word, though
I disagree with Murry's chronology of
the plays.

77. *affection*] disposition.
78. *staunchless*] insatiable.
80. *his*] i.e. one man's.

And my more-having would be as a sauce
To make me hunger more; that I should forge
Quarrels unjust against the good and loyal,
Destroying them for wealth.

Macd.   This avarice
Sticks deeper, grows with more pernicious root   85
Than summer-seeming lust; and it hath been
The sword of our slain kings: yet do not fear;
Scotland hath foisons to fill up your will,
Of your mere own. All these are portable,
With other graces weigh'd.   90

Mal. But I have none: the king-becoming graces,
As Justice, Verity, Temp'rance, Stableness,
Bounty, Perseverance, Mercy, Lowliness,
Devotion, Patience, Courage, Fortitude,
I have no relish of them; but abound   95
In the division of each several crime,
Acting it many ways. Nay, had I power, I should

---

85. Sticks] Strikes *Hanmer* (*conj. Theobald*).   86. summer-seeming] *F;*
summer-teeming *Theobald* (*Warburton*); summer-seeding *Steevens* (*1785*), *conj.*
Heath; summer-seaming *conj. Staunton.*   88. foisons] Poisons *F3–4.*

82–3. *forge Quarrels*] Rushton, *Shakespeare Illustrated by the Lex Scripta,* quoted a statute of Henry IV's reign about the making of faulty arrowheads and defective quarrels (i.e. square-headed arrows for a crossbow) and argued that Malcolm here and 137 *post* ('warranted quarrel') was using the word in a double sense, because the verbs 'forge' and 'warrant' might both be applied to arrows. I think this is very unlikely, though the double meaning might have been at the back of Shakespeare's mind.

85. *Sticks*] Theobald's change is unnecessary. Cf. III. i. 49 *ante*, and *Meas.*, v. i. 480.

root] See Holinshed, Appendix, p. 177.

86. *summer-seeming*] i.e. either summer-beseeming, or summer-like. Lust fades with the winter of age, but avarice does not. Malone compared

Donne's 'Love's Alchymy': 'So, lovers dreame a rich and long delight, / But yet a winter-seeming summer's night.' Here *winter-seeming* = winter-like, i.e. long. Lust and summer are often juxtaposed in Shakespeare, e.g. *Oth.*, IV. ii. 66.

87. *slain kings*] see Holinshed, Appendix, p. 177.

88. *foisons*] plenty, abundance. The plural form is unusual. Cf. *Tp.*, IV. i. 110.

89. *Of your mere own*] i.e. royal property.

portable] Holinshed uses the word 'importable' in this dialogue. See Appendix, p. 176.

90. *weigh'd*] i.e. counterbalanced.

93. *Perseverance*] The accent is on the second syllable.

95. *relish*] savour, trace. Cf. *Ham.*, III. iii. 92: 'Some act / That hath no relish of salvation in't.'

96. *division*] variation, descant.

    Pour the sweet milk of concord into Hell,
    Uproar the universal peace, confound
    All unity on earth.
Macd.   O Scotland! Scotland!   100
Mal. If such a one be fit to govern, speak:
    I am as I have spoken.
Macd.   Fit to govern?
    No, not to live.—O nation miserable!
    With an untitled tyrant bloody-scepter'd,
    When shalt thou see thy wholesome days again,   105
    Since that the truest issue of thy throne
    By his own interdiction stands accus'd,
    And does blaspheme his breed? Thy royal father
    Was a most sainted King: the Queen, that bore thee,
    Oft'ner upon her knees than on her feet,   110

98. Pour] Sow'r *Hanmer.*   Hell] hate *Hanmer.*   99. Uproar] Uproot *or*
Uptear *conjs. Keightley.*   102–3. Fit . . . miserable!] *so Pope; one line,* F.
107. accus'd] *Grierson, Harrison, Wilson;* accust *F1;* accurst *F2–4, most Edd.*

98. *milk of concord*] Cf. I. v. 17 *ante.*

99. *Uproar*] throw into confusion (*O.E.D.*).

99–100. *confound . . . earth*] 'This is what Macbeth has done' (Knights, *op. cit.*, p. 29). As this is not in Holinshed, Wilson suspects an interpolation by Shakespeare to please James I, who had ambitions as a peacemaker and hoped for the unity of Christendom. 'It seems that the crowning horror in Malcolm's self-indictment is violent opposition to James's cherished foreign policy.' Later (125–31) Malcolm recants three vices—lechery, avarice, and falsehood, as in Holinshed—though he has not accused himself specifically of falsehood; and in his recantation he does not mention his hatred of peace. This is an ingenious theory. But it should be noted that Malcolm does accuse himself of lack of verity (92) and that the 'milk of concord' is a main theme of the play (cf. the chapter of that title in Knight, *The Imperial Theme*). But although there is insufficient evidence of an insertion to please King James, there may have been a cut at 89 or

90 of a passage in which Malcolm spoke in detail of the third vice, falsehood.

101. *such a one*] Cf. 'such an one', 66 *ante.*

107. *interdiction*] An interdiction was normally an authoritative or peremptory prohibition, particularly in ecclesiastical matters; but it seems here to be a term in Scots law = 'a restraint imposed upon a person incapable of managing his own affairs on account of unsoundness of mind, improvidence, etc.' (*O.E.D.*). Such an interdiction might be 'voluntary', when a man resigned the conduct of his affairs to another. N.

accus'd] Nearly all editors follow F2 reading, 'accurst'. But 'accus'd' (F1 'accust') makes better sense if 'interdiction' is interpreted as above, and makes a tolerable sense even if 'interdiction' is interpreted in the ordinary way. N.

108. *blaspheme*] slander, defame. Cf. Bacon, *Advancement of Learning*, I. ii. 9: 'And as to the judgment of Cato the Censor, he was well punished for his *blasphemy* against learning.'

Died every day she liv'd. Fare thee well!
These evils thou repeat'st upon thyself
Hath banish'd me from Scotland.—O my breast,
Thy hope ends here!

Mal.   Macduff, this noble passion,
Child of integrity, hath from my soul   115
Wip'd the black scruples, reconcil'd my thoughts
To thy good truth and honour. Devilish Macbeth
By many of these trains hath sought to win me
Into his power, and modest wisdom plucks me
From over-credulous haste: but God above   120
Deal between thee and me! for even now
I put myself to thy direction, and
Unspeak mine own detraction; here abjure
The taints and blames I laid upon myself,
For strangers to my nature. I am yet   125
Unknown to woman; never was forsworn;
Scarcely have coveted what was mine own;
At no time broke my faith: would not betray
The Devil to his fellow; and delight
No less in truth, than life: my first false speaking   130
Was this upon myself. What I am truly,
Is thine, and my poor country's, to command:

---

111. liv'd] *F;* lived *Capell, Wilson.*   113. Hath] Have *Rowe.*   126. woman]
women *F2–4.*   forsworn] foreswore *F2–4.*

111. *Died . . . liv'd*] Malone compared 1 Cor., xv. 31: 'I die dayly.'

liv'd] Most editors correct this to 'lived'; but although Shakespeare uses the dissyllabic word in *Caes.*, III. i. 257, 'That ever lived in the tide of times', it is better here to retain the Folio reading and assume a pause, which is natural and necessary. Cf. Flatter, *op. cit.*, p. 43.

113. *Hath*] Rowe's emendation is unnecessary. Macduff means either that Malcolm's sins, which he has just confessed, or the same sins in Macbeth, have banished him.

118. *trains*] stratagems, artifices, plots. Cotgrave defines 'Traine' as 'a plot, practise, conspiracie, deuise'. Cf.

1H4, v. ii. 21. In hunting and hawking the term was used for a bait trailed or drawn along the ground to entice an animal; or for a lure of some kind to reclaim a hawk. Baynes, *Shakespeare Studies*, 1896, p. 312, quotes Turberville, *Book of Hunting*, 1908, p. 210: 'When a huntsman would hunt the wolfe, he must trayne them by these means . . . there lette them lay downe their traynes. And when the wolves go out in the night to pray and to feede, they will crosse upon the trayne and follow it.'

123. *mine own detraction*] my detraction of myself.

125. *For strangers*] as being strangers.

Whither, indeed, before thy here-approach,
Old Siward, with ten thousand warlike men,
Already at a point, was setting forth.   135
Now we'll together, and the chance of goodness
Be like our warranted quarrel. Why are you silent?
Macd. Such welcome and unwelcome things at once,
'Tis hard to reconcile.

Enter a Doctor.

Mal.   Well, more anon.
Comes the King forth, I pray you?   140

133. thy] *F2;* they *F1.*   here-approach] *Pope;* heere approach *F1.*   135.
Already] *F;* All ready *Rowe.*   forth.] foorth? *F2–3.*   136–7. the chance . . .
quarrel] our chance, in goodness . . . quarrel *Hanmer;* the chance, O goodness
. . . quarrel *conj. Johnson;* the chance of good success Betide our . . . quarrel
conj. Bailey; the grace of Goodness Betide . . . quarrel *conj. Cuningham.*   139–
40. 'Tis . . . you?] *Muir;* Well, . . . you? *one line F.*

133. *here-approach*] Cf. 'here-remain',
148 *post.*

134. *Siward*] the son of Beorn, Earl
of Northumberland. He assisted King
Edward the Confessor in suppressing
the rebellion of Earl Godwin and his
sons in 1053.

135. *at a point*] in readiness, prepared, in agreement. The Clar. Edd.
quote Foxe's *Acts and Monuments,* 1570,
p. 2092: 'The Register there sittyng
by, beying weery, belyke, of tarying or
els perceauyng the constant Martyrs
to be at a point, called vpon the chaun-
celour in hast to rid them out of the
way, and to make an end.' Cf. *Ham.,*
I. ii. 200: 'armed at point'.

136–7. *the chance . . . quarrel*] i.e. may
the chance of success be proportionate
to the justice of our cause. *goodness =*
good fortune. (Or, might it mean 'may
our just cause be Goodness's (i.e.
God's) opportunity to overthrow evil
in the shape of Macbeth'?)

139. *Well, more anon*] The pause
comes better after this phrase than
before it, for during the pause the
doctor comes down stage.

140–59. *Comes . . . grace*] Although
one motive for the introduction of this
passage may have been to flatter

James I, and although the fact that
' 'Tis hard to reconcile' (139) and 'See
who comes here' (159) might be
joined to make a line suggests that the
intervening lines might be an interpolation, it can still be justified on
dramatic grounds. The good supernatural described here is a contrast to
the evil supernatural of the Weird
Sisters (cf. Knight, *The Wheel of Fire,*
1949, p. 148). Knights, *op. cit.,* p. 31,
links the passage with the disease
imagery of Act v; and there is an
obvious contrast between the holy king
of England and the unholy king of
Scotland. There has been some preparation for the account of Edward in
III. vi and in the list of the king-
becoming graces. It is also arguable
that the entrance of Rosse, with his
tragic news, comes more dramatically
after an undramatic interlude than it
would at 139. The passage is based on
the account of Edward the Confessor
in Holinshed, *Hist. Eng.,* 195*a:* 'As hath
beene thought he was inspired with
the gift of prophesie and also to haue
had the gift of healing infirmities and
diseases. He vsed to help those that
were vexed with the disease, commonlie called the kings euill, and left that

Doct. Aye, Sir; there are a crew of wretched souls,
        That stay his cure: their malady convinces
        The great assay of art; but at his touch,
        Such sanctity hath Heaven given his hand,
        They presently amend.
Mal.   I thank you, Doctor.   145
                                        [*Exit Doctor.*
Macd. What's the disease he means?
Mal.   'Tis call'd the Evil:
        A most miraculous work in this good King,
        Which often, since my here-remain in England,
        I have seen him do. How he solicits Heaven,
        Himself best knows; but strangely-visited people,   150
        All swoln and ulcerous, pitiful to the eye,
        The mere despair of surgery, he cures;
        Hanging a golden stamp about their necks,
        Put on with holy prayers: and 'tis spoken,
        To the succeeding royalty he leaves   155
        The healing benediction. With this strange virtue,
        He hath a heavenly gift of prophecy;
        And sundry blessings hang about his throne,
        That speak him full of grace.

                    Enter ROSSE.

Macd.   See, who comes here.
Mal. My countryman; but yet I know him not.   160

148. here-remain] *Pope;* heere remaine *F.*   150. strangely-visited] *Pope;* strangely visited *F.*   160. not] nor *F.*

vertue as it were a portion of inheritance vnto his successors the kings of this realme.'

142. *convinces*] conquers.

143. *great . . . art*] greatest effort of medical skill.

146. *the Evil*] the king's evil—scrofula.

148. *here-remain*] i.e. stay.

149. *solicits*] prevails by entreaty. King James in 1603 ascribed the effect of his 'touch' to prayer. Cf. Gardiner, *History of England*, I. 152.

152. *mere*] utter.

153. *stamp*] i.e. stamped coin: an

angel. Cf. *Wint.*, IV. iv. 747: 'we pay them for it with stamped coin.' The gift is not mentioned in Holinshed, but was customary in Shakespeare's day. Paul supposes that Shakespeare was asked to insert this reference to the coin to overcome the King's reluctance to use it in the ceremony.

156. *virtue*] healing power.

160. *My countryman*] Malcolm recognizes him by his dress—Wilson suggests a blue bonnet. There are no signs of Scottish costume in the earliest illustration to the play (1709) and Macklin is reputed to have introduced

Macd. My ever-gentle cousin, welcome hither.
Mal. I know him now. Good God, betimes remove
    The means that makes us strangers!
Rosse.   Sir, amen.
Macd. Stands Scotland where it did?
Rosse.   Alas, poor country!
    Almost afraid to know itself. It cannot   165
    Be call'd our mother, but our grave; where nothing,
    But who knows nothing, is once seen to smile;
    Where sighs, and groans, and shrieks that rent the air
    Are made, not mark'd; where violent sorrow seems
    A modern ecstasy: the dead man's knell   170
    Is there scarce ask'd for who; and good men's lives
    Expire before the flowers in their caps,
    Dying or ere they sicken.
Macd.   O relation,
    Too nice, and yet too true!
Mal.   What's the newest grief?
Rosse. That of an hour's age doth hiss the speaker;   175
    Each minute teems a new one.
Macd.   How does my wife?

---

161. ever-gentle] *Pope;* euer gentle *F.*
meanes *F2–4.*   makes] make *Hanmer.*
4. O . . . true!] *so Theobald; one line, F.*
Steevens.   What's] What is *Hanmer, etc.*
one. / children? / too. *Arden (ed. 1).*

163. The means] The meanes, the
meanes *F2–4.*   168. rent] *F;* rend *Rowe.*   173–
174. and . . . true] yet true *conj.*
176–7. Each . . . too] *lines end*

---

it in 1773. R. Walker, *op. cit.,* p. 167,
suggests that Malcolm refuses to know
Rosse, diplomatically, because he is a
collaborator. I doubt this; but Walker
also draws a suggestive parallel between this entry and Rosse's first entry
in I. ii: 'Again it is Ross who comes to
the King of Scotland, again with news
of a treacherous thane of Cawdor—
and again from Fife.'

  167. *once*] ever, at any time. Cf. *Ant.,*
v. ii. 50.

  168. *rent*] used indifferently with
rend, as the present tense of the verb
(Clarendon).

  170. *A modern ecstasy*] i.e. a common-
place emotion. Cf. *Rom.,* III. ii. 120:
'modern lamentation'; *All's W.,* II. iii.

2: 'to make modern and familiar
things supernatural and causeless'. For
'ecstasy' see III. ii. 22 *ante.* The words
may mean a sham trance or fit of
hysteria and allude to the sham
demoniacs exposed in Harsnett's
Declaration (Paul).

  171. *who*] for 'whom'.

  172. *flowers*] H. Rowe thought there
might be a reference to the way High-
landers stick heather in their bonnets.

  174. *nice*] elaborate. Cf. *Rom.,* v. ii.
18: 'The letter was not nice, but full of
charge.'

  175. *hiss*] cause to be hissed.

  176. *teems*] also in the active sense
in *H5,* v. ii. 52: 'nothing teems / But
hateful docks, rough thistles.'

Rosse. Why, well.

Macd.   And all my children?

Rosse.   Well too.

Macd. The tyrant has not batter'd at their peace?

Rosse. No; they were well at peace, when I did leave 'em.

Macd. Be not a niggard of your speech: how goes't?   180

Rosse. When I came hither to transport the tidings,
    Which I have heavily borne, there ran a rumour
    Of many worthy fellows that were out;
    Which was to my belief witness'd the rather,
    For that I saw the tyrant's power afoot.   185
    Now is the time of help. Your eye in Scotland
    Would create soldiers, make our women fight,
    To doff their dire distresses.

Mal.   Be't their comfort,
    We are coming thither. Gracious England hath
    Lent us good Siward, and ten thousand men;   190
    An older, and a better soldier, none
    That Christendom gives out.

Rosse.   Would I could answer
    This comfort with the like! But I have words,
    That would be howl'd out in the desert air,
    Where hearing should not latch them.

Macd.   What concern they?
    The general cause? or is it a fee-grief,   196

---

179. 'em] *F;* them *Capell.*   180. goes't] *Capell;* gos't *F.*   195. latch] catch
Rowe.   195–6. What . . . cause?] *Theobald;* What . . . they, . . . cause, *F;*
What? concern they The gen'ral cause? *Rowe.*

177. *well*] Cf. *Ant.,* II. v. 32: 'We use
To say, the dead are well.' Craig
quotes Heywood, *Faire Maid of the
West* (ed. Pearson, II. 299): 'Why well
. . . He's well in heaven, for, mistresse,
he is dead.'

children] The metrical pause after
this word suggests Rosse's embarrass-
ment.

179. *at peace*] Cf. 'sent to peace',
III. ii. 20 *ante,* and *R2,* III. ii. 127–8.

181. *tidings*] i.e. of the murder of
Macduff's family. Rosse twice shies
away from his message.

183. *out*] i.e. in the field, in rebellion.

The followers of the two Pretenders
were frequently spoken of as 'out' in
the '15 and '45.

186. *Your*] i.e. Malcolm's.

188. *doff*] clothing image. Cf. 33 *ante.*

189. *Gracious England*] Cf. 43 *ante.*

192. *gives out*] proclaims.

194. *would*] should.

195. *latch*] i.e. catch. See Palsgrave,
Lesclarcissement, 1530, p. 604: 'I latche,
I catche a thynge that is throwne to
me in my handes, *je happe.*' Cf. *Sonn.,*
cxiii. 6.

196. *fee-grief*] An estate in fee simple
is the largest estate in land known to

Due to some single breast?

Rosse.   No mind that's honest
But in it shares some woe, though the main part
Pertains to you alone.

Macd.   If it be mine,
Keep it not from me; quickly let me have it.   200

Rosse. Let not your ears despise my tongue for ever,
Which shall possess them with the heaviest sound,
That ever yet they heard.

Macd.   Humh! I guess at it.

Rosse. Your castle is surpris'd; your wife, and babes,
Savagely slaughter'd: to relate the manner,   205
Were, on the quarry of these murther'd deer,
To add the death of you.

Mal.   Merciful Heaven!—
What, man! ne'er pull your hat upon your brows:
Give sorrow words; the grief, that does not speak,
Whispers the o'er-fraught heart, and bids it break.   210

Macd. My children too?

Rosse.   Wife, children, servants, all
That could be found.

Macd.   And I must be from thence!
My wife kill'd too?

Rosse.   I have said.

---

203. Humh!] Hum! *Rowe;* Humh: *F;* Humph! *Malone.*   211–13. Wife . . .
too?] *so Capell; two lines, the first ending* found *F.*

the English law, and Shakespeare here
may convey a twofold idea of boundless grief, i.e. the utmost which could
be contained in 'some single breast',
and of particular ownership as opposed
to ownership in common. But Shakespeare may have meant no more than
'a peculiar sorrow, a grief which hath
a single owner' (Johnson).

197. *Due to*] i.e. owned by.

198. *in . . . woe*] continuation of legal
metaphor.

202. *possess*] inform precisely (Dyce).

203. *Humh*] Cf. note on III. ii. 42 *ante.*

206. *quarry*] game killed in hunting
or hawking. Cf. *Ham.*, v. ii. 375.

deer] a pun.

209–10. *the grief . . . break*] a variation on one of the favourite lines in
Seneca, *Hippolytus*, 607: 'Curae leves
loquuntur, ingentes stupent.' Florio,
Essayes, I. ii, translates: 'Light cares
can freely speake, / Great cares heart
rather breake.' Shakespeare uses the
same rhyme. Cf. Ford, *Broken Heart*,
v. iii. 76: 'They are the silent griefs
which cut the heart-strings'; and
Webster, *White Devil*, II. i. 279: 'Those
are the killing greifes which dare not
speake.'

211–13.] Perhaps the F lineation,
suggesting dramatic pauses in the
metrical gaps, is preferable.

212. *must*] preterite.

Mal.   Be comforted:
  Let's make us med'cines of our great revenge,
  To cure this deadly grief.   215
Macd. He has no children.—All my pretty ones?
  Did you say all?—O Hell-kite!—All?
  What, all my pretty chickens, and their dam,
  At one fell swoop?
Mal. Dispute it like a man.
Macd.   I shall do so;   220
  But I must also feel it as a man:
  I cannot but remember such things were,
  That were most precious to me.—Did Heaven look on,
  And would not take their part? Sinful Macduff!
  They were all struck for thee. Naught that I am,   225
  Not for their own demerits, but for mine,
  Fell slaughter on their souls: Heaven rest them now!
Mal. Be this the whetstone of your sword: let grief
  Convert to anger; blunt not the heart, enrage it.
Macd. O! I could play the woman with mine eyes,   230
  And braggart with my tongue.—But, gentle Heavens,
  Cut short all intermission; front to front,

214–15. *Let's . . . grief*] One passion
was thought to drive out another. Cf.
H. Craig, *The Enchanted Glass*, 1936,
pp. 116 *seq.*

216. *He . . . children*] There are three
explanations of this passage. (i) He
refers to Malcolm, who if he had children of his own would not suggest
revenge as a cure for grief. Cf. *John*,
III. iv. 91: 'He talks to me that never
had a son.' This was supported by
Malone and Bradley. (ii) He refers to
Macbeth, on whom he cannot take an
appropriate revenge (Clarendon, New
Clarendon, Cuningham). (iii) He
refers to Macbeth, who would never
have slaughtered Macduff's children
if he had had any of his own. Cf. *3H6*,
v. v. 63: 'You have no children,
butchers if you had, / The thought of
them would have stirred up remorse'
(Delius). I adhere to (ii).

217. *Hell-kite*] Cf. note on III. iv.
71–2 *ante*, and *deer* (206), *chickens* (218),

slaughter, souls (227) and *Lr.*, I. iv. 260.

218. *dam*] used of birds as well as of
quadrupeds.

219. *swoop*] i.e. of the hell-kite. But
Wilson suggests there is also present
the sense of losing all in a sweepstake.
Cf. *Ham.*, IV. v. 142.

220. *Dispute*] struggle against.

225. *Naught*] wicked.

226. *Not . . . mine*] He is not blaming
himself for his flight from Scotland, but
for his sinful nature. The word 'demerits' is used by Holinshed of Donwald (p. 151).

229. *Convert*] turn; here used in-
transitively, as in *R2*, v. i. 66: 'The love
of wicked men converts to fear'; and
ibid., v. iii. 64: 'Thy overflow of good
converts to bad.' Anderson, *Elizabethan
Psychology and Shakespeare's Plays*, p. 99,
comments that 'to weep . . . is to make
less the fuel of revenge.'

232. *intermission*] interruption, delay, interval of time. Cf. *Mer.V.*, III.

Bring thou this fiend of Scotland, and myself;
Within my sword's length set him; if he 'scape,
Heaven forgive him too!
Mal.   This tune goes manly.   235
Come, go we to the King: our power is ready;
Our lack is nothing but our leave. Macbeth
Is ripe for shaking, and the Powers above
Put on their instruments. Receive what cheer you may;
The night is long that never finds the day.   [*Exeunt.*

---

235. Heaven] *F;* Then Heaven *Pope;* O God *or* Then God *or* May God *or* God,
God *Camb.*   tune] *Rowe (ed. 3);* time *F.*

---

ii. 201 : 'You loved, I loved, for intermission / No more pertains to me, my
lord, than you', and *Lr.*, II. iv. 33:
'spite of intermission'.

235. *Heaven*] 'Probably the original
MS. had "May God", or "Then God",
or "God, God", as in v. i. 72, which
was changed in the actors' copy to
Heaven for fear of incurring the
penalties provided by the Act of
Parliament against profanity on the
stage' (Clarendon). The Act 3 James I,
cap. 21, *An Act to Restrain the abuses of
Players*, 'For the preventing and avoid-
ing of the great abuse of the holy
Name of God, in Stage-playes, Enter-
ludes, May-games, Shews, and such-
like', enacted that 'if . . . any person do
or shall in any Stage-play . . . jestingly
or prophanely speak, or use the holy
Name of God, or of Jesus Christ, or of
the Holy Ghost, or of the Trinity . . .
shall forfeit for every such offence . . .
ten pounds'; half of the fine going to
the king and half to 'him or them that
will sue for the same'. I suspect that
'God' rather than the conjectures of
the Camb. and Clar. Edd. was what
Shakespeare wrote.

too] because if he escapes, it will be a
sign that my hatred is appeased.
Wilson compares *Ham.*, I. ii. 182–3 and
III. iii. 73–95.

tune] Rowe's emendation for 'time'

is generally accepted. But Cuningham
defends the Folio reading by quoting
Ham., III. i. 166 (Q2): 'Like sweet bells
jangled out of *time* and harsh' and two
other passages from Elizabethan plays.
Though the *Hamlet* 'time' was probably a misprint, which was corrected
in the Folio, and though the other
passages by Cuningham are not decisive, it is possible that Malcolm here
means 'time'; for the time of manly
music would differ from that of a plaint
or dirge.

236. *power*] army. Cf. 238 *post.*

237. *Our lack . . . leave*] i.e. we have
only to take our leave of the king.

238. *ripe for shaking*] Noble compares
Nahum, iii. 12: 'All thy strong cities
shall be like figge trees with the first
ripe figs: for if they bee shaken, they
fall into the mouth of the eater.'

Powers] Cf. note on II. i. 7–9 *ante.*

239. *Put . . . instruments*] i.e. arm
themselves; not 'set us, their instruments, to the work' (Steevens, Clarendon, Cuningham).

239–40. *Receive . . . day*] Wilson and
others suspect the hand of the interpolator; but the tag makes an easier
finish to the act, and the alexandrine
(239) is insufficient evidence of an interpolation. Cuningham argues that
'Put on' (239) should be printed in the
previous line.

ACT V

SCENE I.—[*Dunsinane. A room in the castle.*]

Enter a Doctor of Physic and a Waiting-Gentlewoman.

Doct. I have two nights watch'd with you, but can per-
ceive no truth in your report. When was it she last
walk'd?

Gent. Since his Majesty went into the field, I have seen
her rise from her bed, throw her night-gown upon   5
her, unlock her closet, take forth paper, fold it, write
upon't, read it, afterwards seal it, and again return
to bed; yet all this while in a most fast sleep.

Doct. A great perturbation in nature, to receive at once
the benefit of sleep, and do the effects of watching!   10
In this slumbery agitation, besides her walking and

ACT V

Scene 1

S.D. *Dunsinane.*] Capell.   *A . . . castle*] Rowe (subst.).   1. two] too *F.*   9.
nature,] *F;* nature,— *Dyce.*   10. watching!] *Dyce, Wilson;* watching. *F.*

4. *into the field*] Steevens complains
that Shakespeare 'forgot he had shut
up Macbeth in Dunsinane and surrounded him with besiegers. That he
could *not go into the field* is observed by
himself with a splenetic impatience,
v. v. 5–7.' But Macbeth was not yet
surrounded by besiegers; and in IV.
iii. 185 Rosse speaks of having seen 'the
tyrant's power afoot', probably to
suppress the rebels 'that were out';
and Macbeth would not necessarily be
beleaguered in his fortress until the
arrival of the English forces under
Siward. Holinshed mentions 'light
skirmishes'. See Appendix, p. 178.

5. *night-gown*] See II. ii. 69 *ante.*
6. *closet*] private repository of
valuables. Cf. *Lr.,* III. iii. 11: 'I

have lock'd the letter in my closet.'

paper] Critics suggest that she writes
a letter to Macbeth; perhaps indica-
ting that she still wishes to control him,
though he no longer consults her. But
it might be a confession. Paul thinks
she is writing to warn Lady Macduff.

fold it] probably to mark a margin.
Cf. Florio's *Montaigne,* I. 39: 'a sheete
without folding or margine'.

9. *perturbation in nature*] constitu-
tional disorder (Wilson).

10. *watching*] i.e. waking. Cf. *Rom.,*
IV. iv. 8; and Holland, *Pliny,* XIV. 18
(cited Clarendon): 'two kindes of wine
of contrary operations, the one pro-
cureth sleepe, the other causeth
watching'.

11. *slumbery*] Cf. Phaer, *Virgil* (sig.

other actual performances, what, at any time, have
you heard her say?

Gent. That, Sir, which I will not report after her.

Doct. You may, to me; and 'tis most meet you should.   15

Gent. Neither to you, nor any one; having no witness to
confirm my speech.

Enter LADY MACBETH, *with a taper.*

Lo you! here she comes. This is her very guise; and,
upon my life, fast asleep. Observe her: stand close.

Doct. How came she by that light?   20

Gent. Why, it stood by her: she has light by her continually; 'tis her command.

Doct. You see, her eyes are open.

Gent. Ay, but their sense are shut.

Doct. What is it she does now? Look, how she rubs her   25
hands.

Gent. It is an accustom'd action with her, to seem thus
washing her hands. I have known her continue in
this a quarter of an hour.

Lady M. Yet here's a spot.   30

Doct. Hark! she speaks. I will set down what comes from
her, to satisfy my remembrance the more strongly.

14. report] *F;* repeat *conj. Warburton.*   17. *Lady Macbeth*] *Rowe;* Lady *F.*
24. sense are] *F;* senses are *Keightley;* sense' are *Dyce (conj. S. Walker), Arden*
(*ed. 1*); sense is *Rowe and many Edd.*   32. satisfy] satisfie *F;* fortifie *Warburton.*

1. 4, ed. 1620): 'the place of sleepe and
slumbry night'.
   agitation] physical activity, not
mental. 'slumbery agitation = sleep-
walking' (Wilson).
   12. *actual*] exhibited in deeds
(*O.E.D.*).
   15. *You may ... should*] blank verse.
   16–17. *Neither ... speech*] Liddell
comments: 'The gentlewoman's canny
reluctance to shelter herself under the
physician's professional privilege is
probably due to Shakespeare's knowledge of law ... her unsupported statement as to what Lady Macbeth has
said would amount to treason if the
doctor chose to betray her confidence.'
This is most unlikely.

18. *Lo ... guise*] blank verse.
   This ... guise] 'This is the way she
has done it before' (New Clarendon).
   19. *close*] concealed. Cf. *Caes.*, I. iii.
131.
   21. *light*] because she is now terrified
of the dark.
   24. *are*] often emended; but Shakespeare probably wrote 'are' on account
of the plural contained in 'their', and
because the sense of two eyes is referred
to (Delius). Walker compares *Sonn.*,
cxii. 10–11: 'that my adder's sense /
To critic and to flatterer stopped are'.
   30. *spot*] Cf. II. ii. 66–7.
   32. *satisfy*] furnish with sufficient
proof, i.e. support. Cuningham thinks
it means 'assure' and quotes *H5*, III. ii.

Lady M. Out, damned spot! out, I say!—One; two:
why, then 'tis time to do't.—Hell is murky.—Fie,
my Lord, fie! a soldier, and afeard?—What need   35
we fear who knows it, when none can call our power
to accompt?—Yet who would have thought the old
man to have had so much blood in him?
Doct. Do you mark that?
Lady M. The Thane of Fife had a wife: where is she   40
now?—What, will these hands ne'er be clean?—
No more o'that, my Lord, no more o'that: you mar
all with this starting.

34. murky.] *F;* murky! *Steevens.*   36–7. fear who . . . accompt?] feare? who
. . . accompt: *F1–2;* fear who . . . account? *Theobald;* fear? who . . . account:
F3–4.   38. him?] *Rowe;* him. *F;* him! *Knight.*   43. this] *not in F2–4.*
starting] *F1;* stating *F2.*

105; *Tw.N.*, III. iii. 22; and Coles, *Lat.
Dict.* (1677): 'satisfied, certior factus.'
33–65. *Out . . . to bed*] Lady Macbeth's speeches might be printed as
rough blank verse (cf. Bayfield, *Shakespeare's Versification*) though Shakespeare probably intended them as
prose. The verse fossils (cf. notes to 15,
18 *ante*) may indicate a revision of this
scene. It must be in prose, writes J.
Wilson, *Dies Boreales* (Blackwood's,
1849), 'because these are the *ipsissima
verba*—yea, the escaping sighs and
moans of the bared soul. There must
be nothing, not even the thin and
translucent veil of the verse, betwixt
her soul showing itself, and yours
beholding.'
33. *One; two*] Lady Macbeth thinks
she hears the clock strike—not, I think
as Wilson suggests, the bell she struck
at II. i. 61; cf. Marston, *2 Antonio and
Mellida*, I. i. 9.
34. *Hell is murky*] The Folio punctuation, i.e. with the full stop, is correct
here and not Steevens's emendation.
Bradley, *Shakespearean Tragedy*, p. 334,
remarks: 'The failure of nature in Lady
Macbeth is marked by her fear of darkness: "She has light by her continually." And in the one phrase of fear
that escapes her lips even in sleep, it is
of the darkness of the place of torment

that she speaks.' Steevens thought she
imagined herself here talking to Macbeth, who (she supposed) had first said
Hell is murky, and repeats his words in
contempt of his cowardice: and he
punctuated with a note of exclamation
accordingly. But, as Bradley further
remarks, 'He would hardly in those
days have used an argument or expressed a fear that could provoke
nothing but contempt.' In I. vii
Macbeth never appeals to moral prin-
ciples, and he would jump the life to
come.
36–7. *none . . . accompt*] Rushton,
Shakespeare a Lawyer (1858), p. 37, says:
'Reference seems to be here made to
the ancient and fundamental principle
of the English Constitution that the
King can do no wrong.' Cuningham
supported this view by a quotation
from Blount's *Law Dictionary* (1670).
But I agree with Case that 'a more
ancient and fundamental' principle is
that tyrant power cannot be brought
to book.'
40. *Fife . . . wife*] The doggerel
rhyme is used with superb effect.
41. *clean*] imitated by Webster,
White Devil, v. iv. 76: 'Heere's a white
hand: / Can bloud so soone bee washt
out?'
43. *starting*] Cf. III. iv. 62.

Doct. Go to, go to: you have known what you should not.

Gent. She has spoke what she should not, I am sure of   45
that: Heaven knows what she has known.

Lady M. Here's the smell of the blood still: all the
perfumes of Arabia will not sweeten this little hand.
Oh! oh! oh!

Doct. What a sigh is there! The heart is sorely charg'd.   50

Gent. I would not have such a heart in my bosom, for the
dignity of the whole body.

Doct. Well, well, well.

Gent. Pray God it be, sir.

Doct. This disease is beyond my practice: yet I have   55
known those which have walk'd in their sleep, who
have died holily in their beds.

Lady M. Wash your hands, put on your night-gown;
look not so pale.—I tell you yet again, Banquo's
buried: he cannot come out on's grave.   60

Doct. Even so?

Lady M. To bed, to bed: there's knocking at the gate.
Come, come, come, come, give me your hand.
What's done cannot be undone. To bed, to bed, to
bed.   [*Exit.*   65

Doct. Will she go now to bed?

Gent. Directly.

Doct. Foul whisp'rings are abroad. Unnatural deeds

---

44. Go . . . not.] *one line, Pope; two lines, the first ending* to: *F.*   51–2. the
dignity] *F1–2*; dignity *F3–4*.

44. *Go . . . not*] This line is not addressed to the Gentlewoman, as some
have imagined.

47. *smell*] Grierson contrasts Macbeth's visual imagination with Lady
Macbeth's sense of smell.

50. *sorely*] heavily.

52. *dignity*] worth, value. Cf. *Troil.*,
I. iii. 204.

55. *practice*] art.

59–60. *I tell you . . . grave*] Adams
thinks that these words indicate that a
scene has been lost, because there is
nothing like it in the Banquet scene.
But Shakespeare does not attempt to
chronicle every hour of the lives of his

characters; and this sentence is merely
a retrospective indication of the terrible dreams and hallucinations which
once afflicted Macbeth nightly, but no
longer. Direness cannot once start him.
Cf. v. v. 9 *post*.

60. *on's*] i.e. of his. Cf. *Lr.*, I. iv. 114:
'two on's daughters'; and 'on' for 'of',
I. iii. 84 *ante*.

64. *What's . . . undone*] Cf. III. ii. 12.

68. *Foul whisp'rings*] insinuations,
slanders, rumours. Cf. 2 Cor., xii. 20.

68–70. *Foul . . . secrets*] Knight, *New
Adelphi*, 1927, pp. 69–73, compares
2H6, III. ii. 374–6: 'he calls the King /
And *whispers* to his *pillow*, as to him, /

Do breed unnatural troubles: infected minds
To their deaf pillows will discharge their secrets.   70
More needs she the divine than the physician.—
God, God forgive us all! Look after her;
Remove from her the means of all annoyance,
And still keep eyes upon her.—So, good night:
My mind she has mated, and amaz'd my sight.   75
I think, but dare not speak.

Gent.   Good night, good Doctor.

                                                        [*Exeunt.*

SCENE II.—[*The country near Dunsinane.*]

Enter, with drums and colours, MENTETH, CATHNESS, ANGUS,
LENOX, *and Soldiers.*

Ment. The English power is near, led on by Malcolm,
His uncle Siward, and the good Macduff.

---

72. God, God] *F;* God, God, *Theobald;* Good God *Pope.*

Scene II

S.D.] *The . . . Dunsinane.*] *Capell.*

The *secrets* of his over-*charged* soul.'

73. *annoyance*] injury, harm to herself; 'annoy' and 'annoyance' were
used in a stronger sense than at present. This hint prepares us for Lady
Macbeth's suicide.

75. *mated*] bewildered, confounded.
Cotgrave's *Dict.* gives the two senses:
'Mater: *To mate, or giue a mate unto;
to . . . amate, quell, subdue, ouercome.*' Both
senses are played upon in *Err.*, III. ii.
54: 'not mad but *mated*'. Cf. Marlowe,
1 Tamb., I. i. 107: 'How now, my lord,
what mated and amazed?' The
original form, *amate*, occurs in Greene,
Orlando Furioso, II. i. 488: 'Hath love
amated him?' Sidney, *Arcadia*, III. vii,
uses the expression 'mated minde' (ed.
Feuillerat, I. 385).

Scene II

S.D. Angus] R. Walker, *op. cit.*, p.
204, remarks that the 're-appearance

of Angus . . . in the rebel ranks in Scotland suggests an almost organic relationship between the invaders and the
rebels, for Angus is almost as much
Rosse as Rosse himself! The same
qualities of Scottish manhood march
with Malcolm and march to meet
Malcolm, the union of the two armies
is not merely an Anglo-Scottish alli-
ance but an organic union of the sun-
dered parts of the snake which Macbeth scotched but could not kill.'

2. *His uncle Siward*] Holinshed speaks
of him as the grandfather of Malcolm:
'Duncane, hauing two sonnes by his
wife which was the daughter of Siward,
Earle of Northumberland'. Cuningham points out that 'nephew' with
Elizabethans clearly meant 'grandson' as well as our 'nephew', as in
Spenser, *Ruines of Rome*, 8: 'Of vertuous
nephewes, that posteritie / Striuing in
power their grandfathers to passe.' But

Revenges burn in them; for their dear causes
Would, to the bleeding and the grim alarm,
Excite the mortified man.

Ang.   Near Birnam wood   5
Shall we well meet them: that way are they coming.

Cath. Who knows if Donalbain be with his brother?

Len. For certain, Sir, he is not. I have a file
Of all the gentry: there is Siward's son,
And many unrough youths, that even now   10
Protest their first of manhood.

Ment.   What does the tyrant?

Cath. Great Dunsinane he strongly fortifies.
Some say he's mad; others, that lesser hate him,
Do call it valiant fury: but, for certain,
He cannot buckle his distemper'd cause   15
Within the belt of rule.

---

4. bleeding] bleeding, *F.*   5. Birnam] *F3–4;* Byrnan *F1–2.*   6. well] *not in*
F3–4, Chambers.   10. unrough] *Theobald;* vnruffe *F;* unruff'd *Pope.*   11.
tyrant?] *F4;* Tyrant. *F1–3.*

Duncan in the play seems to be at least as old as Siward; Shakespeare made him older than in the *Chronicle* and made Siward Malcolm's uncle instead of grandfather to harmonize with the other alteration.

3. *Revenges*] used in the plural, meaning either the desire for vengeance or the act of revenge. Cf. *Cym.*, II. v. 24.

dear causes] heartfelt grounds of accusation, grievous wrongs (Wilson); or grounds of action; or grievous diseases (Liddell). The last meaning suggested 'bleeding' (4) and 'mortified' (5) and 'cause' (15). Cf. *All's W.*, II. i. 113: 'toucht With that malignant cause'.

4. *the bleeding . . . alarm*] i.e. the battlefield. But 'bleeding' may have been suggested by the word 'burn' in the previous line and by 'causes', bleeding being the remedy for a fever (Liddell). 'Bleeding' may also have been suggested by the superstition that the corpse of a murdered man bled afresh in the presence of the murderer (Clarendon), which Shakespeare

might have been reminded of by Holinshed's account of Donwald, where it is mentioned.

5. *Excite . . . man*] either (i) raise up the dead, or (ii) stir up the numbed. Cf. *Caes.*, II. i. 324: 'Thou, like an exorcist, hast conjured up / My mortified spirit.' 'Excite' (from *excitare*) would thus mean 'call forth' or 'quicken'. The whole passage is discussed in *M.L.N.*, XXIX. 94–5, and thus paraphrased: 'The justice of their cause should rouse even the dead to an interest in the bloodshed and din of the battle.' This is, I believe, what Shakespeare meant, though there may have been unconscious or concealed puns.

8. *file*] list, roll. Cf. III. i. 94 *ante*.

10. *unrough*] unbearded.

11. *Protest*] proclaim. Cf. III. iv. 104 *ante*, and *Ado.*, v. i. 149.

15–16. *He . . . rule*] For the metaphor compare *Troil.*, II. ii. 30: 'And buckle in a waist most fathomless / With spans and inches so diminutive / As fears and reasons.' Cf. note to 3 *ante: cause* = sickness. It may mean that Macbeth,

Ang.   Now does he feel
His secret murthers sticking on his hands;
Now minutely revolts upbraid his faith-breach:
Those he commands move only in command,
Nothing in love: now does he feel his title   20
Hang loose about him, like a giant's robe
Upon a dwarfish thief.
Ment.   Who then shall blame
His pester'd senses to recoil and start,
When all that is within him does condemn
Itself, for being there?
Cath.   Well; march we on,   25
To give obedience where 'tis truly ow'd:
Meet we the med'cine of the sickly weal;
And with him pour we, in our country's purge,
Each drop of us.
Len.   Or so much as it needs
To dew the sovereign flower, and drown the weeds.   30
Make we our march towards Birnam.
                                        [*Exeunt, marching.*

like a man with dropsy who cannot get his belt on (cf. Falstaff), cannot restrain his passions (cf. 'mad'). Or, it may mean that the kingdom which he rules is sick and rebellious. Cf. *2H4*, III. i. 38 ff.: 'the body of our kingdom / ... is but as a body, yet distemper'd.'

17. *sticking*] Cf. note on II. ii. 59–62 *ante.*

18. *minutely*] adj. 'very frequent'.

upbraid] used with accusative of things as well as of persons. Cf. *Troil.*, III. ii. 198: 'Upbraid my falsehood'.

his faith-breach] i.e. his own treason.

19. *in command*] i.e. under orders.

21–2. *Hang . . . thief*] The same image is repeated in different forms several times in the course of the play. Cf. I. iii. 108–9 and I. iii. 145–7. Traversi, *Approach to Shakespeare*, 1938, p. 100, comments: 'Before the advancing powers of healing good, evil has shrunk to insignificance.'

23. *pester'd*] embarrassed, troubled, Cotgrave gives: 'Empestrer. *To pester*,

intricate, intangle, trouble, incomber.' The original sense was 'to hobble a horse, or other animal, to prevent it straying'. Cf. *1H4*, I. iii. 50: 'To be so pester'd with a popinjay', and *Troil.*, v. i. 38: 'pester'd with such water flies'.

27. *med'cine*] probably used in the sense of doctor (Fr. *médecin*), though Shakespeare usually uses it in the sense of drug. Cuningham points out that Minsheu's *Spanish Dictionary* (1599) and Cotgrave's *French Dictionary* (1611) have the word only in the latter sense. In either case Malcolm is meant.

28. *purge*] The blood they shed, absorbed by the earth, will act as a purgative drug. Wilson explains the whole passage: 'they are ready to help ... Malcolm purge the land of its fever, even if it means bleeding themselves to the last drop of their blood.'

30. *dew*] bedew. Cf. *2H6*, III. ii. 340.

sovereign] 'Two ideas are suggested by this epithet, royal or supreme, and powerfully remedial, the latter con-

SCENE III.—[*Dunsinane. A room in the castle.*]

Enter MACBETH, *Doctor, and Attendants.*

Macb. Bring me no more reports; let them fly all:
Till Birnam wood remove to Dunsinane,
I cannot taint with fear. What's the boy Malcolm?
Was he not born of woman? The spirits that know
All mortal consequence have pronounc'd me thus: 5
'Fear not, Macbeth; no man that's born of woman
Shall e'er have power upon thee.'—Then fly, false Thanes,
And mingle with the English epicures:
The mind I sway by, and the heart I bear,
Shall never sag with doubt, nor shake with fear.   10

Enter a Servant.

The devil damn thee black, thou cream-fac'd loon!

Scene III

S.D. *Dunsinane . . . castle.*] *Capell.*   2. Birnam] *F3-4;* Byrnane *F1;* Byrnam *F2.*
3. taint] faint *conj. S. Walker.*   5. consequence] *Singer (ed. 1), Wilson;*
Consequences *F;* consequents *Steevens (1793).*

tinuing the metaphor of 27–9' (Clarendon). Fleay and Wilson suspect that
the couplet is interpolated.

Scene III

1. *them*] the thanes.
3. *taint*] go rotten, become weak,
wither. Cf. *Tw.N.,* III. iv. 145. Liddell
quotes Comenius, *Janua linguarum,*
106: 'failing of that moisture it flags,
tainteth, and by and by drieth away'.
4. *spirits*] not the witches but their
'masters' who appear as the apparitions in IV. i.
5. *consequence*] As Shakespeare does
not elsewhere use the plural form, and
as the rhythm is improved by using the
singular form here, 'used collectively
and comprising in its meaning all subsequent circumstances', I have adopted Singer's emendation.
me] 'in my case' or 'me to be circum-
stanced'.

8. *epicures*] Perhaps suggested by
Holinshed, 1587, pp. 179–80, who says
that 'The Scottish people before had
no knowledge nor understanding of
fine fare or riotous surfet . . . those
superfluities came into the realme of
Scotland with the *Englishmen.* . . For
manie of the people abhorring the
riotous maners and superfluous gor-
mandizing brought in among them by
the *Englishmen,* were willing inough to
receiue this Donald for their King,
trusting . . . they should by his severe
order in gouernement recouer againe
the former temperance of their old
progenitors.'
9. *sway*] control myself, direct my
actions. Cf. *Tw.N.,* II. iv. 32.
10. *sag*] droop. Not used elsewhere
by Shakespeare, but in Golding, Ovid's
Metam., xi. 198: 'And made them
downe to sag'.
11. *loon*] a rogue or worthless rascal:

Where gott'st thou that goose look?
Serv. There is ten thousand—
Macb.   Geese, villain?
Serv.   Soldiers, Sir.
Macb. Go, prick thy face, and over-red thy fear,
　Thou lily-liver'd boy. What soldiers, patch?   15
　Death of thy soul! those linen cheeks of thine
　Are counsellors to fear. What soldiers, whey-face?
Serv. The English force, so please you.
Macb. Take thy face hence. [*Exit Servant.*]—Seyton!—I am
　　sick at heart,
　When I behold—Seyton, I say!—This push   20
　Will cheer me ever, or disseat me now.
　I have liv'd long enough: my way of life

12. goose look?] *Capell;* Goose-looke. *F.*　　19. Seyton] *F;* Seton *Wilson.*
21. cheer] cheere *F1-2;* chair *Dyce (conj. Percy).*　　disseat] *Steevens (conj.*
Jennens and Capell); dis-eate *F1;* disease *F2-4;* disseize *conj. Bailey;* defeat *conj.*
Daniel; dis-ease *Furness.*　　22. way] May *Steevens (1778), (conj. Johnson).*

F4 spelling and *Oth.*, II. iii. 95, 'lown',
correspond to the Southern pronuncia-
tion.

12. *goose*] Cf. II. iii. 15 *ante.* Armstrong, *Shakespeare's Imagination,* p. 60,
suggests that the black and white
imagery was 'almost certainly aroused
by the thought of writing with a goose-
quill on white paper'. He also shows
that prick (14), lily-liver'd (15), sick
(19), water (51), and sere (23) all appear elsewhere in Shakespeare in
goose contexts.

15. *patch*] properly, a domestic fool
or clown. It is also used as a term of
contempt. It is perhaps derived from
Ital. *pazzo,* or from the fool's wearing a
'patched', or parti-coloured, coat. Cf.
MND., III. ii. 9: 'a crew of patches'. An
unconscious pun on 'patch' (= also
plaster) would suit the associations of
goose and *disease.* Cf. note on 12 *ante.*

17. *Are . . . fear*] prompt others to
fear (Kittredge).

20. *push*] crisis, assault of fortune,
attack. Cf. III. iv. 81 *ante* and *Caes.,*
v. ii. 5.

21. *cheer*] probably a quibble on *cheer*
and *chair* (which Percy proposed). The

former links up with 'sick at heart' and
the latter with 'disseat' (Wilson).
Cuningham points out that *cheer* is mis-
printed *chair* in *Cor.,* IV. vii. 52, and that
it is quite common in the Folio to find
heare for *hair;* a proof that the pronunciation of our *hair* in Shakespeare's day
must have been close to *heer.* So, Cuningham argues, the *cheere* of the Folio
might easily represent a phonetic
spelling of *chair.* 'Chair' in the sense of
throne is common enough in Shakespeare. Cf. *R3,* v. iii. 251. But Cuningham's arguments for emendation are
more powerful as arguments for a
quibble.

22. *way of life*] course of life. Cf.
Horace, *Epistles,* I. xvii. 26. Baldwin,
Shakespeare's Small Latine, II..518, thinks
Shakespeare was recalling the context.
Johnson supporting his conjecture,
argued that there was no relation between 'way of life' and 'fallen into the
sere', and that Shakespeare had 'May'
in the same sense elsewhere (e.g. *Ado.,*
v. i. 76, and *R2,* III. iv. 48–9). Steevens,
in support of Johnson, quoted Sidney,
Astrophel and Stella, XXI: 'If now the
May of my years much decline'. The

Is fall'n into the sere, the yellow leaf;
And that which should accompany old age,
As honour, love, obedience, troops of friends,   25
I must not look to have; but in their stead,
Curses, not loud, but deep, mouth-honour, breath,
Which the poor heart would fain deny, and dare not.
Seyton!—

Enter SEYTON.

Sey. What's your gracious pleasure?
Macb.   What news more?   30
Sey. All is confirm'd, my Lord, which was reported.
Macb. I'll fight, till from my bones my flesh be hack'd.
    Give me my armour.
Sey.   'Tis not needed yet.
Macb. I'll put it on.
    Send out moe horses, skirr the country round;   35

32. be] *F1*; is *F2–4*.   35. moe] *F1–2*; more *F3–4*.   skirr] skirre *F1–2*;
skir *F3–4*.

Clar. Edd. object to the mixture of meta-phors in the Folio reading; and Cun-ingham points out that 'may' is mis-printed for 'way' at II. i. 57 *ante*. But the lines from *Sonn*. lxxiii, which Cuning-ham cites in support of Johnson, are used by Wilson in support of Folio: 'That time of year thou may'st in me behold / When yellow leaves, or few, or none, do hang. . .' Wilson also quotes Seneca, *Her. Fur.*, 1258–9: 'Cur animam in ista luce detineam amplius/ Morerque nihil est; cuncta iam amisi bona.' The parallel is not very close. But certainly no emendation is desir-able. The image 'way of life' is not sufficiently vivid to conflict with the image of 'the yellow leaf' and may refer also to the 'process of the seasons' (*Sonn*. civ, in which Shakespeare men-tions 'Three beauteous springs to yellow autumn turn'd'). See Empson, *op. cit.*, pp. 104–6.

23. *sere*] the withered state (Onions, who points out in *T.L.S.*, 24 Oct. 1935, that the word is printed with a capital

in the Folio, that Shakespeare often converted adjectives into nouns, and that 'the withered state, i.e. yellow-leaf state' makes better sense than 'the withered, i.e. the yellow, leaf'.

25. *As*] i.e. namely.

27. *mouth-honour*] Cf. Isa., xxix. 13: 'Because this people come neere vnto me with their mouth, and honour me with their lippes, but haue remooued their heart farre from me'.

29. Seyton] French, *Shakespeareana Genealogica*, p. 296, says: 'The Setons of Touch were (and are still) heredi-tary armour-bearers to the Kings of Scotland; there is thus a peculiar fit-ness in the choice of this name.' One critic suggests wildly that Shakespeare intended a quibble on *Satan*.

35. *moe*] Shakespeare used both forms, *moe* and *more*; the former usually relating to number, the latter to size. But the distinction, if any there really were, was not always observed.

skirr] move rapidly, scour. Cf. *H5*, IV. vii. 64.

Hang those that talk of fear. Give me mine armour.—
How does your patient, Doctor?
Doct.   Not so sick, my Lord,
As she is troubled with thick-coming fancies,
That keep her from her rest.
Macb.   Cure her of that:
Canst thou not minister to a mind diseas'd,   40
Pluck from the memory a rooted sorrow,
Raze out the written troubles of the brain,
And with some sweet oblivious antidote
Cleanse the stuff'd bosom of that perilous stuff

36. talk of] *F1;* stand in *F2–4.*   armour.—] *Wilson adds S.D.: Seton goes to fetch it.*   39. Cure her] *F2–3;* Cure *F1.*   of] *F1–2;* from *F3.*   44. stuff'd] *Theobald;* stufft *F1;* stuft *F2–4.*   stuff] *F3;* stuffe *F1–2. See note below.*

37. *How . . . doctor?*] Cuningham suggests that the doctor should enter at this point. As there is no occasion for his presence until now, and as the names of characters who appear in a scene are sometimes given at the beginning, though they do not appear until later, I agree.

39–45. *Cure . . . heart?*] Cf. Daniel, *The Queenes Arcadia,* 1240–51, where Daphne laments the insomnia caused by her guilty conscience which presents 'Those onely formes of terror that affright / My broken sleepes, that layes vpon my heart / This heauy loade that weighes it downe with griefe; / And no disease beside, for which there is / No cure I see at all, nor no redresse.' The parallel is discussed in K. Muir, *Shakespeare's Sources,* I. 167.

40. *Canst . . . diseas'd*] Cf. Seneca, *Her. Fur.,* 1261–2: 'nemo polluto queat / Animo mederi.' Heywood translates: 'no man may heale and loose from gylty bandes / My mynd defyled.'

42. *written . . . brain*] 'written' and hence fixed or permanent. Cf. *Ham.,* I. v. 103.

43. *oblivious*] Cotgrave, *Dict.,* 'Oblivieux: *causing forgetfulnesse.*' Cf. Horace, *Odes,* II. vii. 21: '*Obblivioso* levia Massico Ciboria exple.' Other critics quote Spenser, *F.Q.,* IV. iii. 43; Virgil, *Aen.,* VI. 714–15. See note to

II. ii. 34 *ante,* and compare the following lines from Seneca, *Herc. Fur.,* 1077–81: 'placidus fessum lenisque fove, / preme devinctum torpore gravi; / sopor indomitos alliget artus / nec torva prius pectora linquat, / quam mens repetat pristina cursum.' Heywood translates: 'Keepe him fast bound with heavy sleepe opprest, / Let slomber deepe his Limmes untamed bynde, / Nor soner leave his unright raginge breaste / Then former mynd his course agayne may fynd.'

44. *stuff'd . . . stuff*] Editors suspect that one of these words is a corruption. For 'stuff'd' (F 'stufft') numerous words have been proposed: full, foul, steep'd, fraught, clogged, slufft, press'd, charg'd. For 'stuff' the following: load, matter, freight, fraught, slough, sluff. Wilson voted for *charged,* and failing that, *pressed* = oppressed. Cf. *2H6,* III. ii. 376: 'the secrets of his over-charged soul' (cf. v. i. 50 *ante*), and *3H6,* II. v. 78: 'o'ercharged with grief'. *Oth.,* III. iv. 177: 'I have this while with leaden thoughts been pressed', and *Per.,* III. ii. 84: 'the o'erpressed spirits'. I think we should rule out words which rhyme with 'stuff' as the jingle would be more offensive than the repetition. But I believe that Shakespeare wrote the text as printed. If an alteration were necessary, 'fraught' for 'stuff'd'

Which weighs upon the heart?
Doct.   Therein the patient   45
Must minister to himself.
Macb. Throw physic to the dogs; I'll none of it.—
Come, put mine armour on; give me my staff.—
Seyton, send out—Doctor, the Thanes fly from me.—
Come, sir, despatch.—If thou couldst, Doctor, cast   50
The water of my land, find her disease,
And purge it to a sound and pristine health,

46. to] *F1;* unto *F2–4.*   himself.] *Wilson adds* S.D.: *Seton returns with armour and an armourer, who presently begins to equip Macbeth.*   48. mine] my *F4.* 52. pristine] *F2;* pristiue *F1.*

would be comparatively harmless. The Folio spelling 'stufft' might conceivably have been a misreading of 'fraught', the initial *fr* being read as *st* and the concluding *ght* as *fft.* Cf. *Oth.,* III. iii. 449: 'Swell bosom with thy fraught, for 'tis of aspics' tongues'; and IV. iii. 210 *ante,* 'o'erfraught'.

45. *Which . . . heart*] There would seem to be echoes in this scene and in Scene v of Seneca, *Agam.,* tr. Studley (Chorus 1): 'Sleepe that doth ouercome and breake the bonds of griefe, / It cannot ease theyr heartes, nor mynister reliefe.' Cf. 'minister' (46 *post*) and II. ii. 36–8 *ante*). 'Can not bestow on them her safe and quiet rest'. Cf. 39 *ante.* 'No banners be displayed'. Cf. v. v. 1: 'Hang out our banners.' 'castell strongly built'. Cf. v. v. 2: 'castle's strength.' 'From high and proude degre driues downe in dust to lye'. Cf. v. v. 23: 'The way to dusty death'. It may be added that the 'paynted pomp' and wretchedness of the monarch described in the chorus may be compared with Macbeth's speech, v. iii. 22 ff.; that the repetition of 'fear' (3, 10, 14, 17, 36 *ante*) may have been suggested by the lines: 'Fayne would they dreaded bee, and yet not settled so, / When as they feared are, they feare, and lyue in woe'; that v. v. 19 ff. resembles 'To-morrow shall we rule, as wee haue done to-day. / One clod of croked care another

bryngeth in, / One hurly burly done, another doth begin'—the 'clod of croked care' being 'the perilous stuff' (44 *ante*) and the 'hurly burly' is echoed in I. i. 3; and finally that 'those *Erennys* wood turmoyles' links up, by a quibble, with Birnam wood (2, 60, *ante* and *post*). It may be worth noting that the same chorus contains the phrase 'light and vaine conceipt' (cf. *R2,* III. ii. 166), and the line 'The bloudy Bellon those doth haunt with gory hand' (cf. I. ii. 55 and II. ii. 60–3 *ante*), and a parallel with IV. i. 56. Cf. note on that line.

45–6. *Therein . . . himself*] Baldwin quotes from *Ciceronis Sententiae,* which Shakespeare may have read at school: 'Corpora curari possunt, animorum nulla medicina est.' Timothy Bright, *Treatise on Melancholy,* p. 189, says: 'Here no medicine, no purgation, no cordiall, no tryacle or balme are able to assure the afflicted soule and trembling heart, now painting [i.e. panting] vnder the terrors of God.'

50. *cast*] the term employed in the diagnosis of ailments by inspection of the urine. Shakespeare would find it in Lyly, *Euphues* (ed. Arber), 296: 'An Italian . . . casting my water . . . commaunded the chamber to be voyded'; and in Greene, *Menaphon* (ed. Arber), p. 35: 'Able to cast his disease without his water'. Cf. *Tw.N.,* III. iv. 114.

52. *purge*] Cf. III. iv. 75.

I would applaud thee to the very echo,
That should applaud again.—Pull't off, I say.—
What rhubarb, cyme or what purgative drug,　　　55
Would scour these English hence?—Hear'st thou of
　　them?
Doct. Ay, my good Lord: your royal preparation
Makes us hear something.
Macb.　　　　　　　　　Bring it after me.—
I will not be afraid of death and bane,
Till Birnam forest come to Dunsinane.　　[*Exit.*　60
Doct. [*Aside.*] Were I from Dunsinane away and clear,
Profit again should hardly draw me here.　　[*Exeunt.*

55. cyme] *F1; Cæny F2–3;* senna *F4;* Sirrah *conj. Bulloch. See note below.*
60. Birnam] Birnane *F.*

55. *cyme*] Some think that this word
is a misprint of *cynne,* an earlier spelling
of senna. Hunter defends F2, whose
spelling 'correctly represents the pronunciation'. Cotgrave spells it *Sene* and
Senne, and Dodoens, *New Herball,* 1586,
mentions that 'The cods and leaues of
Sena taken in the quantitie of a dram
do loose and purge the belly, scoure
away fleume and choler, especially
blacke choler and melancholie.' The
curious may be referred to a long con-
troversy in *M.L.N.,* where the following suggestions were made: *Tyme* (liv),
sium = wild parsley (lvi), a doublet of
cumin (lvii), and *Ocyme* = basil (lx).
The last, which is mentioned in Burton's *Anatomy of Melancholy,* is super-
ficially attractive because, as Gerard,
Herbal, p. 548, says, 'the seede cureth
the infirmities of the hart, taketh away
sorrowfulnesse which cometh of melancholie, and maketh a man merrie and
glad.' This links up with Macbeth's
previous speech (40–5 *ante*) but it does
not suggest a purgative drug, which
the sense requires. The various Her-
bals I have consulted make no mention
of the use of basil as a purge. Dodoens,
op. cit., p. 272, is typical: 'The later
writers say, that it doth fortifie and
strengthen the hart and the brayne,
and that it reioyceth and recreateth

the spirits, and is good against melancholie and sadnesse, and that if it be
taken in wine, it cureth an old cough.'
Cynne or *senna* therefore gives the best
sense. But as Rea points out (*M.L.N.,*
xxxv) the word *cyme* is used in Holland's *Pliny,* 1634, bk. xix, vol. 2, p. 26:
'Moreouer, like as Coleworts may be
cut at all times of the years for our vse,
so may they be sown and set all the
yere long. . . The tender crops called
Cymæ after the first cutting, they
yeeld the Spring next following: now
are these Cymæ nothing els but the
yong delicat tops or daintier tendrils
of the maine stem . . . and yet none
put forth their Cymes or tender buds
more than they.' Coleworts (*op. cit.,*
pp. 48–9) 'be good for the stomack, and
gently loosen the belly . . . they purge
cholerick humours, being taken with
sweet grosse wine'. Rea comments
that the reading of the First Folio is
perfectly intelligible, 'meaning the
tops and tendrils of the Colewort'.
But *cyme* is the top of any plant,
not specifically of the Colewort (cf.
O.E.D.). The later contributors to
M.L.N. seem not to have noticed this
passage.
　58. *it*] i.e. some part of his armour.
　61–2. *Were . . . here*] Fleay thought
this couplet spurious and beneath the

SCENE IV.—[*Country near Dunsinane. A wood in view.*]

Enter, with drum and colours, MALCOLM, *old* SIWARD, *and his Son,*
MACDUFF, MENTETH, CATHNESS, ANGUS, LENOX, ROSSE, *and*
Soldiers, marching.

Mal. Cousins, I hope the days are near at hand,
    That chambers will be safe.
Ment.   We doubt it nothing.
Siw. What wood is this before us?
Ment.   The wood of Birnam.
Mal. Let every soldier hew him down a bough,
    And bear't before him: thereby shall we shadow   5
    The numbers of our host, and make discovery
    Err in report of us.
Soldier.   It shall be done.
Siw. We learn no other but the confident tyrant
    Keeps still in Dunsinane, and will endure
    Our setting down before't.
Mal.   'Tis his main hope;   10
    For where there is advantage to be gone,

Scene IV

S.D. *Country . . . view.*] *Capell subst.*   1. Cousins] Cousin *F3–4.*   3. Birnam]
F3–4; Byrnam *F2;* Birnane *F1.*   11. advantage to be gone,] *Capell, Wilson;*
aduantage to be giuen, *F;* a vantage to be gone, *conj. Johnson;* advantage to be
got *conj. Steevens;* advantage to be gotten *Collier (ed. 2) ;* advantage to be ta'en
Dyce (ed. 2), (conj. S. Walker) ; advantage to 'em given, *conj. Clar.*

dignity of tragedy. 'But when Shakespeare saw a chance to salt the meats
of his plays with such touches he did
not stand upon tragic dignity' (Granville-Barker).

Scene IV

2. *chambers . . . safe*] Shakespeare may
refer to the espionage mentioned in
III. iv. 130–1. But there is more likely to
be a reference to Duncan's murder,
the phrase meaning: 'When we can
sleep in our beds without fear of being
murdered'.

4–7. *Let . . . us*] This incident is in
Holinshed, and there is therefore no
point in tracing its origins to the

Romance of Alexander or to the battle of
Lamberkine, in 1332.

6. *discovery*] i.e. reconnaissance. Cf.
Lr., v. i. 53.

9. *endure*] allow.

10. *setting down before*] i.e. laying
siege to. Cf. *Cor.*, I. ii. 28: 'Let us along
to guard Corioli: / If they set down
before's.' Cuningham thinks that the
above should read *sit* and the *Macbeth*
passage *sitting*.

11. *advantage*] opportunity.

gone] Johnson's conj. makes sense,
which the Folio reading does not. The
compositor's eye obviously hit on the
'giuen' in the following line. This
means that 'giuen' is more likely to be

Both more and less have given him the revolt,
And none serve with him but constrained things,
Whose hearts are absent too.
Macd.   Let our just censures
Attend the true event, and put we on   15
Industrious soldiership.
Siw.   The time approaches,
That will with due decision make us know
What we shall say we have, and what we owe.
Thoughts speculative their unsure hopes relate,
But certain issue strokes must arbitrate;   20
Towards which advance the war.   [*Exeunt, marching.*

SCENE V.—[*Dunsinane. Within the castle.*]

Enter, with drum and colours, MACBETH, SEYTON, *and Soldiers.*

Macb. Hang out our banners on the outward walls;
The cry is still, 'They come!' Our castle's strength

14–15. Let our just censures Attend] *F1;* Let our best Censures Before *F2–4.*

S.D. *Dunsinane . . . castle.*] *Malone subst.*   1–2. Hang . . . come!'] Hang . . . banners! On . . . walls The cry is still, "They come!" *Keightley;* Hang . . . banners! On . . . walls The cry is still. They come. *Robert Nichols.*

wrong than 'to be', so that the Clarendon conj. should be rejected. Kittredge retains F, and explains: 'Wherever the circumstances are such that an opportunity can offer itself'.

12. *more and less*] great and small. Cf. *2H4,* I. i. 209.

14–15. *Let . . . event*] i.e. we shall know after the battle if the rumours about the morale of Macbeth's army are true or not.

19. *Thoughts . . . relate*] Siward, as well as Mucduff, warns Malcolm of the dangers of optimism.

20. *certain . . . arbitrate*] i.e. actual fighting must decide the issue and make it a certainty. Steevens cites Chapman, *Odyssey,* bk. XVIII: 'Can

arbitrate a war of deadliest weight'. Fleay thought that this and the preceding couplet could not be Shakespeare's, and Wilson suspected 19–20 because 'due decision' (17) makes a good antecedent to 'which' (21). But 'certain issue' (20) is an equally good antecedent.

Scene v
1–2. *Hang . . . cry*] Keightley justified his emended punctuation by declaring that it was from the keep, not the walls, that the banner was hung. But the rhythm of the line is against Keightley and Nichols. Cf. also *1H6,* I. vi. 1: 'Advance our waving colours on the walls'.

Will laugh a siege to scorn: here let them lie,
Till famine and the ague eat them up.
Were they not forc'd with those that should be ours,   5
We might have met them dareful, beard to beard,
And beat them backward home. What is that noise?

                    [*A cry within, of women.*
Sey. It is the cry of women, my good Lord.   [*Exit.*
Macb. I have almost forgot the taste of fears.
The time has been, my senses would have cool'd   10
To hear a night-shriek; and my fell of hair
Would at a dismal treatise rouse, and stir,
As life were in't. I have supp'd full with horrors:
Direness, familiar to my slaughterous thoughts,
Cannot once start me.

                    Re-enter SEYTON.

                    Wherefore was that cry?   15
Sey. The Queen, my Lord, is dead.
Macb. She should have died hereafter:

---

5. forc'd] 'forc'd *Hanmer.*   8. S.D.] *Dyce; not in F.*   9. fears] tears *conj.*
Bayliss.   15. S.D.] *Dyce; not in F.*   17–18. died hereafter: There] died:
hereafter There *Jackson.*

5. *forc'd*] reinforced, strengthened.
In *Troil.*, v. i. 64, 'wit larded with
malice and malice forced with wit',
where forced = farced, stuffed; the
metaphor is from the kitchen. In the
present passage there is a quibble on
the two meanings.
6. *dareful*] bold or boldly; or de-
fiantly. Not used elsewhere by Shakespeare.
8. cry] Lady Macbeth has not died
a natural death.
10. *cool'd*] used in a stronger sense
than at present. Cf. *John*, II. i. 479, and
Florio's *Montaigne*, iii. 5: 'In like case,
incorporeal pleasures, is it not injustice
to quaile and coole the minde, and say
it must thereunto be entrained as unto
a forced bond, or servile necessity?'
(Temple ed., v. 179). Collier's reading
'quail'd' may have come first to
Shakespeare's mind, and may then

have recalled the word near it in the
Florio context.
11. *fell of hair*] skin with the hair on.
Florio, *Worlde of Wordes*, for 'Vello' has
'a fleese of wooll, a fell or skin that hath
wooll on'. Cf. Job, iv. 15.
12. *treatise*] story, recital. Cf. *Ado*,
I. i. 317, and *Ven.*, 774.
13. *with*] Cf. IV. ii. 32 *ante*.
14–15. *Direness . . . me*] Horror can
never make me start . . .
17. *She . . . hereafter*] This apparently
simple statement is ambiguous. Either
'She would have died sometime'
(Wilson, Arrowsmith) or 'Her death
should have been deferred to a more
peaceful hour; had she lived longer
there would have been a more convenient time for such a word.' On
this, Johnson's interpretation, Murry,
Shakespeare, p. 335, comments: 'Macbeth's meaning is stranger than that.

There would have been a time for such a word.—
To-morrow, and to-morrow, and to-morrow,
Creeps in this petty pace from day to day,   20
To the last syllable of recorded time;
And all our yesterdays have lighted fools
The way to dusty death. Out, out, brief candle!

23. dusty] study *F2–4;* dusky *Hanmer (conj. Theobald).*

"Hereafter", I think, is purposely vague. It does not mean "later"; but in a different mode of time from that in which Macbeth is imprisoned now. "Hereafter"—in the not-Now: *there would have been a time for such a word* as "The Queen is *dead.*" But the time in which he is caught is tomorrow, and to-morrow, and to-morrow—one infinite sameness, in which yesterdays have only lighted fools the way to dusty death. Life in this time is meaningless—a tale told by an idiot—and death also. For his wife's death to have meaning there needs some total change —a plunge across a new abyss into a Hereafter.' That Shakespeare would have been puzzled by this explanation is not necessarily a condemnation of it. Perhaps 'should' is used indifferently to denote either what will be or what ought to be; cf. 31 *post.*

18. *time . . . word*] i.e. such a phrase, expression, intelligence, as 'the queen is dead.' Cf. *R2*, I. iii. 152: 'The hopeless word of "never to return" '; and Ecc., iii. 2, 'a time to die'.

19–28. *To-morrow . . . nothing*] 'Expresses in Shakespeare's terms the hopelessness of a hardened sinner, to whom the universe has now no meaning . . .'; 'merely implies the atheism . . . which has resulted from his gradual hardening in crime' (Bethell, *Shakespeare and the Popular Dramatic Tradition,* pp. 74, 98). See Introduction, p. liii. Halliwell thought the lines were suggested by 'a remarkable engraving' in Barclay's *Ship of Fooles,* 1570, p. 61: 'They folowe the crowes crye to their great sorowe, / *Cras, cras, cras,* to-morrowe we shall amende.' / Cuning-

ham thinks Shakespeare may have been influenced by his recent perusal of Florio's *Montaigne,* I. xix: 'That to Philosophie, is to learne how to die.'

21. *recorded time*] the record of time (Hudson). This seems to be the best and simplest explanation. Johnson suggests: 'the time fixed in the decrees of Heaven for the period of life'. Steevens thinks recorded was used for *recording* or *recordable.* Elwin thinks the line means 'till the last judgment'. Cf. Rev., x. 5, 6.

22. *fools*] not 'foules' = crowds, as Hunter conjectured, but just ordinary foolish people.

23. *dusty*] Theobald's conj. 'dusky' has little to recommend it; cf. Ps., xxii. 15: 'dust of death'. Steevens suggests that *dusty* refers to 'dust to dust' of the burial service. Collier cites Copley, *Fig for Fortune* (1596, Spenser Soc., p. 55): 'Inviting it to dusty death's defeature'. But Cuningham supports *dusky* on the ground that Shakespeare often used the word in connection with death. He cites *1H6,* II. ii. 27; *2H6,* III. ii. 104; *R3,* IV. iv. 70: 'dusky graves'. Cuningham proceeds to summarize Elwin's arguments: Light lights folly on its way to darkness; this is connected with the idea of darkness as a *shadow;* the living man is the shadow walking between the light and that dusky death to which it is lighting him. Life has only a delusive resemblance to an endurable substance, and the poor player is but the shadow of the substance or reality whose semblance he has assumed. I agree with some of Elwin's analysis of the passage, but not with his conclusion: 'With the term *dusty* the shadow

> Life's but a walking shadow; a poor player,
> That struts and frets his hour upon the stage,   25
> And then is heard no more: it is a tale
> Told by an idiot, full of sound and fury,
> Signifying nothing.

Enter a Messenger.

> Thou com'st to use thy tongue; thy story quickly.
> *Mess.* Gracious my Lord,   30
> I should report that which I say I saw,
> But know not how to do't.
> *Macb.*   Well, say, sir.
> *Mess.* As I did stand my watch upon the hill,
> I look'd toward Birnam, and anon, methought,
> The wood began to move.
> *Macb.*   Liar, and slave!   35
> *Mess.* Let me endure your wrath, if't be not so.

28–30. Signifying . . . Lord] *two lines, the first ending* tongue, *conj. Lettsom.*
30. Gracious my] My gracious *F2–4.* 30–1. Gracious . . . which] *one line
Keightley.* 34, 44. Birnam] *F4;* Byrnaın *F2–3;* Byrnane *F1.*

---

has no affinity: and by retaining this word the otherwise exquisitely preserved unity of thought would consequently be destroyed.' Shakespeare would cheerfully violate a unity of impression for his own purposes—in this case to extend the associations of the word 'death'.

candle] Cf. Job, xviii. 6: 'The light shall be darke in his dwelling, and his candle shall be put out with him.' Cf. Ps., xviii. 28. Wilson contrasts Prov., xx. 27.

24. *shadow*] Cf. Ps., xxxix. 7: 'For man walketh in a vain shadow'; Job, viii. 9: 'For wee are but of yesterday, and are ignorant: for our dayes vpon earth are but a shadow.'

player] suggested by *shadow.* Cf. *MND.*, v. i. 213: 'The best in this kind are but shadows'; and *MND.*, v. i. 430. *Poor* player does not mean a *bad actor*— or not primarily—but one who is to be pitied because his appearance on the

stage of life is so brief (Kittredge).

26–7. *it . . . Told*] Cf. Ps., xc. 9: 'We bring our years to an end as a tale that is told.' N.

28. *Signifying nothing*] 'The theme of the false appearance is revived—with a difference. It is not only that Macbeth sees life as deceitful, but the poetry is so fine that we are almost bullied into accepting an essential ambiguity in the final statement of the play, as though Shakespeare were expressing his own "philosophy" in the lines. But the speech is "placed" by the tendency of the last Act (order emerging from disorder, truth emerging from deceit)' (Knights, *op. cit.*, p. 36).

28–30. *Signifying . . . my Lord*] The text could be printed in two lines, the first ending with 'use' or 'tongue'.

31. *should*] Cf. 17 *ante.*

32. *say*] Pope's insertion of 'it' is essential to neither the rhythm nor the meaning of the line.

Within this three mile may you see it coming;
I say, a moving grove.

Macb.   If thou speak'st false,
Upon the next tree shalt thou hang alive,
Till famine cling thee: if thy speech be sooth,   40
I care not if thou dost for me as much.—
I pull in resolution; and begin
To doubt th'equivocation of the fiend,
That lies like truth: 'Fear not, till Birnam wood
Do come to Dunsinane';—and now a wood   45
Comes toward Dunsinane.—Arm, arm, and out!—
If this which he avouches does appear,
There is nor flying hence, nor tarrying here.
I 'gin to be aweary of the sun,
And wish th'estate o'th'world were now undone.—   50
Ring the alarum bell!—Blow, wind! come, wrack!
At least we'll die with harness on our back.   [*Exeunt*.

---

37. may you] *F1–2;* you may *F3–4.*   39. shalt] shall *F.*   42. pull] *F;* pall
conj. Johnson, A. Hunter, Wilson.   48. nor flying] *F1–2;* no flying *F3–4.*

---

37. *mile*] Cf. *Wiv.*, iii. ii. 33: 'This
boy will carry a letter twenty mile';
and *Ado*, ii. iii. 17: 'he would have
walked ten mile afoot.'

39. *the next tree*] Cf. *Tp.*, iii. ii. 42.

40. *cling*] shrink up, wither. Used of
the drawing together and shrinking up
of animal or vegetable tissue; and still
used in dialect. *O.E.D.* quotes *Cov.
Myst.*, 54: 'My heart doth clynge and
cleve as clay.'

42. *pull in*] rein in. Kittredge explains: 'I can no longer give free rein
to confidence and determination.' He
cites as illustration of alternative meanings Dekker, *Old Fortunatus*, Prol.
('feare . . . makes her pull in her fainting pinions'), and Fletcher, *The Sea
Voyage*, iii. i; ('All my spirits . . . Pull in
their powers'). Johnson's conj. 'pall'
is, however, possible. Cf. *Ham.*, v. ii. 9,
and *Ant.*, ii. vii. 88.

43. *equivocation*] Cf. ii. iii. 9; Introduction, pp. xv–xviii; Scot, *The Discouerie of Witchcraft*, xiii. xv ('How men
have beene abused with words of

equivocation, with sundrie examples
thereof'); and *2H6*, i. iv. 60–75.

47–50.] The Clar. Edd. thought
these lines were interpolated.

47. *avouches*] Cf. iii. i. 119 *ante*.

50. *estate o'th'world*] the universe. Cf.
iii. ii. 16 *ante*: 'frame of things'. Wilson
suggests that the phrase implies both
structure and organization.

51. *Ring . . . bell!*] Theobald believed
these words to be a 'Stage-direction
crept from the Margin into the text'
because the line was 'deficient without
them, occasioned probably by a Cut
that had been made in the Speech by
the Actors. They were a Memorandum
to the Prompter to ring the *Alarum-
bell*.' I see no sufficient warrant for
Theobald's belief in this instance,
though I think he was right on ii. iii. 79
ante.

wrack] The usual spelling in Shakespeare. Cf. i. iii. 114.

52. *At . . . back*] If Macbeth had not
sallied forth the attackers might have
stayed 'till famine and the ague eat

SCENE VI.—[*The same. A plain before the castle.*]

Enter, with drum and colours, MALCOLM, *old* SIWARD,
MACDUFF, *etc., and their army, with boughs.*

Mal. Now, near enough: your leavy screens throw down,
And show like those you are.—You, worthy uncle,
Shall, with my cousin, your right noble son,
Lead our first battle: worthy Macduff, and we,
Shall take upon's what else remains to do,   5
According to our order.
Siw.   Fare you well.—
Do we but find the tyrant's power to-night,
Let us be beaten, if we cannot fight.
Macd. Make all our trumpets speak; give them all breath,
Those clamorous harbingers of blood and death.   10
                    [*Exeunt. Alarums continued.*

SCENE VII.—[*The same. Another part of the plain.*]

Enter MACBETH.

Macd. They have tied me to a stake: I cannot fly,
But, bear-like, I must fight the course.—What's he,

Scene VI
S.D. *A plain . . . castle.*] Rowe, *subst.*   1. Now . . . down,] *so Rowe; two lines, the first ending* enough: *F.*   leavy] *F;* leafy *Collier.*

Scene VII
S.D. *The . . . plain.*] Capell, *subst.*

them up'. By leaving the castle, he enables the prophecies to be fulfilled.

harness] gear, equipage, furniture,
and specifically, armour for a man or
horse. Shakespeare uses it in both
senses. See Bible (A.V.), 1 Kings, xxii.
34.

Scene VI
1. *leavy*] Cf. *Ado,* II. iii. 75, where the
word rhymes with 'heavy'. Cotgrave
has 'Feuillu: leauie.'
2. *uncle*] See note to v. ii. 2 *ante.*

4. *battle*] Nares defines as 'the main
or middle body of an army, between
the van and the rear'. But it is often
used of a whole army in order of battle,
e.g. *John,* IV. ii. 78. Probably Shakespeare took the word from Holinshed.
See Appendix, p. 169.
9–10. *Make . . . death*] Fleay regarded
this couplet as an interpolation.
10. *harbingers*] Cf. note on I. iv. 45.

Scene VII
2. *bear-like . . . course*] Bear-baiting

That was not born of woman? Such a one
Am I to fear, or none.

Enter young SIWARD.

Yo. Siw. What is thy name?
Macb.   Thou'lt be afraid to hear it.   5
Yo. Siw. No; though thou call'st thyself a hotter name
Than any is in hell.
Macb.   My name's Macbeth.
Yo. Siw. The devil himself could not pronounce a title
More hateful to mine ear.
Macb.   No, nor more fearful.
Yo. Siw. Thou liest, abhorred tyrant: with my sword   10
I'll prove the lie thou speak'st.
                    [*They fight, and young Siward is slain.*
Macb.   Thou wast born of woman:—
But swords I smile at, weapons laugh to scorn,
Brandish'd by man that's of a woman born.   [*Exit.*

Alarums. Enter MACDUFF.

Macd. That way the noise is.—Tyrant, show thy face:
If thou be'st slain, and with no stroke of mine,   15
My wife and children's ghosts will haunt me still.
I cannot strike at wretched Kernes, whose arms
Are hir'd to bear their staves: either thou, Macbeth,
Or else my sword, with an unbatter'd edge,
I sheathe again undeeded. There thou shouldst be;   20

---

10. abhorred] *F1;* thou abhorred *F2–4.*   12. swords] words *conj. Daniel.*

---

was a favourite old English sport; and
a 'course' was the technical term for a
bout or round between the bear and
the dogs. Cf. *Lr.*, III. vii. 54: 'I am tied
to the stake, and I must stand the
course.'

11. *born of woman*] Cf. Job, xiv. 1, and
the Burial Service: 'Man that is born
of a woman'.

13. *born*] 'Shakespeare designed
Macbeth should appear invincible till
he encountered the object destined for
his destruction' (Steevens).

17. *Kernes*] Cf. I. ii. 13 *ante.* Macbeth
has to rely on Irish mercenaries, upon
whom Macdonwald had relied before
(Wilson).

18. *staves*] spear-shafts. Cf. *R3*, v.
iii. 341.

thou] Commentators have worried
themselves over the grammar. 'We
must supply some words like *must be my
antagonist*' (Clarendon).

20. *undeeded*] i.e. not having performed any deeds: the word was probably coined by Shakespeare.

> By this great clatter, one of greatest note
> Seems bruited. Let me find him, Fortune!
> And more I beg not.   [*Exit. Alarum.*

Enter MALCOLM *and old* SIWARD.

Siw. This way, my Lord;—the castle's gently render'd:
The tyrant's people on both sides do fight;   25
The noble Thanes do bravely in the war.
The day almost itself professes yours,
And little is to do.
Mal.   We have met with foes
That strike beside us.
Siw.   Enter, Sir, the castle.
                    [*Exeunt. Alarum.*

SCENE VIII.—[*Another part of the field.*]

Enter MACBETH.

Macb. Why should I play the Roman fool, and die

Scene VIII

S.D. *Another . . . field.*] Dyce. *Scene vii continued F, Rowe, Arden (ed. 1); sc. viii
Pope, Camb. etc.*

21. *clatter*] another word not found
elsewhere in Shakespeare's works.

22. *bruited*] announced, reported,
with the idea of clamour. Cf. *1H6*, ii.
iii. 68: 'I find thou art no less than
fame hath bruited.'

Let] Although the line wants a foot,
we need not assume that a word has
dropped out. There is room for a
pause, a move, or a gesture after
bruited.

23. Enter Malcolm and old Siward]
Siward does not notice his son's body;
and we hear later (v. ix. 10) that it has
been 'brought off the field'. This was,
perhaps, just before the entrance of old
Siward, as Macduff should obviously
enter immediately after the exit of
Macbeth. In which case 24–9 would
be virtually a separate scene, its effectiveness depending mainly on the
ironical juxtaposition of the removal of

young Siward's body and the entrance
of his father. Granville-Barker, however, suggests (Preface, xxxi) that
young Siward has been killed in the
gallery, and that his body is concealed
by the drawing of a curtain.

24. *gently render'd*] i.e. tamely surrendered.

29. *strike beside us*] i.e. by our side.
Some, however, interpret 'deliberately miss us' and cite *3H6*, ii. i. 130–2.

Scene VIII

S.D.] There is no scene division in
the Folio at this point, but most editors
follow Pope and Johnson in beginning a new scene. Siward and Malcolm enter the castle, and Macbeth
is obviously on another part of the
field.

1. *Roman fool*] e.g. Cato, Brutus,
Antony.

On mine own sword? whiles I see lives, the gashes
Do better upon them.

Re-enter MACDUFF.

Macd.   Turn, Hell-hound, turn!
Macb. Of all men else I have avoided thee:
But get thee back, my soul is too much charg'd   5
With blood of thine already.
Macd.   I have no words;
My voice is in my sword: thou bloodier villain
Than terms can give thee out!   [*They fight.*
Macb.   Thou losest labour:
As easy may'st thou the intrenchant air
With thy keen sword impress, as make me bleed: 10
Let fall thy blade on vulnerable crests;
I bear a charmed life; which must not yield
To one of woman born.
Macd.   Despair thy charm;
And let the Angel, whom thou still hast serv'd,
Tell thee, Macduff was from his mother's womb   15
Untimely ripp'd.
Macb. Accursed be that tongue that tells me so,
For it hath cow'd my better part of man:
And be these juggling fiends no more believ'd,

5-6. *my ... already*] 'the only touch of real remorse in Macbeth' (Chambers). Or is he rationalizing his fear?

9. *intrenchant*] incapable of being cut: the active in a passive sense. Shakespeare uses *trenchant* in an active sense in *Tim.*, IV. iii. 115: 'trenchant sword'.

12. *charmed life*] Cf. Spenser, *Faerie Queene*, I. iv. 50: 'he beares a charmed shield, / And eke enchaunted armes, that none can perce'; and *Cym.*, V. iii. 68.

13. *Despair*] i.e. despair of; the preposition being omitted after verbs regarded as transitive.

14. *Angel*] i.e. bad angel, demon.

16. *Untimely ripp'd*] Furness quoted Virgil, *Aen.*, x. 315: 'Inde Lichan ferit, exsectum jam matre perempta / Et tibi,

Phoebe, sacrum'. Shakespeare may have read the passage in Virgil; but he probably relied on Holinshed; see Appendix A, p. 179. Flatter, *op. cit.*, p. 27, notes that the line is filled out by a pause, before Macbeth's speech.

18. *better part*] This seems to mean simply the mind, soul, or spirit: not 'the better part of my manhood' (Clarendon). Cf. *Sonn.*, lxxiv. 8: 'My spirit is thine, the better part of me'; and Peele's *Arraignment of Paris*, II. i. 76: 'And look how much the mind, the better part, / Doth overpass the body in desert.'

19-20. *these ... sense*] Simpson (*apud* Wilson) cites Spenser, *Faerie Queene*, III. iv. 28: 'So tickle be the termes of mortall state, / And full of subtile sophismes, which doe play / With

That palter with us in a double sense;   20
That keep the word of promise to our ear,
And break it to our hope.—I'll not fight with thee.

Macd. Then yield thee, coward,
And live to be the show and gaze o'th'time:
We'll have thee, as our rarer monsters are,   25
Painted upon a pole, and underwrit,
'Here may you see the tyrant.'

Macb.   I will not yield,
To kiss the ground before young Malcolm's feet,
And to be baited with the rabble's curse.
Though Birnam wood be come to Dunsinane,   30
And thou oppos'd, being of no woman born,
Yet I will try the last: before my body
I throw my warlike shield: lay on, Macduff;
And damn'd be him that first cries, 'Hold, enough!'

[*Exeunt, fighting. Alarums. Re-enter fighting, and Macbeth slain.*

22–3. And ... coward] *lines end* hope! / coward, *and read* I will *for* I'll *S. Walker.*
30. Birnam] *F4;* Byrnam *F2–3;* Byrnane *F1.*   31. being] be *Theobald.*
34. S.D.] *F subst.*   Re-enter ... slain] *not in Pope, etc.; restored by Wilson.*

double sences, and with false debate, /
T'approue the vnknown purpose of
eternal fate.'

20. *palter*] shuffle, equivocate. Cf.
Caes., II. i. 125: 'Secret Romans, that
have spoke the word, / And will not
palter.' Cotgrave has '*Harceler: to
haggle, hucke, dodge, or paulter long in the
buying of a commoditie.*'

22–3. *I'll ... coward*] S. Walker's
arrangement may be right.

24. *show*] Cf. *Ant.,* IV. xii. 36: 'most
monster-like be shown'.

26. *Painted ... pole*] i.e. painted on a
cloth or board suspended on a pole. Cf.
Benedick's jest, *Ado,* I. i. 267: 'and let
let me be vilely painted'. Craig conj.
that *Painted* should be *Paunched* =
disembowelled. But Macduff threa-

tens Macbeth with life in captivity.

32–3. *before ... shield*] The Clar. Edd
thought this sentence must be interpolated. It would certainly be improved by Hilton's conj. (*apud* Wilson)
of 'warlock' for 'warlike'.

34. *Hold*] The cry of the heralds,
'Ho! Ho!' commanding the cessation
of a combat, is probably corrupted
from 'Hold, hold' (Clarendon).

S.D.] I have retained the substance
of the Folio directions. On the Elizabethan stage the fight would be concluded either on the inner stage
(Wilson), or in the gallery (Granville-
Barker, *op. cit.,* p. xxxii), in either case
the curtain being drawn on Macbeth's
body.

SCENE IX.—[*Within the castle.*]

Retreat. Flourish. Enter, with drum and colours, MALCOLM, *old* SIWARD, ROSSE, *Thanes, and Soldiers.*

Mal. I would the friends we miss were safe arriv'd.
Siw. Some must go off; and yet, by these I see,
   So great a day as this is cheaply bought.
Mal. Macduff is missing, and your noble son.
Rosse. Your son, my Lord, has paid a soldier's debt: 5
   He only liv'd but till he was a man;
   The which no sooner had his prowess confirm'd,
   In the unshrinking station where he fought,
   But like a man he died.
Siw.   Then he is dead?
Rosse. Ay, and brought off the field. Your cause of sorrow
   Must not be measur'd by his worth, for then   11
   It hath no end.
Siw.   Had he his hurts before?
Rosse. Ay, on the front.
Siw.   Why then, God's soldier be he!
   Had I as many sons as I have hairs,
   I would not wish them to a fairer death: 15
   And so, his knell is knoll'd.
Mal.   He's worth more sorrow,
   And that I'll spend for him.

Scene IX
S.D.] *Pope, Wilson (conj. Kittredge); sc. vii continues,* F.

S.D.] I follow Kittredge and Wilson in assuming that a new scene begins at this point, inside the castle. There is no reason to believe that Shakespeare intended Malcolm to leave the castle once he had entered it. The Clar. Edd. questioned the authenticity of the whole of this scene; but it has been convincingly defended by Nosworthy, *R.E.S.*, April 1948, p. 139.
2. *go off*] a stage metaphor, signifying the exit from life's stage. Cf. *Ant.*, IV. xiii. 6, and the similar expressions I. vii. 20 and III. i. 104 *ante*.
7. *prowess*] probably a monosyllable,

though elsewhere in Shakespeare it is a dissyllable. Butler, *Hudibras*, III. iii. 357, rhymes *prowess* and *cows*.
8. *unshrinking station*] i.e. the station whence he did not shrink.
9. *he died . . . dead?*] Nosworthy compares Laertes' reception of Ophelia's death.
12–15. *Had he . . . death*] Shakespeare closely follows Holinshed. See Appendix A, p. 180.
14. *Had . . . hairs*] quibble on hairs/heirs. Nosworthy compares Marlowe, *Doctor Faustus*, 339: 'Had I as many soules as there be starres'.

Siw.   He's worth no more;
They say he parted well and paid his score:
And so, God be with him!—Here comes newer comfort.

Re-enter MACDUFF, *with* MACBETH'S *head.*

Macd. Hail, King! for so thou art. Behold, where stands   20
Th'usurper's cursed head: the time is free.
I see thee compass'd with thy kingdom's pearl,
That speak my salutation in their minds;
Whose voices I desire aloud with mine,—   24
Hail, King of Scotland!
All.   Hail, King of Scotland! [*Flourish.*
Mal. We shall not spend a large expense of time,
Before we reckon with your several loves,
And make us even with you. My Thanes and kinsmen,
Henceforth be Earls; the first that ever Scotland
In such an honour nam'd. What's more to do,   30
Which would be planted newly with the time,—
As calling home our exil'd friends abroad,
That fled the snares of watchful tyranny;
Producing forth the cruel ministers
Of this dead butcher, and his fiend-like Queen,   35
Who, as 'tis thought, by self and violent hands

20. Hail . . . stands] *so Rowe; two lines, the first ending* art. F.   22. pearl] peers
Rowe; pearls *Var. '73.*   26. expense] extent *conj. Steevens;* expanse *conj.*
Singer.   28. My] *not in Pope.*

18. *parted*] Cf. *H5*, II. iii. 12 (of the
death of Falstaff): 'a' parted even just
between twelve and one.'
20–1. *stands . . . head*] 'vpon a pole'
(Holinshed).
21. *the time*] See I. v. 63 and IV. iii. 72
ante, etc.
22. *pearl*] used collectively for the
nobles of Scotland, and probably suggested by 'the row of pearls which
usually encircled a crown' (Clarendon). Florio, *Worlde of Wordes*, called
Southampton 'Braue Earle, bright
Pearle of Peeres'. Cf. *Ham.*, IV. vii. 93:
'he is the brooch indeed and gem of all
the nation.'
26. *spend . . . expense*] Cf. *Err.*, III. i.
123: 'This jest shall cost me some ex-

pense,' and Num., xxiii. 10: 'die the
death of the righteous'. There is no
reason to think that the passage is
corrupt.
time] Cf. 21 *ante*, 31, 39 *post.*
27–8. *Before . . . you*] before we reward you for your services, so that we
are no longer in your debt.
29. *Earls*] from Holinshed. See
Appendix A, p. 180.
34. *Producing forth*] bringing out of
hiding.
36. *self and violent hands*] Cf. *R2*, III. ii.
166: 'Infusing him with self and vain
conceit'. 'Self is used by Shakespeare
as an adjective, as in *Tw.N.*, I. i. 39,
"one self king", so that he felt no
awkwardness in separating it from the

Took off her life;—this, and what needful else
That calls upon us, by the grace of Grace,
We will perform in measure, time, and place.
So thanks to all at once, and to each one,   40
Whom we invite to see us crown'd at Scone.

[Flourish. Exeunt.

37. what] what's *Hanmer.*

substantive, whose sense it modifies, by a second epithet' (Clarendon).

38. *the grace of Grace*] Theobald compares *Gent.*, III. i. 146; *All's W.*, II. i. 163. Cuningham compares his own emendation for IV. iii. 136: 'the grace of Goodness'.

39. *measure*] due proportion (Wilson).

40. *So . . . one*] Manly suggested that this was addressed to the audience rather than the *dramatis personæ.*

41. *Scone*] See note on II. iv. 31 *ante.*

APPENDIX A

HOLINSHED

Holinshed in his *Chronicles of Scotland* describes how various noblemen were put to death for conspiring with witches against King Duff. Amongst them were certain kinsmen of Donwald, 'capteine of the castell', who 'had been persuaded to be partakers with the other rebels, more through fraudulent counsell of diuerse wicked persons, than of their owne accord: wherevpon the foresaid Donwald lamenting their case, made earnest labor and sute to the king to haue begged their pardon; but hauing a plaine deniall, he conceiued such an inward malice towards the king (though he shewed it not outwardlie at the first), that the same continued still boiling in his stomach, and ceased not, till through setting on of his wife, and in reuenge of such vnthankefulnesse, hee found meanes to murther the king within the foresaid castell of Fores where he vsed to soiourne. For the king being in that countrie, was accustomed to lie most commonlie within the same castell, hauing a speciall trust in Donwald, as a man whom he neuer suspected.

'But Donwald, not forgetting the reproch which his linage had susteined by the execution of those his kinsmen, whome the king for a spectacle to the people had caused to be hanged, could not but shew manifest tokens of great griefe at home amongst his familie: which his wife perceiuing, ceassed not to trauell with him, till she vnderstood what was the cause of his displeasure. Which at length when she had learned by his owne relation, she as one that bare no lesse malice in hir heart towards the king, for the like cause on hir behalfe, than hir husband did for his friends, counselled him (sith the king oftentimes vsed to lodge in his house without anie gard about him, other than the garrison of the castell, which was wholie at his commandement) to make him awaie, and shewed him the meanes wherby he might soonest accomplish it.

'Donwald thus being the more kindled in wrath by the words of his wife, determined to follow hir aduise in the execution of so heinous an act. Whervpon deuising with himselfe for a while, which way hee might best accomplish his curssed intent, at length gat opportunitie, and sped his purpose as followeth. It chanced that the king vpon the daie before he purposed to depart foorth of the castell, was long in his oratorie at his praiers, and there continued till it was late in the night. At the last, comming foorth, he called such afore him as had faithfullie serued him in pursute and apprehension of the rebels, and giuing them heartie thanks, he bestowed sundrie honorable gifts amongst them, of the which number Donwald was one, as he that had been euer accounted a most faithfull seruant to the king.

'At length, hauing talked with them a long time, he got him into his priuie chamber, onelie with two of his chamberlains, who hauing brought him to bed, came foorth again, and then fell to banketting with Donwald and his wife, who had prepared diuerse delicate dishes, and sundrie sorts of drinks for their reare supper or collation, wherat they sate vp so long, till they had charged their stomachs with such full gorges, that their heads were no sooner got to the pillow, but asleepe they were so fast, that a man might haue remooued the chamber ouer them, sooner than to haue awaked them out of their droonken sleepe.

'Then Donwald, though he abhorred the act greatlie in heart, yet through instigation of his wife hee called foure of his seruants vnto him (whome he had made priuie to his wicked intent before, and framed to his purpose with large gifts) and now declaring vnto them, after what sort they should worke the feat, they gladlie obeied his instructions, & speedilie going about the murther, they enter the chamber (in which the king laie) a little before cocks crow, where they secretlie cut his throte as he lay sleeping, without anie buskling at all: and immediatlie by a posterne gate they caried foorth the dead bodie into the fieldes. . .

'Donwald, about the time that the murther was in dooing, got him amongst them that kept the watch, and so continued in companie with them all the residue of the night. But in the morning when the noise was raised in the kings chamber how the king was slaine, his bodie conueied awaie, and the bed all beraied with bloud; he with the watch ran thither, as though he had knowne nothing of the matter, and breaking into the chamber, and finding cakes of bloud in the bed, and on the floore about the sides of it, he foorthwith slue the chamberleins, as guiltie of that heinous murther and then like a mad man running to and fro, he ransacked euerie corner within the castell, as though it had beene to haue seene if he might haue found either the bodie, or anie of the murtherers hid in anie priuie place: but at length comming to the posterne gate, and finding it open, he burdened the chamberleins, whome he had slaine, with all the fault, they hauing the keies of the gates committed to their keeping all the night, and therefore it could not be otherwise (said he) but that they were of counsell in committing of that most detestable murther.

'Finallie, such was his ouer earnest diligence in the seuere inquisition and triall of the offendors heerein, that some of the lords began to mislike the matter, and to smell foorth shrewd tokens, that he should not be altogether cleare himselfe. But for so much as they were in that countrie, where he had the whole rule, what by reason of his friends and authoritie togither, they doubted to vtter what they thought, till time and place should better serue therevnto, and heerevpon got them awaie euerie man to his home. For the space of six moneths togither, after this heinous murther thus committed, there appeered no sunne by day, nor moone by night in anie part of the realme, but still was the skie couered with continuall clouds, and sometimes such outragious windes arose, with lightenings and tempests, that the people were in great feare of present destruction. . .

'Monstrous sights also that were seene within the Scotish kingdome that yeere were these: horsses in Louthian, being of singular beautie and swiftnesse, did eate their owne flesh, and would in no wise taste anie other meate. In Angus there was a gentlewoman brought foorth a child without eies, nose, hand, or foot. There was a sparhawke also strangled by an owle. Neither was it anie lesse woonder that the sunne, as before is said, was continuallie couered with clouds for six moneths space. But all men vnderstood that the abhominable murther of king Duffe was the cause heereof' (pp. 149–52).

A later passage describes a mysterious voice after King Kenneth had slain his nephew:

'Thus might he seeme happie to all men, hauing the loue both of his lords and commons; but yet to himselfe he seemed most vnhappie, as he that could not but still liue in continuall feare, least his wicked practise concerning the death of Malcolme Duffe should come to light and knowledge of the world. For so commeth it to passe, that such as are pricked in conscience for anie secret offense committed, haue euer an vnquiet mind. And (as the fame goeth) it chanced that a voice was heard as he was in bed in the night time to take his rest, vttering vnto him these or the like woords in effect: "Thinke not Kenneth that the wicked slaughter of Malcolme Duffe by thee contriued, is kept secret from the knowledge of the eternall God: thou art he that didst conspire the innocents death, enterprising by traitorous meanes to doo that to thy neighbour, which thou wouldest haue reuenged by cruell punishment in anie of thy subiects, if it had beene offered to thy selfe. It shall therefore come to passe, that both thou thy selfe, and thy issue, through the iust vengeance of almightie God, shall suffer woorthie punishment, to the infamie of thy house and familie for euermore. For euen at this present are there in hand secret practises to dispatch both thee and thy issue out of the waie, that other maie inioy this kingdome which thou doost indeuour to assure vnto thine issue."

'The king, with this voice being striken into great dread and terror, passed that night without anie sleepe comming in his eies' (p. 158).

'After Malcolme succeeded his nephue Duncane the sonne of his daughter Beatrice: for Malcolme had two daughters, the one which was Beatrice, being giuen in mariage vnto one Abbanath Crinen, a man of great nobilitie, and thane of the Iles and west parts of Scotland, bare of that mariage the foresaid Duncane; the other called Doada, was maried vnto Sinell the thane of Glammis, by whom she had issue one Makbeth a valiant gentleman, and one that if he had not beene somewhat cruell of nature, might haue beene thought most woorthie the gouernement of a realme. On the other part, Duncane was so soft and gentle of nature, that the people wished the inclinations and maners of these two cousins to haue beene so tempered and interchangeablie bestowed betwixt them, that where the one had too much of clemencie, and the other of crueltie, the meane vertue betwixt these two extremities might haue reigned by indifferent partition in them both, so should Duncane haue prooued a woorthie king, and Makbeth an excellent capteine. The beginning of Duncans reigne was verie quiet and peaceable, without anie notable trouble; but after it was perceiued how negligent he was in punishing offendors, manie misruled persons tooke occasion thereof to trouble the peace and quiet state of the common-wealth, by seditious commotions which first had their beginnings in this wise.

'Banquho the thane of Lochquhaber, of whom the house of the Stewards is descended, the which by order of linage hath now for a long time inioied the crowne of Scotland, euen till these our daies, as he gathered the finaunces due to the king, and further punished somewhat sharpely such as were notorious offendors, being assailed by a number of rebelles inhabiting in that countrie, and spoiled of the monie and all other things, had much a doo to get awaie with life, after he had receiued sundrie grieuous wounds amongst them. Yet escaping their handes after hee was somewhat recouered of his hurts and was able to ride, he repaired to the court, where making his complaint to the king in most earnest wise, he purchased at length that the offendors were sente for by a sergeant at armes, to appeare to make answer vnto such mater as shoulde be laid to their charge: but they augmenting their mischiefous act with a more wicked deede, after they had misused the messenger with sundrie kindes of reproches, they finallie slew him also.

'Then doubting not but for such contemptuous demeanor against the kings regall authoritie, they should be inuaded with all the power the king could make, Makdowald one of great estimation among them, making first a confederacie with his neerest friends and kinsmen, tooke vpon him to be chiefe capteine of all such rebels as would stand against the king, in maintenance of their grieuous offenses lately committed against him. Manie slanderous words also, and railing tants this Makdowald vttered against his prince, calling him a faint-hearted milkesop, more meet to gouerne a sort of idle moonks in some cloister, than to haue the rule of such valiant and hardie men of warre as the Scots were. He vsed also such subtill persuasions and forged allurements, that in a small time he had gotten togither a mightie power of men: for out of the westerne Iles there came vnto him a great multitude of people, offering themselues to assist him in that rebellious quarell, and out of Ireland in hope of the spoile came no small number of Kernes and Galloglasses, offering gladlie to serue vnder him, whither it should please him to lead them.'

Makdowald defeats an army sent against him and beheads its captain, Malcolm. Duncan thereupon called a council.

'At length Makbeth speaking much against the kings softnes, and ouermuch slacknesse in punishing offendors, whereby they had such time to assemble together, he promised notwithstanding, if the charge were committed vnto him and vnto Banquho, so to order the matter, that the rebels should be shortly vanquished & quite put downe, and that not so much as one of them should be found to make resistance within the countrie.

'And euen so it came to passe: for being sent foorth with a new power, at his entring into Lochquhaber, the fame of his comming put the enimies in such feare, that a great number of them stale secretlie awaie from their capteine Makdowald, who neuerthelesse inforced thereto, gaue battell vnto Makbeth, with the residue which remained with him: but being ouercome, and fleeing for refuge into a castell (within the which his wife & children were inclosed) at length when he saw how he could neither defend the hold anie longer against his enimies, not yet vpon surrender be suffered to depart with life saued, hee first slue his wife and children, and lastlie himselfe, least if he had yeelded simplie, he should haue beene executed in most cruell wise for an example to other.'

Macbeth entered the castle and found Makdowald lying dead with the rest of the corpses:

'which when he beheld, remitting no peece of his cruell nature with that pitifull sight, he caused the head to be cut off, and set vpon a poles end, and so sent it as a present to the king. . . Thus was iustice and law restored againe to the old accustomed course, by the diligent means of Makbeth. Immediatlie wherevpon woord came that Sueno king of Norway was arriued in Fife with a puissant armie, to subdue the whole realme of Scotland' (pp. 168–9).

'The crueltie of this Sueno was such, that he neither spared man, woman, nor child, of what age, condition or degree soeuer they were. Whereof when K. Duncane was certified, he set all slouthfull and lingering delaies apart, and began to assemble an armie in most speedie wise, like a verie valiant capteine: for oftentimes it happeneth, that a dull coward and slouthfull person, constreined by necessitie, becommeth verie hardie and actiue. Therefore when his whole power was come togither, he diuided the same into three battels. The first was led by Makbeth, the second by Banquho, & the king himselfe gouerned in the maine battell or middle ward, wherein were appointed to attend and wait vpon his person the most part of all the residue of the Scotish nobilitie.

'The armie of Scotishmen being thus ordered, came vnto Culros, where incountering with the enimies, after a sore and cruell foughten battell, Sueno remained victorious, and Malcolme with his Scots discomfited. Howbeit the Danes were so broken by this battell, that they were not able to make long chase on their enimies, but kept themselues all night in order of battell, for doubt least the Scots assembling togither againe, might haue set vpon them at some aduantage. On the morrow, when the fields were discouered, and that it was perceiued how no enimies were to be found abrode, they gathered the spoile, which they diuided amongst them, according to the law of armes. Then was it ordeined by commandement of Sueno, that no soldier should hurt either man, woman, or child, except such as were found with weapon in hand readie to make resistance, for he hoped now to conquer the realme without further bloudshed.

'But when knowledge was giuen how Duncane was fled to the castell of Bertha, and that Makbeth was gathering a new power to withstand the incursions of the Danes, Sueno raised his tents & comming to the said castell, laid a strong siege round about it. Duncane seeing himself thus enuironed by his enimies, sent a secret message by counsell of Banquho to Makbeth, commanding him to abide at Inchcuthill, till he heard from him some other newes. In the meane time Duncane fell in fained communication with Sueno, as though he would haue yeelded vp the castell into his hands, vnder certaine conditions, and this did he to driue time, and to put his enimies out of all suspicion of anie enterprise ment against them, till all things were brought to passe that might serue for the purpose. At length, when they were fallen at a point for rendring vp the hold, Duncane offered to send foorth of the castell into the campe great prouision of vittels to refresh the armie, which offer was gladlie accepted of the Danes, for that they had beene in great penurie of sustenance manie daies before.

'The Scots heerevpon tooke the iuice of mekilwoort berries, and mixed the same in their ale and bread, sending it thus spiced & confectioned, in great abundance vnto their enimies. They reioising that they had got meate and drinke sufficient to satisfie their bellies, fell to eating and drinking after such greedie wise, that it seemed they stroue who might deuoure and swallow vp most, till the operation of the berries spread in such sort through all parts of their bodies, that they were in the end brought into a fast dead sleepe, that in manner it was vnpossible to awake them. Then foorthwith Duncane sent vnto Makbeth, commanding him with all diligence to come and set vpon the enimies, being in easie point to be ouercome. Makbeth making no delaie, came with his people to the place, where his enimies were lodged, and first killing the watch, afterwards entered the campe, and made such slaughter on all sides without anie resistance, that it was a wonderful matter to behold, for the Danes were so heauie of sleepe, that the most part of them were slaine and neuer stirred: other that were awakened either by the noise or other waies foorth, were so amazed and dizzie headed vpon their wakening, that they were not able to make anie defense; so that of the whole number there escaped no more but onelie Sueno himselfe and ten other persons, by whose helpe he got to his ships lieng at rode in the mouth of Taie' (pp. 169–70).

Holinshed goes on to describe how Sueno escaped with only one ship back to Denmark. While the Scots were rejoicing in their victory word was brought that a new Danish fleet had arrived at Kingcorne, sent by Canute, king of England, to avenge his brother Sueno's overthrow.

'To resist these enimies, which were alreadie landed, and busie in spoiling the countrie; Makbeth and Banquho were sent with the kings authoritie, who hauing with them a conuenient power,

incountred the enimies, slue part of them, and chased the other to
their ships. They that escaped and got once to their ships, obteined
of Makbeth for a great summe of gold, that such of their friends as
were slaine at this last bickering, might be buried in saint Colmes
Inch. In memorie whereof, manie old sepultures are yet in the said
Inch, there to be seene grauen with the armes of the Danes, as the
maner of burieng noble men still is, and heeretofore hath beene
vsed.

'A peace was also concluded at the same time betwixt the Danes
and Scotishmen, ratified (as some haue written) in this wise: That
from thencefoorth the Danes should neuer come into Scotland to
make anie warres against the Scots by anie maner of meanes. And
these were the warres that Duncan had with forren enimies, in the
seventh yeere of his reigne. Shortlie after happened a strange and
vncouth woonder, which afterward was the cause of much trouble
in the realme of Scotland as ye shall after heare. It fortuned as
Makbeth and Banquho iournied towards Fores, where the king
then laie, they went sporting by the waie togither without other
company saue onelie themselues, passing thorough the woods and
fields, when suddenlie in the middest of a laund, there met them
three women in strange and wild apparell, resembling creatures of
elder world, whome when they attentiuelie beheld, woondering
much at the sight, the first of them spake and said: All haile
Makbeth, thane of Glammis (for he had latelie entered into that
dignitie and office by the death of his father Sinell). The second of
them said: Haile Makbeth thane of Cawder. But the third said:
All haile Makbeth that heereafter shalt be king of Scotland.

'Then Banquho: What manner of women (saith he) are you,
that seeme so little fauourable vnto me, whereas to my fellow heere,
besides high offices, ye assigne also the kingdome, appointing
foorth nothing for me at all? Yes, (saith the first of them) we
promise greater benefits vnto thee, than vnto him, for he shall
reigne in deed, but with an vnluckie end: neither shall he leaue
anie issue behind him to succeed in his place, where contrarilie
thou in deed shalt not reigne at all, but of thee those shall be borne
which shall gouern the Scotish kingdome by long order of continuall descent. Herewith the foresaid women vanished immediatlie out of their sight. This was reputed at the first but some
vaine fantasticall illusion by Mackbeth and Banquho, insomuch
that Banquho would call Mackbeth in iest, king of Scotland; and
Mackbeth againe would call him in sport likewise, the father of
manie kings. But afterwards the common opinion was, that these
women were either the weird sisters, that is (as ye would say) the

goddesses of destinie, or else some nymphs or feiries, indued with knowledge of prophesie by their necromanticall science, bicause euerie thing came to passe as they had spoken. For shortlie after, the thane of Cawder being condemned at Fores of treason against the king committed; his lands, liuings, and offices were giuen of the kings liberalitie to Macbeth.

'The same night after, at supper, Banquho iested with him and said: Now Mackbeth thou hast obteined those things which the two former sisters prophesied, there remaineth onelie for thee to purchase that which the third said should come to passe. Wherevpon Mackbeth reuoluing the thing in his mind, began euen then to deuise how he might atteine to the kingdome; but yet he thought with himselfe that he must tarie a time, which should aduance him thereto (by the diuine prouidence) as it had come to passe in his former preferment. But shortlie after it chanced that king Duncane hauing two sonnes by his wife which was the daughter of Siward earle of Northumberland, he made the elder of them called Malcolme prince of Cumberland, as it were thereby to appoint him his successor in the kingdome, immediatlie after his deceasse. Mackbeth sore troubled herewith, for that he saw by this his hope sore hindered (where, by the old lawes of the realme, the ordnance was, that if he that should succeed were not of able age to take the charge vpon himselfe, he that was next of bloud vnto him should be admitted) he began to take counsell how he might vsurpe the kingdome by force, hauing a iust quarrell so to doo (as he tooke the matter) for that Duncane did what in him lay to defraud him of all manner of title and claime, which he might in time to come, pretend vnto the crowne.

'The woords of the three sisters also (of whom before ye haue heard) greatlie incouraged him herevnto, but speciallie his wife lay sore vpon him to attempt the thing, as she that was verie ambitious, burning in vnquenchable desire to beare the name of a queene. At length therefore, communicating his purposed intent with his trustie friends, amongst whome Banquho was the chiefest, vpon confidence of their promised aid, he slue the king at Enuerns, or (as some say) at Botgosuane, in the sixt yeare of his reigne. Then hauing a companie about him of such as he had made priuie to his enterprise, he caused himselfe to be proclaimed king, and foorthwith went vnto Scone, where (by common consent) he receiued the inuesture of the kingdome according to the accustomed maner. The bodie of Duncane was first conueied vnto Elgine, & there buried in kinglie wise; but afterwards it was remoued and conueied vnto Colmekill, and there laid in a sepulture amongst his predecessors, in the yeare after the birth of our Sauiour, 1046.

'Malcolme Canmore and Donald Bane the sons of king Duncane, for feare of their liues (which they might well know that Mackbeth would seeke to bring to end for his more sure confirmation in the estate) fled into Cumberland, where Malcolme remained, till time that saint Edward the sonne of Etheldred recouered the dominion of England from the Danish power, the which Edward receiued Malcolme by way of most friendlie enterteinment: but Donald passed ouer into Ireland, where he was tenderlie cherished by the king of that land. Mackbeth, after the departure thus of Duncanes sonnes, vsed great liberalitie towards the nobles of the realme, thereby to win their fauour, and when he saw that no man went about to trouble him, he set his whole intention to mainteine iustice, and to punish all enormities and abuses, which had chanced through the feeble and slouthfull administration of Duncane' (pp. 170–1).

Holinshed gives a number of examples of Macbeth's reforms and mentions that among the thanes who were slain for sedition was Ros. After giving a list of some of Macbeth's laws, Holinshed adds:

'These and the like commendable lawes Makbeth caused to be put as then in vse, gouerning the realme for the space of ten yeares in equall iustice. But this was but a counterfet zeale of equitie shewed by him, partlie against his naturall inclination to purchase thereby the fauour of the people. Shortlie after, he began to shew what he was, in stead of equitie practising crueltie. For the pricke of conscience (as it chanceth euer in tyrants, and such as atteine to anie estate by vnrighteous means) caused him euer to feare, least he should be serued of the same cup, as he had ministred to his predecessor. The woords also of the three weird sisters, would not out of his mind, which as they promised him the kingdome, so likewise did they promise it at the same time vnto the posteritie of Banquho. He willed therefore the same Banquho with his sonne named Fleance, to come to supper that he had prepared for them, which was indeed, as he had deuised, present death at the hands of certeine murderers, whom he hired to execute that deed, appointing them to meet with the same Banquho and his sonne without the palace, as they returned to their lodgings, and there to slea them, so that he would not haue his house slandered, but that in time to come he might cleare himselfe, if anie thing were laid to his charge vpon anie suspicion that might arise. It chanced yet by the benefit of the darke night, that though the father were slaine, the sonne yet by the helpe of almightie God reseruing him to better fortune, escaped that danger: and afterwards hauing some inkeling (by the admonition of some friends which he had in the court) how his life was sought no lesse than his fathers, who was slaine not by chancemedlie (as by the handling of the matter Makbeth woold haue had it to appeare) but euen vpon a prepensed deuise: wherevpon to auoid further perill he fled into Wales' (p. 172).

Holinshed goes on to describe how the founder of the Stuart dynasty, Walter Steward, who married the daughter of Robert Bruce, and also 'the earles of Leuenox and Dernlie', were descended from Fleance.

'But to returne vnto Makbeth, in continuing the historie, and to begin where I left, ye shall vnderstand that after the contriued slaughter of Banquho, nothing prospered with the foresaid Makbeth: for in maner euerie man began to doubt his owne life, and durst vnneth appeare in the kings presence; and euen as there were manie that stood in feare of him, so likewise stood he in feare of manie, in such sort that he began to make those awaie by one surmized cauillation or other, whome he thought most able to worke him anie displeasure.

'At length he found such sweetnesse by putting his nobles thus to death, that his earnest thirst after bloud in this behalfe might in no wise be satisfied: for ye must consider he wan double profite (as hee thought) hereby: for first they were rid out of the way whome he feared, and then againe his coffers were inriched by their goods which were forfeited to his vse, whereby he might the better mainteine a gard of armed men about him to defend his person from iniurie of them whom he had in anie suspicion. Further, to the end he might the more cruellie oppresse his subiects with all tyrantlike wrongs, he builded a strong castell on the top of an hie hill called Dunsinane situate in Gowrie, ten miles from Perth, on such a proud height, that standing there aloft, a man might behold well neere all the countries of Angus, Fife, Stermond and Ernedale, as it were lieng vnderneath him. This castell then being founded on the top of that high hill, put the realme to great charges before it was finished, for all the stuffe necessarie to the building, could not be brought vp without much toile and businesse. But Makbeth being once determined to haue the worke go forward, caused the thanes of each shire within the realme, to come and helpe towards that building, each man his course about.

'At the last, when the turne fell vnto Makduffe thane of Fife to builde his part, he sent workemen with all needfull prouision, and commanded them to shew such diligence in euerie behalfe, that no occasion might bee giuen for the king to find fault with him, in that he came not himselfe as other had doone, which he refused to doo, for doubt least the king bearing him (as he partlie vnderstood) no great good will, would laie violent handes vpon him, as he had doone vpon diuerse other. Shortly after, Makbeth comming to behold how the worke went forward, and bicause he found not Makduffe there, he was sore offended, and said: I percieue this man will neuer obeie my commandments, till he be ridden with a snaffle: but I shall prouide well inough for him. Neither could he afterwards abide to looke vpon the said Makduffe, either for that he thought his puissance ouer great; either else for that he had learned of certeine wizzards, in whose words he put great confidence (for that the prophesie had happened so right, which the three faries or weird sisters had declared vnto him) that he ought to take heed of Makduffe, who in time to come should seeke to destroie him.

'And suerlie herevpon had he put Makduffe to death, but that a certaine witch, whom hee had in great trust, had told that he should neuer be slaine with man borne of anie woman, nor vanquished till the wood of Bernane came to the castell of Dunsinane. By this prophesie Makbeth put all feare out of his heart, supposing he might doo what he would, without anie feare to be punished for the same, for by the one prophesie he beleeued it was vnpossible for anie man to vanquish him, and by the other vnpossible to slea him. This vaine hope caused him to doo manie outragious things, to the greeuous oppression of his subiects. At length Makduffe, to auoid perill of life, purposed with himselfe to pass intoe England, to procure Malcolme Canmore to claime the crowne of Scotland. But this was not so secretlie deuised by Makduffe, but that Makbeth had knowledge giuen him thereof: for kings (as is said) haue sharpe sight like vnto Lynx, and long ears like vnto Midas. For Makbeth had in euerie noble mans house one slie fellow or other in fee with him, to reueale all that was said or doone within the same, by which slight he oppressed the most part of the nobles of his realme.

'Immediatlie then, being aduertised whereabout Makduffe went, he came hastily with a great power into Fife, and foorthwith beseiged the castell where Makduffe dwelled, trusting to haue found him therein. They that kept the house, without anie resistance opened the gates, and suffered him to enter, mistrusting none euill. But neuertheless Makbeth most cruellie caused the wife and children of Makduffe, with all other whom he found in that castell, to be slaine. Also he confiscated the goods of Makduffe, proclaimed him traitor, and confined him out of all the parts of his realme; but Makduffe was alreadie escaped out of danger, and gotten into England vnto Malcolme Canmore, to trie what purchase hee might make by means of his support to reuenge the slaughter so cruellie executed on his wife, his children, and other friends. At his comming vnto Malcolme, he declared into what great miserie the estate of Scotland was brought, by the detestable cruelties exercised by the tyrant Makbeth, hauing committed manie horrible slaughters and murders, both as well of the nobles as commons, for the which he was hated right mortallie of all his liege people, desiring nothing more than to be deliuered of that intollerable and most heauie yoke of thraldome, which they susteined at such a caitifes hands.

'Malcolme hearing Makduffe's woordes, which he vttered in verie lamentable sort, for meere compassion and verie ruth that pearsed his sorrowful hart, bewailing the miserable state of his countrie, he fetched a deepe sigh; which Makduffe perceiuing, began to fall most earnestlie in hand with him, to enterprise the deliuering of the Scotish people out of the hands of so cruell and bloudie a tyrant, as Makbeth by too manie plaine experiments did shew himselfe to be: which was an easie matter for him to bring to passe, considering not onelie the good title he had, but also the earnest desire of the people to haue some occasion ministred, whereby they might be reuenged of those notable iniuries, which they dailie susteined by the outragious crueltie of Makbeths misgouernance. Though Malcolme was verie sorowfull for the oppression of his countriemen the Scots, in maner as Makduffe had declared; yet doubting whether he were come as one that ment vnfeinedlie as he spake, or els as sent from Makbeth to betraie him, he thought to haue some further triall, and therevpon dissembling his mind at the first, he answered as followeth.

'I am trulie verie sorie for the miserie chanced to my countrie of Scotland, but though I haue neuer so great affection to relieue the same, yet by reason of certeine incurable vices, which reigne in me, I am nothing meet thereto. First, such immoderate lust and voluptuous sensualitie (the abhominable founteine of all vices) followeth me, that if I were made king of Scots, I should seeke to defloure your maids and matrones, in such wise that mine intemperancie should be more importable vnto you than the bloudie tyrannie of Makbeth now is. Heerunto Makduffe answered: this suerly is a verie euill fault, for manie noble princes and kings haue lost both liues and kingdomes for the same; neuerthelesse there are women enow in Scotland, and therefore follow my counsell. Make thy selfe king, and I shall conueie the matter so wiselie, that thou shalt be so satisfied at thy pleasure in such secret wise, that no man shall be aware thereof.

'Then said Malcolme, I am also the most auaritious creature on the earth, so that if I were king, I should seeke so manie waies to get lands and goods, that I would slea the most part of all the nobles of Scotland by surmized accusations, to the end I might inioy their lands, goods, and possessions; and therefore to shew you what mischiefe may insue on you through mine vnsatiable couetousnes, I will rehearse vnto you a fable. There was a fox hauing a sore place on him ouerset with a swarme of flies, that continuallie sucked out hir bloud: and when one that came by and saw this manner, demanded whether she would haue the flies driuen beside hir, she answered no: for if these flies that are alreadie full, and by reason thereof sucke not verie egerlie, should be chased awaie, other that are emptie and fellie an hungred, should light in their places, and sucke out the residue of my bloud farre more to my greeuance than these, which now being satisfied doo not much annoie me. Therefore saithe Malcolme, suffer me to remaine where I am, least if I atteine to the regiment of your realme, mine inquenchable auarice may prooue such; that ye would thinke the displeasures which now grieue you, should seeme easie in respect of the vnmeasurable outrage, which might insue through my comming amongst you.

'Makduffe to this made answer, how it was a far woorse fault than the other: for auarice is the root of all mischiefe, and for that crime the most part of our kings haue beene slain and brought to their finall end. Yet notwithstanding follow my counsell, and take vpon thee the crowne. There is gold and riches inough in Scotland to satisfie thy greedie desire. Then said Malcolme againe, I am furthermore inclined to dissimulation, telling of leasings, and all other kinds of deceit, so that I naturallie reioise in nothing so much, as to betraie & deceiue such as put anie trust or confidence in my woords. Then sith there is nothing that more becommeth a prince than constancie, veritie, truth, and iustice, with the other laudable fellowship of those faire and noble vertues which are comprehended in soothfastnesse, and that lieng vtterlie ouerthroweth the same; you see how vnable I am to gouerne anie prouince or region: and therefore sith you haue remedies to cloke and hide all the rest of my other vices, I praie you find shift to cloke this vice amongst the residue.

'Then said Makduffe: This yet is the woorst of all, and there I leaue thee, and therefore saie; Oh ye vnhappie and miserable Scotishmen, which are thus scourged with so manie and sundrie calamities, ech one aboue another! Ye haue one curssed and wicked tyrant that now reigneth ouer you, without anie right or title, oppressing you with his most bloudie crueltie. This other that hath the right to the crowne, is so replet with the inconstant behauiour and manifest vices of Englishmen, that he is nothing woorthie to inioy it: for by his owne confession he is not onelie auaritious, and giuen to vnsatiable lust, but so false a traitor withall, that no trust is to be had vnto anie woord he speaketh. Adieu Scotland, for now I account my selfe a banished man for euer, without comfort or consolation: and with those woords the brackish tears trickled downe his cheekes verie abundantlie.

'At the last, when he was readie to depart, Malcolme tooke him by the sleeue, and said: Be of good comfort Makduffe, for I haue none of these vices before remembered, but haue iested with thee in this manner, onelie to prooue thy mind: for diuerse times heeretofore hath Makbeth sought by this manner of meanes to bring me into his hands, but the more slow I haue shewed my self to condescend to thy motion and request, the more diligence shall I vse in accomplishing the same. Incontinentlie heereupon they imbraced ech other, and promising to be faithfull the one to the other, they fell in consultation how they might best prouide for all their businesse, to bring the same to good effect. Soone after, Makduffe repairing to the borders of Scotland, addressed his letters with secret dispatch vnto the nobles of the realme, declaring how Malcolme was confederat with him, to come hastilie into Scotland to claime the crowne, and therefore he required them, sith he was right inheritor thereto, to assist him with their powers to recouer the same out of the hands of the wrongfull vsurper.

'In the meane time, Malcolme purchased such fauor at king Edwards hands, that old Siward earle of Northumberland, was appointed with ten thousand men to go with him into Scotland, to support him in this enterprise, for recouerie of his right. After these newes were spread abroad in Scotland, the nobles drew into two seuerall factions, the one taking part with Makbeth, and the other with Malcolme. Heerevpon insued oftentimes sundrie bickerings, & diuerse light skirmishes: for those that were of Malcolmes side, would not ieopard to ioine with their enimies in a pight field, till his comming out of England to their support. But after that Makbeth perceiued his enimies power to increase, by such aid as came to them foorth of England with his aduersarie Malcolme, he recoiled backe into Fife, there purposing to abide in campe fortified, at the castell of Dunsinane, and to fight with his enimies, if they ment to pursue him; howbeit some of his friends aduised him, that it should be best for him, either to make some agreement with

Malcome, or else to flee with all speed into the Iles, and to take his
treasure with him, to the end he might wage sundrie great princes
of the realme to take his part, & reteine strangers, in whome he
might better trust than in his owne subiects, which stale dailie from
him: but he had such confidence in his prophesies, that he beleeued
he should neuer be vanquished, till Birnane wood were brought to
Dunsinane; nor yet to be slaine with anie man, that should be or
was borne of anie woman.

'Malcolme following hastilie after Makbeth, came the night
before the battell vnto Birnane wood, and when his armie had
rested a while there to refresh them, he commanded euerie man to
get a bough of some tree or other of that wood in his hand, as big as
he might beare, and to march foorth therewith in such wise, that
on the next morrow they might come closelie and without sight in
this manner within viewe of his enimies. On the morrow when
Makbeth beheld them comming in this sort, he first maruelled
what the matter ment, but in the end remembred himselfe that the
prophesie which he had heard long before that time, of the comming of Birnane wood to Dunsinane castell, was likelie to be now
fulfilled. Neuertheless, he brought his men in order of battell, and
exhorted them to doo valiantlie, howbeit his enimies had scarsely
cast from them their boughs, when Makbeth perceiuing their
numbers, betooke him streict to flight, whom Makduffe pursued
with great hatred euen till he came vnto Lunfannaine, where
Makbeth perceiuing that Makduffe was hard at his backe, leapt
beside his horsse, saieng: Thou traitor, what meaneth it that thou
shouldest thus in vaine follow me that am not appointed to be
slaine by anie creature that is borne of a woman, come on therefore,
and receiue thy reward which thou hast deserued for thy paines,
and therewithall he lifted vp his swoord thinking to haue slaine
him.

'But Makduffe quicklie auoiding from his horsse, yet he came at
him, answered (with his naked swoord in his hand) saieng: It is
true Makbeth, and now shall thine insatiable crueltie haue an end,
for I am euen he that thy wizzards haue told thee of, who was neuer
borne of my mother, but ripped out of her wombe: therewithall he
stept vnto him, and slue him in the place. Then cutting his head
from his shoulders, he set it vpon a pole, and brought it vnto
Malcolme. This was the end of Makbeth, after he had reigned 17
yeeres ouer the Scotishmen. In the beginning of his reigne he accomplished manie woorthie acts verie profitable to the commonwealth (as ye haue heard), but afterward by illusion of the diuell,
he defamed the same with most terrible crueltie. He was slaine in

the yeere of the incarnation 1057, and in the 16 yeere of king
Edwards reigne ouer the Englishmen.

'Malcolme Canmore thus recouering the relme (as ye haue
heard) by support of king Edward, in the 16 yeere of the same
Edwards reigne, he was crowned at Scone the 25 day of Aprill, in
the yeere of our Lord 1057. Immediatlie after his coronation he
called a parlement at Forfair, in the which he rewarded them with
lands and liuings that had assisted him against Makbeth, aduan-
cing them to fees and offices as he saw cause, & commanded that
speciallie those that bare the surname of anie offices or lands,
should haue and inioy the same. He created manie earles, lords,
barons, and knights. Manie of them that before were thanes, were
at this time made earles, as Fife, Menteth, Atholl, Leuenox,
Murrey, Cathnes, Rosse, and Angus. These were the first earles
that haue beene heard of amongst the Scotishmen (as their his-
tories doo make mention)' (pp. 174–6).

'It is recorded also, that in the foresaid battell, in which earle
Siward vanquished the Scots, one of Siwards sonnes chanced to be
slaine, whereof although the father had good cause to be sorrowfull,
yet when he heard that he died of a wound which he had receiued in
fighting stoutlie in the forepart of his bodie, and that with his face
towards the enimie, he greatlie reioised thereat, to heare that he
died so manfullie. But here is to be noted, that not now, but a little
before (as *Henrie Hunt* saith) that earle Siward went into Scotland
himselfe in person, he sent his sonne with an armie to conquere the
land, whose hap was there to be slaine. When his father heard the
newes he demanded whether he receiued the wound whereof he
died, in the forepart of the bodie, or in the hinder part: and when
it was told him that he receiued it in the forepart; I reioise (saith
he) euen with all my heart, for I would not wish either to my sonne
nor to my selfe any other kind of death' (*History of England*, p. 192).

Prof. M. C. Bradbrook pointed out in a lecture, printed in
Shakespeare Survey, 4, that Shakespeare may have derived some hints
for the character of Lady Macbeth and particularly for her speech
1. vii. 54 ff. from Holinshed's *Description of Scotland* prefixed to the
Chronicles: 'And sith it was a cause of suspicion of the mothers
fidelitie toward hir husband, to seeke a strange nurse for hir
children (although hir milke failed) each woman would take
intollerable paines to bring vp and nourish hir own children. They
thought them furthermore not to be kindlie fostered, except they
were so well nourished after their births with the milke of their
brests, as they were before they were borne with the bloud of their
owne bellies, nay they feared least they should degenerat and grow

out of kind, except they gaue them sucke themselues, and eschewed strange milke, therefore in labour and painfulnesse they were equall, and neither sex regarded the heat in summer or cold in winter. . . In these daies also the women of our countries were of no lesse courage than the men; for all stout maidens and wiues (if they were not with child) marched as well in the field as did the men, and so soone as the armie did set forward, they slue the first liuing creature that they found, in whose bloud they not onelie bathed their swords, but also tasted thereof with their mouthes, with no lesse religion and assurance conceived, than if they had alreadie been sure of some notable and fortunate victorie. When they saw their owne bloud run from them in the fight, they waxed neuer a whit astonished with the matter, but rather doubling their courages with more egernesse they assailed their enimies' (ed. 1587, p. 21).

APPENDIX B

BUCHANAN

From *Rerum Scoticarum Historia*. Translated by J. Aikman (1827).

XXII. . . . When Donald, the governor of the castle, requested the release of some of his relations, and was denied their pardon, he conceived the most unbounded rage against the king; and, as if he had received a signal affront, turned all his thoughts upon revenge, for he valued the services he had rendered Duff so highly, that he imagined he ought to be refused nothing which he chose to ask. Donald's wife, too, when she found that some of her own relations were condemned to death, inflamed her already incensed husband, not only by her bitter speeches, but by her persuasion incited him to murder the king; telling him that as keeper of the royal castle he had the life and death of his sovereign in his hands, and that he might thereby not only perpetrate the act, but conceal it when it was done. Wherefore, after the king, fatigued with business, had fallen into a deep sleep, and his attendants, who had been made drunk by Donald, were also overcome with drowsiness, assassins were secretly admitted, who murdered the king, and carried out the body so circumspectly by a back way, that not a single drop of blood betrayed the deed. . . Next day, when the report was spread abroad that the king was nowhere to be found, and that the bed was spotted with blood, Donald, as if suddenly struck with the atrocious act, rushed into the bedchamber, and apparently transported with anger, murdered the servants, and then diligently searched everywhere round about to see if any traces of the dead man could be found. . .

XXXVIII. (The following passages refers to King Kenneth.)

His soul, disturbed by a consciousness of his crime, permitted him to enjoy no solid or sincere pleasure; in retirement the thoughts of his unholy deed rushing upon his recollection, tormented him; and, in sleep, visions full of horror drove repose from his pillow. At last, whether in truth an audible voice from heaven addressed him, as is reported, or whether it were the suggestion of his own guilty mind, as often happens with the wicked, in the silent watches of the night he seemed thus to be admonished: 'Dost thou think that the murder of the innocent Malcolm, perpetrated secretly by thee with the most consummate villany, is either unknown to me, or can remain longer unpunished? Even now snares are spread for thy life, which thou canst not escape. Nor shalt thou leave, as thou imaginest, a stable and secure throne to thy posterity. They shall inherit an agitated and tempestuous kingdom.'

IV. Macbeth was a man of penetrating genius, a high spirit, unbounded ambition, and, if he had possessed moderation, was worthy of any command, however great; but in punishing crimes he exercised a severity which, exceeding the bounds of the laws, appeared oft to degenerate into cruelty.

VIII. After this tide of success, both at home and abroad, when peace was re-established throughout the whole of Scotland, Macbeth, who had always despised the inactivity of his cousin, cherished secretly the hope of seizing the throne, in which he is said to have been confirmed by a dream. On a certain night, when he was far distant from the king, three women appeared to him of more than human stature, of whom one hailed him thane of Angus, another, thane of Moray, and the third saluted him king. His ambition and hope being strongly excited by this vision, he re-volved in his mind every way by which he might obtain the king-dom, when a justifiable occasion, as he thought, presented itself. Duncan had two sons, by the daughter of Sibard, governor of Northumberland, Malcolm Canmore (great head) and Donald Bane (white). Of these he made Malcolm, while yet a boy, governor of Cumberland. This appointment highly incensed Macbeth, who thought it an obstacle thrown in the way of his ambition, which— now that he had obtained the two first dignities promised by his nocturnal visitors—might retard, if not altogether prevent, his arriving at the third, as the command of Cumberland was always considered the next step to the crown. His mind, already sufficiently ardent of itself, was daily excited by the importunities of his wife, who was the confidant of all his designs. Wherefore, having consulted with his most intimate friends, among whom was Bancho, and having found a convenient opportunity, he waylaid the king at Inverness, and killed him, in the seventh year of his reign; then, collecting a band together, he proceeded to Scoon, where, trusting to the favour of the people, he proclaimed himself king. The children of Duncan, amazed at this sudden misfortune, their father slain, and the author of the murder upon his throne, surrounded on every side by the snares of the tyrant, who sought, by their death, to confirm the kingdom to himself, for some time endeavoured to save themselves by flight, and shifting frequently the places of their concealment. But when they saw they could be no where safe, if within the reach of his power, and having no hope of mercy from a man of so barbarous a disposition, they fled in different directions, Malcolm into Cumberland, and Donald to his relations in the Æbudæ.

LXXXV.   Macbeth

IX. Macbeth, in order to establish himself on the throne he had so iniquitously acquired, won the favour of the nobles by large gifts. As he was secure of the king's children, on account of their age, and of the neighbouring kings, on account of their mutual animosities, having gained the more powerful, he determined to procure the affection of the people by his equity, and retain it by his strict administration of justice. Wherefore, he determined to punish the robbers, who had grown insolent through the lenity of Duncan. But when he saw that this could not be effected without raising a great commotion, he contrived, by men selected for the purpose, to scatter the seeds of dissension among them, and induce them to challenge each other to decide their disputes by battle, in small parties of equal numbers, in places widely distant, and upon the same day. On which day, when they assembled according to appointment, they were all seized by trusty officers, whom the king had stationed for apprehending them, and their execution struck terror into the rest. He, likewise, put to death the thanes of Caithness, Ross, Sutherland, and Nairn, together with some other powerful chieftains, by whose feuds the people were terribly harassed. He, afterwards, went to the Æbudæ, where he executed severe justice, and returning thence, he summoned repeatedly Macgill, or Macgild, the most powerful chief of Galloway, to stand trial. But he—Macgill—more afraid of being charged with having belonged to the party of Malcolm, than dreading any crime of which he could have been accused—refused to obey; on which, Macbeth sent some detachments against him, who, having vanquished him in battle, put him to death. By these means, perfect tranquility being restored, he applied himself to frame laws, an object which had been much neglected by the preceding kings, and enacted very many and very useful statutes, which now, to the great detriment of the public, are allowed to remain unnoticed, and almost unknown. Thus, for ten years, he so governed the kingdom, that, if his obtaining it by violence were forgotten, he would be esteemed inferior to none of the kings who preceded him.

X. But when he had strengthened himself by so many safeguards, and thus gained favour of the people; the murder of the king—as is very credible—haunting his imagination, and distracting his mind, occasioned his converting the government which he had obtained by perfidy, into a cruel tyranny. He first wreaked his unbounded rage on Bancho, his accomplice in the treason, instigated, as is reported, by the prophecy of some witches, who predicted that Bancho's posterity would enjoy the kingdom. Wherefore, fearing that so powerful and active a chief, who had already dipt his hands in royal blood, might imitate the example which he himself had set, he familiarly invited him, along with his son, to an entertainment, and caused him to be assassinated on his return, in such a manner, as if he had been accidentally killed in a sudden affray. Fleanchus, his son, being unknown, escaped in the dark, but, informed by his friends that his father had been killed by the treachery of the king, and that his own life was sought after, fled secretly to Wales. This murder, so cruelly and perfidiously committed, inspired the nobles with such dread, each for his own safety, that they all departed to their houses, few of them, and they but rarely, ever venturing to court; so that the cruelty of the king, being openly exercised upon some, and secretly suspected by all, mutual terror produced mutual hatred between him and his nobles, and then, when concealment became impossible, he began to exhibit an undisguised tyranny. He publicly executed the most powerful chieftains, upon the most frivolous pretences, and frequently upon fictitious accusations; and with the produce of their confiscations, he supported a band of ruffians, under the name of Royal Guards.

XI. The king, however, not yet thinking his life sufficiently protected, commenced building a castle upon Dunsinnan hill, whence there is an extensive prospect upon every side; and when the building proceeded but slowly, on account of the difficulty of the carriage of the materials, he commanded all the thanes, throughout the whole kingdom, to provide by turns for the work labourers and carriages, and ordered that they should themselves superintend the operations, as inspectors. Macduff, thane of Fife, was then exceedingly powerful, but not daring to trust his life in the king's hands, frequently sent workmen thither, and, likewise, several of his most intimate friends to urge their labour. The king, either desirous to see how the work proceeded, as he pretended, or, as Macduff feared, to apprehend him, came to view the building, when, by chance, a yoke of oxen, unequal to the task, could not drag a load over a steep ascent. The king eagerly seized the occasion to vent his indignation, threatening that he would subdue the contumacious spirit of the thane, which was already well known to him, and place the yoke on his own neck, which speech being reported to Macduff, he commended his family to his wife, and, without delay, passed over to Lothian, in a little vessel hastily rigged out for the occasion, and thence proceeded to England. Macbeth, having heard of his intended flight, proceeded immediately with a strong force to Fife, if possible to prevent him. At his arrival, he was immediately admitted into Macduff's castle, but not finding the thane, he wreaked his vengeance upon his wife, and his children who remained. He confiscated also his estate, proclaimed himself a rebel, and threatened to inflict a severe punishment on any one who dared to hold any communication with him. He likewise behaved with great cruelty towards the rest of the rich, and the powerful, without distinction; and, in contempt of his nobility, administered the internal affairs of the kingdom, by the advice of his household, without ever deigning to consult them.

XII. In the meantime, Macduff, having arrived in England, found Malcolm living in a royal style, at the court of king Edward; for Edward having been recalled from exile to the throne, when the power of the Danes was broken in England, was for many reasons interested in behalf of Malcolm, who had been presented to him by his maternal grandfather, Sibard, either because his father and grandfather, when they commanded in Cumberland, were always attached to his ancestors, or, because a similarity of circumstances, and a recollection of their mutual dangers, had produced a mutual friendship, for both kings had been driven into exile unjustly, by tyrants, or, because the misfortunes of kings easily interest the minds of the greatest strangers. The thane, therefore, as soon as he could find a proper opportunity, addressed Malcolm in a long speech, in which he lamented the unhappy necessity of his flight, represented the cruelty of Macbeth towards all ranks, and the universal hatred of all ranks towards him, and strongly urged Malcolm to attempt the recovery of his paternal throne, especially, as he could not without the greatest guilt leave the impious murder of his father unpunished, neglect the miseries of a people committed to him by God himself, or turn a deaf ear to the just petitions of his friends. Besides, he might rely on the assistance of his ally, the excellent king Edward, and on the affections of the people, who hated the tyrant, nor would the favour of the Deity, to aid a just cause against the wicked, be withheld. In fine, nothing would be wanting, if he were not wanting to himself. Malcolm, who had often before been solicited to return, by spies, sent from Macbeth to draw him into a snare, determined, before he should commit himself to fortune in so great an affair, to prove the fidelity of Macduff. He therefore replied, I am not indeed ignorant of what you tell me, but I am afraid that you are wholly unacquainted with me, whom you invite to assume the crown; for the same vices which have destroyed many kings, lust and avarice, exist in me also, and although now hid in a private station, would break forth in the licence of a regal state. Beware then, lest you do not rather invite me to destruction, than to a kingdom. Macduff answered, that licentious desires after variety, might be counteracted by a lawful marriage, and avarice removed, by being placed above the fear of penury. Malcolm rejoined, that he now rather chose to confess to him ingenuously as a friend, than hereafter to be caught in faults, which might prove dangerous to both; that he did not believe in the existence, either of truth or sincerity; that he confided in no man; that he was apt to change his designs with every breath of suspicion, and, that from the inconstancy of his own disposition, he formed his judgment of every other person. On which, Macduff exclaimed, away! dishonour of thy royal blood and name, more fit to dwell in a desert, than to reign; and was about to retire in anger, when Malcolm taking him by the hand, explained to him the reason of his simulation, that he had so often been deceived by the emissaries of Macbeth, that he dared not rashly trust himself to every body, but with regard to Macduff, his lineage, his manners, his character, and his circumstances, claimed his confidence. Then mutually plighting their faith, they proceeded to consult on the means for accomplishing the destruction of the tyrant. Having, by secret messengers, sent previous information of their design to their friends, they received from

King Edward, ten thousand soldiers, under the command of Sibard, Malcolm's maternal grandfather.

XIII. The report of this army's march, excited a great commotion in Scotland, and many daily flocked to the new king. Macbeth, being almost wholly deserted, when in this so sudden defection he saw no better alternative, shut himself up in the castle of Dunsinnan, and sent his friends with money into the Æbudæ, and Ireland, to procure soldiers. Malcolm hearing of his intentions, marched directly against him, accompanied, wherever he went, by the acclamations of the people, and their prayers for his success. The soldiers joyfully seized this as an omen of victory, and placing green boughs in their helmets, represented an army rather returning in triumph, than marching to battle. Astonished at this confidence of the enemy, Macbeth immediately fled and the soldiers, deserted by their leader, surrendered to Malcolm, Macduff having followed the tyrant, overtook him, and slew him. Here some of our writers relate a number of fables, more adapted for theatrical representation, or Milesian romance, than history, I therefore omit them. Macbeth reigned seventeen years over Scotland, during the first ten of which, he performed the duty of the best of kings, but in the seven last, he equalled the cruelty of the most barbarous tyrants.

APPENDIX C

JOHN LESLIE

From *De Origine, Moribus, et Rebus Gestis Scotorum*. Translated by C. Collard.

Chapter lxxxiv: DUNCAN

Malcolm's grandson Duncan then became king with the assent of all;[1] a man whose nature was unmarked by any roughness, resentment or bitterness, he was of the sort which does not retaliate even when provoked by the most grievous outrage. The common people shamefully abused this remarkable and merciful disposition of their king, and indulged their wicked cravings like wild beasts freed of all bonds; because Duncan was himself quite unable to act otherwise than mercifully, he entrusted his powers of government to Macbeth, a man a little more disposed to stern measures. Macbeth seized the earliest opportunity to repress the general

[1] Malcolm was murdered at Glamis, 1040 (end of chap. lxxxiii).

lawlessness of the nation by inflicting the harshest punishment on the inhabitants of Lochaber (they had despoiled Banquo, the Royal Thane of Lochaber, of the royal estates and of much money, besides wounding him severely). Macbeth also drove into Lochaber Castle MacDonald of the Isles, who supported these robbers and had fought stubbornly for them; he was there put under so close a siege that no way of escape was left to him. MacDonald became so terrified by the imagination of the penalties he would suffer if he fell into his enemies' hands, and so blinded by obstinacy of kind, that he took the lives both of himself and of his family.

Meanwhile the King of Norway crossed to Scotland with an army, bringing about a wholly unjustifiable war on the pretext of avenging an ancient massacre of his countrymen. Besieging Duncan in Perth Castle he pressed him so hard that he would without doubt have been forced to surrender to his enemy, had he not taken quick advantage of a chance to attack the Danes while they were buried in their drinking. Nor long after, Macbeth came to his help with reinforcements; thereupon King Sven hastily broke camp and fled to his ships, for he had not only sustained a great defeat but was himself in extreme danger of his life. Duncan did not allow the opportunity to destroy the Danes to slip away, but with Macbeth's counsel and assistance overcame and scattered their fleet at Kingorn. The tombs of the Danes survive there to this day, and memorials graven in stone mark the everlasting glory of the action.

Within a few days, however, Macbeth had become so swollen with vainglory, and his resolution so tortured by a mad lust for power, that he hideously murdered Duncan his most holy King, who had rewarded him with such great honours, in the sixth year of his reign; though fearful of the deed, his wife urged him to it with high promises of its happy outcome. Duncan's two sons Malcolm Canmoir and Donald were seized by fear upon their father's murder, and most wisely decided to flee the country.

Chapter lxxxv : MACBETH

Thus Macbeth forcibly seized the throne; he was the son of Doada, the daughter of Malcolm the Second.

Though Macbeth was famed for his prowess in war, and by nature disposed to cruelty, he thought to secure his ill-won kingdom by favouring the nobles through total suppression of brigandage, and indulging the common people with beneficial laws; thus he might bind both to himself in the closest ties of goodwill. In the end, however, the conscience of his hideous deeds so worked upon him and caused him such fear for his life from those about him, that his mildness changed to ruthlessness. He began either openly to execute his nobles or to induce them by his cunning to intrigue one another's deaths.

Banquo and, above all, Macduff he thought particularly dangerous. He destroyed Banquo at the first opportunity, while he contrived to ensnare Macduff by cunning. In short, like any tyrant, he went in fear of all men, and all men of him. The people thereupon wisely grew concerned for the state of their kingdom, and for their own safety; they sent Macduff to England, where Malcolm Canmoir was in exile, to invite him to recover his rightful inheritance and to assure him under holy oath of their allegiance to him against Macbeth. At this news Malcolm was generously furnished with 10,000 English soldiers by King Edward. Returning to Scotland, he pursued Macbeth in a number of fierce engagements first to Dunsinane, and then to Lumphanan. There Macduff, the Earl of Fife, had Macbeth put to death (he had a little before ordered the execution of Macduff's wife and children), and took his head to Malcolm, who gave him fine praise and abundant reward. Macbeth's death occurred in the sixth year of his tyranny.

APPENDIX D

ADDITIONAL NOTES (1984)

I. ii. 13. *Gallowglasses*]Joseph J. Egan, *ELN*, 15 (1978), 167–71, points out that this term, anachronistic in Duncan's Scotland, refers to Scots foot soldiers employed as mercenaries in Ireland.

I. iii. 51–2. *fear . . . fair*] a quibble. Cf. III. i. 2–3.

I. vii. 12. *double trust*] Arthur Melville Clark, *Murder Under Trust* (1981), p. 46, suggests that Shakespeare was referring to an act of 1587 by which a murder 'vnder the traist, credit, assurance and power of the slayer' was regarded as treason.

I. vii. 27 *Vaulting*] C. Belsey, *ELN*, 10 (1972), 198–201, points out that this may relate to the traditional representation of Pride as a figure falling from a horse.

II. iii. 1–21.] Cf. Dekker and Massinger, *The Virgin Martyr*, III. iii. 179–82, where Harpax, an evil spirit, answers questions about the devil: '*Spung.* How if he come to any great mans gate, will the Porter let him come in sir? *Harpax.* Oh, hee loues Porters of great mens gates, because they are euer so neere the wicket.'

II. iii. 14. *stealing*] quibbling on *staling* = urinating (Waith).

III. i. 71. S.D.] Joan Hartwig, 'Macbeth, the Murderers and the

Diminishing Parallel', *Yearbook of English Studies* 3 (1973), 39–43, shows that the resemblance between the hired murderers and Macbeth himself reduced his actions 'to the level of absurdity'; but that 'the shallowness of the murderers heightens the complexity of Macbeth when he finds himself in similar situations'. She compares III. i. 107–13 with Macbeth's despair in Act v.

III. ii. 32. *Unsafe . . . we*] unsafe so long as we must continue to flatter (Gomme).

III. iv. 99. *rugged Russian bear*] Cf. Dekker, *Whore of Babylon* (1607), II. i. 42–3, 'hearts more rugged/Then is the Russian Beare'.

III. iv. 123. *understood relations*] Ann Pasternak Slater, *EC*, 27 (1978), 125, quotes from Lavater's *Of Ghostes and Sprites* a story from Plutarch about Bessus, who had murdered his father, 'espying a swallowes neast with his speare he thrust it downe', defending the action by asking 'haue they not falsely accused me a great while crying out on me, that I haue slaine and murthered my father?'

III. vi. 31. *Northumberland . . . Siward*] Either Shakespeare had forgotten that Siward was Earl of Northumberland, or the name refers to the county.

III. vi. 40. *Sir, not I*] spoken by Macduff.

III. vi. 41. *turns me*] i.e. turns.

IV. i. 61. *Speak*] In Davenant's adaptation this is spoken by Hecate, and E. B. Lyle argues, *The Library* (1970), 150–1, that Hecate should not exit at 43, and that she should speak this and other speeches ascribed by F to 1 (Witch), i.e. 61–2, 64–7, 69–70, 75–6. This is unlikely, as Hecate would hardly refer to 'our masters'.

IV. i. 121. *two-fold . . . sceptres*] E. B. Lyle, *SQ*, 28 (1977), 516–19, argues that the double orb indicates the union of England and Scotland, and the treble sceptre the king's rule over Britain, France, and Ireland.

IV. ii. 32. *birds*] Slater (see III. iv. 124 n.) suggests that the bird imagery later in this scene (32–6, 82) and in IV. iii. 217 ff. was suggested by the Bessus anecdote.

IV. ii. 34–5. *net . . . gin*] See Introduction, p. xliii.

IV. iii. 107–8. *interdiction . . . accus'd . . . blaspheme*] Rogers, pp. 13–14, argues that to take 'interdiction' as a term in Scots law is to obscure the significance of the passage; nor does 'blaspheme' merely mean slander. Malcolm is damned, beyond God's grace, guilty of blasphemy, accursed, rather than accused. I concur.

v. v. 27. *idiot*] F. Pyle, *NQ* (1972), 29 ff., in a wayward analysis of this speech suggests that Macbeth is referring to himself and that this proves that he has attained to self-knowledge. He is referring rather to the meaninglessness of all human existence, not realizing that he himself has drained it of meaning.